PRAISE FOR *ELECTRIC*

Parthenon has made some of my favorite records and now he's produced one of my favorite books. *Electric Light Odyssey* is a beautifully written and often laugh-out-loud look at one man's determination to penetrate the cutthroat but intoxicating world of professional rock 'n' roll. If you love strivers with a wry perspective, you'll love this memoir.
—**Dr. Daniel J. Levitin**, *New York Times* best-selling author of *This Is Your Brain On Music*

Electric Light Odyssey showcases Parthenon's many literary gifts, such as knowing which details will carry his story into the reader's heart. It's impressive, but not surprising, if you know his lyrics and music. Parthenon's unpredictable and adventurous life is a tale worth telling, and as his past bandmate, co-writer and good friend, I'm honored to be a small part of his story's fabric. Well done, brother.
—**Rusty Anderson**, recording artist, guitarist for Paul McCartney

P. Hux can not only conjure a great song out of thin air, his talent for raucous storytelling is on full, shining display throughout *Electric Light Odyssey*. A self-taught musician who dove into the super tough world of the music business, these missives detailing his highs and lows along the journey are quirky, heart-felt, and fun. When I met P. Hux at a fund-raising show I instantly recognized his immense talent...and humor! His story is amazing and I'm so pleased he decided to tell it here.
—**Duff McKagan**, bassist, singer, founding member of Guns N' Roses and *New York Times* best-selling author of *It's So Easy: And Other Lies*

I've read hundreds of great memoirs and biographies by and about musicians from Charles Mingus, Tina Turner and Johnny Cash, who were never my friends, to Amy Rigby, Ivan Bodley and Robert Crenshaw, who are. Parthenon Huxley, who I consider a dear friend, has managed to do something rare in this genre. With his unique wit, style and rhythm he has captured what it's like to wade waist-deep in the crazy world of rock while never going under, illuminating that indescribable yearning for more. *Electric Light Odyssey* proves that talent and tenacity are their own rewards.
—**Don Dixon**, recording artist, producer for Marshall Crenshaw, Smithereens, Hootie and the Blowfish, Kim Carnes, R.E.M.

With a singer-songwriter's soul, a novelist's observant eye, and a musician's spirit, Parthenon Huxley has crafted a riveting memoir that takes readers inside the creative process and on the road.
–**Holly George-Warren**, author of *A Man Called Destruction: The Life and Music of Alex Chilton* and *Janis: Her Life and Music*

Parthenon has been one of my favorite songwriters since the first time I heard his songs. The music is always engaging and fun to hear and play, and his enviable way with lyrics tends to capture both his and the human experience, with no grandiloquence. For instance, he'd never write that previous sentence, especially in a book as well-written as *Electric Light Odyssey*.
–**Dan Rothchild**, writer, producer, bassist for Heart, Fiona Apple, Sheryl Crow, Beck, Tonic

ELECTRIC LIGHT ODYSSEY

My Zigzag Life and the Iconic Band
that Changed Everything

A Memoir by Parthenon Huxley

An award-winning musician's rollicking blind faith rock 'n' roll journey from fringe to front man starring Electric Light Orchestra Part II with appearances by Brian Wilson, Paul McCartney, Stephen Stills, Iggy Pop, Rick Wakeman, Linda Ronstadt, Roger McGuinn, Don Dixon, Cheap Trick, Duff McKagan, KISS, Muzak, the North Carolina indie scene, David Lee Roth, and many others.

HIGHPOINT
LIT

Copyright © 2024 by Parthenon Huxley

All rights reserved. Published in the United States of America. No part of this book may be reproduced or transmitted in any form or by any means, graphic, electronic or mechanical, including photocopying, recording, taping or by any information storage or retrieval system, without permission in writing from the publisher.

This edition published by Highpoint Lit
For information, write to info@highpointpubs.com.
First Edition
ISBN: 979-8-9908488-1-8

Library of Congress Cataloging-in-Publication Data
Huxley, Parthenon
Electric Light Odyssey: My Zigzag Life and the Iconic Band that Changed Everything

Summary: "Singer, songwriter, and guitar ace Parthenon Huxley takes readers on a high-voltage global adventure through his amazing life and career as a member of classic rock band ELO Part II, its successor the Orchestra, and as a Columbia recording artist, acclaimed songwriter and record producer. This memoir is packed with unforgettable stories, some starring luminaries of the rock 'n' roll world."—Provided by publisher.

ISBN: 979-8-9908488-1-8 (paperback)
1. Memoir 2. Music

Library of Congress Control Number: 2024918860

> "Do something you really like, and hopefully, it pays the rent. As far as I'm concerned, that's success."
>
> — Tom Petty

CONTENTS

Preface... xi

Mea Culpas... xii

PART ONE – IN WHICH I GET A CALL OUT OF THE BLUE

Chapter 1: The Audition... 3

Poster Boy ❂ A Call Out of the Blue ❂ Woodshedding ❂ The Audition ❂ Cookie Monster ❂ We'll See You in Uruguay ❂ Woodshedding Part II ❂ An Earful at the Audiologist ❂ A Day at the Opera ❂ Music of Your Own ❂ Rich Bitch Part II ❂ Modus Operandi ❂ Ringing

Chapter 2: Sex, Mugs, and Rock 'n' Roll... 27

The Airport Question ❂ Two or Three Little Things ❂ Show Number One ❂ Wedges ❂ Ego Ramps and Go-Go Girls ❂ Hodgenizer ❂ It's Not Always Like This ❂ Sex, Mugs, and Rock 'n' Roll ❂ Meet the New Press, Same as the Old Press ❂ Dinosaurs

Chapter 3: Who's the Boss... 51

The Ukraine Really Knocks Me Out ❂ Lost Soul ❂ Boss of Water ❂ You Kyiv Me Hangin' On ❂ Ukraine Girls ❂ Victory for the People ❂ International News ❂ Home Turf

Chapter 4: Beatle Nerd... 63

Goin' Home ❂ Boss of Songs ❂ Over London Skies ❂ Let There Be Bev ❂ Tears in Truro ❂ Showdown ❂ The Name ❂ Da Man ❂ The Love You Make ❂ Now They Know How Many Holes ❂ She's So Heavy

Chapter 5: Uh-Oh... 85
Hard Work ☙ Same and Sane ☙ Uh, Oh ☙ Dark and Tidy ☙ You're No Good ☙ David Lee Roth is Fun to Hang with Man Alright! ☙ Never Again ☙ New, New Guy ☙ What'd He Say?

PART TWO – IN WHICH I GET A CHANCE TO BE LOVED

Chapter 6: First Verse... 111
The Secret's Out ☙ Gifts ☙ Rick Hours ☙ Live at the Pool Party

Chapter 7: Behind the Olive Curtain... 117
New Kid ☙ Summer of '67 ☙ Behind the Olive Curtain ☙ Baseball and Black Sabbath ☙ Band Life ☙ Who the Hell Are the Move? ☙ Bands Banned ☙ Recording Stars ☙ I Didn't Know You Could Do That ☙ A Hellas of an Ending

Chapter 8: How To Rock... 131
Back in the USA ☙ The New Greece ☙ Work? ☙ Call of the Wild ☙ Crawdaddy Was Right ☙ The Shop ☙ A New Way of Life ☙ Who Are These Guys? ☙ Sneakers, Dixon, and TGS ☙ School Daze ☙ The Blazers ☙ How to Rock ☙ Every Musician's Dream

Chapter 9: The Waiting Room... 149
Look, Mom, I'm Using My Degree ☙ In Deep ☙ Better Late Than Never ☙ Dads Social Club ☙ Nooooo ☙ And Your Bird Can Freak Me Out ☙ Girl of My Dreams ☙ Rick Rock ☙ Landing a Marlin ☙ Encores and Onward ☙ Musi-Call ☙ The Waiting Room ☙ Unforgettable ☙ Me & Dixon

Chapter 10: Guy In Band... 171
Parthenon Huxley ☙ The M-Word ☙ Star Search ☙ The Sound of Silence ☙ Hey, Hey, Ve're Don Dixon Band (With Norwegian Accent) ☙ Be More Careful Next Time ☙ What's That? ☙ A Fork ☙ I Love LA ☙ Guy in Band ☙ But the Best Was... ☙ Harmony Sandwich ☙ Is This Your First Time?

Chapter 11: Weirdest A&R Meeting Ever... 189

Picture a Sphere ❂ Nobody Knows Who I Am ❂ Digital? ❂ My Coffee's On Fire ❂ Not Wendy ❂ Trust Me ❂ Echo Park ❂ Tricky ❂ Genius or Clueless ❂ My Chance to Be Loved ❂ Glub, Glub, Glub ❂ A Titch Sad

Chapter 12: My Expanding Portfolio... 209

The Handmade Tale ❂ Next ❂ The Wrong Lord-Alge ❂ Workin' for MCA ❂ A Job Called E ❂ The Other CBS ❂ Foreigner Policy ❂ I Want 62.5% ❂ Hot Shot ❂ Purgatory Falls, the Farm ❂ Rent-A-Kid ❂ Senses Working Overtime ❂ VeG Is a Buzzword ❂ Birmingham American Style ❂ Goin' To the Go-Go ❂ Over and Out

Chapter 13: The Easiest Album Ever Made... 233

Now With Even Less Cruelty ❂ A Walk in the Park ❂ P. Hux ❂ Alain ❂ The Easiest Album Ever Made ❂ Dishes ❂ Parthenon Huxley's Off Day ❂ It Needs More Oboe

Chapter 14: A Final Tour... 243

Everything's Weird ❂ 180 Degrees ❂ The Battle ❂ Rock 'n' Roll to the Rescue ❂ Slow Dancing ❂ P. Hux Redux ❂ A Final Tour ❂ P. Hux 2.0 ❂ And in the End ❂ Livin' On the Edge ❂ Steer Clear ❂ Helle ❂ Purgatory Falls, the Album

PART THREE – IN WHICH WE FIGHT FOR OUR MUSICAL LIVES

Chapter 15: No Rewind... 269

Heavenly ❂ In the Year 2000 ❂ No Rewind ❂ A Twist on Twist ❂ April Is the Cruelest Month ❂ Worst Name in Rock ❂ Identity Crisis ❂ Meet the Nuptials ❂ Addition by Subtraction ❂ Best Name in Rock ❂ Follow That! ❂ Pulling Strings

Chapter 16: The Orchestra... 283

Let There Be Drummers ☯ Den ☯ Hey, Trommeslager! ☯ Machine Guns and Bananas ☯ The Center Holds ☯ We'd Better Get on It ☯ Who's the Orchestra? ☯ A Calamitous Miscalculation ☯ 9/11 and 10/01 ☯ To Bev or Not to Bev

Chapter 17: Leaving The West Behind... 295

Getting Better ☯ Echo, Banned ☯ Getting Worse ☯ Fab Five ☯ Here Comes My Baby ☯ He's Sam and I'm Out ☯ House Concert ☯ Homemade Spaceship ☯ Workin' for MCA, Again ☯ Go East, Old Man ☯ Elementary, My Dear Huxley ☯ Canadian Idol ☯ Smart Fi ☯ The King ☯ Leaving the West Behind ☯ Russian Idol ☯ Clang, Clang ☯ Getcha Ufa Two-fa ☯ Safe at Last ☯ Swingin' '70s

Chapter 18: Dad... 325

OK in the UK ☯ Dad ☯ Revolver

Chapter 19: Back in the (Former) USSR... 331

We Are Travel ☯ Same, Same ☯ Good Pipe ☯ Cowboys ☯ Why Would You Go? ☯ From Salt Lake to Samara ☯ Deep Tour ☯ Boss of Banner ☯ One for the Money ☯ Two for the Show ☯ A Ray of Sunshine ☯ 78.5 Hours ☯ Split Decision ☯ Love and Marriage ☯ Tits for Tatts

Chapter 20: Thank You, Bethesda... 351

Dream Number One ☯ How The Mighty Have Fallen ☯ Seriously, Muzak? ☯ Union Jack's ☯ Too Tall Indeed ☯ Thank You Bethesda ☯ Hey, These Guys Are Good ☯ Coke and Red Wine ☯ Big Leagues ☯ KISSing Ass ☯ What Goes Around ☯ You'll Never Guess Who ...

Epilogue: Back In The Fold... 371

ELO: With or Without You ☯ Apostrophe or Possessive? ☯ ...Comes Around ☯ Lou Clark ☯ The Hillis Is Alive with the Sound of Music ☯ Pretty Good for Americans ☯ Seasoned Stars ☯ Guns & McKagan ☯ Job #1 ☯ Imogen ☯ Woman Reappears ☯ Where Are They Now? ☯ Electric Light Odyssey

Appendix A: Learning the Repertoire... 381

Appendix B: Travels with ELO Part II and The Orchestra... 383

Appendix C: Amazon Reviews of No Rewind... 385

Appendix D: Every Show 1999 to 2024... 389

Appendix E: P. Hux Discography... 407

Thank you... 417

Index... 419

PREFACE

As a teenager in the late '60s and early '70s, lying in bed at night, eyes closed, listening to my favorite albums on headphones, I often imagined myself center stage, singing my guts out, playing heroic guitar solos and egging on the crowd. Whether it was *Led Zeppelin II*, Bowie's *Ziggy Stardust* or Black Sabbath's debut, there I was in my mind, easily performing the greatest tracks of the hard rock era. Imagining I was Ziggy Zeppelin was fun, but I never thought, "Maybe I could join a famous band." Who aspires to such a thing?

I wrote songs from an early age and once I began taking songwriting seriously, all I wanted in life was to get the music in my head onto records, hear it on the radio, and learn how to play it live like a pro. Those were my dreams.

Thanks to luck, stubbornness, talent, and the good will of countless friends, those dreams came true. I've recorded thirteen studio albums for major and indie labels, heard plenty of my music on the radio, and become a reliable performer. Then, in 1998, the thing I never aspired to do miraculously happened anyway. I joined a successor version of one of my favorite bands: ELO.

In *Electric Light Odyssey*, I tell the story of my determination to build a music career, warts and all, with special emphasis on my unexpected association with ELO Part II and the Orchestra Starring ELO Former Members. I hope you have a great time reading all about it.

MEA CULPAS

Electric Light Odyssey contains stories I pulled from my journals, random personal notes, concert reviews, interviews, and so on—what I'd call "reliable sources." Some stories came straight from my memories and strike me as equally vivid and reliable. "I was there!" I tell myself. Still, is it possible I've misremembered stuff? Sure. Have I perhaps mixed up events that were unrelated? *Definitely maybe.* Others who were also "there" may remember things differently—I'd be surprised if they didn't. My friends' and bandmates' memories are likely just as reliable, or as unreliable, as mine. So, are my stories true? From my perspective, absolutely yes. I've told these stories precisely the way I remember them, as accurately as my memory allows. When I've put quotations around statements by people other than me, I've relied on memories etched in my mind, and done my very best to quote others verbatim. If I've made mistakes, they were made in the spirit of capturing the truth.

Electric Light Odyssey describes events from the 1950s up to 2024. Societal norms and expectations related to race, gender roles, language, privilege, and so on have radically evolved during the last sixty-eight years. I pay attention to that stuff, and I have two daughters and a wife who keep me culturally updated from their perspectives. That said, I've tried to be respectful of how people behaved and how language was commonly used in the past, how it reflected cultural norms of the time, and even how it sounded. When appropriate for this memoir, I've used some (pretty innocuous, really) language that best suits the story I'm telling and the decade in which the story occurred.

PART ONE

IN WHICH I GET A CALL OUT OF THE BLUE

CHAPTER 1

THE AUDITION

I needed to repair my tattered life. In 1998, I was forty-two and surviving month to month. I shared a rented house with two musician friends in the Echo Park hills, on the cheaper margin of Los Angeles. My once-upon-a-time recording contract with Columbia Records had terminated after one album, and I hadn't seen a steady paycheck since the end of my run as a staff songwriter with MCA Music Publishing six years earlier. I was no longer the intriguing new guitarist/singer in town, much less the Next Big Thing, and I wasn't getting any younger in a young man's game.

POSTER BOY

To pay my bills, I performed my original music in LA clubs, wrote songs with other artists, and composed instrumental music for film and television. I was happy to take odd jobs—anything I could do to make a buck in the music biz. I once spent two weeks teaching Harvey Keitel how to look and act like a guitar player for his *Finding Graceland* movie. Harvey was fun to be around, but not overly interested in learning guitar. After one lesson, he said, "I don't think I can do this." I said, "Harvey, think of all the guitar players who struck gold using three chords. How hard can it be?" Harvey chuckled. He stuck with me, and I earned my paycheck.

I won Album of the Year awards three times. My records received glowing press but rarely sold in numbers beyond "cult" status. I appreciated being a critic's darling, but I'd never met a landlord willing to accept a four-star review in place of a month's rent. I was a poster boy for the artist cliche: good at creating music, not so good at creating commerce.

I drove a banged-up white Ford Ranger pickup that I'd bought for $1 from an in-law (keeping it on the road was a lot more expensive). Health insurance and personal savings were out of the question. I'd long ago given up on middle-class security. On top of everything else, I was recently widowed. The curtain fell on my happily married life with screenwriter Janet Heaney when she succumbed to brain cancer the previous year, aged thirty-eight. Her death had devastated me, and there was nothing I could do but learn to live with it. I'd steadily progressed from shock to depression to black-humored stoicism, but normalcy, or heaven forbid, happiness, was still a long way off. I needed something to pull me upward.

A CALL OUT OF THE BLUE

Seen from my living room, downtown Los Angeles squatted on the horizon, barely visible in the smog, just a few miles south of my low-rent hillside home. Cheap sliding windows let in a questionably healthy breeze. The walls of my California bachelor pad were crowded with outsider art. Some pieces rose no higher than thrift store kitsch, but I did have one excellent small painting called "Heaven Everwhere" (yes, the title is spelled correctly) by folk legend Howard Finster, which I'd bought with money from my publishing deal with MCA. I also found space for treasured posters of underappreciated rock heroes such as Dwight Twilley and Pierce Turner.

I was camped in my living room with a young husband and wife duo who called themselves Splendid. They were in the writing phase for their debut album and had sought my help. I didn't have a string of chart-topping smashes to my credit (some in the industry thought my songs coulda-shoulda been hits), but I had a solid reputation as a good writer, thoughtful lyricist, and collegial collaborator. I enjoyed writing with other artists, even if it was essentially unpaid spec work. The odds of writing a hit song and making a living from music are daunting at best, but I was determined to keep trying. Here's what I needed to do:

1. Tap into the cultural zeitgeist, pinpoint a universal emotion, and merge the two into singable lyrics and irresistibly catchy music.
2. Match my song with an extraordinary artist, producer, and record label.
3. Create a recording unlike anything ever heard before.
4. Pray the label's promotional staff will pay, I mean, convince hundreds of radio program directors that my song is a surefire number-one hit.
5. In the likely event of failure, return to step 1.

Fueled by coffee, we strummed acoustic guitars and jotted down our best lyric ideas. I had just mentioned I had a song they might like called "Come Clean" when my phone rang. I crossed the room to my wall-mounted landline.

A man's voice said, "Uh, hi. Is this Parthenon? 'P. Hux?' I'm not sure what to call you."

"This is Parthenon."

Chapter 1: The Audition

"Okay. My name's Eric Troyer. I play in a band called Electric Light Orchestra Part II."

I wasn't expecting that. I signaled to my guests that I needed to take the call. I was intrigued.

Eric continued. "We have a mutual friend, Jeffrey Foskett."

I smiled. "Oh, okay! Yeah, I love Jeff. He's my 'new best friend.'"

A few months earlier, I'd met the former Beach Boy and surf music aficionado at the Garden Grove Amphitheater in Orange County, south of LA. My band, P. Hux, had preceded Foskett at the International Pop Overthrow Festival. We'd watched each other from the side of the stage and come away impressed. Jeff and I spoke backstage and hit it off immediately. With Foskett in the mix, the phone call became less strange. I figured this would be about a favor for a friend—maybe someone needed to borrow a guitar.

Eric told me he'd recently called Foskett asking for a favor. *Bingo*. He continued, "I sang on John Lennon's *Double Fantasy*, but I never received a Gold Record from Geffen. I asked Foskett if he could get me one, since he's good at that stuff, hobnobbing with the labels and everything. I normally don't care much about these kinds of things, but, you know, it was John Lennon and if there's one Gold Record I'd like on my wall, it's *Double Fantasy*."

"Yeah, no kidding," I said, pretending I knew what it would be like to sing with John Lennon or earn a Gold Record. Good story.

Eric went on. "So anyway, kind of as an aside, I mentioned my band was looking for a new guitarist and Foskett recommended you."

"Did he really?"

I must've spoken a little loudly. My songwriting guests looked at me and picked up on the change in my tone. I tried to focus. Through the open living-room window, I could hear chained-up dogs barking from the bottom of the canyon. I closed the window. This apparently wasn't just a conversation about Jeffrey Foskett and gold albums.

"Well, that was nice of him," I said idiotically. "What did he say?"

"He said he played a show with you recently and that we should cancel the auditions because you were the perfect guy."

"Ha!" How much did I love my New Best Friend Jeffrey Foskett?

Eric laughed, too. "So, what do you think? Are you the perfect guy?" I could picture this Eric dude kind of smiling on the other end of the line.

"Of course, I'm the perfect guy!" What else was I going to say?

With the landline phone cradled on my shoulder, I reached into a closet where my vinyl LPs languished on shelves. I pulled out my four ELO albums and found one with a good picture of the group.

"So, who's still in the band?" I asked, ready to match current members to the guys from the classic '70s lineup.

"Well, it's Bev of course on drums, Kelly Groucutt on bass, Mik Kaminski on violin, Lou Clark on orchestral keyboards, and I sing and play keyboards...".

"Is Jeff involved?" I asked, referring to Jeff Lynne, ELO's singer, songwriter, and producer.

"No. Jeff's not involved."

That was disappointing, but it made sense. If Lynne was still in the band, I wouldn't be needed. At least Bev was in, and that was huge. Bev had drummed for the Move, ELO's predecessor, and one of my all-time favorite bands. That was *cool*. And ELO Part II had three more guys from the glory days of ELO—a high percentage for a classic rock band.

Eric went on. "Anyway, we're looking for a guitarist and singer, but we also want to find someone who can write songs for a new album."

This was sounding better by the minute.

Eric and I talked some more and eventually agreed that I would send him some of my music and we'd talk after he'd had a listen. When the call ended, I apologized to my guests for interrupting our songwriting session. I shook my head and muttered, "That was weird."

They waited for me to spill the beans.

"I think I might be joining a band."

WOODSHEDDING

The day after speaking with Eric, all I could think about was ELO and the band's predecessor group, the Move. I'd spent a lot of time in college listening to ELO's *Out of the Blue* under headphones. It was a richly produced double slab of post-Beatle perfection and I knew it well. In high school, my friends and I had marveled at the sound of albums by the Move such as *Shazam*, *Looking On*, and *Message From the Country*. Thundering bass guitar, dry compressed drums, reedy vocals, and layers of crunchy guitars mixed with oddball sounds from cellos and recorders. To our ears, the Move were the coolest thing, especially since they weren't super-famous. Post-college, my band played Move songs such as "Down On The Bay," and I'd even written a song called "Dino's Laughing Now," which mentioned the Move in the lyrics. I was a fan.

I flashed back to another memory from the late 1970s. I was on the Greek Island of Ios when the *International Herald Tribune* showed two photos of a "British rock group's spaceship," which looked like a giant white clamshell. In the top photo, the spaceship was closed; in the bottom photo, it was open, with laser beams shooting out of it above the (relatively) tiny members of ELO arrayed inside. The idea of inserting myself into the Move/ELO scenario seemed like a farfetched fantasy.

In 1998, the internet was still in its infancy, so I packaged up some of my CDs along with a three-page letter detailing why I'd be a great fit for the band. I began with "Dear Eric: I've had some time to think about this gig, and I've decided you want me." I was being funny (but not). Soon after receiving my package, Eric called to say I sounded like a good candidate and asked if I'd be willing to learn a batch of ELO songs and audition for the band in England.

Yes. Yes, I would.

In my excitement, I thought, "If I get this gig, it's as close as I'll ever get to being in the Beatles." Joining the Beatles was a fantasy, of course, but, in reality, I could hardly do better than ELO, even if it was the less-known successor group, ELO Part II. John Lennon himself had declared ELO "Son of Beatles" and ELO's marriage of rock and hard-chugging strings evoked the Fabs' exquisitely progressive Strawberry Fields/I Am the Walrus period. How cool if I could be a part of all that.

The audition for ELO Part II required that I learn guitar and vocal parts for "Do Ya," "Rockaria!," "Evil Woman," "Getting To The Point," and "Ma-Ma-Ma Belle." My favorite ELO song at the time was "10538 Overture." It had a killer descending guitar riff and a great vocal melody. It wasn't on the list they'd sent me, but I decided to learn it anyway, just in case (always over-prepare).

As I studied Lynne's songs, I discovered they contained certain naughty chords—diminished and augmented—which I rarely used in my own music. I had to work extra hard to train my left (chord-shaping) hand to learn these ELO tricks. There was no faking this stuff. My playing had to be fluid. No clams (mistakes) allowed. Two of the songs also required that I employ a slide, so I boned up on my slide guitar skills, as well.

Eric instructed me to learn the lead vocals on each song. If I joined the group, I might wind up singing harmony instead of lead on certain songs, but for the audition it was best to keep things simple.

As I rehearsed, there were times when I confused an evil woman with a sweet talkin' one, but I dug in and learned the songs note for note. During every moment of woodshedding in LA, I knew that waiting for me in Birmingham were musicians whose pictures I'd studied on album covers. I'd soon be plugging in with Bev Bevan, Kelly Groucutt, Mik Kaminski, and Lou Clark, as well as my newest best friend Eric Troyer. These were the real guys. I had to be ready.

THE AUDITION

The band flew me from LA to England and put me up at the Jarvis Hotel in Solihull, a leafy town near Birmingham. ELO Part II's accountant, a kindly and quick-to-laugh English gentleman in his fifties named Phil Ackrill, drove me from my hotel to the audition. It was late morning. We wound past verdant parks and endless blocks of tidy brick duplexes ("semi-detached houses" in *English* English). Phil pointed out some of the local landmarks as we headed into urban Birmingham, home of Black Sabbath, the Moody Blues, and (my favorite) the Move. Phil complained lightly about the Moodies' reputation as kings of classical rock. "They don't have *half* the hits of ELO. Not even close." I hadn't expected this outbreak of rock 'n' roll jousting, but game on, Phil.

After about twenty-five minutes, we turned down a narrow alley between generic brick buildings. "Here we are, Parthenon. Rich Bitch."

I looked out the window. I wasn't sure what Phil was referring to.

"Rich Bitch. That's the name of the rehearsal studio."

Ah. Had a ring to it, for sure.

I stepped inside and Phil steered me into Rich Bitch's biggest rehearsal room. Large black road cases on steel caster wheels rested against the walls and doubled as seating. Padded sound proofing covered the ceiling. The room hummed with conversation and light laughter. A dozen men mingled about, sipping hot drinks and chatting. Most were dressed in the standard-issue rock 'n' roll uniform: black clothes, big sneakers or boots, and longish hair.

Arranged in a large circle were two electric keyboards, drums, a bass amp, guitar amp, and mic-stands. All very familiar. Rehearsal rooms are rehearsal rooms. The difference here in Rich Bitch was the large team of road crew. Nice to have help from half a dozen guys.

Bev Bevan's enormous drum set dominated one side of the room. It would look impressive on stage, but to my taste it had far too many toms and cymbals. But what do I know? Bev's a legend, right? A long-haired guy who wasn't Bev stood near the kit polishing Bev's cymbals. A drum roadie.

Just then, a man, a good bit shorter than me, walked in my direction. He sported a below-the-knees black leather "duster," tight black jeans, a silver-studded belt, cowboy boots, and a ponytail popping out the back of his otherwise shiny, bald head. Clearly not a roadie. He stopped directly in front of me, looked up, and declared with a brassy voice, "You're too tall!"

Kelly Groucutt laughed at his joke and introduced himself as "the bass player." I liked him right away.

Across the room, I picked out Eric Troyer, the band's keyboardist, singer, and, most significantly, my champion. Like me, he was an American in a room full of Brits. Eric had bluntly told me that the band's preference was to find an English guitar player instead of another (bloody) American, but here I was. We were both under added pressure to make this audition go well.

Eric came over and greeted me warmly. "You made it!"

"I did! Thanks for having me here."

He gave me a half-serious look of concern. "You learned the parts, right?"

"Oh, was I supposed to?" We laughed. "Yeah, I should be okay."

Eric walked me over to Bev Bevan. Six-foot-three, thick brown hair, and dressed in denim from head to toe, Bev asked about my flight, was the hotel okay, etc., nothing earth-shattering. Then he said he'd listened to my CDs and liked my music. I was thrilled. Moments like this were weird and wonderful. In high school, I'd spent hours nodding my head in time to Bev's drumming on albums by the Move. In a few minutes, we'd be playing "Do Ya" together.

Additional polite introductions were made around the room. I felt welcomed but not too welcomed. If the audition went poorly, I'd be shown the door. Guitar tech Barrie "Barru" Evans (a Welshman very handy with a guitar himself) led me to my place in front of the Vox AC30 amp I'd requested. When in doubt, use Beatles amps. I removed my guitar from its gig bag. Barru helped me set up my effects pedals and made sure I was happy with the sound of the amp.

I should've been nervous, but I remember thinking, "In a few minutes, I'm going to hear what Bev Bevan sounds like in person." I was eager to play. I knew I'd have to quickly get over being excited by who was in the room and pay attention to the racket we were making. As much as this audition was about me, I wanted us to sound like a band. I tuned the strings on my guitar, propped my cheat sheets on a music stand, and adjusted the height of the vocal mic.

I watched the members of ELO Part II head to their instruments. Each guy sported a de rigueur classic rock hairstyle. Kelly topped the bill with his kung fu ponytail, the rest of the English guys sported long hair and goatees, and Eric's layered cut safely sidestepped a shag. The animated Mr. Groucutt strapped on a dark blue bass guitar and adjusted his vocal mic, brawny Bev settled behind his Pompidou Center of drums, the impossibly youthful Eric Troyer (50, could've passed for 35) situated himself at the keyboards, the slight Mik Kaminski tuned his blue violin, and the gentlemanly Lou Clark settled in behind his orchestral keyboards. The crew guys receded to the perimeter. Right on cue, the awkward feel of "audition" settled over the room. It was now or never.

I asked if we might start with "Do Ya." Nods all around. Good. Okay.

A few seconds passed and no one played anything.

Kelly said, smiling, "*You* start it, you know."

I laughed. "Oh, right! So I do." So, I did.

"Do Ya" begins with three very satisfying power chords (D, A-A, G). If you're a guitarist auditioning for *the band that plays this song*, you've got to get at least three things right:

1. The guitar must produce a satisfying crunch. Not too clean, not too fuzzy. The sound must be *crunchy*.
2. The tempo must be restrained. Tempting as it might be to let adrenaline rule the day and blast through the three opening chords quickly, one must, instead, pull back on the throttle a little bit. "Do Ya" has what we musical sophisticates refer to as "balls." Played too quickly, the balls won't swing. (Trust me, the *cahunas* metaphors go on forever.)
3. You must deploy a slide (a short tube of metal or glass) on your fretting hand's pinky finger. "Do Ya" features a guitar element that sounds like a downshifting bus. It's created by placing the slide on the 7th fret and moving it down the neck toward the headstock. "Do Ya" also has a middle bit that features the slide moving *up* the neck. Both slide parts are critical to the correct execution of the song.

So, I did all those things. And I sang my little heart out. The result was good. The song sounded right, which meant I hadn't ruined it. Bev Bevan hit the drums hard as hell and I thought, "So *that's* what he sounds like." Big sticks, big kit, big dude. He did not pussyfoot around. Kelly and Eric nailed all the super high vocal parts, and Mik and Lou were an amazing two-man orchestra ... what a band!

Chapter 1: The Audition

I stole some looks at Bev, trying not to watch him as a fan, but checking his facial expression to see if he looked pleased. The guys mostly kept their cool, playing along, doing their parts, not letting their faces give too much away (Brits are good at that). But I noticed one very important thing: no stink faces. No grimaces. No expressions that said, "Oh, Christ, this guy's terrible ... are we really gonna let him play four more songs?" That didn't happen.

On we went. "Rockaria!" raced along like the Chuck Berry tribute it was, a fun up-tempo runaway train of rock 'n' roll that, again, required me to play slide, but nothing I couldn't handle. "Ma-Ma-Ma Belle" rocked in a sludgy, grindy way, a good one to not speed up. I sang "Getting To The Point" with real feeling, even though it was the song I knew least well. After four songs, heads around the room had begun to nod in the affirmative.

We reached the last song of the audition, "Evil Woman." I did the "You made a fool of me" bit and then the band launched into the meat of the song. As the intro ended and I began to sing, something didn't sound right. I'd lost the phrasing of the lyrics. I had the words on my cheat sheet in front of me, but I couldn't recall exactly how the phrasing fit with the music. The first verse went badly, and when the second verse started just as poorly, I could feel my skin getting sweaty. I was botching the vocal, pure and simple.

Kelly Groucutt let go of his bass and waved his hands for the band to stop. My brain screamed, "Shit! I blew it." A sinking feeling snaked into my gut.

But instead of acting annoyed or schooling me on the part, Kelly, bless his soul, gently bailed me out. "Don't worry about it," he said with a smile. "I sing this one anyway. Just play along." We re-started the song with Kelly taking the vocal. Chagrined but relieved, I relaxed into the easy guitar parts and sang on the choruses. "Well, I've got at least one vote," I thought. "Kelly's on my side."

The audition ended there. Despite the "Evil Woman" meltdown, no one had a horrified look on their face. I didn't expect applause or a group hug, but as "Evil Woman" hung in the air, and no one said much of anything (note to self: English people often won't speak without a beer in their hand), the quiet in the room kind of got to me. I realized it was premature for the band to say anything definitive since there were more auditions after mine, but still, it was unnerving.

I said into my mic, "Do you guys do '10538 Overture?'" The band members looked around at each other, surprised by my request. Kelly mumbled, "We've done it in the past, but it's been a while." Lou Clark said, "I think we do it in C" and started to leaf through his sheet music. After some more mumbling

11

and group-speak about the arrangement (I asked to play it in the original key of D), it was decided we could proceed.

I thought, "Well, if I don't get the job, at least I'll have played '10538' with these guys."

Bev clicked his sticks to count us in and I opened with the cool descending guitar part. I focused intently, playing the arpeggiated notes cleanly and not allowing the tempo to speed up. Lou's strings came in, Bev's drums tumbled down a musical cliff and, voila, it sounded mountainous. I dug into the vocal and, all bets off, lost myself in the joy of playing "10538 Overture" with ELO Part II. It was among the greatest four minutes of my life. Hardly anyone in America even knows this song, and here I was in England with Bev bashing, Eric and Kelly harmonizing, Mik sawing away, and Lou nailing the orchestral parts. I was in the middle of a loud, heavenly hurricane.

The atmosphere in the room changed. The crew guys were smiling openly. I could see them exchanging looks that said, "This one's keen for the gig." The band looked happier, too. Bev looked over and said, "Good job." Eric looked pleased as well. And relieved.

At that moment, I was content to pack up and get out of there. I had survived my clammy "Evil Woman." My ace in the hole, "10538 Overture," had perhaps done the trick. I could leave on a high note. Good vibes aside, I knew it was possible I wouldn't get the job. It was a big ask to fill the position created by Jeff Lynne. At least one more audition was scheduled for that afternoon. I could be blindsided by some hotshot. Someone younger. Someone hipper. Someone British. I hated the thought.

COOKIE MONSTER

Phil Ackrill drove me back to my hotel in Solihull. We chatted a bit, but Phil conspicuously said nothing about the audition. Not his call. The band would decide my fate. I couldn't help but think that this day, December 4, 1998, could be a major turning point. Had I done enough at the audition to change my life? Could I really become a bandmate of the guys from ELO?

Phil dropped me off. I was jet-lagged, eight time zones from my home in Los Angeles. My adrenaline was wearing off and I couldn't wait to collapse into bed. With my black Fender Telecaster secure in its gig bag on my back, I dragged my roller bag noisily over terracotta pavers in the hallway of the Jarvis Hotel.

Wait. What's that?

I stopped. I heard singing. It was coming from a room adjacent to mine. It had to be the next guy—the hotshot. The hairs stood up on my neck and I unashamedly placed my ear to the door. I could hear the tinny strum of an unplugged electric guitar. Then a voice sang, "DOOO-yah DOOO-yah wan' my LUVVVVV?" The voice was gruff. Unpleasant. And an octave too low. It sounded like Cookie Monster.

It was the most beautiful thing I'd ever heard.

WE'LL SEE YOU IN URUGUAY

I was startled awake by the loud *brrrrrrrrring* of an odd-sounding phone. Ugh. What time was it? I didn't see a clock. I sat up in bed, but it wasn't my bedroom. Where was I? The foreign phone rang again. It was dark outside. I reached to turn on a bedside lamp and glanced around the room. England. Right! I'm in England. I grabbed the phone.

"Hel-lo-oh," I said, with groggy politeness.

"Good evening, Parthenon. It's Phil Ack. I know I'm probably waking you up. Did you get some kip?"

It was Phil. The nice guy. The band accountant.

"If kip means sleep, yeah. I did. Thanks, Phil."

I groggily became aware that this evening was the same day as the audition. Wow, that's weird. Seemed like a million years ago. Wait a minute. The audition! Why was Phil calling me and not one of the guys in the band? Oh, no. Here comes the bad news. Don't tell me Cookie Monster got the gig? No fucking way. I couldn't believe it. Phil interrupted my thoughts. "The band would like to take you out to dinner. Can you be ready in a half hour?"

Dinner? Yes! Yes! Yes!

"That sounds great, Phil," I said, trying to sound nonchalant. Uncool to be overeager. "Yeah, I can be ready. Should I meet you in the lobby?"

"I'll be there. See you in a half hour then, Parthenon."

"Okay, Phil. Thanks."

I GOT THE GIG!

Wait. Did I? The band wouldn't take me out to dinner to tell me I *didn't* get the gig, would they? The unlikely scenario flashed through my head: "Order anything you like, old boy. This is the last you'll ever see of ELO Part II." That seemed ungentlemanly. Un-British.

I got in the shower. The alarmingly hot water helped remove my lingering jet lag. I fantasized about how I'd share the news with my girlfriend. How I'd tell my brothers. My mom and dad. My friends. I felt fantastic, excited about the future. As I soaped up, I broke into "Sweet Talkin' Woman" in a swinging Sinatra-like croon that echoed off the tiled shower walls. I told myself to calm down. Nothing has happened yet. They're taking you to dinner. That's all. Stay in the moment.

I got out of the shower, got dressed, and said aloud, "Thank you, friends." That's my blanket gesture of gratitude to whomever is on my side, living or dead, seen or unseen, real or not. It's basically, "Thank you, God" without specifying an all-powerful bearded dude or sword-wielding Amazon.

On my way to joining Phil in the lobby, I again put my ear to the adjacent room's door. Nothing. Did they send Cookie Monster home already? Good sign.

Phil drove us out of Solihull and into the very dark countryside. The headlights of his comfy car were solitary beacons on the wrong side of the road. We discussed English history, a subject about which Phil was very enthused. He pointed out a red and white flag dramatically lighted atop a looming castle. "Flag of St. George, there, Parthenon. Wouldn't be right if it were the Union Jack." I didn't pretend to know the difference but thought it would be cool to return to this part of the world and learn more. If I got this new job, perhaps that could happen.

We pulled into the parking lot of the cheerfully lighted Pearl Palace Restaurant. This was it. Polite kiss-off or bright future. Phil and I entered a carpeted front room. Through a set of open double doors, I could see all five members of ELO Part II in the restaurant bar, pints of beer and glasses of wine in hand.

"Ah, there he is!" Bev announced in his chesty voice, as Phil and I entered the bar area. "You've decided to come after all!" Bev laughed. He was in good spirits. I began to relax. A little. Mik Kaminski, speaking with a wooly, nearly indecipherable Yorkshire drawl, advised me, "There's still time to back out, you know." More laughs.

I liked these guys.

I attempted to assimilate to British culture and ordered a Newcastle Brown Ale. Once my pint of just-below-room-temp ale was in hand, we stood together and Bev said, "We all thought you did a very good job today, Parthenon, and we've made a unanimous decision. We'd like you to join the group."

My face broke into a huge smile. I didn't know what to say. The moment may have been even bigger than I'd understood. We clinked glasses all around. I still hadn't said anything.

Bev rescued me and asked, "So, would you like to join the group?"

Chapter 1: The Audition

It was my turn to laugh. "Yeah! I'd be honored to join the group." Hurrah. My brain and voice still worked. God, that felt great to say.

"We just want to be sure," Bev said.

"Yeah," chimed in the suddenly animated Lou Clark, "because we're tired of fucking auditioning people!"

Bev went on. "You'll join as an equal member. One sixth. You'll make the same money as everyone else."

"Or lose the same money," Mik Kaminski noted, to yet more laughs.

I hadn't even thought about the money.

I loved Bev's up-front, above-board presentation. He'd taken the worry out of something I wasn't even worried about.

"We have some dates coming up in South America," Bev continued. "Plus, some shows in Eastern Europe and then a good, long, proper tour of the UK." (For a complete list of my travels with ELO Part II and the Orchestra, see Appendix B.)

"That sounds amazing," I said. On the outside I was calm, but I was turning cartwheels inside. Damn—this was no joke. I'd played music for years but toured only rarely in the U.S. and Europe. My life was on a whole new trajectory.

As I sipped my beer, I enjoyed a brief out-of-body experience watching Bev "drummer-of-the-Move" Bevan talk to me as a member of his band. An equal member. It was like my planet was suddenly orbiting a much brighter sun. It also struck me that Bev was acting as spokesman and presumed leader of the band. In my experience it was unusual for a drummer to take that role, but in ELO Part II, it made sense. Besides owning a commanding presence, Bev was a founding member of ELO. Seniority ruled.

"So," Bev continued as I re-entered my body, "There's a lot of catching up you'll have to do between now and the new year when we start. We'll bring you over for a rehearsal in January before the tour, here in Birmingham at Rich Bitch, but we'd like you to start learning the full show—about thirty-eight songs—and then we'll see you in Uruguay!"

Uruguay. Of course. As you do. Jeez.

"Cheers!" Bev raised his pint glass and nodded in my direction. Another round of clinks with Bev, Kelly, Mik, Lou, and Eric. No teetotalers in ELO Part II. Ceremony over, the guys chatted among themselves. Eric Troyer stepped over to me and offered congratulations. "Alright, man, you got the job! Nice goin'." Eric was pleased. I was happy not just for me, but for Eric as

15

well. He'd taken a shot on Jeff Foskett's recommendation, and it had worked out. He said I'd handled the pressure of the audition and done well.

"Except for 'Evil Woman,'" I admitted.

"Yeah, there were some things here and there that you missed," Eric agreed, "but overall, it was obvious you'd done your homework." That was praise I was happy to accept. Luck and some talent got me a shot, but putting in the work sealed the deal. I had studied the songs and gotten deep enough into the details of the writing to convincingly perform them as if they were mine. I'd also proved to myself that if I wanted something badly enough, I had the capacity to go get it. That felt good.

Kelly Groucutt tipped his pint glass toward me in salutation. "You did okay for an American," he said through a shit-eating grin.

The host of the Pearl Palace indicated that our table was ready.

"One more thing," Bev said, looking me straight in the eye. "There's no possible way we can call you 'Parthenon.' So, from now on, you're 'Hux,' alright?"

I suppose I could've told Bev that James Earl Jones really liked the name Parthenon, but I decided not to bring it up. "Alright, Bev," I agreed. "Hux it is."

I'd been in the band less than five minutes, and I already had a cool new nickname. As we sat down to dinner, I wondered if anyone ever dared call ELO Part II's brawny drummer "Beverly"?

I sat down next to Eric. The first question he asked me clearly illustrated ELO Part II's priorities. He said, "I'm interested to hear what you think about joining the band, but what I need to know right now is, would you like to try a curry?"

WOODSHEDDING PART II

Prepping for my audition was nothing compared to learning ELO Part II's live set. The show pulled songs from all eleven ELO studio albums, the *Xanadu* soundtrack, and two albums by my new best friends in ELO Part II. (See Appendix A for the list of songs I was asked to learn.) I had about six weeks to learn two-and-a-half hours of music. That's a lot of coffee.

In the mail, I received a cassette tape of ELO Part II's most recent show. The band's front-of-house sound man Dennis York had taken the guitar and vocal parts performed by departing member Phil Bates and panned them hard to the left channel. By turning the balance knob on my stereo, I could isolate Phil's performance from the rest of the band and study it in detail. The cassette was my entire training manual. No chord sheets, no lyric sheets. No video.

Chapter 1: The Audition

Listening to Phil sing, I grew concerned that I wouldn't be able to handle some of my vocal assignments. Phil had a strong, bluesy vocal tone. He could reach high notes with his voice in full throttle. My tone is more on the John Lennon side of things. In my upper register, I can get a little screechy. When that happens, I default to a smoother, but not as powerful, falsetto. I didn't want the band to think I wasn't as good a singer as Phil. Not much I could do about it until we reconvened in England for rehearsals. Crap.

Analyzing Phil's guitar sound on tape, I could tell he was using a Fender Stratocaster with its distinctive out-of-phase "poinky" banjo sound (a la Eric Clapton on "Lay Down Sally"). Phil was a very good player, and I owned a Strat myself, but I didn't think the Stratocaster's thin-ish sound was appropriate for most ELO music other than "Hold On Tight." My guitar of choice in 1999 was a black Fender Telecaster, cousin to the Strat, but a little more aggressive. Think Led Zeppelin's first album. (Within a year, I would ditch the Tele in favor of more muscular-sounding Gretsch and Gibson guitars.)

To prep for my first tour, I committed to a routine. Every day, my coffee and I commuted from my kitchen to the giant McDowell & Craig Steel Tanker desk in my living room. I studied the cassette tape of ELO Part II live, mapping out the chords for all thirty-eight songs. I made notes where melodies took unexpected turns. I underlined where my assigned singing part switched from a lead vocal to a background harmony. I starred chords that were hard to play and made diagrams of the especially naughty chords that were new to me. I noted where choruses were doubled in length, where verses were shortened by a bar, and where outros modulated to new keys. In no time, I'd filled a looseleaf notebook.

You may wonder why I didn't just write out the music and lyrics on staff paper? Good question. The answer is that I don't read or write music. I'm completely self-taught. I attempted to learn music notation in high school and college and bombed out both times. Musical notation doesn't resonate with me—it looks like birds on power lines. I understand music by its feel, its sound, its rhythm, its emotion, its dreaminess. I feel inadequately educated sometimes, but Paul McCartney and Bruce Springsteen don't read music either, so, I'll happily goof off in the back of class with *those* two dunces.

ELO songs are precisely put together. They don't lend themselves to blues jams, boring middle sections, or long improvisations. All unnecessary musical fat is carved away, leaving tight, lean, fast-moving songs that keep you on your toes. Chord changes occur frequently. On my first attempts to learn some of the more ornate songs like "All Over The World" and "Sweet Talkin' Woman,"

I fell behind quickly. The only cure was to go back to the start and play along again and again. With each attempt, I would get a clearer understanding of the sequence of events. *Intro, verse, pre-chorus, chorus, weird little riff, b-section, breakdown, etc.* I was caught less by surprise as each section came racing at me.

After loads of rehearsal, a cool thing happened—songs began to slow down. My fingers acquired the requisite muscle memory to let me anticipate each onrushing part, to be poised and ready for every chord, every note. The first time I got through "Mr. Blue Sky" without making a mistake—nirvana.

For my audition, I'd worked on a half dozen songs to impress five people. Tour prep was a different ritual. I had to memorize a ton of material and be ready to perform it for an audience of strangers. In a scant few weeks, three dozen songs had to meld with my voice, my fingers, my body, and, in time, my feelings. I leaned on my twenty-plus years of writing songs and playing live to get me through. There are certain things I do as a musician that *work*. It might be an aggressive way of strumming, a softer approach to a background vocal, an unusual way of bending a note. As I grew more comfortable with the songs, I began to substitute my own stylings in place of Phil Bates'. I didn't change a *lot* of things (Phil's a really good player) but I did enough to put my stamp on the songs.

I also listened carefully to the original ELO albums. If I felt a part was iconic and deserved to be played note for note like the original, I did it. A good example of this is the guitar solo on "Mr. Blue Sky." It's a perfect little solo, a charming blend of whimsy and blues. It features a fuzzy tone with all the high end rolled off. I learned the solo note for note because there's no reason to change it and every reason to nail it.

AN EARFUL AT THE AUDIOLOGIST

Eric called me from New Jersey during my woodshedding period. "We'd like you to go to an audiologist and get fitted for some in-ear monitors." Eric explained that the band had successfully switched to in-ear monitors and no longer used wedges, the black-box floor speakers commonly seen arrayed onstage, blasting music back at the band. The problem with wedges is that they're loudspeakers and they add significantly to the noise level on stage. By using in-ear monitors and eliminating wedges, the overall stage noise goes down, making it easier for singers to hear their voices and sing in tune.

I found an audiologist out in the Valley, part of LA's infamous suburban sprawl. She filled my ears with warm molding wax to make impressions of the left and right ear canals. Talk about deep silence. Both ears went absolutely dead to the outside world. Very weird and disconcerting. When the wax had cooled, she removed the molds. They looked like little cornucopia baskets. The molds would be used to make custom mini-monitors that would fit snugly in each of my ears.

A DAY AT THE OPERA

With a new guitarist and fifty-plus gigs booked for 1999, ELO Part II needed to update its publicity photos. The challenge was getting all six band members together in one spot for a photo shoot. Mik Kaminski, Kelly Groucutt, and Bev Bevan, all Brits, lived in England. Lou Clark resided in Cleveland, Ohio, with his American wife Gloria. Eric Troyer had a house in western New Jersey. I lived in Los Angeles where, after all, budding classic rock stars are *supposed* to live.

ELO Part II's final shows with their soon-to-be former guitarist Phil Bates included a date at the Opera House in Wilmington, Delaware, on December 29. My girlfriend, Helle, and I planned to spend Christmas with her family in Maryland, so a jaunt up to Delaware was doable. We arranged to take new band pictures on December 30. When the day came, Helle and I traveled by train from DC to Wilmington. It was a cold, bright morning and a bitter wind whipped down the streets. We walked a half-dozen blocks to the Wilmington Opera House, shivering like the LA weather-wimps we'd become.

I hadn't seen the guys since my induction dinner at the Pearl Palace a month earlier. I was excited to reconnect. I couldn't think of a better Christmas present than photos of ELO Part II with me in them. At forty-two years old, I felt like a kid on a great new adventure.

Band and crew arrived at the backstage area of the Opera House, where coffee and donuts beckoned. It was 11 am, crack-of-dawn musician time. Helle and I'd been up for hours, but it was apparent some members of ELO Part II had enjoyed a late night.

"It's too bloody early," mumbled violinist Mik Kaminski. "I'm still knackered." (Brit for tired.) Lou Clark arrived and, politely, shook Helle's hand. I asked how he was doing. "Alright, I suppose," Lou chuckled. "I could use a beer." Mik agreed that was a good idea, if just a tad early. It soon became apparent that Mik and Lou were, in fact, *Mik 'n' Lou*, a sympatico string section and drinking duo.

The normally effervescent bassist, Kelly Groucutt, joined Helle and me in a warm dressing room. He dropped himself sideways into a padded armchair and rested a snakeskin boot on an adjoining table. He looked fried. Before we could even say "good morning," Kelly removed his glasses, rubbed his eyes, and moaned, "I'm getting too bloody old for this…"

Although I didn't take him literally, the sudden idea of Kelly quitting, or, God forbid, the band breaking up, threatened to turn my donut into a lump of coal. I was reminded that my new bandmates were men in their fifties, all sporting years of rock 'n' roll wear and tear. I wasn't exactly a spring chicken in my early forties.

Rather than discuss his fatigue, I left Kelly in the dressing room with Helle, gambling that the company of a gorgeous, engaging twenty-eight-year-old (just stating facts) might cheer him up. I decided to get more coffee. Barrie "Barru" Evans, the band's guitar tech, joined me at the craft services table.

"D'ya mind if we discuss a few things?" Barru asked in his melodic Welsh drawl.

"No. Not at all." I wondered what there was to discuss. Turned out, a lot.

Barru asked me, what brand of strings did I use on my Telecaster? What gauges? What kind of picks did I prefer? Did I use pedals? Which ones? Did I have a road case for them? No? Could I send him a diagram of my pedal board so he could build a road case for me? Did I have a road case for my *guitar*? It should be easy to get one in LA but let him know if I ran into any problems. Make sure the handles are recessed, otherwise the airlines won't take them. What kind of guitar tuner did I use? Was I interested in a nice strobe tuner for greater accuracy?

That was "a few things"? Wow. Barru was grilling me like Guitar Santa. If he'd been sitting, I might've jumped on his lap.

But Barru St. Nick wasn't finished. His eyes, dancing behind prescription aviators, stayed locked on me. He asked, would I like him to put strap locks on my guitar? We don't want an expensive guitar to fall off my shoulder during a show, do we? He noted I had asked for a Vox AC30 amp at the audition, but was I concerned with their unreliability on the road? Would it be okay if I went with something like a Marshall 800, which is a great sounding and more reliable amp? Did I want to play through just one amp or two? Did any of my pedals have stereo outs? What mics did I prefer for my amps? Shure 57s or something more to my specific tastes?

All this attention to my guitar needs was new and wonderful, but it felt a bit weird to a DIY guy like me. I'd always minded my own gear, carried my own amps, strung my own guitars. I'd never imagined having a guitar tech whose job was to take care of *me*. What a luxury. I thanked Barru for all his attention and assured him I'd be fine with Marshall amps and whatever mics he thought would serve me best. I don't know if he was relieved (*Hux is easy*) or disappointed (*Hux is no fun*).

As I re-filled my coffee and headed back to Helle and Kelly, Barru's survey questions nudged me to ponder my approach to guitar sound. I was not a gearhead. I'd never bothered to learn which pickups were better for what sound, or which woods made the best bodies and necks. If a guitar felt good, played well, sounded nice, and looked cool, I liked it. The same with amps. If an amp's speaker moved lots of air and teamed with my guitar to produce a full range of frequencies from tight low end to clear crispy high, I liked it. My favorite amps were vintage 1960s Vox AC30s (I had three of them). They were loud and awesome sounding—when they behaved. AC30s were favorites of the Beatles and bands like Queen, U2, and Tom Petty. Good company.

I also used a custom-made pedal deliciously called the *P-Hux1 Blue Buddha Tone Rehabilitator*. It was a fantastic-sounding natural distortion pedal designed for me by Jeorge Tripps, the now-famed creator of Way Huge guitar pedals. Jeorge and I met when my band played his high school prom in Monterey, California. We'd been friends ever since.

But, more than anything, my guitar sound depended on my hands. Most guitarists, truth be told, sound like themselves no matter what gear they play. I'll never forget seeing Wally Bryson, the phenomenal guitarist of the Raspberries, playing live with a Parker Fly guitar. In Wally's hands, the thin carbon-fiber guitar sounded like a vintage Les Paul. Wally couldn't help sounding like Wally. Whatever Barru arranged on my behalf, if I sounded like me, I'd be fine with it. (I can't help but mention that, after that Raspberries show, I introduced myself to Eric Carmen backstage. He said, "You're P. Hux? I'm a huge fan of your music!" I nearly fell over.)

A hotshot New York photographer arrived and set up his flash umbrellas in a large room backstage at the Opera House. The band changed into dark (slimming) clothes. I was in a black turtleneck, black jeans, and my favorite black John Fluevog boots. We lined up shoulder to shoulder, all the same distance from the camera, not unlike a police lineup ("identity parade" in *English* English). Dressed in black in a dark room, our faces really popped in those photos. Bev and Eric were the tallest, with me a close third and Mik 'n' Lou next. Kelly was about a foot shorter than the rest of us. The top of his head was level with my shoulder. The new band photo would adorn hundreds of posters and print ads for our 1999 UK Tour. The poster for our Royal Albert Hall show is framed in my home office. Every time I look at it

Electric Light Odyssey

and notice poor Kel's diminished positioning in the photo I think, *we at least could've had Kelly stand on a box.*

The photographer then moved us into the opera house itself and arranged us in the plush seats. The six of us dressed in black against the red seats was a nice image. When I see these photos today, my relaxed pose doesn't fool me. My brain was spinning cartwheels. Sitting for these band photos seemed like the final confirmation that I'd passed the audition and joined the group as an equal member. It was a happy day. Ironic, because less than a year after we posed for those photos at the Wilmington Opera House, my fear of someone quitting the band would turn into reality. The defection by one of our key members would create tremendous financial fallout and torment the band in other ways for years to come.

MUSIC OF YOUR OWN

In January 1999, I returned to England for pre-tour rehearsals. The friendly band accountant, Phil Ackrill, met me at Manchester Airport and we drove to Birmingham together. Phil was easy to talk to. I discovered he loved golf, British history, and Florida, among other things. His wife was a Disney nut, and she filled their house with Mickey and Minnie paraphernalia. I told him I'd been up to my ears in ELO music, studying hard to learn the show.

Phil was kind enough to ask, "Are you working on any new music of your own?"

I didn't know how deep I should go with a relatively new acquaintance, but I decided to dive in anyway. I said, "I'm working on an album called *Purgatory Falls*. That's the name of my late wife's family farm in New Hampshire. She passed away almost exactly two years ago."

Phil said, "Yeah, I heard about that, Parthenon. I'm sorry."

"Thanks." I said, "The thing is, the songs on the album are very intense, as you might imagine, and I'm determined to finish recording them...while still in the throes of my, well, suffering. I didn't want too much time to pass and have them just become normal songs. I felt like I owed it to her to do the best job possible, you know? I'll never, God willing, make another album like this, so I'm trying hard to get it right."

Phil said, "Well, I look forward to hearing it, if that's even the right thing to say."

Chapter 1: The Audition

RICH BITCH PART II

Phil Akrill dropped me off at the Jarvis/George Hotel in suburban Solihull, where I'd stayed during my audition. I was greeted by the same doorman in top hat and long coat. He wasn't particularly helpful with bags, but he made up for it by talking a lot. Good to be back.

The next morning, I headed for the breakfast buffet. I found Kelly Groucutt happily wading into a Full English: fried eggs, baked beans, sliced tomato, hash brown patty, fried bread, cooked mushrooms, cold toast, and, diving in where only the brave dared to go, blood sausage. "Oh, that's gorrrrgeous," he said, offering compliments to the crusty, black meat while chewing happily.

I was a pescatarian. I'd never know the pleasure.

Mik Kaminski arrived, light on his feet as usual, since he weighed about 110 pounds. Mik greeted me, his voice, as always, muffled by Yorkshire wool, "Hello, Hux. Was Norman the Doorman happy to see you again?" Kelly and I laughed.

Eric and Lou, who'd also both flown in from the States, joined us at breakfast. We empathized with each other's jet lag, chugged hot coffee, and discussed what we needed to accomplish in the coming days. With so much music to go over, the band had scheduled me for a full week of rehearsal.

"How'd the woodshedding go?" Eric asked.

"Good. I've got a few questions about some spots where I wasn't sure what Phil was playing on the tape, but I think I know what's going on in most of the songs."

"Well, we'll find out, won't we?" Eric laughed.

We finished breakfast, and back to Rich Bitch we went. The site of my audition had become my workspace. I felt like I'd made a triumphant return. Bev lived near Birmingham and had arrived before us. I found him sipping tea by his drums. He smiled and said, "Hux! You made it! Welcome back." We shook hands. I kept things a tad more businesslike with Bev. He felt a bit like my boss, even if he wasn't. Bev was born on the same day as my dad, so maybe a paternal thing was at play, too.

I greeted the friendly guitar tech Barru and the rest of the crew: gentlemanly Dennis (front of house sound, sage advice), feisty Greg (lights, tour management, sarcastic abuse), affable Nick (cymbal polisher, curly mullet), and mischievous Simon (monitors, short pants).

I arranged my cheat sheets on a music stand in front of my vocal mic. I carefully inserted my new in-ear monitors, red dot for right ear, blue dot for left ear. I flipped on my amp's standby switch, checked my guitar sound, and tapped my vocal mic. I was ready for rehearsal to begin.

First things first. I dreaded the moment, but I had to confess to Kelly and Eric that some of my vocal parts were above my full-voice range. I sheepishly apologized, saying I would have to employ falsetto on some of my high parts. I expected them to be disappointed and I was prepared to get an earful. Amazingly, that didn't happen. They both just shrugged.

"Falsetto's fine," Eric said.

"There's three of us singing most o' the time," Kelly added, "we don't need full voice from everyone."

My angst blissfully plummeted. I'd been worried about nothing. I loved these guys.

MODUS OPERANDI

By the end of the first day of rehearsal, I noticed that ELO Part II employed two distinct modes of operation. Mode One spoke to the band's understated English professionalism and efficiency. We'd launch into a song, everyone listening to everyone else. If something wasn't right, we'd stop to fix it.

"The guitar doesn't come in until such and such time." Right. Got it.

"The chord leading into the bridge is actually a diminished chord, not a minor." Oh, okay.

"We're playing it too fast. Start again." Check.

No one raised their voice or sounded annoyed. It was all business.

We continued that way, playing each song until we were satisfied that every vocal phrase, guitar chord, vocal harmony, string part, solo, pause, build, breakdown, modulation, etc., was in its proper place. Once a song's arrangement was fully agreed upon, woe unto thee who made a mistake. The smallest error was fair game for merciless mocking. Whenever I blew a lyric or sang an errant note of harmony, the devilish Mr. Groucutt would grimace and thrust an accusing black-fingernail-polished digit at me and declare, "You said you could do it when you wrote in!" In this manner, we set about rehearsing thirty-eight songs, methodically piecing together two-and-a-half hours of music. It would take the full week to get it done.

Mode Two spoke to the band's understated English ability to fuck off. Eric, speaking into his vocal mic so everyone in the large room could hear, might say, "Okay, are we ready to go over 'Poker'? Hux, do you and Kelly have the harmonies worked out? Oh, wait—where's Kel?"

Crew member: "He's stepped out for a smoke."

Chapter 1: The Audition

Eric, to crew: "Can one of you guys go get him? We've got a ton of stuff to go over." This kind of talk earned Eric the title "typical pushy American." A crew member would shuffle out of the room, perhaps in search of Kelly as requested, or perhaps in search of tea and a sandwich. Without our bassist/singer, momentum for rehearsing "Poker" dissipated. The rest of us would noodle on our instruments or visit some other part of the room where a story or joke might be in progress. Ten minutes would pass. Kelly would finally reappear.

Eric, back on his mic: "Alright, Kelly's back. Shall we go over 'Poker'? Hux, do you have the lyrics memorized yet?"

Me: "Working on it . . .".

Eric, sarcastically: "O-*kay*-ayy . . .".

Me: "I'll be fine. Let's do it."

Eric: "Yes, let's. We left off working on the middle part. We had a question about the string parts...oh, Christ! Where're Mik 'n' Lou?"

Crew member: "I believe they've just nipped down to the pub."

Eric: "What? It's only noon!"

Crew member: "That's never stopped them before."

Eric: "How long will they be down there?"

Crew member: "I would imagine until they're fetched."

Eric: "Oh, for Chrissakes! Can someone please run down there and bring them back?"

The crew would exchange glances to gauge whether any of them were interested in interrupting Mik 'n' Lou during their first pints of the day. It was easy to read their thoughts about Eric's request: *Pushy American!*

RINGING

After a week at Rich Bitch with ELO Part II, I felt relatively secure about my guitar and vocal parts. The work had paid off. In addition, the guys had introduced me to several excellent local curry houses and encouraged me to drink near-room-temperature English draught beer during nightly sessions at our hotel's low-ceilinged 250-year-old pub, The George. All in all, it had been a solid week of band bonding. In a month, I would see them in Uruguay.

The morning after our final rehearsal, I bid adieu to Norman the Doorman in Solihull and caught a train to London. I stayed the next few days at the home of Monelle and Morley Speed. I'd known Monelle since fifth grade. During my first night in their elegant and quiet Highgate home, I awoke, distracted by a high-pitched sound. I turned on a bedside lamp and walked around the guest room, trying to locate the source of the shrill signal. I couldn't figure out where it was coming from. It sounded the same, no matter where I stood. I sat back down on the bed and put my hands over my ears. The sound was still there.

"Oh, no."

A shot of fear-infused adrenaline raced through my body. The ringing sound was in my head. I couldn't get away from it. Or turn it off. I felt like I might have a panic attack. I was not only panicky, I was pissed off. In-ear monitors had to be the culprit. Loud music had directly pounded my ear drums for a week at Rich Bitch without much of a break. I cursed the in-ear technology.

The irony of my situation wasn't lost on me. I'd joined ELO Part II and was about to embark on my first tour with the band. My life had literally taken a huge turn for the better. But at what cost? Tinnitus? *Can't get it out of my head*, indeed. After trying to distract my brain by reading a book, I lay back down on the bed and prayed the noise would go away. I somehow managed to get back to sleep.

The next morning, the ringing was still audible, but I found that conversing with my hosts enabled me to temporarily ignore it. If that was the trick to dealing with tinnitus, I'd just have to avoid being alone in quiet places for too long.

CHAPTER 2:

SEX, MUGS, AND ROCK 'N' ROLL

I hadn't played a note as the new guitarist for ELO Part II, but I was already convinced I'd landed the greatest gig in the world. Here I was—in Business Class—on a flight to South America, an exotic continent I'd never expected to visit, much less tour. I sat comfortably in my roomy seat, stretched my legs, and drank complimentary wine. My guitar case was safely in a closet, not buried below with the freezing Samsonites. To top things off, a Chilean flight attendant had just leaned over my seat and asked me in her adorable accent, "Please, what group are you?"

Ah. *The Airport Question.*

THE AIRPORT QUESTION

Bands are easily spotted in airports. We are the untidy huddle of black-clad, scruffier-than-thou, guitar-toting dudes and dudettes. I have a theory that, because we perform in public, we are seen as public property. Strangers approach us. They'll either do it nervously ("Hate to bother you guys, but ...") or full of balls ("What's in your case? I play a pretty mean axe myself ..."). Either way, the question will be the same.

"Uh, hey, excuse me, you guys in a band?"

We reply, "Yep."

"You on tour?"

"Unn-hunh."

So far, no harm, no foul.

"What's the name of your band?"

That's the Airport Question.

"What's the name of your band?" is code for "Have I heard of your band?" which is code for "Are you famous?" which really means "Am I going to get a good story out of this interaction or not?" If you happen to be in a famous band, the Airport Question is a win-win. The musicians get to confirm their standing atop the brutal music business and the inquisitor goes home with

"Guess who I met today?" For instance, I have four talented friends, Rusty Anderson, Stevie Salas, Winston Watson, and Rob Ladd, who've all had excellent responses to the Airport Question: "Paul McCartney," "Mick Jagger," "Bob Dylan," "Roger Daltrey." *Boom.*

If you're not obviously famous, "What's the name of your band?" translates to "After chasing your dream all these years, has your career amounted to doodle-y squat or not?" For all of you who don't work as musicians, you're welcome for us shouldering this high risk of public humiliation.

My responses to the Airport Question have included "Me & Dixon," "E," "VeG," "Kyle Vincent," "Head Popping Through," plus of course "P. Hux" and "Parthenon Huxley," among others. There are good bands on that list (as some of you will know) and, yes, occasionally, we would be approached by fans who knew us, but it's not exactly a murderer's row of Top Ten Recognizable Names.

Typically, if I respond to your Airport Question with "Parthenon Huxley," your expression, which seconds earlier was hopeful and maybe even excited, will go blank. You'll say, "Sorry, *who?*" or "Parmesan *what?*" or "Okay, cool…have a good…show, or whatever." You'll walk away disappointed with no story to tell and I'll stand there with my so-so career in my carry-on bag.

But in 1999, things were suddenly different. For the first time in forever my answer was going to kick some Airport Question ass. I told the flight attendant the name of my group and her face lit up like a lottery winner. "E-*LEK*-treek? Ohhhhhh! Thank you! Thank you!" She excitedly scurried off to tell her flighty friends. Adjacent passengers stole looks in my direction. I was loving every second of this, but feigning indifference. My body language said, "Nothing to see here, folks. It's just me…famous guitarist for a famous band…no big deal."

I know, I know. I hadn't earned an ounce of adulation. I didn't care. I loved it. I was no longer *Parmesan Whatsley: Airport Question Fail.* I was the guitarist for fucking E-LEK-TREEK!

TWO OR THREE LITTLE THINGS

I slid off the comfy vastness of the king-sized bed and opened the blackout curtains. February summer light poured into my sixth-floor room at the Conrad Hotel and Casino in Punta Del Este, Uruguay.

I thought about what Bev Bevan had said to me just a few months earlier when he'd welcomed me into the band: "Learn thirty-eight songs and we'll see you in Uruguay." It's one of my favorite quotes. It spoke to the big picture—the sense of adventure, the promise of opportunity that lay before me. Well, here it was. The big picture was all true. I was on tour with a world-class band in an exotic country on a continent I'd never seen. I'd flown thousands of miles in business class. I had an enormous room to myself (into which I could've easily squeezed one of my old power trios) and it overlooked a beach. I couldn't wait to rent a Vespa so I could tool around the area and check me out some Uruguay. I loved my new job.

Except for two things.

One, my ear was ringing, with a sound like crickets in crystal. I didn't notice my tinnitus if I was distracted or in a noisy environment, but when I went to bed, it drove me crazy and made me incredibly afraid that it would get worse. I didn't know what to do about it except "don't panic." Ugh.

Two, my girlfriend in Los Angeles was in the dumps. We'd spoken on the phone after I arrived. Instead of an excited "How is everything?" I got a sad, muttered "Hi...". Of course, I hadn't thought about Helle's part of the deal, left behind, alone in our house—the side of my new job that *wasn't* fun. Our phone call had knocked me right off my cloud. I loved being on the road and I loved Helle. We had some figuring out ahead of us.

In the Conrad showroom, I got my first look at ELO Part II's stage setup. We were three in front, three in back. I was front-stage-left (facing the audience) with Kelly center stage and Mik stage right. Behind me was Bev, on a drum riser. Next were Eric and Lou, who stood at their keyboards on a separate riser completing the back line.

Guitar savant Barru had arranged my pedals in front of my mic. My guitar was tuned and ready for me. I still couldn't get over that. A guitar roadie. Such decadence. Then I saw my amp.

"Uh, Barru... what happened to our Marshall 800?"

"I'd hoped you might not notice," Barru said bleakly.

Instead of a dependable Marshall 800 amp atop a tall four-speaker enclosure, the backline company responsible for supplying us with amps, drums, spare guitars, and so on, had delivered a squat Fender Twin Reverb. I'd never liked Twins. Their sound quality swung crazily depending on the year they were made. This one had a silver facing behind the knobs, indicating a non-vintage year. More alarming than that, it was beat to shit. The black Tolex and the silver grill cloth were both ripped to shreds. Parts of the amp were even a little *sticky*. Yikes. It must've come straight from a wild scene the night before.

Tinnitus. Sad girlfriend. Shitty amp. Make that *three* little problems.

Eric joined Barru and me at the beaten-up amp. He shook his head and said, "Oh, crap. The backline company must've followed an old equipment rider. Phil always used Twins. Sorry, dude. I'll make sure it gets updated." Eric looked at me. "Can you make this amp work?"

"We'll see."

We plugged my Telecaster into the sad, abused Twin Reverb. I struck a chord and the amp farted out an awful, woofy sound that I'm sure Phil Bates would've hated, too. Barru and I got to work, trying to wrestle a tone out of the damned thing. We fiddled with the volume, bass, middle, and treble controls, searching for a combination that might create a sweet spot.

"Now you know why I prefer Marshalls," Barru said. "The worst Marshall would sound better than this piece of shite."

Eventually, Barru and I dialed up a tone we deemed least horrible. My guitar sounded like a guitar, just void of personality. Welcome to the perils of using backline in faraway places. Despite my farty amp, the rehearsal was exciting. Instead of facing each other in a circle at Rich Bitch, I now looked out at a thousand seats. They'd soon be filled with a noisy crowd excited to hear the hits. Behind me was the Move's Bev Bevan and to my right ELO bassist Kelly Groucutt. My corner of the stage would make a damned good power trio. My new job became distinctly less theoretical. I could feel the songs forming in my throat and buzzing in my hands as I held my guitar.

SHOW NUMBER ONE

The next night, alone in my room just prior to my debut, I felt compelled to write a note to posterity. Corny, but I did it.

So, here I am.

In about fifteen minutes, I'll walk downstairs...and get ready for my first show with ELO Part II.

I'm a little nervous.

I'm in love with Helle O'Connell.

I've come a long way and changed practically nothing.

My left ear is ringing.

I'm glad my folks are okay. I'm blessed.

Now it's 9:18. Go get 'em tiger.

Clearly, I felt that I was embarking on a life-changing journey. For the other guys in ELO Part II—not so much. Just another gig. If they had any concerns about facing a thousand punters (*English* for paying customers) with a new guy on guitar and vocals, they didn't show it. Four of my bandmates being British—stiff upper lip and all that—perhaps they felt it would be untoward to telegraph any doubts about my preparedness. Better to sip booze and talk about anything else. I guess it's also possible they had confidence in me.

More than an hour before showtime, I arrived backstage in my show clothes. Mik Kaminski, carrying a suit-bag and his violin case, looked at me with mock horror and exclaimed, "You're already dressed!" I thought, "Note to self: arrive backstage in street clothes (even if your room is just upstairs from the gig)." I wore blue-grey sharkskin pants, a black T-shirt and new Beatle boots I'd bought in England (couldn't resist). "You'll be soaked afterwards," Mik added. Second note to self: Bring dry clothes to change into after the show.

Lou, Bev, Kelly, and Eric arrived in the dressing room and began their routines. Lou blasted his wavy mullet with hairspray, the treacly mist forcing everyone to flee the dressing room. Brawny Bev looked positively domestic standing at an ironing board de-creasing a black shirt. Guileless Kelly Groucutt strolled around the room blindly guiding a noisy electric razor over his bald head. Eric sucked Ricola throat lozenges and ran his tenor voice through various scales in the bathroom where the acoustics were livelier.

I tried to relax as our start time grew ever closer. I ran through my own vocal warm-ups, tried a handful of jumping jacks, and checked my outfit a dozen times. Not to get too insider, but there're just enough nerves involved with going onstage that most musicians feel the need to pee multiple times prior to hitting the stage.

Our set for Punta Del Este would be two hours long, but not the full thirty-eight songs I'd learned. Right before we were to go on, Eric put on a mock cheery smile and said, "So! Hux! Ready for your big debut? Lots of people out there, all extremely anxious to see if you've learned your parts. Don't blow it!" *Nice.*

We all moved to the side of the stage, just out of view of the audience. Our intro music would cue us when to take our places. I checked that my in-ears were snug. They doubled as earplugs, so I felt a bit detached from my surroundings, a bit like being underwater. The wires from my earplugs ran down my back underneath my shirt and plugged into a radio receiver clipped to my belt. I reached back and turned the volume knob clockwise. My receiver clicked on, and I set the volume halfway up. I could hear the murmuring of the crowd through the mics on stage.

I said to Bev, "I've been looking forward to this." He smiled and said, "Enjoy it." The lights went down to a smattering of whoops and whistles. Up came our intro music, a spooky pastiche of sound effects and stringed instruments. The show had begun. With butterflies in my guts, I stepped over black cables duct-taped to the floor, around my amp, and headed to my position at stage left.

Barru was waiting for me, holding my guitar. He lifted the strap, and I ducked my head through, putting the guitar's weight on my left shoulder. The strap was secured to the body of my Telecaster by Barru's new strap-locking system. It wouldn't fall. I turned the volume knob on my guitar until it stopped at full, something I would habitually do throughout the show. Always be sure you're at full volume. I lightly hit a string. I could hear it loudly in my earphones and distantly in the room. I then tapped on my vocal mic. It, too, could be heard clearly in my earphones. If nothing else, I would be able to hear my voice and guitar. I was ready to go. In my journal, I would describe my first moments on stage as, "A trippy slow-motion weird-but-okay experience. Flying on adrenaline and not wanting to fuck up." That sounds about right.

Bev clicked his sticks to count us in. "Fire On High" began with a series of big staccato chords and then a dramatic orchestral section. As Eric played a long series of rapid triplets on his keyboard, I turned my attention to the crowd. Woah. Crouching photographers three rows thick were jostling for position and snapping away at us. Damn. This was serious. I tried my best to ignore the photographers and breathe through the butterflies that were partying in my belly.

As we performed "Fire On High," I nervously anticipated the tricky series of rapid-fire barre chords I had to play without the band. When it arrived, I bent both knees and dug in. I was playing it well. But I was also watching myself playing it well and thinking, "*I'm playing it well.*" That had to stop. I booted the observer out of my head, took a breath, and focused on my hands and on the guitar resting against my body. When the tricky part was over, I allowed myself to glance at the other guys. We were all playing as one. Despite my hyper-focus on guitar parts and the aural claustrophobia of the in-ears, I let my confidence build just a little.

Apparently, we sounded pretty good out in the room. When "Fire On High" ended and we tore into "All Over The World," the sold-out crowd erupted with applause and heartily sang along. It dawned on me that I'd never seen a crowd react to this new band I was in. It looked like Uruguay was with us.

I stayed on high alert, determined to keep up with the avalanche of parts bearing down on me. After each song, I had ten or fifteen seconds to congratulate myself for not ruining the show and then mentally prepare for the next number. "Okay. 'Rockaria!' down. *Woo-hoo!* Next: 'Livin' Thing.' First chord: C. Second chord: Bbm. *Got it.*" Click, click, drum, stick. Boom. Off we'd go, ready or not.

After a half-dozen numbers, I began to settle into a rhythm. Once a song was safely in progress and I was confident I knew what I was doing, I would engage Kelly, Eric, or Bev with a rock pose or a mock-smug look that said, *Hell, yeah, we're rockin' this tune.* But only briefly. I knew if I enjoyed goofing off too much, instant karma would surely nudge me into some horrible mistake.

When I wasn't mugging with my bandmates, I faced the crowd and did my best to assume the posture of a cocky, capable performer (fake it 'til you make it). Happily, my voice felt strong, and I sang well. Reaching for notes and nailing them is singer's nirvana. I also remembered my words and knew where to go with every melody line. I experienced a few brain farts but nothing serious enough to earn a mock-smoldering glare from Kelly.

Meanwhile, everybody else onstage just went about their business. No one resorted to overly flashy moves or hackneyed posturing to get a rise from the audience. Everyone just did their bit, and the crowd was with us.

Effervescent Kelly Groucutt stood center stage, engaging the first few rows and playing master of ceremonies on behalf of the band. His black-nail-polished fingers deftly handled a blue German-made "Esh" electric bass nearly as big as himself. Kelly wore snakeskin boots and pants to match. Garish colored scarves hung like peacock tails from the samurai ponytail sprouting from the back of his head. His outfit was a hot mess, but somehow it said, "Kelly!" He smiled and laughed throughout the show and his brassy vocals easily punched through the rock 'n' roll din.

Sly Mik Kaminski was clearly a crowd favorite. He'd stroll around, treating the stage like it was a park on a summer day. When a song reached a particularly iconic violin part, he'd plant his feet, bend his body back like Gumby posing as a crescent moon, and let fingers fly. In Mik's expert hands the electric violin became a crowd-slaying weapon.

Directly behind me at stage left, brawny Bev bashed the hell out of his oversized rock star drum kit: two huge floor toms, four rack toms, thunderous snare, eight cymbals…nuts. He gazed out from his drum throne, a king surveying the field of battle.

Eric "Impossible Fifty" Troyer handled all the insanely busy piano and synth parts. High-flying arpeggios danced under his fingers and his versatile tenor gave our vocals a sheen on the upper end that most bands can't match.

Mild-mannered Lou Clark, lined up next to Eric, played his original orchestral string bits on a keyboard. Oddly, Lou read from sheet music while he played, even though he'd written the parts himself twenty years earlier. Didn't he know them by now? Dressed in a blazer, reading sheet music, Lou was kind of a quaint classical addition to a rock band. (A few weeks later Lou would abandon his keyboard and move to a conductor's podium. He'd lead three different symphony orchestras during shows in Eastern Europe. Conducting got Lou's juices going. He became a different animal.)

The guys knew their stuff forwards and backwards. ELO music can be busy and up-tempo but Kelly, Mik, Bev, Eric, and Lou made it look easy. Me? I *pretended* to make it look easy. Mid-show, Bev emerged from behind his kit to speak to the crowd and introduce the band. When it came time to introduce me, Bev made a big fuss about it being my first night and called my performance "Fantastic!" That felt beyond wonderful to hear. My woodshedding with the cassette tape in Echo Park had paid off.

After the show, our King's English-speaking soundman Dennis York rushed into the dressing room laughing loudly and jumping pogo-like as he hugged me and shouted, "You were absolutely, smashingly brilliant, Hux!" Wait, check that. Dennis actually approached me calmly, smiled, gave me a firm handshake and said, "Well *done*, Hux. Well done." *That's* the British version of going bonkers.

WEDGES

Our second show was a rowdier affair before a rabid Friday night crowd. Afterward, a super-fan of the band, whom I'd seen hanging out in the hotel lobby with multiple albums waiting to be signed, said my vocals on "Do Ya" were the best ever, and he liked how I moved around more than Phil Bates or Jeff Lynne. Wow. I had at least one fan in South America. A beaming hotel rep told me that the crowd's over-the-top reaction was very unusual at the Conrad. Looks like we were doing something right.

I went for a drink in the hotel bar. A young guitarist from the better-than-they-had-to-be hotel lounge band approached me. He said he'd caught our show and that my guitar sound was "amazing, like something I've never heard."

I nearly spat in my cocktail. The tone I was getting from that punch-drunk frat boy of an amplifier was like something *I'd* never heard, either. I thanked him, though, for saying he liked my tone. I wasn't about to punish a fan for a compliment. And it was possible, I supposed, that Dennis had been able to improve my guitar sound from his perch in the sound booth.

Back in my comfy bed after our second show, I awoke before dawn with a new ringing tone in my head. I plugged my ears to confirm it wasn't a noise somewhere in the room. It wasn't. A new shot of adrenaline/fear blitzed through my body. Fucking in-ear monitors! After a few minutes, I entered a self-induced state of calm, trying not to freak out…I told myself to stay cool, love life, and have faith that the ringing would go away. I managed to get back to sleep, and the new tone was gone by breakfast to my immense relief. Still, it made me more determined than ever to stop using in-ears. I was sure they were the cause. I found Barru and asked him to set up some wedges in front of my vocal mic. I would use floor monitors and wear normal ear plugs.

Before Saturday night's show, our lighting director Greg Szabo came into the dressing room and said, "What's with the wedges? Looks like shit on stage." Eric reassured him, "It's only a temporary thing, it's gotta be the last resort. We've worked really hard to reduce the noise on stage …"

I sat there boiling. I thought, "Fuck the fucking stage. They're *my* ears!"

The show went great. The wedges and ear plugs worked fine (for me, at least) and I felt more connected to the sound on stage and the vibe in the room. Afterwards Eric said, "God, we gotta work on the vocals. We were terrible at times. Sometimes it was good, but man …" I thought his reaction was overblown and maybe a veiled dig at me using wedges. We weren't perfect on vocals, but we were still great. Kelly, Eric, and I had blended beautifully from our first rehearsal in a Solihull hotel room. Still, I kept my thoughts to myself.

After showering in my room, I cooled down and realized I was exactly like Eric. I was just as critical of my guitar playing as he was of the vocals. Although I'd performed perfectly well, I knew where every cringey guitar clam had occurred and that they all had to get cleaned up. If Eric was overly critical of the vocals, that would only be a good thing. I wasn't sure what to do about the wedges versus in-ears thing, though. I still had a defensive attitude about it.

The next day at breakfast, to my great relief, Eric greeted me with "How are your ears?" He said, "The most important thing is of course your health, sanity, and future, but if we could exhaust all possibilities, it would be good." My bile receded. I appreciated that he had acknowledged my tinnitus, while keeping his concerns about stage noise in the picture. Fair is fair. It was just something we'd have to figure out.

Electric Light Odyssey

EGO RAMPS AND GO-GO GIRLS

We were booked to perform three songs on daytime Argentine television. The show would air live, with no chance for re-takes, so the producers insisted that we do the safe thing and mime to tracks. Ugh. Fine, but what tracks? We couldn't use the original ELO recordings. Eric worked out a solution. During rehearsals in Punta, we recorded three songs live to a digital mini-disc. The TV audience would hear a recording that was truly us. If there's a good version of faking it, this was it. The producers were happy.

One of the more interesting things about the ELO catalog's worldwide popularity is *which* songs were hits *where*. For Argentine TV, we would present "Evil Woman," "Confusion," and "Last Train To London." In the States, "Last Train To London" would be an odd choice, as it wasn't nearly as popular as a dozen other ELO hits. But in South America, "Last Train To London" is huge. It may as well be "Hey Jude." Over the years, whenever we've played down there, "Last Train" is the climax of our set. The audiences, literally, go mad with joy. Who knew "Last Train To London" was so big in South America? Well, a few years earlier, ELO Part II didn't.

Before I joined the band, ELO Part II made its first ever trip to South America. Arriving in Buenos Aires, the band was immediately hustled to a press conference. The press asked which songs they could expect to hear. The band threw out some titles. The reporters said, "What about 'Last Train To London'?" The promoters jumped in and said of course the band would play "Last Train To London." Bev said, "Uh, we don't currently have that song in our repertoire." Reporters and promoters both seemed aghast that ELO Part II would come to Argentina and not play *their biggest song*. According to Eric, Bev was reluctant to rehearse the song on short notice, but that's exactly what they did. Twenty-four hours after arriving in South America, ELO Part II performed "Last Train" for the first time, on Argentine national television. It's been a staple of the South American set ever since.

The day after our fifth and final show at the Conrad Resort, band and crew boarded a small chartered plane and flew west across Uruguay to Buenos Aries. It was a beautiful sunny day and our plane's shadow skipped across the vast, brown Plata River. Buenos Aires is the epitome of a megalopolis. Even from the air, it's not possible to see where it ends. Maybe it doesn't. We began our descent to Aeroparque Jorge Newbery, a small in-town airport built in the late 1940s when it was reasonable to land planes within two miles of downtown. We hit the short runway with the Plata River on one side and dense modern Buenos Aries on the other.

Our promoters ushered us into a couple of vans, and we melted into the thick Buenos Aries traffic, which seemed to follow no rules. Creative drivers filled four lanes on three-lane roads. Obeying red lights appeared to be optional. After a forty-five-minute thrill ride, the city morphed into a neighborhood called Tigre. Our vans came to a stop on a leafy quasi-residential street, and we were hustled into a backstage area of steel scaffolding and blue tarps. A makeshift plywood walkway lay atop muddy, trampled grass. Hand-drawn signs pointed us to a "Green Room."

We were on the set of *La Movida del Verano* ("The Summer Move"), a hugely popular show hosted by a TV personality named Juan Alberto Mateyko. I got the impression that the energetic Mr. Mateyko was something like Argentina's Regis Philbin.

ELO Part II's arrival jarred the show's staff into action. Harried production people were everywhere, shouting orders into walkie-talkies. Our handlers led us to an improvised makeup room, where a crew of delightfully chatty women did their best to get us TV-presentable. We were instructed to change into our stage clothes. My pulse quickened. The nervous energy in the air was contagious. Live National TV. I wished for a minute I could be a local so I could appreciate the significance of appearing on *La Movida del verano*. It seemed like a big deal.

Dressed for stage, faces powdered, and donning our instruments, we were quick-marched by our handlers through a labyrinth of scaffolding. Crowd buzz became audible as we ascended a metal staircase. We emerged onto the stage and looked out at a thousand kids, packed in tight and ready to go. They screamed and shouted when we appeared. Thick showbiz smoke filled the air, lit by hundreds of colored lights. Stagehands ran busily around the set. Fans held banners including one that read "Michael Jackson" over a phone number. Not sure what that was about.

We found our positions. A tanned, dark-haired stage manager wearing headphones indicated we would start in just a few minutes. He gave us a thumbs-up and a quick smile. In front of us, three stage spurs jutted into the crowd, left, right, and center—ego ramps for preening performers. Were we supposed to go out there? Nope: six raven-haired Carnival dancers dressed in giant heels, skin-tight sequined outfits, and feather boas appeared from below stage and found their spots on the left and right ramps. *La Movida del verano* was a lot sexier than American daytime TV. I wanted to soak it all in, but host Juan Alberto Mateyko was speaking excitedly into a camera about "E-lek-treek." Time to fake it, boys.

We opened with "Confusion," a song not well known in the States but popular in South America. The crowd roared. Next was "Last Train To London" and, as predicted, the audience erupted into delirium. I exchanged looks with Kelly. With a smile and one raised eyebrow, he acknowledged that we'd hit the South American audience's sweet spot.

While I pantomimed playing my guitar parts, Eric Troyer banged away on his Keytar, an over-the-shoulder keyboard last seen in the '80s. The Keytar is a mostly uncool relic, but in its defense, it freed keyboard players like Eric from being stuck behind a stationary piano. Aren't I fair-minded?

After we'd finished "Last Train To London," it occurred to me that the poor go-go-dancers were all on their lonesome, separate from the band. Before "Evil Woman," I approached Eric and shouted into his ear over the crowd noise, "Let's hit those ego ramps! I'll go left, you go right!" While Kelly sang the opening verse, Eric and I headed toward the dancers. I stopped next to the first dancer on the left ramp and continued my guitar pantomime to our pre-recorded track. I looked over to see how Eric was doing. *Hey, now!* Eric was strutting down the length of the right ramp, sliding between dancers with his Keytar, shaking his ass like a pro. What an entertainer! I've never been prouder of him. (You can watch it on YouTube: "ELO Part II La Movida Del Verano TV Argentina 1999".)

We ended "Evil Woman," the crowd screamed even louder, and that was that. We'd been on for about ten minutes. I've played on TV a few times, and it's weird when you finish your bit. There's no hanging around. You wave and get the hell out. Back we went into the blue tarp labyrinth below.

While we changed back into street clothes, two of the exotic dancers appeared in our dressing area. They each had jet black hair and shining eyes. One of the dancers spoke excitedly and, when it was clear we couldn't understand her, a handler stepped in to translate for us. Apparently, the dancer was saying that Eric and I were the first musicians brave enough to approach them onstage, on national TV no less. We laughed. It hadn't exactly been bravery. She then asked if we would please go out dancing and drinking with them that night in Buenos Aires? Eric and I looked at each other and...

Hey, sorry for the deception, but the previous paragraph never happened. If it had, Eric and I would've politely declined the girls' offer. Eric will confirm that.

HODGENIZER

ELO Part II's monitor engineer, Simon Hodge, was a pleasantly mischievous fellow with a shock of black hair perpetually dangling over his forehead, making him look a bit like a slimmer Bob's Big Boy. Simon's other distinguishing feature was his choice of pants. Winter, spring, summer, fall: Simon wore shorts. It was an interesting look for a skilled sound engineer who would go on to work for Elton John, Kylie Minogue, and numerous productions on London's West End theatre circuit.

But this is not about shorts. One day in Punta Del Este, Simon and I were chatting about our favorite amplifiers. I told him how much I loved Vox AC30s, despite their fickle nature. Simon was a bit of a gear head and mentioned how cool it would be to someday design his own amp. He said it with an undercurrent of wonder and passion. To put his name on a piece of gear would be the nazz. Marshall. Fender. Hodge.

Back in my hotel room after our chat, Simon's dream led my eyes to an oval-shaped waste bin by the desk. I picked it up and turned it upside down. The bottom was a cheap, shiny gold-colored metal. A great color for a small, oddly shaped guitar amplifier. Or facsimile of one.

Hmmm.

Using a pencil and hotel stationery, I drew a loudspeaker. I patiently drew mesh lines for the speaker grill and added realistic screw holes where the speaker enclosure would attach to the amp. I cut it out and taped it onto the side of the waste bin. Ten-inch speaker: done. From my hotel room bath, I harvested four small shampoo bottle tops, serendipitously colored gold, lined them up and glued them to the bin's upright bottom. Knobs: done. Black Sharpie in hand, I labeled the trashbin/amp's potentiometers "Hodge," "Hodge Podge," "Dodgey Hodgey," and "Hodgenize!" I wasn't sure what each knob, theoretically, did, but since they were shampoo tops on an upside-down waste bin it didn't much matter, did it? I then applied the final touch. I created the amp's logo: *Hodgenizer*, with the first and last letters acquiring lightning bolts and the "i" dotted with a star. Sweeeeeet.

Beaming with satisfaction, I concealed the *Hodgenizer* in a white plastic hotel laundry bag, rushed out of my room and went looking for Simon. I eventually found him with his crewmates Dennis, Greg, Nick, and Barru as they were heading into a hotel elevator.

"Simon!" I ran with my bag and joined them in the lift, "I've got a little surprise for you."

The elevator doors closed and quiet enveloped the six of us. I felt the awkwardness of a *band guy* suddenly inserting himself into *crew guy* space. Things weren't unfriendly between band and crew, but we tended to be separate gangs that kept to their own. Right on cue, Greg said, "Is that a bag of your dirty laundry, Hux? Do you want us to clean your room for you, too?"

I ignored Greg and handed the bag to Simon.

Simon mused, "What could this *possibly* be?" He gingerly opened the bag. When Simon laid eyes on the *Hodgenizer*, his face morphed to unadulterated delight. "*Ohhhh, YEAHHHH!*" Simon exclaimed, laughing. "That is *ab-so-lute-ly* fantastic!" Dennis, Greg, Nick, and Barru crowded around to examine the functions of the knobs and exploded into laughter like I'd hoped they would. The crew heartily approved. A beaming Greg said, "Good one, Hux!" Almost reverently, Simon said, "We'll have to build a road case for it ..." More laughter. Sometimes there's nothing better than a well-intentioned dumb-ass gag.

The *Hodgenizer* acquired a special reverence from me and the crew. More than once, we placed the former waste bin on stage as part of ELO Part II's backline. Den, with his proper accent, would ask, "Will you be running your guitar through the *Hodgenizer* tonight, Mr. Huxley?"

"Yes, please, Den. But no louder than 'Hodge Podge'...we don't want the crowd to get *too* excited."

"Sound policy, for sure." Giggle, giggle.

Six weeks after South America, ELO Part II performed on BBC Manchester's National Lottery Show. Because we were lip-syncing to track, the Hodgenizer sounded just as good as the other amps sitting idly on the set. Maybe even better. You can spot the *Hodgenizer* atop my Marshall amp on YouTube. https://www.youtube.com/watch?v=8rRrdz1wKBk

With the Hodgenizer's successful rollout, Simon pointed out that he needed a name for his fictional amp company. My ridiculous brain immediately sent me *Hodgenization Across the Nation Organization,* or HATNO. Sometimes silly writes itself. I may be reading too much into it, but I believe it's possible the *Hodgenizer* helped to bring band and crew a little closer.

IT'S NOT ALWAYS LIKE THIS

After our successful appearance on *La Movida del Verano* and the short flight back to Uruguay, we had one more day to enjoy the Conrad Hotel and Casino. It was hard to beat the Conrad buffet, an all-you-can-eat masterpiece of beautifully presented fresh food. I sat, once again, at an elegant table and prepared to enjoy my umpteenth plate of glazed salmon, pristine shrimp, seared scallops, fresh salad, warm bread, perhaps a glass of wine, an elegant dessert, espresso coffee, maybe another dessert, maybe another glass of wine... you get the picture.

Bev Bevan, grizzled tour veteran and bandmate, dressed head to toe in black, drifted into the buffet. He joined me at my table with his own heaving, colorful plate of fresh food and inquired, "So, Hux—alright?"

"Yeah, Bev. I'm trying to limit myself to forty or fifty shrimp, but I'll get by."

Bev laughed and took a bite of buttery roast beef with creamy garlic sauce. He then leaned toward me and said, "It's not always like this, you know."

I stopped mid-shrimp.

"Whattya mean, Bev?"

He wagged his fork at our heaving plates and said, "I just mean it's not always like this," eyeing me seriously before his baritone voice rose to an ironic laugh.

I thought, "Is there something about this band that no one's told me?"

Fine. So sometimes the hotel buffet won't have seven kinds of fish. My room won't always look onto a beach. I resolved not to worry. I shrugged and finished off my eighth prawn. Whatever happens, happens.

It happened. Rock 'n' roll reality check, thy name is Antofagasta, our next stop on the South American tour. Antofagasta is a port city in Chile's northern desert. If California falls into the sea and the armpit of Nevada acquires a coast it will look like Antofagasta. Barely any measurable rain has fallen in this part of Chile for four hundred years. The palette of the place is overwhelmingly tan with occasional flourishes of beige. A golf course by the airport is all sand, no grass. Antofagasta exists because of copper mines. *Sexy*.

If Antofagasta is not officially the middle of nowhere, it's close. The European Southern Observatory (an organization for astronomical research) built their Very Large Telescope array in the Atacama Desert, the most remote, atmosphere-less place they could find on Earth. It's just 150 miles from Antofagasta.

As we were bussed from the airport into the city, the promoter told us that the best hotel in town was unfortunately full. We would be staying instead at the Hotel Ancla Inn. I thought, second best can't be so bad. And if it's both a Hotel and an Inn...it's gotta be special, right? I thought differently once we parked before the Ancla Inn's faded façade. The sad, down-on-its-luck exterior was topped only by its poorly lit, depressing lobby. Ancla translated to *Anchor*, as in a sinking feeling.

The elevator wasn't working so I grunted my bags and guitar one dirty marble step at a time to the second floor. I inserted a skeleton key and swung open the door. Yikes. My room featured a rickety bed, unmatched fifty-year-old dressers, and a cigarette-scarred night table. My outside view? A jerry-rigged constellation of electrical wires, some swaying and sparking as noisy streetcars battled through traffic below. The clamor and dust filled the room. I slammed the windows shut and decided to turn on the AC.

No AC.

I sat resignedly on the lumpy mattress with metal springs. The room smelled like a wrestling match: cigarettes versus Lysol. It may've been rigged—cigarettes were winning. Memories of my beachfront room in Punta Del Este were fading fast. As sweat ran down my back beneath my clinging shirt, I had to let out a small laugh. Okay, Bev. I get it now. I know what you mean by "it's not always like this." That didn't take long. Despite its shortcomings, I wanted to give Antofagasta some credit. In the very least, it was the most far-flung place on Earth I'd ever been. And for that, I dug it.

I also enjoyed the chewy syllables of "Antofagasta." It sounded like an obscure form of torture Goldfinger might inflict on James Bond. "Mr. Bond, rest assured...you will return in good time to your beloved England...but first...ANTOFAGASTA!"

As much as I tried to put lipstick on my Chilean pig of a hotel, I couldn't bear the idea of staying in the airless room. I decided to unpack and then explore my exotic new surroundings. A photo-copied hotel leaflet bragged about the Ancla Inn's rooftop pool. I ran up four flights of stairs and emerged on the roof in bright sunlight. There was a pool, yes, but it lacked one crucial element: water. It also smelled bad. How can an empty pool stink?

I took in the rooftop view. Antofagasta's graceless urban sprawl crept upward to barren mountains on one side and tumbled down to the roiling blue Pacific on the other. I'd never seen oceanfront property look so forlorn. The city didn't exactly beckon, but it was hours until dinner. Nothing else to do but check out the town.

SEX, MUGS, AND ROCK 'N' ROLL

Antofagasta rewarded my exploratory walk with a handful of sad strip joints, spartan cafes, and kiosks selling cigarettes, drinks, and candy. Dusty mom-and-pop shops sold third-world goods that didn't even rise to the level of kitsch: plastic flowers, cheap cameras, cookie tins, framed religious posters, and ugly clocks. The global economy hadn't yet set up shop in northern Chile.

A motley pack of scarred and dusty stray dogs lay flat on the sidewalk, sunbaked and panting. An unshaven balloon salesman sported a "Goofy" costume that was so threadbare, Disney lawyers wouldn't have bothered filing a lawsuit. Despite its desolate appearance, I appreciated Antofagasta's tired-ass, stuck-in-the-'70s vibe. It reminded me of provincial Greek towns my parents dragged me to as a kid. There's something romantic about a place adrift behind the times.

I wandered the hot, dusty streets for an hour or more and peeked into shop after shop, hoping Antofagasta might spring a retail surprise on me. I figured there had to be cool relics from a bygone era still on the shelves. Maybe some weird albums or ancient rock magazines. It didn't happen. I found nothing worth buying, not even as a gag. I started to head back to the Ancla. Maybe I'd play guitar up by the stinky pool. Sigh.

There was one last souvenir shop on my route back to the hotel. With low hopes and nothing better to do, I walked inside. The young Chilean couple behind the counter greeted me warmly. The shop was spacious, and the quality of goods appeared to be a tad above super tacky. Maybe my luck would change. I scanned the aisles, looking for something, anything, that might jump out at me. I passed on painted seashells, leather doodads, more clocks, pen sets. Everything was run-of-the-mill touristy stuff. Let down yet again, I headed for the door.

I glanced at one last shelf before exiting and—boom! *Pay dirt*. I couldn't believe my eyes. It was like an invisible hand had kept me waiting until the last shopping second for this amazing discovery. Before me were a dozen exquisite souvenirs of Antofagasta. I instantly envisioned giving each member of the band and crew one of these special little somethings to commemorate The New Guy's First Tour. The miraculous items appeared to be made of high-quality glazed ceramic, which pleased me greatly. I wouldn't want to gift my new professional cohorts with anything less than the very finest penis mugs.

The male proprietor picked up on my excitement and joined me at the display. I announced grandly that I would take them all. "You want ALL?" he said, waving a hand over the full battalion. "Yes," I said. "I want to purchase your entire stock of penis mugs, please." I must have been his best-ever dong-ware customer. He seemed both puzzled and delighted by my decision. I was puzzled and delighted by the mere existence of the mugs. Why were these

Electric Light Odyssey

God-awful things here? Nothing else in the store even came close. Just my cosmic luck.

The proprietor's wife joined us at the display, picked up one of the mugs and gamely demonstrated how to drink from the, uh, spout. I nodded with a smile and thanked her. I wanted to ask her to show me again, but her husband was right there. They gathered the mugs and we met at the cash register.

As he carefully wrapped each mug, the shopkeeper employed his limited English and asked, "You are tourist?" I told him no...I was in a group. I pantomimed strumming a guitar. I got across that I was playing at the Rock & Soccer Arena the next night. He nearly dropped one of my Man Mugs. "Eee-LEK-Treek? You are Eee-LEK-Treek?!" He hurriedly pulled out his wallet from under the cash register. "I have my TEE-kets! I SHOW you!"

His reaction confirmed that ELO Part II's appearance in far-flung Antofagasta was quite a big deal. The last band through these parts had been KISS the year before. I felt like we were ambassadors visiting the furthest reaches of the Classic Rock empire. He found his tickets and held them out to me. He helpfully pointed to the name of my band. Yep. There we are. I smiled and nodded in an agreeable way. I said, "I'll look for you tomorrow night."

Now that we were getting to know each other, I felt a little conspicuous as The Guitarist for Eee-Lek-Treek Who Loves Penis Mugs, but they didn't seem fazed at all. He and his wife spoke excitedly about the concert while they placed the wrapped mugs in a large plastic shopping bag. I think the price of the penis mugs may've gone down. Hell, maybe it went up. Either way, their mugs and my pending show made all three of us very, very happy. I loved this town!

I left the store with my bulging sack (of mugs! *Please*). I couldn't help but smile, imagining the guys' reactions to their souvenir from Antofagasta. Wives and girlfriends back home might not be so thrilled. Or maybe they would be.

I snuck the bounty up to my sad, hot, little room and arranged the mugs on a rickety table with its oil cloth covering. I decided to personalize each mug with a black Sharpie. In my most elegant handwriting, I wrote "Memories of Antofagasta" and the name of each band and crew member. Classy! Although I was alone, I was giggling out loud. I couldn't wait to present the gifts at the tour's end.

MEET THE NEW PRESS, SAME AS THE OLD PRESS

The next morning, Antofagasta's charms returned to form. Mik and I ordered breakfast at the grimy restaurant adjoining the Ancla. We were served...well, we weren't sure what we were served. It might've been omelet soup in olive oil. We pulled that rarest of restaurant moves and asked for a check without touching our food.

The venue wasn't much better.

Antofagasta's Rock & Soccer Arena was a giant dusty gym. The nine-foot-tall, sponsor-brand, beer-can-shaped balloons tethered to the upper decks did offer a splash of class. At sound check, Bev's first snare drum hit echoed off the back wall and bounced right back at us a moment later with barely a decrease in volume. Wow. Good luck keeping time to THAT. With all of us playing, and all of us echoing off the walls, this was gonna be one loud-as-hell rock show.

A few hours later, we took the stage and were greeted by a tidal wave of applause and shouting. Each song was met with a tremendous roar and each roar would morph into a full-throated football chant, OLAAAAY, OLAY-OLAY-OLAAYYYY. The bellowing crowd stayed on its feet the entire show. This was not the civilized showroom at the Conrad Hilton in chic Punta Del Este. This was my first exposure to a blue-collar Chilean crowd hungry to hear the music they loved from down the years and across the pond. Their energy was so palpable, I completely forgot about any nerves I might've had. On this night, we could do no wrong, even if we did. I surrendered to the joyful chaos and enjoyed every minute.

After our encore of "Last Train To London" and "Don't Bring Me Down," we slumped onto folding chairs in our cramped cinderblock dressing room, soaked in sweat, ears ringing. Security couldn't seem to keep fans from coming backstage, so we bolted the door to get some privacy. I opened a small window to let in some air. A flock of fans in the parking lot immediately spotted us and jammed our little window with delighted faces and a half-dozen hands holding pens and tickets for us to sign. So much for privacy. I gamely signed as the fans laughed and shouted and jostled for position. The other guys in the band would've preferred the window to be closed, but I thought it was hilarious and fun. *New guy.*

After one last luxurious night at the Ancla Inn, we left Antofagasta for Santiago, Chile's capital. As we checked our bags at the airport, Mik spotted the shopping bag I was carrying and asked, "What's in the ungainly package, Hux?"

"Oh, I bought a mandolin on our day off," I lied. "I didn't want to crush it in my suitcase." *If you only knew, Kaminski. There's a penis mug in your very near future.*

As we flew south, Antofagasta's arid landscape gradually gave way to vineyards and farmland. Back to civilization. Our promoters eagerly greeted us at Santiago airport and shuffled us into a fluorescent-lighted meeting room filling up with reporters and photographers. We sat at a long folding table crowded with microphones and small tape recorders. Behind us were banners glorifying our tour sponsors and a Chilean flag. A translator stood by our table. A TV cameraman signaled he was ready, and we began. Even at this early stage of my journey with the band, the charm was rapidly leaking from the good ship Press Conference. We appreciated the publicity it provided us and our sponsors, but if this fourth session in six days was anything like the others, we knew exactly how it would go.

Translator: "Welcome to (our city). Please, how is your impressions of (our country)?"

ELO Part II: *Very beautiful. We love coming here. The audience is always so great.*

Translator: "Congratulations for your concert. What can be expected from the show?"

ELO Part II: *All the hits that people love to hear. A few acoustic numbers. Bev will even sing "Summertime Blues."*

Translator: "What is the differences or the same from classical music and rock?"

ELO Part II: *The Beatles and other bands successfully mixed classical motifs with rock music in the '60s. ELO music was initially an expansion of that idea. People still like it today.*

I wished we'd had something more newsworthy to report (penis mugs?), but other than me being the new guy, we were simply in town to play the hits. We had nothing in the way of drug arrests, celebrity divorces, or creative differences to share. All we could do was crack a few jokes and try to put a charming spin on things, but that was about it. Classic rock bands are essentially selling history. They don't make news unless they reunite against all odds, make an acceptably good new album, or announce that an original member has died. (I'd vote for making a new album.)

What I *did* find surprising was that the press remained interested in a band like us, or at least felt obligated to be interested because of our history. Here we were, decades removed from the music's peak popularity, but still playing to packed houses. The real story was that music had the capacity to resonate across time and beyond borders. But that's not exactly hot news.

After our admittedly flat press conference, we were driven to the Carrera Hotel in the center of Santiago. A pair of awestruck giggling girls with cameras and a bouquet of flowers greeted us as we got out of the car. Mik and Bev happily posed with them. A plaque near the reception desk read, "Five Stars: One of the World's Great Hotels." The Carrera looked the part. The lobby radiated old school elegance with its marble floors and wrought iron staircases.

We were informed lunch was waiting for us. I dropped my bags in my handsome room overlooking the presidential palace and headed to the rooftop. A poolside restaurant featured a splendid buffet, tables in the sun, and waiters ready to serve us drinks. Ahhhhh. That's better.

Mik, Kelly, and I settled into comfy seats, ready to dig in. We put crisp white cloth napkins on our laps and took in the view of what would become one of my favorite cities. It was already getting hard to recall the Ancla Inn.

Mik said, "This is more like it, eh boys?"

Yeah. It was almost as if…it was always like this.

DINOSAURS

Our final South American show sold out Santiago's Teatro Monumental (now called Teatro Caupolican), a cavernous 5,000-seat arena. During the sound check, a young fan with arena access and a camera rushed to the front of the stage and shouted, "Parthenon!" He wanted me to pose for a picture, so I gave him a pose. I thought, "How in the world does someone in South America know my name? I've been in the band for twelve minutes …"

Backstage, in the hallway outside our dressing room, a small team of smiling elderly ladies in flower-print smocks and worn slippers sat in folding chairs shooting the shit. I wasn't sure of their function. Turned out they were our rock 'n' roll ironing service. Pressed pants and shirts? Hell, yeah. Rock on, damas de planchado! That was a first.

From the moment we took the stage in our pressed pants at Teatro Monumental, five thousand full-throated Chilean rock fans stood up screaming and never sat down. After every song, the crowd noise would cascade over us in waves like a pulsing, living thing (song-pun intended). We were forced to delay the start of several songs because we couldn't hear the count-off. We'd step back from our mics, smiling and shaking our heads. There was no hope of addressing the crowd or announcing the next song until the roar subsided. We weren't doing anything radically different from our other shows, but we must've been doing something right.

After our final number, Mik had to guide me offstage as I was waving to fans and throwing picks without watching where I was going. Still the new guy. Eric and I stood backstage waiting to go out for the encore. The roar of the crowd was unceasing. Insane. I looked at Eric, who shook his head in wonder at the intensity of the crowd. He said, "I gotta remember what this sounds like."

As always, our encore was "Don't Bring Me Down." It's not ELO's best song, but it's a crowd-pleasing rocker that allows the audience to sing along with us. After the last notes rang through the arena, we waved a long goodbye and then flopped our sweaty selves into chairs in our dressing room, all of us buzzing. It was hard to imagine a more satisfying end to my first tour.

The next morning, band and crew gathered in a sitting area on the Carrera Hotel's second floor. Tour manager Greg had conspired with me to get everyone together for a meeting to "tidy up business." With my speech prepared, I stood and addressed the band. "Mik, you can see I have my ungainly package with me. I apologize for telling you I'd bought a mandolin. That was a cover-up. In fact, I've got a small parting gift for each of you, to thank you for making me feel so welcome on my first tour." I detected nervous laughter and mumbles from the Brits. This was not band business as usual. I loved their discomfort. I continued, "I hope this will always remind you of our wonderful stay in Antofagasta, and please know that this gift comes to you from the bottom of my bollocks."

The mugs were wrapped in the white paper from the store in Antofagasta. I began handing them out. Bev was the first to unwrap his mug. I snapped a picture to capture the moment, which I treasure. His jaw dropped and he shouted, "Where on Earth did you FIND this horrible thing?" Guys gathered round and howled. Mik opined, "Not exactly suitable for the mantel, are they, Hux?" Kelly pantomimed drinking from the spout, naturally. Nothing like a dozen dick mugs to wrap up a tour. Worth every Chilean peso.

Off to the airport we went. I felt like my first adventure with the band couldn't have gone better. Before boarding my flight back to LA, I bought copies of all the Santiago newspapers. I was excited to see our picture on every front page. I found even more photos and articles in the entertainment sections. We were the hottest thing in town. I couldn't wait to glory in it all.

I took my seat in Business Class, already feeling entitled. *Yeah, I rocked Santiago pretty hard...need my rest after such a grueling tour. Where's my champagne?* An English-speaking Chilean woman sat next to me. We began having a pleasant chat. She asked what had brought me to Chile. I showed her the newspapers. Her eyes widened. "Oh! Is it *you?*" I smiled and sang a little melody in my head, "*Grea-test...gig in the wor-orld...*".

I asked her if she wouldn't mind translating what the papers said about our show. "Of course, no problem," she said. I handed her the front page with my picture on it. She read to herself for a few seconds and then turned to me with a suddenly downcast face. Uh, oh. That didn't look good. "What does it say?" I asked.

She said, "I'm sorry. It's not so nice."

I smiled, reassuringly. "That's okay. Go ahead..."

"This headline says, 'Dinosaurs invade Santiago'..."

Ha! I'd walked right into that one. I had to laugh at the irony. For as long as I'd been a musician under my own name, my records and CDs had meekly sold in the low thousands. I'd performed in clubs to dozens of fans. My compensation for this mediocre showing had been universally rave reviews from both straight newspapers and rock press. "Genius." "Mesmerizing." "Uncanny talent."

Now that I was in a popular band performing classic hits for thousands of ecstatic fans, I was a bum. Another headline dismissively announced, "Too Much Nostalgia." We caught shit for playing only the old stuff. I guess our attempts at jokes and charm at the press conference hadn't earned us any cred with Santiago's music scribes. Of course, I saw the critics' point. They weren't wrong. At this stage, we were what the biz called a heritage act. Still, I was pissed. And motivated. The only way we'd win over the critics would be to play something other than the old stuff. It was time to write some new material for an old band. That was why they'd hired me, wasn't it?

CHAPTER 3

WHO'S THE BOSS

A week after the glorious Penis Mug unveiling in Santiago, my new job whisked me to another exotic locale: Kyiv, Ukraine.[1]

Approaching Kyiv, our Air Ukraine jet descended over pitch-black terrain, no city lights to be seen. We bounced on the tarmac and taxied to an ice-covered gate. An electric sign on the terminal building announced the temperature as -1C. Sunny South America seemed like a dream now that we were back in the Northern Hemisphere in the dead of winter. The ground crew wore classic Russian-style furry ear-muff hats. Being American, I associated that look with endless rows of gun-toting soldiers marching with missiles in front of the Kremlin. We were not in the West anymore. This would be an adventure, and I was excited to peak behind the former Iron Curtain...*after I got some sleep*. I'd been up for most of a full day, and my mind and body had begun a perilous slide into a danger zone of crispy, buzzy, short-tempered jet lag.

Kyiv International Airport hadn't yet installed jetways, so we descended frozen stairs and shuffled to the terminal like penguins across icy ground. I promptly slipped and fell hard on my ass. I might've laughed, but my jet-lagged mind did not find it funny. Once inside, we trudged through a tediously slow line at passport control. Dour officials toiled in their dimly lit booths. Recently emancipated from the USSR, thanks to Gorbachev's Glasnost, I could see it was going to take a little while for Ukraine to get its freak on with some freedom. My recommendation would've been to start with some paint. Cheer the place up a bit.

THE UKRAINE TOUR REALLY KNOCKS ME OUT

After customs, we pushed our caravan of baggage and road cases toward opaque sliding glass doors. On the other side, we expected to be welcomed by our promoters and taken directly to our hotel. I couldn't wait to get horizontal. The doors slid open, and two dozen cameramen, photographers, and reporters in winter coats and hats all began shouting and jostling for position

---

[1] My story takes place twenty-three years before the 2022 Russian invasion of Ukraine. For the purposes of this memoir, I will stick with my 1999 impressions of Kyiv.

in our cramped corner of the cold terminal lobby. Blinding TV camera lights burst to life. Our little luggage caravan ground to a halt. In the rear, our crew guys, pushing carts loaded down with heavy road cases, cursed, groaned, and finally laughed. They took a seat on the gear. We weren't going anywhere.

I had been first through the doors. New Guy wasn't prepared to handle the press bomb, especially with his buzzing body screaming for a dark room and a soft bed. With reporters pressing in on me, I looked over my shoulder at Bev and Eric. They could see from my expression that I needed reinforcements. Penned in by luggage, they slowly maneuvered their way to my spot at the front, facing the media mob.

A translator pushed her way to the front of the scrum, ready to assist. For the next half hour, we politely answered questions, which sounded awfully similar to the softballs lobbed our way in Chile, but with a different accent. Here are the real questions, followed by answers that may or may not be what we actually said.

"Why do you come now to Kyiv?" *We heard the Russian tanks were gone.*
"What are your impressions of Ukraine?" *Very...airport-y? Dark at night?*
"What do you think about new music?" *Some of it's good, some of it's bad.*
"Before you come here, what do you know about Ukraine?" *That sounds like Chernobyl bait, so instead let's go with everyone loves Chicken Kyiv and the Ukraine girls really knock me out.*

To my great embarrassment, someone in the welcoming party shouted at me, *"Why don't you look more happy?"* I really didn't want to let the Ukrainians down, but my face must've betrayed me. I mumbled something about a long trip from LA and smiled my best weak smile. Damn, I was toast. Did I mention that yet?

I have a theory. Assuming we have souls, I don't think they can handle jet speed. I believe when your body moves thousands of miles in a single day, your soul can't keep up. That's why you don't feel like yourself. You feel soul-less. Jet lag is actually soul lag. Right? No?

After the newspaper and TV guys got what they wanted, a pretty girl holding a bouquet of roses posed with us. Someone indicated it was our duty to kiss her cheek for a photo. Bev said, "Do it, Hux." I did. "That'll haunt you," Mik quipped. Welcome to Ukraine.

Our promoters hustled us into a freezing cold van reeking of diesel for the drive into Kyiv. We headed to town in a steady snowfall. The road was barren except for our police escort with his rotating yellow light. The fanfare was charmingly unnecessary.

We drove through mile after mile of dark forest. Every few minutes, we'd pass empty, ice-encased bus stop shelters. I'd never seen a place look so forlornly cold. After a half hour's drive through darkness, the first hints of city life appeared: classic Soviet-style apartment blocks, each about fifteen stories high. I peered at the lighted windows. Every room had a lone light bulb centered in the exact same spot on the ceiling. Glorious efficiency of the State!

We entered the old city of Kyiv and things got more interesting. Lots of nineteenth-century architecture, busy streets, restaurants, and people on the sidewalks. Whenever I spotted a large hotel, I thought, "That must be where we're staying. We're finally here." Except we weren't. Our vehicle drove past the beckoning nightlife and right on through the city without stopping. The road grew dark again. We all moaned. We'd left the airport an hour ago. Where the hell were we going? "They'll never find our bodies out here," Mik declared.

Our Ukraine itinerary supposedly included *Meet with Ukraine President*. I offered, "Maybe we're going to the President's place?" No one bit. On through the dark suburbs we went, our escort's rotating light keeping absolutely no one at bay. Maybe we said something insulting to the reporters. Maybe we were going to jail.

Finally, we turned into the narrow driveway of a three-story, nineteenth-century building. It didn't look like a hotel, exactly, but at least we were getting out of the van. We gingerly climbed iced-over steps to a pair of twenty-foot-tall doors and stepped into an empty, echoing entrance hall the size of a basketball gym. Three enormous chandeliers, each about fifteen feet wide, hung from forty-foot ceilings. Only one was lit, creating a grandiose yet depressing vibe. A huge central staircase across the way led to shadowy upper floors. We had arrived at Pusha Ozerna.

One youthful promoter in an overcoat and tie stood before us with a translator and welcomed us. He was beaming. "We are so pleased you're here. We'll make you very happy." His words reverberated off the marble walls.

I thought, aww, he's really trying.

He continued, "Just ask for whatever you want."

We started with, "Where's our luggage?"

"Coming. Coming."

Good answer. Alright, man.

The promoter's assistants, two stunning, smiling girls, guided us to a corner of the giant shadowy room, like we were contestants in an underfunded game show. A solemn babushka in her seventies (or fifties...hard to tell) sat behind an old wooden lectern waiting for us. Unsmiling, she reached into her apron pockets and retrieved skeleton keys with huge wooden key fobs. She handed one to each of us, saying nothing. I guess that meant we were already checked in. I think she forgot the warm cookies. I still couldn't tell if Pusha Ozerna was a hotel or an asylum. I learned later it was a sanitorium, so, a bit of both?

A second van arrived and a group of huffing, puffing handlers deposited our bags at the top of the frozen stairs outside. Delivered as promised! We shlepped our bags up the staircase. The third-floor hallway smelled like dirty mop water. I opened the door to my room and felt for a light switch. I found it high on the wall, about seven feet up. *Good placement.*

I lay my six-foot body on the five-foot, nine-inch-long bed. The pillows were three feet square and stiff as a board. Phone? Rotary. Three different colored curtains almost covered the room's windows. In the bathroom, the sink's hot and cold knobs were two different sizes and colors. Instead of a shower curtain, two pieces of oil cloth stretched nearly the length of the tub. I washed my face and dried it with a hand towel. Bad move. The towel was so stiff with starch it scratched my skin. Wow. Pretty much everything about this room was just...*wrong.* Fascinating.

A crew member knocked on my door. We were being taken to dinner. My travel day wasn't finished. We piled unhappily back into the van. We followed the police escort and the promoter's car all the way back to Kyiv proper. By this time, I think my soul had given up and crashed somewhere in England. Sigh. Maybe a good dinner would make me feel better.

LOST SOUL

No dinner. Not just yet. On a quiet street, we stopped in front of a dark, three-story building. Our promoter led us inside and we climbed a set of crumbling marble stairs. The first two floors were unlit and abandoned. What the hell was this place? We reached the third floor, which, surprisingly, was well lit and modernized. We turned left down a gleaming hallway and entered a brightly lit TV studio. We didn't know it, but we were on national television...and I mean *on the air*...as we walked in.

Our four English guys—Bev, Kelly, Mik 'n' Lou—were directed to sit on a couch. Eric and I stood behind them. A young, bearded professor type began to interview us. "Why do you now come to Kyiv? What are your impressions of Ukraine...?" Yep. Same questions. The Brits offered our standard bromides as answers. When Mik spoke, his Yorkshire accent guaranteed the interviewer had no idea what he was saying. I mean, if *we* couldn't understand Mik, what chance did the Ukrainians have? Fortunately, the interview, such as it was, ended quickly enough. The TV people seemed pleased, and we were allowed to leave the haunted broadcasting building.

Still guiding us safely through very little traffic, our police escort led us, at last, to a restaurant. A large table had been prepared for us. We sat and waited. I tried not to nod off. Eventually we were served small bowls of what looked like fish, cold vegetables, and other odd items. More food came out bit by bit, none of it very appetizing. A long, confusing discussion ensued between Greg, the promoter, and the restaurant owner. After a solid fifteen minutes of bantering back and forth between the three parties, the owner/headwaiter disappeared into the kitchen and returned with beers and a bottle of reportedly terrible wine. I think the promoter had only prepaid for food, not alcohol. I avoided the booze and washed my fish bites down with Coke, thinking I was being safe. At last, we took some pictures with the staff and left. Back into the van we went. I couldn't wait to get horizontal at the sanitorium.

After an hour on my small hard bed, I sat up with a terrible stomachache. In a flash, I was in the bathroom puking into the weird toilet. I purposely hadn't drunk any alcohol. I was stone cold sober, but still ended up talking on the big white telephone. I couldn't believe it. What a finish to a lovely day. Must've been the fish. Fortunately, I felt a lot better and even proud of my body for identifying the intruder and kicking his ass out.

Dear soul, can you hear me? I'm in Ukraine. Please find me.

BOSS OF WATER

The next morning, I descended the massive staircase in search of breakfast. One of our promoter's smiling assistants guided me to an enormous banquet room, with seventy tables all set with white tablecloths and formal place settings. The only customers in the entire room were Mik and Kelly, seated together near the middle of the room. I began to sit at an adjacent table, but Mik said, "You can't sit there. We can only sit at these two tables." This place wasn't getting any less weird. I asked how the food was. Mik mused, "Not sure…" On his plate was something he'd not touched that might've been meat with sour cream. Or an omelet. Hard to tell, really. Maybe they'd hired the chef from the Ankla Inn? I asked if there was coffee. Kelly said, "None. And no tea either, so don't get your hopes up." The hell with it. If I couldn't have coffee (Blasphemy!) I'd just go back to sleep. My stomach was still a little iffy, anyway. Maybe lunch would be better. I left.

A couple hours later, feeling slightly more refreshed, I returned to our designated tables and joined some of the guys for lunch. I was served a plate of unrecognizable meat, greasy mashed potatoes, and sad carrots. I ignored what was on my plate, ate some bread and stole a slightly sweet cake off the next table. I didn't care. An elderly babushka stood nearby. I assumed she was our server. I asked her if we could get some water.

She replied, "No."

No? Wait. *Really?* I asked again.

"Sorry. No."

Then she said, "Not boss."

She wasn't boss of water. She, therefore, could not bring us water. Holy fuck. I was speechless. Babushka was done talking, by the way. She'd made it clear she wasn't Boss of Water and that was that. She just stayed in her spot near our table, not really interested in serving us. There was no one who could bring us water. End of story.

I wondered what would've happened if she'd stuck her neck out and gotten us water? Hard to say, but she wasn't willing to take that chance. Maybe it wouldn't even occur to her that she could venture beyond her status and pretend she was at water level. As a Westerner, this Boss of Water thing hit me directly in the conjecture bone. How could a society function, I wondered, when initiative beyond your station was outlawed or even unthinkable? It blew my mind. Just how bad had life been under the Soviets? I guessed it was bad enough to institutionalize timidity. Just stay in your place, keep your head down, don't make waves, and no one will come for you in the middle of the night. Or, maybe Ukrainians just appreciated well-defined roles.

"Boss of Water" became legendary in ELO Part II. It was our model catchphrase for every kind of inefficiency. Later that day we noticed a walkway that led directly to a brick wall, missing its target door by a dozen feet. We imagined Boss of Sidewalk saying, "Not fault. Not Boss of Door."

If Kelly asked to borrow a pick, I'd say, "Sorry. Not Boss of Picks."

Could you please pass the sugar, Mik? "No. Not Boss of Sugar."

After our water-free lunch, we gathered our stage clothes and instruments and headed into Kyiv for a sound check. Boss of Police Escort was still with us, yellow lights flashing, and now he'd added a wailing siren to get us through red lights. It still seemed a bit dangerous and completely unnecessary, but I'd grown fond of him by that point.

YOU KYIV ME HANGIN' ON

The band arrived at Kyiv's Palace of Culture with its high ceilings, swimming pool-sized chandeliers, 2,500 plush red seats, and acres of parquet floor. Our crew had arrived four hours earlier. Lighting Director Greg Szabo walked by us in a hurry. I asked, "How goes it?" Greg said, "Take 'bad' and multiply by three."

Uh-oh.

I found Monitor Engineer Simon Hodge, dressed in his usual winter shorts. Simon shook his head. "Nothing we can't handle, but I've never seen so many fucking blue sparks..." Simon was hinting that the Palace of Culture's electrical circuits might not be up to code. Untethered electricity puts technicians on edge, as it should. It can kill you.

Finally, always-calm Front-of-House-Engineer Dennis York chimed in. "They have...a very different way of doing things. Quite interesting, really." Classic Den.

I headed to the stage and saw the crew were nowhere near ready for us to sound check. What to do? The breakfast failure and coffee-free hotel still stuck in my craw. How can a musician function without coffee? I approached Bev at his drums. He looked a little less chipper than normal. No coffee or tea for Bev, either. I gestured to our surroundings, "This place has fantastic cappuccino by the way." Bev laughed, shaking his head. He said, "Wouldn't that be nice..."

As if on cue, Eric appeared from behind a stage curtain, sipping an espresso. Holy Boss of Coffee! "E.T.! Where'd you get that?"

"There's a café downstairs," Eric said casually, as if we hadn't been stranded all morning behind the Iron Coffee Curtain. I beelined downstairs. Hallelujah. Eric was right. The Palace of Culture had an actual café and even a smiling human who took my order. After my first sip of espresso, life in Kyiv instantly improved. I think I even felt my soul catch up with my body. Souls love caffeine.

Suddenly inspired, I grabbed my Tele from the stage and returned to the café. I strummed through the set for the first time since Santiago. A young couple sitting by themselves at a table across the room were surreptitiously watching. I gave them a friendly nod because I was feeling human again. When they got up to leave, the guy shyly gave me a thumbs-up and a quick smile, which I returned. We were like two polite alien species.

As I quietly played my unplugged guitar, the café began to fill up with the chatter and laughter of well-dressed men and women carrying instrument cases. Without coffee to make my brain work, I'd forgotten we would be accompanied by the National Symphony Orchestra of Ukraine. They looked just like musicians everywhere: happy to have a gig.

Sound check finally began mid-afternoon. I turned on my Marshall amp, and the speaker gave a loud thump. I set the volume at barely above "1" and it was plenty loud. Woah. Strong juice in this part of the world! There was a nasty buzz coming from my amp. I had to stand with my guitar at a specific angle to reduce the level of interference. Not good. Dennis jerry-rigged a grounding device and reduced the buzz to a tolerable level.

I leaned forward and said "Check One" into my vocal mic. *SPITTZZZKKK!* I jerked back from the mic and yelled, "Holy shit!" If you've never felt ungrounded electricity burning your lips, I'm super happy for you. It's not nice.

The crew covered the ball of my mic with not one, but two foam windscreens. The foam would prevent my lips from touching metal while holding my not quite grounded guitar. Scary stuff. Always-practical Dennis said it was "unlikely" I would die. Fair enough.

Behind the band, Lou Clark stood on a riser with the podium and commanded the attention of Kyiv's finest orchestral musicians. Lou's own original arrangements would guide the classical players through our repertoire. Some of the older musicians had probably listened to bootlegs of outlawed rock 'n' roll music under the Soviets in the '70s. It must've been exciting to perform that very music with the guys who played on the records.

We began with "The Eldorado Overture" and I got my first look at Lou with a baton in his hand. The shyest guy in the band was suddenly gesticulating with a fierce precision, moving his body to emphasize bold passages, controlling the tempo with each thrust of his baton. I thought, "So this is what moves Lou." Musically, it was impressive. Personally, it was revealing. Lou might rarely show it, but clearly a sophisticated musical fire burned deep inside the mild-mannered Englishman.

Together, ELO Part II and the orchestra ran through the entire set. I had to pay attention to my guitar and vocal parts, but I gave an ear to the orchestra. I, too, had only heard Lou's string arrangements on ELO records. I'd never heard them like this. Bosses of Violins were no joke. They nailed all the familiar runs with style and precision. If the music sounded this good at rehearsal, I expected it to be mind-blowing by showtime.

UKRAINE GIRLS

A young photographer named Andrei had been hanging around the Palace of Culture all day, documenting our visit. He approached me after sound check and asked if I'd pose for some pictures across the street in the subway. Game for an adventure, off we went. At the entrance to the subway, Andre chatted up a middle-aged fish merchant dressed in layers of dingy clothing. She willingly posed with me, hamming it up and smiling with her remaining teeth. I think I even got a fishy kiss on the cheek. Lucky me.

We repeated the photo op with other hardscrabble fish merchants peddling their wares on overturned plastic buckets. It was a cold, wet, humble scene, but Andre was working it and getting laughs and smiles from his subjects. I played along.

Andre then asked two soldiers with guns to pose with me. Unsmiling, they waved us off. I thought Andre was perhaps pushing his luck. I didn't want any trouble an hour before my show. I said we should get back to the venue and he resignedly agreed. As we walked together, Andre apologized (unnecessarily) for the dirty, cold subway and some of the down-on-their luck merchants we'd encountered. He insisted that "from April to September, Kyiv is very beautiful. The women come out and they are the most beautiful in the world." To prove his point, he said, "All the new prostitutes in Europe are from here." Civic pride, indeed, Andre.

VICTORY FOR THE PEOPLE

Initially, our crowd of 2,500 Ukrainian well-dressed symphonic rock fans sat politely in their seats with a strong sense of propriety. We were performing in Kyiv's Palace of Culture, after all. And, with a full symphony orchestra arrayed behind us, I had to admit our show had taken on a more formal air.

But this was a rock show. As we rolled through our set, which included some Eastern Europe favorites like "Confusion" and "Twilight," our show began to work its magic. The applause grew louder and more sustained. Some "Wooh!"-ing began. Finally, a few fans jumped up from their seats and danced. Things were getting Ukrai-zy, y'all. Ushers rushed to the seats where renegade dancers expressed their joy and demanded the patrons sit back down. At first, the dancers caved. We thought that was silly. In the middle of the show, when Bev stood center stage to introduce the band, he mentioned, "It's okay to dance. We like it." When we resumed playing, Kelly egged the crowd on more. "Are you having a GOOD TIME? Come on, then, let's see you dance!"

That did it. The bond between band and audience had reached the tipping point. Shimmying hips and arms broke out like little wildfires and, finally, there were too many wiggling scofflaws for the culture police to deal with. The ushers backed off and stood helplessly on the perimeter. As we neared the end of our set, the Palace of Culture was truly alive and rocking. Most of the crowd were on their feet, clapping, shouting, singing, and dancing. *Victory for the people!*

As we ended our final song, the desultory but huge-in-Eastern-Europe "Ticket To The Moon," the audience din reached a new crescendo. Instead of leaving the stage, we launched into our encore, "Don't Bring Me Down," and the dam broke. Dozens of not-to-be-suppressed Kyiv rock fans completely broke protocol and rushed to the front of the stage, where they danced with abandon, joyful smiles transforming their faces. Happiness had never looked more hard-won. It was *awesome*. We could barely sing for all our grinning.

With things going so well, Kelly decided we should play "Roll Over Beethoven." I hadn't rehearsed it, but apparently, that was *my* problem. Lou led the orchestra through the dramatic first notes of Beethoven's Fifth Symphony and then Kelly ran at me and shouted, "GO!" I ripped through the Chuck Berry intro riff and we were off. I suddenly remembered it was my job to sing the first verse. I rushed to my mic, but my mouth got there before my brain. I sang something like, "Gonna letter little writer/mocha move it to my local deejay..."

Kyiv didn't care. The Palace of Culture was now at pandemonium level. The fans at the front of the stage shook themselves silly one more time. They'd asserted their right to have some fun and won the battle. Chuck Berry would've been proud.

After the show, our promoter led us to a private café/bar off the lobby. The buzzing VIP crowd was well dressed and sophisticated, enjoying cocktails and beautiful desserts. I struck up a conversation with a Canadian woman who'd lived in Kyiv for eight years, running an art gallery. She told me, "Your show was truly amazing and, really, historic. It was a real breakthrough to have people behave like that at a concert. It's never happened." Wow. Pretty cool that we could move the Kyiv rock history needle a little bit.

INTERNATIONAL NEWS

ELO Part II landed at Sofia, Bulgaria's airport during a nighttime snowfall. We were met on the tarmac by police officers in heavy coats and furry hats who herded the band and crew to one side. We stood shivering, enviously watching the other passengers crossing the frozen tarmac to the warm terminal. Eventually, we were marched in a different direction and ushered into a 30' x 30' featureless, fluorescent-lighted room. A dozen stern-looking Bulgarian officials stood around, not speaking to us. Hmmm. This seemed just a bit odd. I looked at Dennis with eyebrows raised. "Any idea why we're being detained, Den?"

"Not a clue, Hux. Unless they've finally caught up to your smuggling operation."

After an awkward twenty minutes with no explanation for our sequestration, a door flew open, and a dozen bustling media types burst into our holding area. Large black cases were unpacked, and men shouldered heavy cameras. A man speaking heavily accented English said, "We have only one minutes to get ready. Then, please, an interview." Oh. *Of course*. We weren't being detained. We were going on National TV. (How's my hair?) Bright lights suddenly shone in our faces and out came the usual questions: "What is your impressions of Bulgaria?" "What will we expect from your show?" Your answers would've been as good as mine.

In Ukraine, our security had consisted of a police escort. In Bulgaria, we were surrounded by bodyguards, lots of 'em. They hovered near the elevator bays on every floor of our hotel. Whenever we walked to our rooms, one would follow. They were big, dark-suited, unsmiling guys with radio earpieces. Intimidating? Yes. Were they protecting us or watching us? Probably both. On the top floor of our hotel, a different crowd hung around the entrance to a disco: hookers. They seemed friendlier than the bodyguards, which made sense.

As in Kyiv, the Sofia venue was called The Palace of Culture and the fans seemed particularly hungry to hear our formerly degenerate Western music. The Bulgarian crowd responded particularly well to our attempts to speak their language. With cheat sheets at our feet, we shouted "Zdravei, Sofia!" (Hello, Sofia…works just as well as "Cleveland"), "Blagodaria!" (Thank you.), and "Oschte?" (More?)

My favorite memory of Bulgaria took place the next day during breakfast at the hotel. Eric and I observed a young Bulgarian couple navigating what appeared to be their first all-you-can-eat buffet. Their worn, mismatched clothes hinted they were likely rural types, perhaps spending a weekend in the big city. They couldn't stop giggling, holding hands, and kissing. Maybe they were honeymooning. Or maybe they just couldn't get over the limitless buffet. The husband made one trip after another to the baskets of bread, the bowls of fruit, the plates of meats, laughing each time he carried his haul back to his table. His expression said, "Can you believe this, honey?" The finale of the honeymooners' show came when hubby got a bit carried away. Using the bottom of his T-shirt as a basket, he filled it with rolls and bread, far more than he could possibly eat, and then awkwardly headed to his table trying not to spill his bounty. A maître d' finally approached him at this point and asked him to cool it. The kid, clearly chagrined, nodded that he understood. I think he kept the bread.

HOME TURF

Following our dates in South America and Eastern Europe, and prior to our upcoming 1999 UK Tour, ELO Part II returned to American soil for four shows. At the Stranahan Theater in Toledo (or "Tole-Doo" as Kelly enjoyed pronouncing it), I got my first chance to show off for family. My Aunt Bits (younger sister of my dad), Uncle Charlie, and a dozen cousins all drove up from nearby Youngstown to cheer me on with my new band. When we convened backstage after the show, I cracked up to see they were all decked out in vintage Parthenon Huxley T-shirts. Nothing like family loyalty.

The next night in Columbus was at a forgettable club. Literally. I can't remember a thing about it, which is weird because I pretty much remember every show I've ever played and most of the hotels. I couldn't possibly forget our show at Maddies, a charming old-school hotel/restaurant/club hidden in the Pennsylvania countryside not far from Philadelphia. Maddies' owners and staff treated our band and crew like family, stuffing food and drink down our throats and making us feel right at home. Their venue, an outdoor deck with a small stage, couldn't have been more intimate. The packed-in audience was right in our faces, shouting at us like we were a wedding band. That's my favorite way to perform. It reminds me of all the hot sweaty club shows I did in my twenties with barely any space between band and crowd.

We played a sold out show at Lehman Center, a large performing arts center in the Bronx, NY, and then borrowed their stage for three full days of rehearsing in front of our twenty-one-date UK Tour. ELO Part II's home turf beckoned.

CHAPTER 4

BEATLE NERD

At this early juncture in my time with the band, I was still a bit self-conscious as the new guy, doing my best to bring something special to the show while not messing up. As far as I could tell, the four Brits, who'd been playing ELO music together since the band's early days, never got nervous. In South America, Eastern Europe, and the U.S., ELO Part II's grizzled English tour veterans, Bev, Kelly, Mik 'n' Lou would report for sound check, grab dinner, play the show, down a couple drinks, and go to bed. Another day, another dollar, peso, or pound. These Brits went about their business in a methodical, old school, professional way. Ho-hum. I learned a lot from their approach. I learned to relax. *Just do your job*, and the show will take care of itself.

GOIN' HOME

During rehearsals in the Bronx, the Brits bantered back and forth about which cities had the toughest reputations, which venues were the hardest to sell out, which super fans would show up, and so on. Mik was anticipating the gig in Leeds, his hometown. We weren't playing in Birmingham for some reason, but Bev, Kelly, and Lou looked forward to loads of friends coming to see them in other nearby cities. Listening to all the chat about playing on their home turf, it suddenly struck me: *the Brits were kinda nervous*. Bev, Kelly, and Mik'n'Lou—despite their longtime success in ELO—were acting like local lads anxious to put on a good show for family and friends, not to mention fans and press. I almost got the sense that our work in Chile, Uruguay, Ukraine, Bulgaria, and so on had merely been a warm-up for the UK.

All of us, Brits and Yanks, were geeked about the final show of the tour: Royal Albert Hall in London. Like New York, London was one of a handful of cities that truly measured your standing. If you could conquer London, you could play anywhere. It seemed especially meaningful for my bandmates. No matter how successful they'd been, they were still boys from Birmingham and Yorkshire at heart, and the capital city would always stand as the ultimate proving ground.

Electric Light Odyssey

I suspected there was something else contributing to ELO Part II's antsy behavior: the *new guy*. The band had done the unthinkable and brought in another bloody American to replace an Englishman in an English band. I believe my bandmates were—perhaps more than just a little—concerned about the English audience accepting me. There wasn't much I could do about it. My ancestors lived in England in the early 1600s. Did that count?

In advance of the UK run, our setlist would grow by eight songs and include an acoustic interlude. We had a lot of work to do.

We added "10538 Overture," my audition clincher and probably my favorite ELO number at the time. It was less poppy than other songs in the set, and I felt it made the show a little bit cooler. We also learned "Poker," a somewhat obscure rocker from *Face the Music*. I loved that it was guitar heavy as opposed to string dominated. It was also super up-tempo and featured insane drum fills by Bev—kind of a show-off number.

The most exciting addition to our set was "Blackberry Way," a number-one hit for the Move in 1968. Written by ELO founder Roy Wood and produced by Jimmy Miller (Rolling Stones, Traffic, Blind Faith), "Blackberry Way" was a gift to hardcore fans, including me. I couldn't wait to perform it with Bev, who, of course, drummed on the record. It would be as close as I'd ever get to being in the Move.

Another highlight was a beautiful version of "Wild West Hero," which included a stunning *a capella* opening. Eric and Kelly were both tremendous singers, and blending my voice with them was heavenly. There is nothing on Earth like singing three-part harmony. It is, literally, the definition of ecstasy.

The opposite of ecstasy was trying to play a guitar part for "Pavanne," a piece of classical music we'd added to the set. It was in a weird key for guitar, and I couldn't get through it cleanly. It got to the point where I'd curse up a storm after every clam. "Fuck me! Let's do it again, please." We'd try it again. "Fuck!" Repeat.

My bad language led to a quote that's stuck with me from Eric's twelve-year-old daughter Lauren: "Hux sure cusses a lot."

Yep. I do. Sorry about that, Lauren. My bad. And fuck "Pavanne." Oops!

Rehearsals at the Lehman Center were grueling. If a song's vocals weren't coming together properly, Kelly would say, "We can't show up in (insert English city) sounding like *that*." Kelly Groucutt was Boss of Original Vocal Parts. In ELO, he'd been the only other singer besides Lynne. He remembered all the parts from the '70s and '80s and was a stickler for getting them right. Eric Troyer was also a vocal perfectionist. Besides singing on John Lennon's

"Woman," Eric's voice appeared on hits by Billy Joel, Aerosmith, Carly Simon, Kiss, Celine Dion, Ian Hunter, Meatloaf, Lou Reed, and many more. Between the two of them, there was little (zero) room for error.

The same perfectionism applied to string parts, guitar parts, bass bits, piano, drums, everything. It's not that any of us expected to play poorly. We would almost certainly kick ass like we'd done the past few months. But. It was the UK. Home turf.

Get it right!

BOSS OF SONGS

At the end of my first tour with ELO Part II, the Chilean press had called us nostalgia-peddling dinosaurs. They weren't wrong. If we wanted to present ELO Part II as anything other than a heritage act, we'd have to write new material. That process began when Bev approached me during our dates in Eastern Europe and mentioned he'd written some lyrics. He asked me, "Would you mind taking a look? Maybe you could do something with them."

"Sure. Happy to."

As a staff writer at MCA Music Publishing, I'd co-written songs with artists like Foreigner, A Man Called E, Stevie Salas, Sass Jordan, Gina Schock of the Go-Go's, Dave Wakeling of the English Beat and others. When Bev formed ELO Part II, it gave him an opportunity to contribute as a writer, too. That hadn't been the case as a member of the Move and ELO with songwriting bandmates like Roy Wood and Jeff Lynne.

When co-writing, it's often a good plan to divvy up duties—one writer might pitch the lyrics and the other the music (like Elton John and Bernie Taupin, for instance). That would be the model for Bev and me. To my knowledge, Bev had no preconception of how he wanted his lyrics to be sung, or what kind of sound would best support them. He'd let me handle all that. I was glad to oblige.

Before the UK Tour, I'd received a fax from Bev with three sets of lyrics. Of the three, the one I thought had the most potential was "Loving You, Leaving Me." I liked how the words "loving" and "leaving" sounded similar but meant opposite things. That was a good starting point. I could make that work. Here're Bev's lyrics.

LOVING YOU, LEAVING ME

<u>Verses</u>
Deserted railway station, disappearing train
Cold heartless airport, another goodbye plane
Force a carefree smile as the taxi pulls away
Turn my head to hide the tears
Hello again lonely days

<u>Middle Eight</u>
I don't know how much longer
I can watch you leave my life
Is this the way it's always gonna be?
Is this the way it's always gonna be?

<u>Bridge</u>
When you're here and close to me
There's a fire that burns for all to see
But when you're gone all that remains
Are ashes cold as winter rain

<u>Chorus Bridge</u>
You've promised oh so many times
One day you'll stay with me
But deep down I know you'll always have
This longing to be free

<u>Chorus</u>
Yet I keep on loving you
And you keep on leaving me
Yes I keep on loving you
And you keep on leaving me

Setting Bev's lyrics to music wouldn't be just another co-write. It was my audition as a songwriter for the band. I needed to impress Bev and the rest of the guys in ELO Part II.

First, I interpreted how Bev's lyrics made me feel. They described a loving relationship suffering from one partner always going away, so it likely shouldn't be an up-tempo number. The words were better suited to a ballad. Second, I ignored Bev's categories like "Chorus Bridge" and "Middle Eight." Once the music came to me, the chords and melody would dictate the song structure. Third, I liked some of the lyrics, but not all. (I couldn't hear myself singing "force a carefree smile." That sounded like Sinatra or Perry Como.) The raw ingredients of a song were there, but I would have to alter some of the lyrics to make them more singable. Finally, my gut told me that Bev's "Chorus" wasn't really a Chorus. The song needed a more defining statement, a more dramatic summation.

Soon enough, a verse melody and supporting chords came to me that matched the melancholy behind Bev's words. I had a good start, and, once a song starts cooking in my noggin, I take it with me everywhere I go. Driving to Trader Joe's, I came up with an intro. Later, walking my dog, Algonquin, in Elysian Park, my version of the verse lyrics conveniently arrived in my head. Within a few days, I had the outline of quite a nice song. In the spirit of co-writing, I'd kept a lot of Bev's words intact, but I'd moved them around to match my narrative. The biggest change came when I added an entirely new chorus and retitled the song "Over Midland Skies." Here's a portion of the new song, with Bev's retained lyrics in bold.

Another goodbye airport
"I love you" is all we say
Turn my head to hide the tears
Hello lonely days
I don't know how much longer I can watch you leave my life

Tears are falling over Midland skies
Every time you go
Tears are falling over Midland skies
Tears are falling falling falling
Over Midland skies
Is this the way it's gonna be?
I keep loving you, you keep leaving me

I'd turned Bev's original chorus/title into a tag line at the end of my new chorus. It worked great as an alliterative wrap-up of the protagonists' situation. The one nagging question I had was whether it was feasible to reference the "Midlands." I guessed it might be akin to singing "Tri-State Area"

Electric Light Odyssey

or "Southeast Region." Not good. However, the band was truly from the Midlands and I'm always in favor of keeping things real when possible. Other than that, I was confident Bev and I'd written something very good.

When ELO Part II assembled in Croydon just outside of London to begin our UK tour, I couldn't wait to play "Over Midland Skies" for Bev. I grabbed an acoustic guitar and the two of us huddled in a small dressing room backstage. I warned him that I'd added a different chorus and moved his lyrics around quite a bit. He said, "That sounds exciting. Let's hear it."

He smiled as I ran it down. I could see he liked it a lot. Still, I was nervous about the geography in the title. As soon as I finished, I asked him, "So…can you say 'Midland' in a song?" Bev didn't hesitate. "*No*. You can't do it. No one has ever sung about the Midlands, and I doubt anyone ever will." I laughed and said, "I thought that might be the case." Luckily, I had a plan B. I said, "Okay, well, my default is to call it 'Over *London* Skies.'" Bev smiled and said, "Yep! That'll do."

Bev and I presented "Over London Skies" to the guys before sound check. Again, I played it on acoustic guitar, this time in an echoey hallway with natural reverb. With the whole band standing around me, I couldn't have felt more self-conscious, but Bev and I were excited, and we felt the band would like it.

They did. Head nods all around. "Yeah, that's alright." "Good song." Kelly said, "Nice one, Bev." Bev said, "Yeah, well, I had nothing to do with the whole 'Over London Skies' bit. That's all Hux." Bev didn't have to say that, but I was grateful he did. Credit where credit's due and all that. "Over London Skies" likely cemented my value as a member of the band. It also may've kickstarted our efforts to make a new record.

OVER LONDON SKIES

Croydon was a good spot to open the UK tour. No one in the band or crew hailed from the area, so it was a low-pressure gig. We'd taken a two-week break after rehearsals at Lehman, so we were a bit rustier than we would've liked. The crowd seemed to love the show and I'm sure we sounded *fine*, but none of us stepped offstage overly impressed. Opening nights were for sorting things out and I reckon the custodians at Fairfield Halls swept up plenty of clams after our performance. The band decided to drop "Getting To The Point," a lesser known song I'd worked hard to learn but never loved. I was glad to see it go.

Chapter 4: Beatle Nerd

The second show, at Oxford, went well enough, but it wasn't until our third show, in Liverpool, that the band turned a corner. The clams and careless mistakes were all but gone. We played with a palpable precision and purpose. The band sailed through sections of the show that, two days earlier, had sounded like a rehearsal. In Liverpool, I looked over at Eric after a particularly tricky passage and received a confirming smile that signaled, "Hey, we did it right tonight!" Success begat confidence, and confidence is something an audience can read right away. The applause after each song lasted a little longer.

An added highlight at the Liverpool show was knowing that I stood, stage left, in the "Lennon Spot." In the early Beatle days, John would've been strumming and shouting on the very same boards. Even at forty-three years old, I happily gave in to being a grinning, starstruck Beatle tourist.

After Liverpool, we had two days off back in Solihull, where I'd stayed during my audition and rehearsals. It started to feel like a second home. Taking advantage of a sunny spring day, I joined Bev, Den York, and Phil Ackrill at Birmingham's Olton Country Club for a round of rock 'n' roll's dirty little secret: golf. Lots of musicians play, and some, like Alice Cooper and Iggy Pop, play competitively. Den and I paired up and we (mostly Den) managed to tie Bev and Phil. A great way to waste a day outdoors.

The tour picked back up on May 5 in the industrial town of Sheffield, home to Def Leppard and Pulp, among many others. Bev and I stood to the side of the stage waiting to go on. When the house lights dimmed, signaling the show was about to begin, we heard only meager applause and a solitary fan shouting, "Wooo!" Bev turned to me. "Not a good sign, Hux. We're down to one 'wooo' in Sheffield." We both cracked up. The show went fine. I think we got up to at least a dozen "wooos."

The next day on our way to Nottingham, our driver parked the bus so he could rest for the legally required number of hours before resuming driving. At Eric's request, he'd parked directly across from a medieval manor house called Haddon Hall. While the English contingent stayed behind to nurse lagers on the bus ("Who wants to see an old house?"), the curious Americans tromped off to play history buffs. This was the beginning of a tradition Eric Troyer and I would maintain for years to come. When there was cool shit to be seen, we sought to see it. Dating from the eleventh century, Haddon Hall was everything we Americans wanted in an old English castle or estate: a spectacular stone house with huge rooms, high ceilings, stained glass windows, amazing gardens, and a breathtaking country setting on a river. We were especially struck by the Great Room, where, warmed by a huge fireplace in olden times, everyone who lived and worked at the estate would sleep on the floor—adults, kids, animals—everyone. And, whatever happened in that room at night happened with everyone present. Interesting way to live.

During the first few shows of the tour, I'd felt a bit conspicuous as the American new guy making my debut in England. I knew there were Phil Bates fans in the crowd who were checking me out. Of course, the English being English, no one in the band would even think of *talking* about it. Happily, as the tour went on, I could feel my presence become something of a moot point and, possibly, even an added attraction. The audience could see how I'd been accepted by the English guys in the band. We did a lot of laughing together on stage. We were also beginning to develop "bits," such as when Kelly and I would share his mic to sing background vocals. Perhaps most importantly, when Bev left his drums and came center stage to introduce the band members, he was always generous with his comments about me. He'd call me a "smashing chap" or a "bloody nice bloke" and say how well I was fitting in. I'm certain Bev's words went a long way with the fans.

LET THERE BE BEV

Speaking of Bev, our encore always began with the brawny drummer taking a drum solo. Such is the privilege of legends that they're permitted to indulge in this showbiz chestnut from the '60s, (a chestnut outlived, of course, only by the guitar solo.) In the early days of rock, young bands without enough material for a full show could kill a solid twenty minutes by simply having the drummer do a version of In-A-Gadda-Da-Vida. The stoners in the crowd would eat it up. Bev never played *that* long, thankfully. It was 1999, after all.

After half a dozen shows, I noticed that Bev pretty much played the same solo, a heavy-handed thump-fest that didn't come close to revealing the dynamic and creative Bev Bevan I'd admired so much as a kid. The crowd always cheered, but it felt like the applause was for Bev the Legend, not Drums the Solo. One day before sound check, I was backstage when I heard an amazingly complex and powerful drum pattern blasting from the stage. I ran out to see Bev swinging freely, pounding out this ridiculous beat and enjoying himself like a kid hitting drums for the first time. When he was done, I shouted, "*Yeah*, Bev! *That's* the shit! You need to do that for your drum solo!" Bev looked at me, smiling. "You liked that, did you, Hux?" I emphatically said I did.

I noted that Bev had looked surprised by my reaction. I wondered how long it had been since anyone in ELO Part II had found reason to yell something, good or bad, at Bev? Probably years. Of course, the Brits, generally, kept things on the down low. If someone muttered, "Oh, *that's* good," it was high praise.

I wish I had a recording of what it was that Bev played that day. All I know is that I'd never heard anything like it before, and it excited the hell out of me. I remember thinking, "That's the Bev I've been waiting to hear, the guy who did all that amazing drumming for the Move." Bev worked the new beat into his solo that night and it lifted his performance dramatically. As he got more and more into it, the applause sounded different. They were applauding the drumming, not just the famous guy behind the kit.

TEARS IN TRURO

Every day of the tour, we ate dinner backstage at 4:30, courtesy of the wonderful pair of chefs traveling with us. After a hot meal, we'd burp our way through sound check and then kill time until curtain call. I liked to sneak out the rear of the venue by the trash bins and walk around to the typically handsome edifice facing the public. I snapped photos of our name on the marquees of lovely old English theaters. Even better, I watched streams of smiling people dressed up for a big night out in spring, knowing they were all coming to see *us*. It was perversely fun to blend in with the crowd knowing that I'd shortly be up on stage.

The fourteenth date of our tour brought us to Truro in England's southwest corner. Four things stood out during our brief stay in lovely Truro.

One, our venue, the Hall For Cornwall, had no seats on the floor, so the crowd stood, packed in tightly, right up to the stage. I found this arrangement to be much more exciting than playing for customers resting comfortably in theater seats. The energy exchange between band and fans gets amped up considerably.

Two, Bev effusively praised me during the band introductions. I noticed the punters kind of smiling and acknowledging my standing in the group. ("If Bev likes him well enough, he must be awwright...")

Three, we debuted "Over London Skies," my new song co-written with Bev. I gotta say, it's nice to have guys from ELO playing your music. Lou Clark's string arrangement added a magisterial melancholy that made this newborn song sound like a classic. Kelly and Eric sang stratospheric harmonies on top of my lead vocal, sending the choruses soaring, and Mik stuck a brilliant solo in the middle eight. Eric, utilizing his encyclopedic knowledge of musical idioms, had added a single seventh chord to the outro—and the result makes my spine tingle even today. The crowd roared for "Over London Skies"—a real thrill. I felt like I'd rewarded the band's confidence by contributing a new song that fit in well with the classic hits.

And four, the morning after our show, I wandered around picturesque, sunny Truro until I found myself seated in the darkened Cathedral, listening to a plaintive church organ. The atmosphere reminded me how much I love music and life itself, and how lucky I was to be sitting in such a magnificent spot. It wasn't long before the heavenly sounds echoing off soaring Gothic arches did the trick and I began to sob, once again, for my late wife Janet.

As much as I loved life, Janet Heaney had done a better job of living it. She'd turned her thirty-eight years into an incendiary comet ride. She did everything full bore, no half measures. Summa Cum Laude at Boston University. Drove straight out to Hollywood to pursue her dream of filmmaking. Won the Audience Prize at Sundance. Achievements aside, she was just as fiery in everyday life. She made rescuing animals or worshiping Elton John feel like life missions. For the first six months after Janet's death, I'd cried pretty much every day. I'd remember us conversing in silly voices, visualize her beautiful smile, or imagine her laughing—head back, full throat—and that would trigger memories of Janet suffering from brain cancer and the knowledge that I'd never see her again. I hated the unfathomable cruelty of death by disease.

I looked up through teary eyes at the stained-glass windows. In the two-plus years since Janet's death, my life had changed dramatically. I'd joined ELO Part II and begun to tour the world. Fifteen months after Janet's passing, I'd met Helle O'Connell. Surely my new guardian angel had something to do with all my good fortune. As I wiped my eyes, I hoped my deep cry in Truro's Cathedral might be the last of its kind. There are only so many tears. Even the most profound sadness and loss eventually loosen their grip on you. I was certain, too, that Janet would want me to be happy. I could imagine her saying, "Get on with it. Don't worry. I'm *fine*."

Outside the cathedral, I ran into Mik Kaminski. Being a chatty American, I explained why my face was red. He said something kind. We walked back to the hotel to check out. Our big bus was waiting to take us two hundred miles to Cardiff, Wales. A nice long ride sounded good.

SHOWDOWN

A few days later, we arrived in Southend-on-Sea for our eighteenth show. I asked our bus driver to shoot a picture of me in front of the venue, the Cliffs Pavilion. The marquee said, "May 25 ELO PART II IN CONCERT."

The photo taken, Bev eyed my camera and said, "Keep that picture for evidence, Hux."

I shot him a puzzled look. "Evidence of what?"

"The name is correct on the marquee. It says, 'ELO Part II,'" Bev said.

Hmmm. The name of our band was ELO Part II...and that's what it said on the marquee. Was I missing something?

Bev saw I was puzzled. He leaned in and said emphatically, "Whatever you do, Hux, remember that we are *not* 'ELO.' We're 'ELO Part II,' or 'Electric Light Orchestra Part II.' But we're not *just* 'ELO.' We can never use the name 'ELO' or 'Electric Light Orchestra.'"

"Okay..."

The conversation wasn't over. Bev asked me if I'd ever met his former bandmate, Jeff Lynne.

"Nope." A friend of mine, Julianna Raye, had made a record produced by Lynne. That's as close as our crowds ever got to mingling.

"What's the problem?" I asked.

Bev answered with a grave laugh, "The problem is he doesn't want this band to exist."

I took a second to digest what Bev had said. It was incredibly disappointing to hear that Jeff Lynne was not happy with our band. I was a fan of Lynne's going back to his days in the Idle Race. I loved him in the Move and in ELO. I even wrote him a letter in the late '80s asking if he'd produce me. And now I was playing a bunch of his music...and Lynne's my *enemy*? I wondered how that must feel to Bev, who'd played with Lynne for close to twenty years.

I didn't know the details yet, but something didn't make sense. Lynne had quit performing live in 1986, abandoning the stage for the recording studio, an arrangement he'd, apparently, always preferred. Here in 1999, ELO Part II were doing the heavy lifting, traveling to cities all over the world, playing to thousands of fans who loved the music. I'd heard that sales of ELO albums and CDs, not to mention radio play, increased wherever ELO Part II performed. It seemed to me that we were providing Jeff Lynne a nice little service.

But Lynne, apparently, didn't want us to exist. I asked Bev, "Why?"

Bev shook his head. "I wish I had a good answer. I guess he thinks there can't be an ELO if he's not in it."

I understood that line of thinking. Black Sabbath without Ozzy is not—in my opinion as a *fan*—truly Black Sabbath. Deep Purple's guitar player should be Ritchie Blackmore, just as Steve Morse should forever be the guitarist for

Dixie Dregs. Hell, some early fans of the Beatles still feel they should've kept Pete Best. As fans, we love our bands the way we meet them.

But we weren't calling ourselves ELO or claiming to be ELO. We were ELO Part II, and the name tells you straight off that it's a "successor band," and things about it will be different. For instance, heaven forbid, there might be an American guitarist or keyboard player. Music fans are used to this. "Creedence Clearwater Revisited" tells you that John Fogerty is likely not a member. Starship is not the same band as Jefferson Starship. Oddly, Little River Band still has the original name...but zero original members. Personnel changes are often key to a band's longevity. The Rolling Stones rhythm section is now American. Rock bands rarely carry on in their original form. What I didn't understand is why Jeff Lynne, who no longer toured, would resent his former mates carrying on.

As Bev and I headed into the venue, I thought, why do successful bands always seem to have a dark secret? Everything looks groovy from the outside, but when you get on the inside, skeletons start leaping out of the closet. Even the Beatles, God's gift to music, ended up suing each other. The exchange with Bev shook me up. It gave me an unwelcome perspective on my new job. Frankly, I thought the legalities around the name all sounded like a load of unnecessary legal bullshit. Why couldn't ex-bandmates, former friends, just get together and work stuff out among themselves? I guess I'd find out.

Eventually, I decided to distinguish between what I could and couldn't control. I thought, "Okay. We can't be 'ELO' without Lynne. But we *can* be ELO Part II with *me*." I was almost right.

THE NAME

Electric Light Orchestra. It has a nice ring to it. Give credit to Roy Wood of the Move for coming up with a clever modern pun on the quaint "light orchestra." Most Americans don't know the history of light orchestras, including me, so I looked it up. In the 1940s, '50s, and '60s BBC Radio had an agreement with the British musicians' union to limit the amount of airtime given to records. The musicians' union's thinking was that if people could hear records all day on radio, they wouldn't bother buying records for themselves. Yes, once upon a time, recording artists were *against* radio airplay!

With limited airtime for records, the BBC leaned on live performances by "light orchestras" (and dance bands) to fill out their programming. One of the most famous light orchestras was the Midland Light Orchestra, or M.L.O., based in Birmingham. Not hard to see how a Birmingham native like Roy Wood might come up with the name Electric Light Orchestra, or E.L.O. for a rock band with strings...with a pun on *electric light* thrown in for good measure. Woody came up with the name, but apparently, he didn't copyright it for himself. If he had, he might've saved his bandmates a lot of trouble down the road.

The original ELO began in 1970 with three founding members: Roy Wood, Bev Bevan, and Jeff Lynne. After just one album, Wood left to form Wizzard. Lynne, Bevan, and other standout musicians such as Richard Tandy, Kelly Groucutt, Mik Kaminski, Hugh McDowell, and Lou Clark kept ELO going until the band broke up in 1986. A few years after the breakup, Bev was itching to tour and record again, so he decided to put the band back together. Lynne declined to be in the group and a disagreement arose between Lynne and Bevan regarding use of the name "Electric Light Orchestra." A compromise was reached, and Bev called his successor band "ELO Part II."

DA MAN

In Portsmouth, our nineteenth city of the tour, I was on my way to sound check when Greg the Merchandise Guy crossed my path headed in the opposite direction. We exchanged brief greetings. "You da man," Greg said. As is custom, I shot back, "No, *you* da man," and kept walking. To my surprise, Greg stopped and said with emphasis, "No, you *are* the man." I looked at him, not sure what he meant. He said, "You're the guy who's brought this whole thing back around." He gave me a thumbs up and walked off.

I stood there, stunned to have such an unexpected compliment tossed my way. I was flattered, even if I wasn't sure exactly what Greg meant by it. The first thing that came to mind was that the band was having fun onstage. If that was the case, and I had something to do with it, great. The truth was, I was simply enjoying playing in a kick-ass band on a proper tour of England. I supposed my joy might have been a bit contagious.

Just to make sure I didn't get a big head, the next day I awoke with a lousy chest cold and sore throat. The crew arranged for me to visit a "surgery," which isn't what Americans think it is. It's just a doctor's office. The doctor loaded me up with antibiotics and cold medicine.

I also caught a good case of Gig Head, or what normal people call anxiety. Gig Head reminded me every twelve seconds that I could not afford to be sick. Our final UK performance was three days hence, in London, the land of tastemakers, for 5,000 fans. The venue? The Royal "Now they know how many holes it takes to fill the" Albert Hall. The audience would include my

Electric Light Odyssey

girlfriend Helle, her best friend Ursula, Gordon Townsend (drummer from my own band P. Hux), and Rick Shoemaker, who signed me to MCA Music Publishing back in 1986. Lots to fret over.

To top it off—to make things just a *little* more anxiety-inducing—I planned to ask Helle to marry me while she was in England. I would point to her in the crowd during our show at Albert Hall. I'd ask her to come onstage and then propose to her by singing the chorus of "Do Ya." The whole crowd would find out if she wanted my love.

No. I wouldn't do that. That would be stupid. I made other plans.

THE LOVE YOU MAKE

During one of our transatlantic calls, Helle told me she'd dreamt that I'd bought her a Beatle book and a skirt. A week before our show at Albert Hall, I snuck out after sound check and bought Helle a Beatle book and a skirt, making her dream come true, right? Aww-awwww.

I then found a fancy-schmancy paper store and hatched my engagement plan. I bought a small, handsome box, some note cards with envelopes, a Beatles calendar, scissors, and glue. Back in my room I cut out four individual Beatle heads from the calendar. I pasted each head onto a separate envelope. In the John envelope, I inserted a card that read, "The love you take." On a second card I wrote "Is equal to" and placed it in the Paul envelope. The third card read "The love you make" and went in George's envelope. In *Ringo*'s envelope I placed an engagement ring. (See what I did there?)

I imagined Helle patiently opening each envelope, appreciating my heartfelt Beatle-y craftsmanship. She would say, "Oh, baby, this is all so cool and thoughtful. Thank you."

That's not what happened.

NOW THEY KNOW HOW MANY HOLES

The band bus rolled out of the coastal city of Eastbourne and headed to London for our tour-ending show at the Royal Albert Hall. The normally two-hour trip took four hours and Gig Head loved the additional time to torment me. *You've been sick…better take care of your voice…it's LONDON tonight…Helle's coming…you wouldn't wanna fuck up at a big show like this one, would you? Better check your throat again.* Nag, nag, nag.

Slowly, but surely, England's enchanting green countryside gave way to London's Piccadilly Circus, Trafalgar Square, and Buckingham Palace. When we arrived at the iconic theater, a gaggle of fans were waiting with pens and paper. We happily signed autographs and then headed inside.

Two adjacent dressing rooms were tucked into a small space next to the stage doors. Both were tiny and one of them smelled like old lamp oil. Mik and I, simultaneously, wrinkled our noses and quickly scampered, laughing like schoolboys, to the better smelling room.

On a normal show night, we'd have had the backstage area to ourselves. At Albert Hall, we shared it with forty members of the Royal Philharmonic Orchestra. The classically trained musicians crowded into the small cantina and added to the general hubbub. I asked Mik if he felt a kinship with all the violinists in the house. His classically droll answer was, "Why would I do that?"

With a narrow window of time to kill, I decided to explore Albert Hall and soak in the vibe. Who knew if I'd ever be back? (I haven't.) It was a massive place, a huge oval with row after row of floor seating plus five levels of opera boxes. I journeyed to the rear of the hall and turned to look at the stage, which seemed miles away. I pictured us playing up there, backed by the RPO. I couldn't help but think, "Oh boy, this is gonna be good." I felt like I could finally get excited for what promised to be a memorable evening.

At 6:00 pm, I kept an appointment to be interviewed in the backstage cantina by Mick Dillingham. Mick was a journalist/pop rock connoisseur who'd written a nice review of my band VeG for *Mojo* magazine. I'd reached out and thanked him for putting me in my favorite rock rag. When he learned I'd joined ELO Part II, Mick expressed his surprise and suggested we talk about that new development as well as the album I was working on called *Purgatory Falls*. I liked Mick immediately and we chatted for a good half hour, which was all the time I could afford.

An hour before showtime, I began my routine of vocal warm-ups and then the backstage door opened and in walked Helle. Wow. Had I picked the right girl, or what? Besides being smart, funny, caring, thoughtful, and musically savvy beyond her years, Helle was simply drop-dead gorgeous. She was in great spirits, too, happy to be in England with our mutual pal Gordon and reunited with her best friend from high school, Ursula, who was living in London.

I tried not to whine too much about my chest cold but did anyway. She said she and Gordon had laughed all the way from LA, Ursie's apartment was adorable, and they were having a great time.

Exciting as it was to be reunited with my girl, Gig Head reminded me that showtime was fast approaching. I kissed Helle and she scurried off with her gang to get drinks and find their seats. Minutes later, I was continuing my vocal warm-ups while ironing my blue sharkskin suit pants in the dressing room when in walked Rick Shoemaker, Vice President of Warner Chappell Music Publishing. In 1987, while at MCA Publishing, Rick had signed me as an artist/songwriter, my first deal with a major music company. We instantly reverted to our old selves from twelve years earlier. Rick shouted, "P Man!" and I yelled back, "The Publisher of Love!" We acknowledged how weird it was to see each other so far from LA and in such an iconic place as the Beatles-blessed Royal Albert Hall. We held each other by the shoulders and said, "Look at us!"

With Rick was Kenny McPherson, also from Warner Chappell. Kenny had some news that fit snugly into the magic unfolding on this evening. He announced that my song "Come Clean" would be the first single released by Splendid on Mammoth Records. I told Kenny I'd been writing with Splendid in my living room when I first got the call from Eric Troyer about the ELO Part II gig. Those two threads had now convened here in my tiny dressing room. I just shook my head at the ways of the universe.

As fun as it was to see them, Rick and Kenny knew I was getting ready to play. We wrapped up our chat with best wishes all around, exchanged man hugs, and said our farewells.

Alone again in the dressing room with just my idiot brain for company, Gig Head suggested that maybe I should take my second antibiotic pill of the day as vocal insurance. It would keep up the fight against infection. As soon as I swallowed it down, I thought, "Oh, shit. That's gonna dry out my throat." Stupid Gig Head! Our dressing room of course had a plug-in kettle, so I hastily made hot tea with honey and continued with my vocal warm-ups. Gig Head was such an annoying bastard.

I wasn't the only one doing mental gymnastics. I could see that the rest of the guys seemed a little subdued as they went about their business. Kelly, normally loquacious and bouncing off the walls a bit, got dressed without saying much. We all had a bit of a mid-distance look in our eyes, trying to stay calm and somehow chew up the minutes until we could, at last, be on stage and get on with it. Once we'd played a song or two without an amp melting or a string breaking or any other unwanted calamity, we knew we'd be fine. We just had to tough it out until that moment came.

Outside our dressing room, the lights in the Hall went dim and we heard the crowd applaud. The opening act would be our own Lou Clark leading the Royal Philharmonic Orchestra through a set of "Symphonic Beatles." To my ears, Lou's arrangements sounded both magnificent and at times a bit corny, but that was on me. Whenever I hear string arrangements of Beatles songs, I'm painfully reminded of an album my parents bought during the height of the British Invasion: *The Beatles Songbook—Romantic Instrumentals by The Hollyridge Strings*. Released in 1965, it was a misguided attempt to turn that *noisy teenaged Beatle crap* into something pleasing for adults. Featuring godawful saccharine versions of "All My Loving," "Can't Buy Me Love," and so on, the Hollyridge Strings album was pure puke to my young rock 'n' roll ears. Lou's arrangements were a million times better, of course, but the sticky residue of the Hollyridge Strings was hard to nudge out of my memory. Sorry, Lou.

After forty minutes, Lou and his longtime pals in the RPO finished up and took their bows. Now it was our turn. I'll never forget walking out to my spot, stage left, Marshall amp behind me, vocal mic in front. There is no proscenium at Albert Hall. Once you're on stage, you're out in open space, sharing it with 5,000 fans. The ceiling is miles above and everywhere you turn there are faces looking up from the floor or down from the endless balconies. It was a spatially disorienting experience just to stand there, much less perform.

For the first part of the set, Gig Head's poorly timed antibiotic gave me a terrible case of cotton mouth. I sipped water between every song and tried to stay focused and calm. I doubted anyone could tell, but I was truly struggling to push the damned antibiotic out of my mind and enjoy playing at Albert Hall. I kicked myself for worrying about my throat even as I performed and pretended nothing was wrong.

Fortunately, the band sounded great. We were in prime playing condition. After a month on the road, all the trickiest guitar parts had surrendered to my left hand's muscle memory. Nothing flummoxed me. Despite my distracted mind and dry throat, I even handled every note and nuance of the vocals. Kelly smiled, Bev bashed, Mik bowed, Eric belted, Lou conducted, and I tried to soak it all in while giving the fans a show. As usual, I looked to my American buddy on occasion to share a moment. I'd catch Eric's eye and we'd nod our heads toward the hall to say, "Can you believe this?" Wide eyes and big smiles. Happy Americans in London.

Bev, Kelly, and Mik'n'Lou had been a tad nervous to perform for family and friends in the UK, but here we were, all in one piece and playing great at the finale. We'd done it. To see them enjoying themselves, killing it, slaying a sell-out crowd in London…filled me with a special happiness for the Brits—my new buds and bandmates. Well done indeed, as Den might say.

When my favorite lead vocal arrived via "Showdown," I pushed my upper register and thankfully my throat felt fine. I relaxed a bit, enough to tell Gig Head to fuck off and take cotton mouth with him. I finally settled into the show. Yay. I could breathe again.

I wanted to signal something to Helle, but I couldn't find her. The place was just too big. Assuming she was keeping an eye on me, I played a big guitar chord and pointed at the crowd. I aimed for the back middle of the floor. Worth a shot, right? (Helle didn't remember me doing it. She was probably watching Mik.)

Two songs rose to the top for me. It was a massive thrill to stand on that stage and sing "Over London Skies" to a London audience (even if I'd originally targeted the Midlands). The capital crowd gave it a huge response. I suppose it helps to include the name of the audience's town in the title.

The other magical moment was when Bev announced, "Here's one you might know from my old band." We launched into the Move's classic "Blackberry Way," and it, instantly, brought the house down—and me with it. I was so into it, so thrilled to sing one of my favorite songs, to blend my voice with Kelly and Eric, and to do it with Bev bashing away behind me; I thought I might pass out from joy.

The second half of our show began with Lou and the RPO launching into the glorious "Eldorado Overture." Rock band and strings never sounded so good. With no vocals to attend to, this was a moment where I allowed myself to take in the whole shebang. It's a rare pleasure to be a spectator at your own show and there are few things as stirring as a battalion of string players all sawing away, bows like synchronized swimmers all moving in the same direction while carving out magnificent descending runs. All I had to do was chug along on my simple guitar part and enjoy the spectacle.

Settling into an undeniable groove, ELO Part II and the RPO delivered the rest of the set with command and confidence, concluding with our usual rousing sing-along of "Don't Bring Me Down." A standing ovation saw us take our bows and, at the appropriate moment, wave our goodbyes and exit the stage. We'd conquered the capital.

As family and well-wishers joined us backstage, a palpable sense of celebration, relief, and happiness filled the air. The tour was over. We'd played twenty-one shows to heaving, happy crowds on the band's home turf. By all accounts, the American new guy had been accepted by the English fans. In three weeks, we would begin dates in Scandanavia, but, for now, it felt like there was only one place ELO Part II could possibly be, and that was here, on top of the world.

Helle found me backstage. She was beaming. My gal said the show was amazing and the crowd reaction beyond belief. We took pictures, threw down drinks, talked excitedly, and shared lots of laughs. Kelly Groucutt introduced me to his mom. Mik introduced me to his sister. I met Bev's wife, Val. I introduced Ursula and Gordon to everyone in the band.

A good backstage hubbub is one of the best parts of showbiz. I was surrounded by loved ones, old friends, new friends, bandmates—my rock 'n' roll extended family. I savored the feeling that I'd played a small part in bringing all these nice people together for a night filled with music, fun, and happiness. It was hard to beat.

The morning after the show, Helle and I ran into Bev and Val in the lobby of the Grosvenor Hotel. (Bev had recommended the very posh Grosvenor, and I was, technically, a rock star, so I went for it, alright?) They invited us to join them for breakfast. We talked about what to do and see in London, and Bev slyly asked Helle if she was excited about our next day's visit to Abbey Road. I'd told him I planned to propose and swore him to secrecy. After Bev kindly picked up the bill, we headed outside to a lovely spring day in London. Helle remarked, "Bev and Val were so warm to me. It was really nice." I thought, "Why wouldn't they be, *Mrs. Huxley…?*"

SHE'S SO HEAVY

Lou Clark had recorded with the Royal Philharmonic many times at Abbey Road. Through his manager, I'd arranged for a tour of Studio Two on the Sunday after our Friday show at Albert Hall. Helle, Ursula, Gordon, and I arrived at the former EMI Studios fifteen minutes before our appointed time of noon. We took the obligatory *Abbey Road* crosswalk photos and pored over the graffiti that covered the wall in front of the studio entrance.

At noon, we entered the iconic building and were greeted by staff engineer Mike Cox. Mike was expecting us but wasn't sure about our agenda. He asked, "What did you have planned for your session…?" We said, "Oh, we're not doing a session, we're just coming to have a look around." Mike exhaled with relief and said, "Oh, great! In that case, come right this way…"

Mr. Cox led us to the famous control room where producer George Martin and engineers such as Norman Smith, Ken Scott, and Geoff Emerick had recorded the Beatles. It was small, almost cramped, with a large window looking down into Studio Two. At the end of the control room, a door led to stairs, and the four of us made our way down into the live room.

Abbey Road Studio Two is not ornate, architecturally interesting, nor even, necessarily, the most up-to-date live room. It's breathtaking because of the music recorded within its four walls. Here, microphones and tape captured performances that eventually pushed my life off its axis. I became a musician because of the Beatles. I could trace a direct line from my kitchen in New Jersey where I heard "I Want To Hold Your Hand" to the parquet floor on which I now stood in London, my ground zero. (I know, I know. We Beatles-people are dramatically obsessive.)

Gordon and I headed for a Neumann mic and mimicked singing on either side of it, à la Paul and George. Total dweebs. Gordon's a drummer, but he's also nimble on keyboards. He stepped over to an upright piano and played the intro to "Strawberry Fields." Ursula, Helle, and I did our best to soak up the vibes and then Mike, seeing we were entirely useless tourists and wouldn't be needing his attention, headed off to grab us souvenir T-shirts.

Entranced as I was by Studio Two, I was distracted by what was coming next. After a few more minutes of gawking and imagining recording sessions from the '60s, I said to Helle, "Come 'ere a second, baby." I walked her to the bench at the grand piano and we sat next to each other. I reached into my shoulder bag and brought out two wrapped gifts. Awkwardly, she asked, "Why am I opening presents?" She ripped open the Beatles book and the cool skirt. I'd hoped she would say, "A book and a skirt...just like my dream!" No such luck. My plan to share an intimate moment was, instead, making Helle feel self-conscious, while Ursula and Gordon were in the room with us. Nice work, Huxley. I moved the book and skirt aside quickly. I could see she was getting anxious and probably suspicious, like a nervous colt. I had to get control of the situation.

I handed Helle the box I'd bought in Cardiff. She took it nervously and said, "What's this?" She removed the top and then, following my suggestion, ripped open envelope #1, the one with John Lennon's little head taped on it. The card said, "The love you take." Moving at typical Helle Hyper Speed™ she opened the "Paul" envelope ("is equal to") and the "George" ("the love you make") and was about to open envelope number four when I intervened.

She hadn't said a word about the envelopes or asked what I was up to with my (I could see now) far too elaborate presentation. I decided to stop the show before it went any further. I said, "Look at me for a second, baby." I put my arm around her. Helle was shaking. Her body clearly knew what was up even if her mind didn't want to jump to conclusions.

I said, "Will you marry me?"

She repeatedly nodded her head "yes," while half-crying. She then managed to say, "Ye-heh-heh-heh-ah."

I asked, "Was there a 'yes' in there?"

Helle said, "Yes!" and kissed me. I laughed and hugged her shaking shoulders. Phew! That was intense.

Ursula, not privy to my intentions, had innocently been taking photos of us from across the room. (Amazing to have those pictures!) When my grand piano proposal reached its shaky, emotional conclusion, Ursula discretely moved away to where Gordon was playing "Golden Slumbers" on the upright piano. Gordon had heard Helle crying and was afraid we'd had a fight. Ursie suspected otherwise and told Gordon, "I think they just got engaged."

Gordon said, "No way! Are you sure? It sounded like they were getting into something heavy."

We were.

Ursie and Gordon joined us at the piano. They congratulated us and we all had a laugh about the awkward scene I'd badly stage-managed. Soon, Mike Cox returned with our Abbey Road swag. We happily accepted our T-shirts and thanked him for letting us use Beatles Ground Zero as the holy site for our engagement. Mike said, "I've seen a little bit of everything in this room, but that may be a first." Thirty-seven years after the Beatles recorded "Love Me Do," Studio Two was still working its magic.

CHAPTER 5

UH-OH

In late June 1999, less than a month after our glorious sold-out performance at the Royal Albert Hall, the six members of ELO Part II stood huddled together under a sagging tent as heavy rain pummeled the "Hog Wild Cookoff" outdoor concert near Jackson, Mississippi. The concert grounds had turned to mud. A smattering of determined fans stayed put, huddled under umbrellas or wearing rain parkas. "Poor sods," Kelly Groucutt said.

HARD WORK

We took our positions on the tarp-covered stage. I plugged my guitar in, fingers crossed with the hope that I wouldn't get electrocuted. The crowd was a third of what it should have been, but Kelly always said, "Don't punish the ones who show up," and I wholeheartedly, agreed. It was wet, sweaty, and probably a little dangerous. Still, we gamely slogged our way through the set. Apparently, we managed to connect with our audience, because the sopping wet crowd stuck around until the end of our show, cheering us on. God bless 'em.

My brother Tim, along with his wife Carolyn and young daughters, Sarah and Alex, had come all the way from Texas to see his little brother's amazing new job in person. In the tent after the show, I introduced Tim to Bev. Bev said, "You picked a spectacular gig."

Tim replied, "Yeah, well, it was interesting to watch you guys handle a less-than-optimal situation."

"You still sounded good," Tim's always-generous wife Carolyn added.

Kindness and silver linings were nice, but I wished Tim and his family could've seen us anywhere but muddy Mississippi. Sometimes you get Albert Hall, sometimes you get a soggy Hog.

We'd spent the previous afternoon baking in a parking lot outside Three Rivers Stadium in Pittsburgh at a rib fest. I felt like we were on the American Meat Circuit. Everywhere we went, hogs and cows were getting the worst of it. What happened to pescatarian catering? Look at me, complaining about my job. That didn't take long, did it?

When show conditions were truly lousy, Mik Kaminski, who'd been playing ELO music a lot longer than I had, was prone to quip, "This is *harrrrrd* work." I knew what he meant, but I always thought, "Enh. *Not really.*"

I hope I never forget the difference between playing music and, say, my job washing dishes at a restaurant/bar/pick-up lounge/nightmare called Daddy's Money in suburban Atlanta, Georgia, when I was 19. An engineering student from Georgia Tech and I stood for eight hours over steamy sinks of gross greasy water, scrubbing plates and glassware and pots and pans covered with molten cheese, steak fat, and lobster butter. On a particularly harried Saturday night, we turned our misery on its head and began to sing, "To dream...the impossible dream...to fight the unbeatable foe..." Our faces lit up and we actually laughed. My partner in hell fed me the next line and we both sang with full gusto, "To bear...with unbearable sorrow!" That's as far as we got, because on the word "sorrow" a red-faced, hysterical gremlin of a 26-year-old floor manager in a blue button-down shirt and a stupid fucking Daddy's Money tie flew into our grubby cubbyhole and screamed, "*We can HEAR YOU in the DINING ROOM!*"

Perhaps we *had* been a bit boisterous.

We didn't have to say a thing in our defense. The contrast between our disgusting soaked-through aprons and his spotless tan khakis said it all: you don't belong back here, manager boy, and nothing you might say could possibly make conditions worse for us than they already are.

So. I'll play a Hog Fest in the rain *anytime.*

To Mik's point, though, as we toured the States, it became clear that ELO Part II's American gigs paled in status compared to our concerts overseas. In South America, our mere arrival warranted a press conference at the airport. In Bulgaria and Ukraine, we appeared on national television before we could lay our heads down in our hotel rooms. We were a big deal. Front page news.

In the States, we were just another classic rock band making the rounds. We wouldn't be appearing on Leno or Letterman anytime soon. In 1999, acts with current hits such as Smashmouth, Sugar Ray, and Lit were way more relevant than we were in the States. Conversely, could any of those bands sell out The Palace of Culture in Kyiv? Doubtful.

The modest stature of our American gigs hit closer to home on our next show. We were headed to my adopted hometown of Los Angeles, and I was super-excited for my friends to see me in my worldly new band. Unfortunately, the gig was not *really* in LA, but down the 405 Freeway, past LAX airport, to the land where classic rock bands spent the twilight of their career: Redondo Beach. Club Caprice held about 300 people, and customers were encouraged to dine during the show. The stage was tucked in a tight corner and had no room for risers—the mobile platforms on which we normally elevated Bev's drums and Eric and Lou's keyboards. Risers improve sight lines immensely. At Club Caprice, we were all the same level as the bus boys.

Am I complaining again? Damn. Sorry.

On the bright side, our show at the Caprice was sold out and we had forty-three friends on the guest list. Unfortunately, a forty-fourth guest was my old nemesis Gig Head. Ugh. I hadn't heard from him since Albert Hall. But here he was, whispering in my brain, "Wow. Lots of friends here tonight. Big show in your hometown or close enough to it. You've been telling people an awful lot about your fancy-pants, famous band. It sure would be a shame if you chose tonight to play and sing poorly. But, hey, why would you do that? Don't listen to me! Have fun! Just, you know, *don't fuck up.*"

So, of course, right at the get-go I committed a few inexcusable clams, botching several chords during "Evil Woman," which, on any other night, I'd play in my sleep. For the first few songs, instead of losing myself in the moment and letting my muscle memory handle my guitar and vocal tasks, I allowed my mind to drift to my friends in the audience. I wondered, "Are they impressed with the vocals? I've told everybody what a great singing band we are. Should I say something about living here? Can they hear my guitar parts? Should I stop worrying and get back to playing the songs?" Sigh.

Despite my brain wandering in the Gig Head desert for short stretches, I got through the set disaster free. The show was fine, but any honest band knows the difference between a barn burner and an average show. This was closer to the latter, especially concerning my performance. Afterward, my friends all had nice things to say, which is what friends should say when they're on the guest list. One unexpectedly positive comment stuck in my mind. My opinionated pal, Nick Pierone, a fearless musician and singer with whom I've made lots of music, said, "Dude, Kelly's a great singer and everything, but *you* should be in the middle of the stage..."

I loved Nick's vote of support, but I rejected the idea straight away. In my opinion, I was just the new guy. Kelly Groucutt was the brash beating heart of ELO Part II. Kelly brought a street performer's charisma to a thinking man's band. He chatted freely with the front row and shouted enthusiastically to the back. Kelly enjoyed the shit out of himself on stage and there wasn't an audience that didn't feel it. He was a perfect crowd manager.

SAME AND SANE

No matter where we were in the world, our band followed certain routines. We each had our own hotel room and as much private time as needed. When heading to sound check or an airport, we showed up in the lobby on time and ready to go. Sound check was scheduled for mid-afternoon, and dinner was at least three hours before show time. (No one likes to sing on a full stomach.) We generally ate dinner together.

After each show, we'd greet friends and fans, sign autographs, take pictures, and then get in a van back to the hotel. The only variable in our orderly departure after a gig would occasionally be Kelly, who tended to chat with the fans longer than the rest of us. On nights when everyone was ready to depart, except our chatty bass player, we'd tell the driver to start slowly rolling the van to convince Kelly it was time to say goodbye, jump in the van, and go.

Our routines kept us sane. It was good to have structure when plenty of things can go wrong on the road that will upset a carefully planned schedule. Flights delayed or canceled; hotel rooms not ready; a PA company arriving late; a backline company supplying the wrong equipment; a transportation company picking us up in vehicles too small to carry all our luggage and gear, etc.

A big key in our band was that we respected each other and enjoyed each other's company. We had no assholes, no prima donnas, no idiots in our group. No one slept late and missed lobby call (much). None of us disappeared at weird times (much) or missed sound check. None of us were drug addicts, as we much preferred alcohol. I've suffered through bandmates I didn't like and it's the worst. It sucks the joy out of playing music together. Every day I appreciated my good fortune to be a member of ELO Part II.

UH, OH

On July 2, 1999, ELO Part II was booked to play the Skyline Stage, an outdoor amphitheater on Lake Michigan in Chicago. We left our hotel on time and headed to the gig. I sat by Bev, ELO's founder, the loudest drummer I'd ever heard, co-writer of "Over London Skies," and backbeat of my heroes the Move. A few minutes into yet another van ride to a sound check, Bev looked me levelly in the eye and said, "I don't know how much longer I can do this, Hux."

My body suddenly felt heavier on the seat. Oh, shit. "That doesn't sound good. What's going on?"

Bev was frank. "I'm not enjoying touring like I once did. It's gotten stale. I've been playing these songs a lot longer than *you* have," he said with a wry smile. "I just don't know how many more times I can play bloody 'Sweet Talking Woman,' you know?"

I did my best to appreciate where he was coming from. "Sweet Talkin' Woman" was indeed light in the loafers compared to the Move's "Brontosaurus." I also did my best not to freak out. This was way worse than Kelly muttering, "I'm getting too old for this" in Wilmington. Bev went on, "I've always believed I would retire when I turned fifty-five, and I'm just about there. I turn fifty-five in November."

I felt like I retired in my twenties when I decided to become a full-time musician.

Bev continued, "I want you to know, it's nothing on you. You've been *great*. You brought a lot of fresh energy and enthusiasm into the band, and I really enjoy being on stage with you. You've made it fun again. If you hadn't joined the band, I probably would've quit last year when Phil left."

That was nice to hear, but I could tell it wouldn't be enough to keep him around. It seemed like a fait accompli. Bev's words and his weary tone made it clear he wasn't musing aloud. Still, I felt like I'd failed him. If it was so much fun to play with me, why quit now? Damn. This sucked.

As we rode toward the venue, the news sank in. If Bev left, his departure would be a major blow. Besides being the unofficial leader of the band, Bev's status as a founding member of ELO was important for our credibility. I had no doubt that, in the eyes of promoters and fans Bev Bevan legitimized ELO Part II. He was *one of the original guys* and that counted for a lot.

DARK AND TIDY

We arrived at the Navy Pier, and I tried to put aside Bev's deflating news. I hung my stage clothes in the dressing room, grabbed a snack in the green room, and went on stage to check out our backline gear. As I adjusted sounds on the rented Marshall 800 amp, I overheard Bev laugh and say, "Heyyyy! There he is!" I turned to see a familiar looking figure approaching Bev with a big smile and outstretched arms. It was Tony Iommi of Black Sabbath.

I knew that Bev and Tony were old buddies from Birmingham and briefly bandmates in Black Sabbath, but I couldn't help feeling like a fanboy. I was looking at *Tony Fucking Iommi*. His guitar sound had mesmerized my fourteen-year-old brain from the moment I'd heard Black Sabbath's debut album. Tony's a God.

Fiddling with my amp suddenly seemed unimportant, and I wandered over to where Bev and Tony were chatting. I loitered in their vicinity for a few awkward minutes and then Bev introduced me to Tony as ELO Part II's new guitarist.

Tony said, "I've heard you're an amazing player, Parthenon. Maybe we could get together at my mansion in England and write an album."

Wait. Sorry.

Tony said, "Pleased to meet you."

He was pleased to meet *me!*

Tony was noticeably well-groomed. Every black-dyed hair was perfectly in place. He wore fashionable tinted glasses and cool, expensive clothes. He presented himself as a wealthy, well-heeled, English gentleman/rock star. Bev later told me he'd once visited Tony as he was packing for a Sabbath tour. Bev noticed multiple suitcases all filled with identical leather jackets—one for each day. Talk about fastidious. I found all this a little surprising since Tony and his bandmates were supposed to be demon spawn from Hell, but I guess you can work dark and still be *tidy*.

I hung around as Tony and Bev continued chatting and catching up. Tony was in the Chicago area to play a Sabbath reunion gig as part of Ozzfest. He would be bashing out deafening heavy metal hits like "Paranoid" for 20,000 crazed freaks at one of the biggest concerts of the summer. In contrast, Bev would play skipping-thru-the-park "Sweet Talking Woman" for a smattering of tourists.

I found out later from our band's videographer, George Reed, that after our show at the Navy Pier, Bev kicked a chair and threw a wine glass at the wall of the dressing room. Happy as he'd been to see his old pal from Black Sabbath, Bev was apparently mortified to have Tony see him playing for only a few thousand people. That night, Bev told Eric Troyer he'd "never tour the States again" because the gigs just weren't good enough. I knew what he meant (Hog Fest, anyone?) but, in fact, our next three shows were in front of 12,000, 16,000 and 10,000 fans at festivals in Michigan and Minnesota. Pretty good gigs. I held out a slim serving of hope that Bev might change his mind about retiring. Maybe we could take bloody "Sweet Talkin' Woman" out of the set.

I also hoped Bev might consider staying because of "Over London Skies." Our first collaboration had become a staple in our set. Why not continue our songwriting partnership and put together a new album? That was the plan, wasn't it? When Bev asked me to join the group, I was thrilled to have a job, but there was so much more to it than that. I couldn't wait to record new music with such talented bandmates. Any writer my age would die for the chance to record with most of ELO's classic '70s lineup as their band. Eric Troyer and Phil Bates had done a decent job of it on earlier ELO Part II albums. Eric's "Honest Men" had dented the charts in the UK and Germany, and his collaborations with Phil Bates, Bev, Mik, and Kelly were sturdy slabs of classic rock. Before I joined the band, their songs sat in the set alongside Lynne's old hits and had, apparently, held up okay. I wanted some of that action.

"Over London Skies" offered a glimpse of ELO Part II's future. Audiences hearing it for the first time roared for it, like it was an old favorite. I wasn't Jeff Lynne, and it wasn't 1977, but I was surrounded by most of his old band. It gave me a lot of confidence that we could make a great record and expand the repertoire. Lou's string arrangement on "Over London Skies" alone was enough to make my head spin with the possibilities.

After Chicago, we performed on a beautiful Fourth of July summer's day in Muskegon, Michigan. I was heartened to see a review the next day by Anette Buchholz in the *Muskegon Chronicle*:

> ...after a new song titled 'London Skies'...(a) rapport...was developing between the 16,000-capacity audience and the slightly new-sounding band once led by the prominence of lead vocalist/guitarist Jeff Lynne. It took a few songs to accept Parthenon Huxley as Lynne's replacement. But he had us; we were drawn in and wanted more.

Buchholz wasn't writing for *Rolling Stone*, but her assessment carried weight for me. She described precisely what I hoped ELO Part II could be—a "slightly new-sounding" classic rock band. That may seem like a low bar, but it's not. Classic rock bands are expected to serve up tried-and-true songs that everyone knows and loves, and not make fans suffer through new songs they don't know. It's no secret that when bands even as great at the Who, Deep Purple, the Rolling Stones, or even Paul McCartney announce, "Here's a new one for you," people will head to the bar or the bathroom. If we could insert more "slightly new sounding" songs in our set and actually have the audience stay in its seats to listen, it would be a real achievement.

I loved everything about ELO Part II—the guys, the classic hits, the exotic touring, the talent on stage, the harmonizing with Kelly and Eric, the money, the camaraderie, the fun. It was a wonderful new part of my life. But I was also a writer. *That* part of me did not want to lay fallow or look backward. Unless we buckled down and wrote a new album, my job would boil down to playing someone else's songs—something I'd avoided for most of my life. My mission, my favorite thing in the world, was creating new music.

YOU'RE NO GOOD

Before I joined ELO Part II, I met the funniest man in rock, Cheap Trick bassist Tom Petersson. We were introduced by my friend Sass Jordan, the bawdy and talented Canadian singer, at a breakfast joint in LA. After we placed our orders, Sass voluntarily brought Tom up to speed on the nightmare I'd been through the year before, losing my wife to cancer. I hadn't asked Sass to do anything of the kind, but maybe she felt protective of me, who knows? Tom and I sat patiently listening to Sass as she outlined my whole sad story. When she'd finished, Tom turned to me, smiled, and said, "Cool!" I nearly spat out my orange juice, I was laughing so hard. Sass was sweet to look out for me, but I hadn't really wanted my late wife's cancer tale to blanket our breakfast, and with one word, Tom had gotten us all off the hook. It was a neat trick.

A year after that breakfast, ELO Part II was booked at *Moondance Jam VIII,* a festival in Walker, Minnesota, with Joan Jet and the Blackhearts, Blue Öyster Cult, the Outfield, and headliner Cheap Trick. The guys in Cheap Trick, including Tom, were famously huge fans of Roy Wood, the Move, and, by extension, ELO. I doubted Tom was aware that I'd joined ELO Part II, and I was more than a little eager to see his reaction when he found out.

We drove three hours from Minneapolis and arrived at the festival around noon for sound check. Late in the day, Cheap Trick rolled into the muddy backstage area in a ridiculous white stretch limo like the rock stars they were. Rick, Robin, Bun E., and Tommy crawled out of the limo. They all were excited to see Bev and the other ELO guys. Tommy then saw me and said, "Parthy! What are *YOU* doing here?" Only Tom could call me Parthy and make me like it.

I said, "I'm here with Bev and the guys. I'm the new guitarist."

Tom acted incredulous. His face dropped and he said, "You're what? *YOU'RE* in ELO Part II?"

"Yep."

He looked skeptical. "Since when?"

"Since late last year," I said, playing the straight man.

Tommy wasn't having it, and here it came: "No, you're not! *You're no good!*"

Again, only Tommy could say such a thing and make me laugh out loud. He's the quintessential, loveable, asshole prankster.

I asked Tommy if he'd be on-site when we played. I pulled out a set list to show him what we'd be doing. Tom looked it over and said, "Oh, wow. We'll have to be here for *that* one. Oh, *that one*, too. Yeah, I'll get here early."

Tommy showed up halfway through our show. Knowing what a fan he was of ELO made me nervous, like I had to prove to him that I was worthy of being in the band, and that I wasn't "no good." The useless shit that goes on in musicians' minds! I played fine.

After our set, the rest of ELO Part II hightailed it back to Minneapolis. I stayed at *Moondance Jam VIII* so I could see Cheap Trick for the first time. Tommy, generously, invited me to watch the show from the side of the stage. Several times during the midst of the mayhem that is Cheap Trick live, Tommy strolled over to where I stood just to hang for a bit while banging on his insane twelve-string bass that must've weighed twenty-five pounds. They were ridiculously entertaining, as anyone who's seen them knows. Rick Neilson spent as much time throwing picks into the crowd as playing his guitars, and Robin Zander is one hell of a rock singer.

I hitched a ride back to Minneapolis on the Cheap Trick tour bus. After an hour of chatting about music, mutual acquaintances, and creating music for *That '70s Show*, Rick Neilson asked, "Hey, you guys wanna watch a video?"

We all said, "Sure." I thought, "What kind of video would Rick Neilson choose to entertain a tour bus full of dudes? Horror? Porn?" Rick outdid my imagination by a mile. He slapped a video into the VCR. A shaky black-and-white title card appeared, which read *Metamorphose: M.C. Escher, 1898–1972*. M.C. Escher! It was a bio-pic of the Dutch artist whose prints of optical illusions we all bought back in the '70s...at events like classroom fundraisers in Athens, Greece...where they sold posters of the Move.

DAVID LEE ROTH IS FUN TO HANG WITH MAN ALRIGHT!

On August 8, 1999, ELO Part II arrived in Estonia, a country bordering Russia and just across the Baltic Sea from Finland and Sweden. We were in the capital city of Tallinn to play the *Masters of Rock Festival* on a bill with none other than David Lee Roth.

After checking in at the modern Scandic Palace Hotel, Eric and I set off on foot to see the town. Just seven years removed from Soviet control, Estonia had wasted no time embracing the West. They dropped the ruble like a bad beet, linked their currency's value to the euro, and went to work promoting their unique calling card—Tallinn's beautiful, largely intact, medieval city center. Fresh paint and repair work could be seen everywhere on stately, but crumbling, buildings. Under the USSR's economic and administrative control, Tallinn had suffered and remained stagnant. Now that Estonia was free, entrepreneurs were bringing the old city back to life. It was exciting to see.

With a night to kill before our gig the next day, band and crew from ELO Part II and the David Lee Roth Band noisily mobbed the hotel lobby bar, drinking and talking bullshit like schoolboys. About every thirty seconds, the rough and ready rock 'n' roll crowd would turn to look out the bar's large picture window and respectfully go quiet. It seems crazy, but Estonia was like a '60s *Twilight Zone* episode where all the women looked like runway models with long hair, mini-skirts, knee-high boots, doll-like faces and disinterested expressions. They literally shut down two bands just by walking past. We'd shake our heads and mumble, "That's insane," and go back to our conversations.

I ended up chatting with David Lee Roth, or rather, listening to him as his brain sent a million words at light speed through his mouth. As he spoke, Roth's appealing face was cartoonishly animated. He was engaging, hyper, and jivey, but all in a fun, convivial way. I liked him. I asked if he'd been to Tallinn before. DLR said, "No, but I've got ancestors from Minsk, Belarus, just down the road." Wow. What a trip to think that David Lee Roth's forebears had left a wintry outpost like Minsk and ended up in sunny Pasadena, California, where, you know...*Van Halen* happened. Roth looked me in the eye and said, "We're all from *somewhere*, man!"

I asked what had brought him and his band back to the old ancestral neighborhood. He said, pointing his thumb at himself, "Well, when word got around about '*Guess who's in the unemployment line?*' (that made both of us laugh) I had an offer to play an island off the coast of Texas. Then a hurricane wiped out the gig and I thought, well...shit, we've got a band, let's take it somewhere. I hired my old sound guy and made him double as road manager. I asked my monitor guy to do the booking. My old wardrobe gal decked the band out in rock-star clothes, and here we are. We've got a couple of barbecue grills with us and some baseball gloves, so, you know, it's alright. So far, so good."

The next day at *Masters of Rock*, Roth and his band of highly skilled LA guys played all Van Halen hits and they didn't miss a beat. No, it wasn't Eddie, Alex, and Michael on stage, but it *was* David Lee Roth and he owned it. As a singer, DLR is a fabulous front man who works non-stop to engage the audience. He did all his leaps and howls and screams as well as a bit of singing. Did I wish it was Eddie playing guitar? *Yeah*. But I still admired the guitarist who was up there working with DLR and killing it. Stepping in to play Eddie's parts was no picnic and way above my pay grade. The guy was great.

Roth's band wasn't unlike ELO Part II. We would take the stage with four former members of ELO plus me and Eric as the reliable replacement parts. We would play the hits, add a few new wrinkles, engage the audience, and sound great. Was it 1977 inside a spaceship? No. But would you really expect to see a spaceship and lasers in 1999?

NEVER AGAIN

About three weeks later, despite his vow to Eric that he'd never perform again in the States, someone who looked and acted exactly like Bev Bevan showed up for gigs in Texas, Georgia, Missouri, Wisconsin, and Louisiana. I'd like to report that the band was fraught with tension as Bev's fifty-fifth birthday/retirement approached, but it wasn't. Maybe it was an English thing—the ability to face trouble with a stiff upper lip (and a beer), along with the preference to never talk about anything remotely upsetting. Or maybe it was just because bandmates, and men in general, don't like to discuss unpleasant things. For whatever reason, we carried on as normally as ever.

In San Antonio, Texas, my brother Tim came out again to catch ELO Part II, this time at the Farwest Rodeo, a cavernous country music club that held about 3,500. It was not our type of venue, and we might've drawn 2,000. Did I mention our American gigs were weird? At least Tim didn't get rained on as he had in Mississippi.

Two nice things happened in San Antonio. The morning after the show, Tim, Bev, and I convened for a round of golf on a nearby public course. Tim's a good player and I was glad he could add "the drummer of ELO" to his history of playing partners. The second memorable thing happened later that afternoon. Bev found Tim and me hanging out in the hotel lobby before the band left to catch a flight to Atlanta. "Oh, Hux, there you are. I've been looking for you." Bev handed me a paper bag filled with cash. "That's your earnings from the previous run. It's ten thousand dollars. You can count it if you want." Bev chuckled.

I did my best to process the half-wonderful and half-terribly-awkward feeling of sitting in a hotel lobby with $10,000 stuffed in a paper bag. I caught my brother's impressed but skeptical gaze.

Tim said, "That's a nice payday. You'll report every penny of that, of course..."

"Of course. Totally legit, bro."

Besides being profitable, this American run was doing a great job of connecting me with my family. After Tim saw the band in San Antonio, my oldest brother Tom, and his son Buz, caught ELO Part II near Atlanta. My mom and dad attended our show in New Orleans, and my brother Chuck planned to see us in Atlantic City. That covered everybody. My family's attendance got to be a band joke. When Eric would solicit names for the guest list, Mik would ask, "What about it, Hux? Any brothers we haven't met yet?"

NEW, NEW GUY

Although I'd hoped he might change his mind, Bev confirmed he was retiring and informed us that his last two shows would be November 12 and 13 at the Sands Casino in Atlantic City, New Jersey. When those dates arrived, I'd been with the band a year and one week, and that would be the extent of my professional affiliation with Bev Bevan. We played fifty-nine shows together in 1999, some of them the most memorable gigs of my life. I owed Bev a huge thanks for asking me to join his group.

Despite the shock of Bev leaving, the rest of us didn't, for a minute, think of breaking up the band. We just had to find a new drummer, simple as that. The five of us had a meeting to discuss our situation. Band meetings were about as exciting as dry weddings—no one wanted to be there, particularly the English. Mik asked in his classic rhetorical way, "How are we supposed to go about finding a drummer?" Kelly rolled a cigarette and opined, "I might know some guys who could help us..." Lou sipped his wine.

Sigh. The Brits weren't exactly fired up to solve the problem. They'd played with Bev since their twenties. They'd never needed another drummer before, so how would they know how to find one now? They probably assumed the Pushy Americans would fix everything and, of course, they were right.

I had no doubt that Eric knew some great drummers who'd be able to do the job. But Eric wasn't about to start auditioning guys if it wasn't necessary. He knew I had someone in mind. I wanted Gordon Townsend, the drummer in my LA band, P. Hux. To me, it was a no-brainer. He was a great guy and an excellent drummer who'd fit right in with a band like ours. He played perfectly in time and always steered his drumming to the strengths of a song. His taste was impeccable. He wasn't show-offy or sloppy. And Gordon was a Beatles nut. He worshipped the same Liverpool Gods we all did. As a bonus, he was a lot younger than the rest of us. Nothing wrong with bringing down the median age of a classic rock band.

Chapter 5: Uh-Oh

There was just one problem. Gordon was American. The Brits complained, particularly Kelly. "Not another bloody American! This used to be an English band, you know, for Christ's sake!" I pointed out that Gordon's Dad was English, and you couldn't ask for an English-ier rock name than "Townsend" (even if it were missing an "h").

Everyone in the band was entitled to their opinion, of course, especially now that Bev was no longer in the picture. We were all equally permitted to bitch and moan and say how we wanted things to be. But in the end, if something needed to get done, someone had to get off their ass and make it happen. Practicality would win the day.

The band consensus was, "Okay. Give Gordon a call."

On November 10, 1999, Gordon and all the band (except Bev) assembled in a ballroom at the Sands Casino in Atlantic City for the audition. Bev was somewhere in the building, and it felt slightly awkward for us to be with Gordon—like having a new girlfriend at your divorce proceeding. But so be it. It was Bev's choice to leave. We had gigs coming up and we needed a drummer so we could honor our commitments.

Our road crew had assembled our gear and a small P.A. We tuned up and Gordon made some final adjustments to his drum set, setting the height of the cymbals and the angle of his rack tom just so. I can't say what the others were expecting, but I knew exactly what was coming. Gordon was going to kick ass. We'd asked him to learn half a dozen songs. We started with "Turn To Stone." After just a few bars, the band already sounded great. Locked in. Powerful. I quickly grew excited, but I was determined to keep a straight face. Gordon was my guy, so the band knew where I stood. They needed to get there on their own. We followed with "Livin' Thing" and then "Mr. Blue Sky." Gordon was killing it, as I knew he would. After each song, I kept my thoughts to myself.

As it turned out, I didn't need to say a thing. Before we played a fourth song, Kelly stepped away from his mic. He dramatically swung his bass guitar off his shoulder, jammed it on his guitar stand and said, almost angrily, "He's hired! I don't need to hear anyone else. He's fucking great!" We all stood there, surprised. Gordon looked at me, like, *what's happening?* I shrugged my shoulders: *dunno*.

Kelly cleared things up for us. He said, emphatically, "That's the *first* time I've locked into the fucking kick drum *in thirty years*! I wanted an English guy, but if we don't hire Gordon, you can get yourself a new bass player!" Wow. *Looked like Gordon had Kelly's vote.* How did everyone else feel? As he so often did, Mik sealed the deal with a pithy remark. Removing his violin from under his chin, Mik quipped, "Well, I'm quite pleased we've moved on my recommendation. Congratulations, Gordon!" We all laughed and that was that. Gordon was in.

We'd eliminated a huge obstacle to the band's survival. We were down to three former members of ELO, and heaven forbid, half the band members were now Americans, but we could send Bev out in style, wish him the best, and carry on touring with Gordon.

Despite the shockwave Bev's departure represented, a potentially sad weekend quickly acquired the feel of a party. My brother Chuck came up from North Carolina. My pal from Greece who'd turned me on to the Move, Matt Barrett, attended both shows with his wife, Andrea. I was quietly thrilled for Matt to see him hanging out and talking with Bev backstage. Oddly, I think I heard them discussing financial investments.

WHAT'D HE SAY?

It was customary in ELO Part II to pause in the middle of our show and introduce each band member to the audience. At Bev's last gig, I pulled out a speech I'd prepared for his final introduction. I was glad I'd taken the time to compose something instead of just winging it. Here it is:

> Ladies and Gentlemen, music lovers, friends and fans of ELO and ELO Part II, we have an announcement to make. One among us in the band has always had it in mind that upon reaching a certain age he would stop being a member of ELO Part II and "move" on to other interests. With his birthday only twelve days away, that time has arrived, and tonight will be his final show. We remaining members of the band will continue to tour and record without interruption, but for now will you please rise and pay tribute to his twenty-eight-year legacy, the backbeat of the band, the one, the only, Bev Bevan.

As he walked to the mic at center stage, the audience gave him a rousing ovation. Then, from inside his vest, Bev pulled out a speech of his own. He said how much fun he'd had over the years with "the guys" and what an honor it had been to play for the fans with such great musicians and so on. We stood onstage with him, soaking in the nice moment. Toward the end of his speech, Bev said something along the lines of "...my final show as drummer of ELO Part II, and the final show for ELO Part II as a band."

I thought, "Did he just say, 'the final show for ELO Part II'? What does he mean by that?" Kelly's smile dimmed and he looked puzzled as well. Maybe Bev had misspoken. Bev returned to his place behind the drums, and we dove into the second half of our set. My focus shifted away from Bev's speech.

We ended the concert with our usual rousing version of "Don't Bring Me Down." Bev took his final bows to a standing ovation and then we had a bit of a party backstage. Whatever concerns I had about his speech were pushed aside by the usual post-gig high of adrenaline, wine, and companionship. Matt and Chuck came backstage and all of us hung out together, shot the shit, and had a nice time. As the night wound down, Eric Troyer gave Bev a silly going-away present. It was a keychain with a plastic fob that said, "I (Heart) Jeff." Bev posed with it, and I took a picture. What a great joke.

Too bad the joke was on us.

Soon after Bev's retirement, our manager John Regna received a call from Lynne's management. Regna was told that Lynne and Bevan had a deal between them stating that ELO Part II could only exist if Bev was in the band. With Bev out, therefore, ELO Part II no longer existed. All Regna could say was, "Well, nobody told *us*."

And by "nobody," Regna meant Bev. If what Lynne's management said was true, it was shocking news. Tickets were selling briskly for upcoming ELO Part II concerts in the U.S., Spain, Holland, Poland, Denmark, and El Salvador. Surely Bev was aware of that. Would he really leave us holding the bag?

Back on that memorable summer day in Chicago as the band rode to sound check, Bev had told me he was tired of playing "bloody 'Sweet Talkin' Woman'" and that he'd always planned to retire at age fifty-five. But he hadn't mentioned anything about taking our name with him into retirement. That seemed to violate the spirit of our band. We were never called "Bev Bevan's ELO Part II." *All six of us* were ELO Part II. Or so we'd thought.

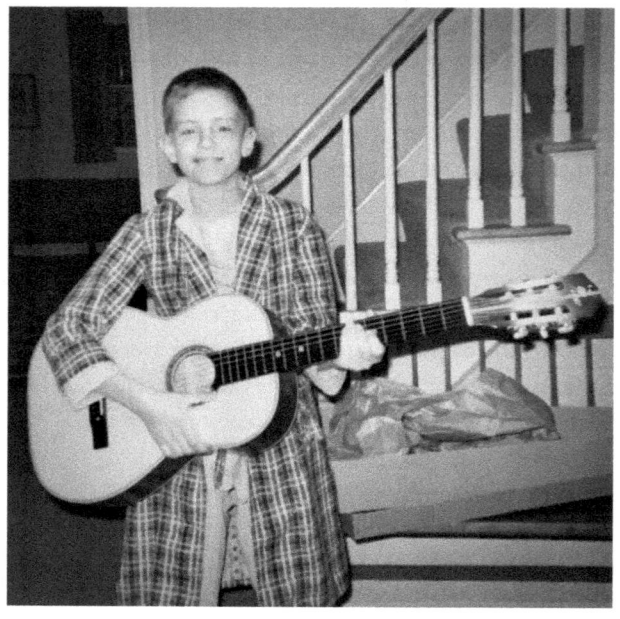

Top: Christmas 1964. After the Beatles played Ed Sullivan I became one of the fifty million kids who couldn't live without a guitar. Bottom: November 1966. The S.S. Cristoforo Columbo Observation Lounge where I began writing songs.

Top: 1972. Improv punk heroes CC Blues King relax backstage at the American Youth Center. L-R: Chuck Saunders, Chris Christ, Pete Christ, PH, George The Mouse, Matt Econopouly. Bottom: 1978. My first pro band, The Blazers. Long sets, lots of laughs. L-R: Lee Gildersleeve, Shakin' Sherman Tate, PH, Ronnie Taylor. Photo: Alex Webb

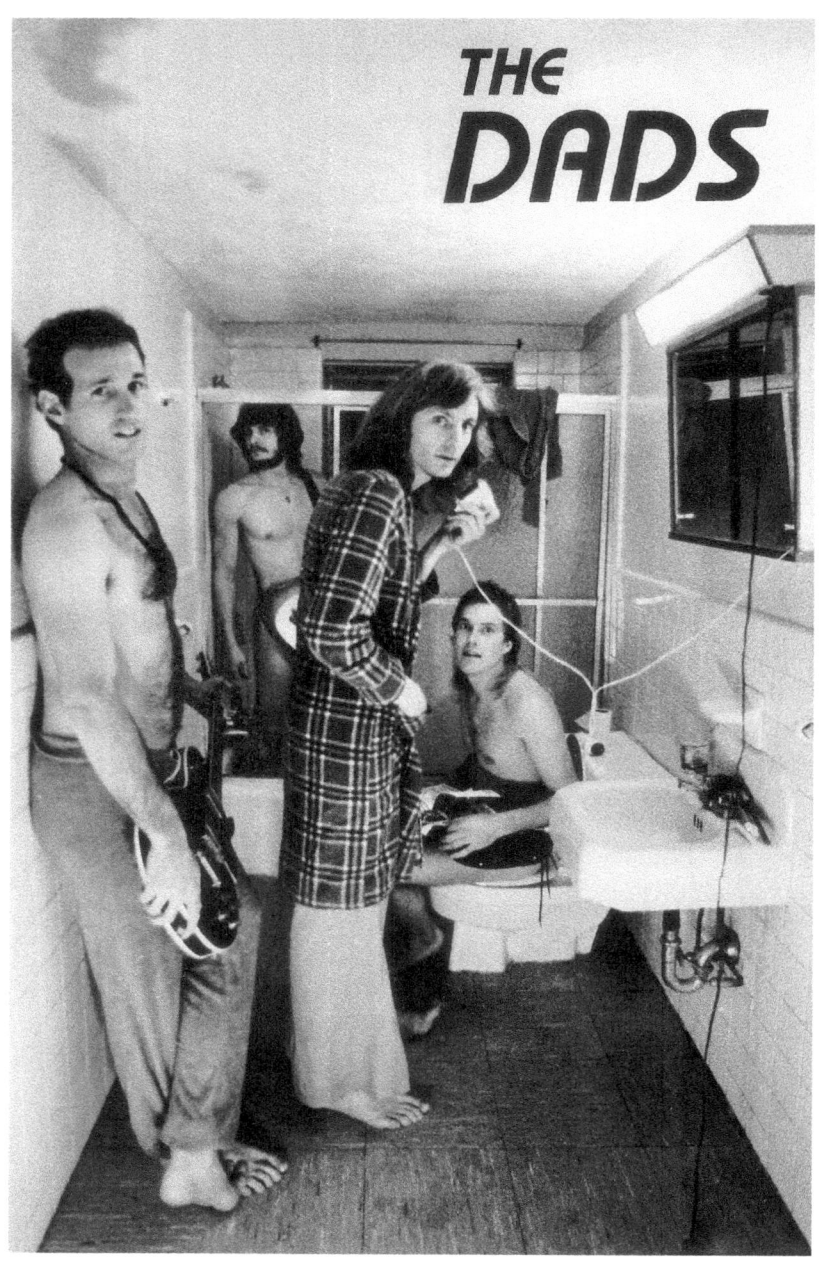

The band that shaves, showers and sh*ts together... stays together. For a while anyway. L-R: Matt (Econopouly) Barrett, Scott Swartzwelder, PH, Zoe Lagergren. Photo: Alex Webb.

Top Left: 1983. Rick Rock rhythm section. L-R: Chip Shelby, Andy Church. Top Right: *Mondo Montage* North Carolina rock compilation. Middle Left: "Buddha, Buddha" was the wind beneath Rick Rock's wings. Poster design: Anistatia Miller, seen Middle Right in 2017. Bottom: 1984. Me & Dixon collage. What a pleasure it was to play with two stars. L-R: PH, Rob Ladd, Don Dixon.

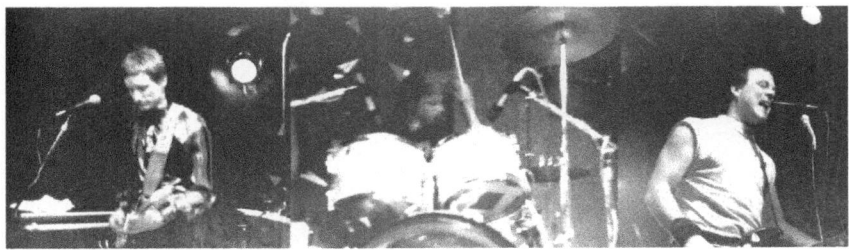

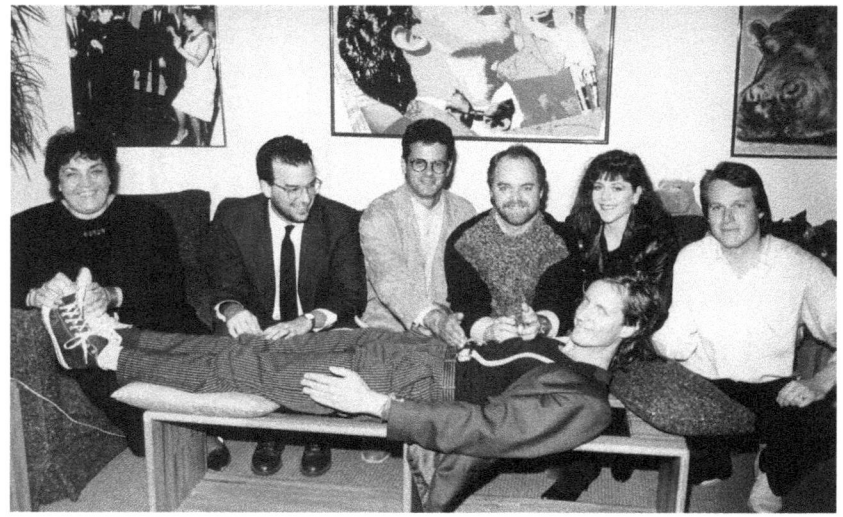

Top: 1987. Manager Michael Solomon and executives at MCA Music Publishing claim their percentages of PH. L-R: Carol Ware, Leeds Levy, Michael Solomon, Rick Shoemaker, Betsy Anthony, Scott James. Photo behind Carol is of Ringo dancing with MCA President Leeds Levy's mom.

Bottom: We performed as "Parthenon Huxley" but I could make a case for being the fourth most talented member of my band. L-R: PH, Jen Condos, Rusty Anderson, Rob Ladd. Photo: Doug Hooper.

Top: 1988. My hometown Record Bar in Chapel Hill went all out to publicize *Sunny Nights*. I loved the support, but I felt really self-conscious as the center of attention among my friends. I got better at this kind of thing after I joined ELO Part II. Bottom: 1991. That's my wife Janet with my songwriting partner E and Janet's all-time favorite artist, Elton John.

Top: 1994. P. Hux. L-R: PH, Gordon Townsend, Rob Miller. Front: Algonquin, looking all badass for the band pic. Photo: Henry Diltz. Bottom: 1993. VeG. Paul Martinez, PH, Winston Watson. Photo: Allen Carrasco.

1998. My first ELO Part II promo shoot at Wilmington DE Opera House convinced me I was truly a member of the band. Back: Louis Clark, Kelly Groucutt, Eric Troyer. Front: PH, Bev Bevan, Mik Kaminski.

Top Left: 1999. Text-heavy Royal Albert Hall Poster. Top Right: After his last show with ELO Part II, Bev joyfully posed with a parting gift from Eric Troyer. Bottom: Eric Called me out of the blue in 1998 and changed my life. After working together for twenty-five years I think he's the best man I know. Photo Kimmy G.

PART TWO

IN WHICH I GET A CHANCE TO BE LOVED

CHAPTER 6
FIRST VERSE

After giving birth to three sons named Tom, Tim, and Chuck, my blue-eyed mom gave it one more go, praying for the girl she planned to name Barbara. On January 19, 1956, at Our Lady of the Lake Hospital in Baton Rouge, Louisiana, one-time schoolteacher-now-housewife Phyllis Miller awaited the gender verdict in her recovery room. The doctor entered and excitedly announced, "You're the proud parent of a baby boy!" My mom, perhaps still coming out of anesthesia's fog, replied, "You son of a bitch!" Like my newborn wiener was the doctor's fault. With Barbara out of the picture, I was named Richard Willett[2] Miller, "Rick" for short. (I dodged the "Dick" bullet.)

My raised-right mom moved past her rare burst of foul language and accepted her fate as the mother of four sons. Among her many thoughtful actions as we grew up, Mom kept hardcover Baby Books for all of us. I came across mine not long ago and a written entry caught my eye. In 1958, my mom noted, "Rick likes to pantomime playing a ukulele." I prefer to think I was imagining a Les Paul in my stubby little baby hands, but, yeah, a uke would've been easier to handle. I was two years old and already exhibiting my ambitions.

With his degree in chemical engineering from Carnegie Tech, my dad worked for Esso at the petrochemical plants by the Mississippi River. In 1960, Esso promoted him to an office job in New York City. We moved to suburban New Jersey, a half-hour commuter train ride from the city. We arrived during a historic snowstorm and Dad immediately bought four sleds, hats, coats, and mittens for his boys. He'd grown up in the Upper Peninsula of Michigan. Dad knew snow. He also knew that sleds and warm clothes would keep us outside and out of Mom's hair as she settled us into our suburban house in the town of Summit. Smart guy.

---

2 My middle name Willett has been traced back to Thomas Willett, first mayor of New York City, 1665. His appointment apparently was helped by Willett's ability to get along with the English, the Dutch, and the Native Americans. He was reappointed in 1667, or, as I like to think of it, three hundred years B.S.P. (Before Sgt. Pepper).

One freezing-cold evening, just after dusk, I was trudging home alone across tire-packed snow. Laboring to pull my sled behind me, I stopped to take a breather and looked up. Softly and slowly, millions of near-weightless flakes descended to Earth from their dark gray origins. I held my breath so I could better appreciate the rare outdoor silence. I remember thinking the world was wondrous and I had a place in it.

THE SECRET'S OUT

Several winters later, in December 1963, I stood in our suburban New Jersey kitchen listening to the radio, transfixed. That song about wanting to hold your hand was playing again. I was seven years old, and I'd never heard anything like it. The excited shouting. The pounding beat. The metallic tension of electric guitar strings. The Beatles' music came out of nowhere—like it had been kept a secret. Now the secret was out, and the world was a completely different place.

I stared out the kitchen window at leafless trees behind our basketball hoop and absorbed every note. After a few breathless minutes, "I Want To Hold Your Hand" pumped the brakes (I later learned these were called "triplets") and slammed to a stop. As a glib New York deejay raved about the Beatles, the song's magical afterglow filled the room. My oldest brother, Tom, strutted into the kitchen. He knew how much I loved this new sound. He liked it, too. With all the bored confidence of a worldly thirteen-year-old, he looked down at me and said, "That's four guys, you know."

I didn't know. I shook my head. "No, it's not."

"Yes, it is. The Beatles are just four guys, making all that sound."

I couldn't believe it. "I Want To Hold Your Hand" sounded like a stampede of horses with maybe a dozen guys and definitely some girls. Who was doing the high singing? Four guys? That's crazy.

Before the Beatles, my parents' taste in music ruled the house. We heard their records on a Heathkit monophonic hi-fi my dad built in the basement. I liked the Smothers Brothers, Allen Sherman, and Henry Mancini just fine, but the other stuff was sappy and boring. I'm looking at you, Ray Conniff. And you, Perry Como.

Tom bought *Meet The Beatles*. The album roared from his bedroom. "I Saw Her Standing There." "Hold Me Tight." "Little Child." "All My Loving." Each tune more thrilling than the last. I'd crouch outside his closed door or even hide in a large laundry basket so he wouldn't find me eavesdropping. When he was feeling beneficent, Tom let me listen inside his room after I paid him a nickel. I paid. And paid. And paid. (Maybe that's why I was so broke at forty-two.) Soon a headline on the front page of *The New York Times* announced, "Mop Tops Invade U.S." I remember the picture of four smiling faces under hillsides of hair. How could anyone possibly look like that? I didn't understand! My dad kept me and my brothers in butch cuts. Was there something wrong with us?

On February 9, 1964, my three older brothers, my mom, and even my dad gathered to watch *The Ed Sullivan Show* on our black-and-white RCA. This was it. The Beatles. On TV. As 8 o'clock approached, it felt like the world was about to rip apart. I'd never seen the Beatles play or sing a note. If they acted as crazy as they sounded...what would that look like? Would they blow up? Catch fire? It was beyond my imagination.

Ed Sullivan appeared on screen. He said some nice things about "the boys" and then finally, "Ladies and Gentlemen...THE BEATLES!" A shot of screaming girls and then holy crap! There they were. A Beatle on the left (Paul, but I was too excited to be sure) counted off and they launched into "All My Loving." They were smiling and singing and playing guitars and drums and, oh my God, the Beatles were real. Tom was right—four guys really could make this huge sound. Four guys dressed alike but looking so different from anything ever before. And the hair—the hair was primitive mammalian. They were boys who wore their hair like girls, sang like girls, and all the girls were in love with them. I nearly lost my boyhood mind. This was the best thing in the world.

The Beatles finished "All My Loving." They then each took a backward step and bowed. Wow! They're not only out-of-this-world exciting, but they're also polite. I looked over at my parents and saw Mom smiling. Even Mom likes them! That was enough for me. Move over Starting Pitcher for the New York Yankees. Move over Spiderman. I wanna be a Beatle!

GIFTS

The Christmas after the Beatles had blown my mind on *Ed Sullivan*, two gifts cemented my new obsession with rock 'n' roll music. My dad bought me a nylon-stringed "Lori"-brand classical guitar. It was cheap and hard to play, but I didn't care. I could plink and strum and felt like I was on my way. (It would take three years to play something listenable.) More surprisingly, my gray, ancient grandparents (probably in their fifties) surprised me with a portable record player along with a 45-rpm single, "Oh, Pretty Woman" by Roy Orbison. Good start for a record collection. I wore out the grooves of "Pretty Woman," marveling at the crack of the drums, the endless repeatability of the guitar riff, and the heavenly singing.

Hoarding my modest allowance, I soon shelled out 78 cents for "Hanky Panky" by Tommy James and the Shondells. "Hanky Panky" introduced me to the mysteries of fuzz tone and tremolo. I invested another small fortune in "Set Me Free" by the Kinks, latching my own nascent emotions to Ray Davies' aching melody. One day after school, I must've played "Set Me Free" a dozen times over the phone for a friend, marveling at the sound of the guitars and the majesty of the background vocals.

Every week, something new and amazing seeped out of my transistor radio AM dial and destroyed any desire to save my allowance. I bought "For Your Love" by the Yardbirds and tried to puzzle out the trick of one voice descending while others stayed put. The B-side was just as incredible. "Got To Hurry" had no singing. It was one long lead guitar solo, with whip-cracking riffs that steadily built to a climactic crescendo before finally cooling down as the record faded. I played it over and over, spellbound. I learned, many years later, that "Got To Hurry" was the work of a twenty-year-old guitarist named Eric Clapton.

RICK HOURS

I began daydreaming about music. It seemed to always be in my head, like a soundtrack to my life. There were so many great songs to think about. "Satisfaction" by the Rolling Stones. "Baby Love" by the Supremes. "Mr. Tambourine Man" by the Byrds. "She's Not There" by the Zombies. Was it possible to be mesmerized all day long? It may have just been my personality, but with music transforming my mind into a dreamy playground, I found I was completely disinterested in work or chores. Schoolwork was never a problem. I was always a good student. Sports were great. My brothers and I were all good at sports. But chores? Or a real job? Nah. Not my thing. I had stuff to think about. Leave me alone and let me dream.

My brothers took note of my slackness. They even coined a new unit of time to account for my inefficient performance of household duties: Rick Hours. A job like raking leaves that a normal person would finish in fifteen minutes would take me an unspecified but gigantic number of Rick Hours. I'd rake some leaves, look at the clouds, check out the squirrels, give the leaves another rake, rub my tired arm, sigh, pick up a stone and toss it at a tree, check the angle of the sun to see if it was time to go inside, spit, wipe my chin, and rake again.... My brothers would gleefully ask, "Geez, how many Rick Hours did you put in today? Fifty? A hundred?" You'd think their playful abuse might've bothered me or inspired me to work harder. It didn't. My pride never even blinked. I was fine daydreaming about music and living in my head—two of my greatest skills.

LIVE AT THE POOL PARTY

My ear for rock 'n' roll grew sharper with every record I added to my collection. One typical New Jersey summer evening in 1966, I was walking home from a friend's house (before parents tracked kids with GPS) enjoying the smell of cut grass, the early evening's soft humidity, and the comforting percussion of crickets. I stopped suddenly when I heard the unmistakable guitar riff from "Day Tripper." It wasn't the record—it was live. I knew it couldn't be the Beatles, but who could it be? I forgot about going home and ran toward the source of the sound, "Day Tripper" growing louder and louder until my black high-top Keds brought me to the community pool.

A real live band was playing for a teen party on the concrete apron around the pool. I was underaged, and not allowed in, so I stood outside the chain-link fence directly behind the drummer. His right foot aggressively stomped on a pedal, causing a mallet to hit a big bass drum. His drumsticks flailed against the cymbals and snare. His view and mine was of the backs of three guys with guitars. They all wore tight corduroy pants with wide belts and cool boots. Each guy had longish hair.

Wow. So, this was what the real thing looked and sounded like. Curly cords stretched from plugs on their instruments to the open-back amplifiers. The volume coming out of the speakers was astounding. The difference between a record player and a live band was like a toy plane and an actual jet. My little universe crackled with excitement. I stayed for a few more songs, including "Keep On Dancing" by the Gentrys, to which I mouthed the lyrics. Not wanting to wear out my eavesdropping welcome, I practically flew home. I'd been baptized.

CHAPTER 7

BEHIND THE OLIVE CURTAIN

Later that summer, in our pale yellow, two-story home on tree-lined Seven Oaks Drive, my mom and dad shouted from the center of the house, "Family meeting! Everyone to the living room, please!" My brothers and I all dropped what we were doing and took seats on our living room's upholstered furniture. What could possibly warrant such a dramatic announcement?

Mom said to us, "You may've noticed that your father and I have been doing some traveling recently." We had noticed that, yes. My mom continued, "You may have also noticed that I had a Pan Am carry-on bag..." I didn't know what that meant. Our oldest brother Tom said, "That means they were traveling overseas, dum-dums." Oh.

We sat there blankly. Mom saw we weren't following her, undoubtedly, well-rehearsed guessing game. She cut to the chase. "Okay. Well. We're moving to Greece."

What? We're leaving New Jersey? Holy cow. Then I thought, "What's Grease?"

I had three months to say farewell to my friends and watch the last episodes of *Batman*, *Shindig*, and *The Man From U.N.C.L.E.* I'd see for a long time. That November of 1966, we boarded the Italian ocean liner *Cristoforo Columbo* in New York harbor, destination Athens, with stops in Boston, Spain, and Italy. Before we'd even sailed past the Statue of Liberty, I'd slipped on a wet deck, separated my left wrist and had a cast put on me by the ship's doctor. Putting up with a cast for the whole voyage was a drag, especially when bathing, but it wasn't any less amazing to be on an ocean liner. We watched movies every day and ate some of the best food I'd never heard of. Leaving New Jersey no longer seemed so traumatic.

I went exploring. On the top deck, I discovered an observation room with a panoramic view of the ocean. I sat on a cushioned bench in front of a writing table. I opened a drawer and found it filled with light blue *Cristoforo Columbo* stationery and sharpened pencils. Nice. I sat alone, overlooking the vast blue Atlantic Ocean. The motion of the boat, the endless horizon, the sound of the sea and wind, the privacy of the room…I loved my place in the world. The world must've loved me, too, because, at that moment, I began to write songs.

I could hear a song in my head as usual, but this time it was music that I was making up. Guitars, drums, all doing whatever I wanted them to do. A singer joined in, and I gave his voice an expressive rock 'n' roll attitude. A vocal melody took shape and I matched words to the notes and rhythm. I wrote lyrics on the blue *Cristoforo Columbo* stationery. I'd never written a song before, but apparently I'd absorbed a trick or two from popular music. My themes were girls and heartbreak—with a smidgen of biblical gravitas:

> *The night I left her was sad*
> *The night I left her was bad*
> *That night I left her in the dark*
> *It was just like Noah's Ark*
> *You leave the people behind!*

Hmmm. I hadn't consciously thought about it, but here I was, a guy on a boat, moving to Greece, leaving his friends behind. This songwriting thing was kind of magical. "The Night I Left Her" thrilled this young songwriter and still sounds pretty good today. (The original lyric sheet is framed in my office.)

When I got up the courage, I sang my nascent songs to my brothers. They immediately made fun of my lyrics, poking holes in my imaginary scenarios. "You left her in the dark? Where, in a basement? Why didn't she just turn on a light?" I was accustomed to fraternal sarcasm, but I noticed something else—they kept singing my songs even though they made fun of them. My songs were catchy.

I journeyed back to the observation room often. Songwriting was my first true communion with something beyond myself, something vast, something amazing. No offense to Catholicism (my dad took us to church each week to give my mom a Sunday morning breather), but it wasn't until I began writing songs that I felt plugged into the mysteries of the universe. Whatever the songwriting wavelength was, I was on it, and it pointed my ten-year-old imagination toward a bold, new, romantic horizon.

NEW KID

Speaking of romantic horizons, after twelve days at sea and visits to a bull ring in Malaga and ruins in Pompeii, the *Cristoforo Columbo* at last arrived at

Chapter 7: Behind the Olive Curtain

Piraeus, the port for Athens. Filling a basin formed by three mountain ranges, Athens was huge. And sunny. And dry. And beautiful. And right on the water. Wow. We weren't in New Jersey anymore.

Our furniture was on a ship that wouldn't arrive for months, so we settled into two rooms at the Athens Hilton with just the contents of our suitcases. The Hilton was a bustling place with a massive marble lobby, giant chandeliers, and, off in a corner, the Byzantine Café, our dining room away from home. Traffic streamed past on wide boulevards out front, mostly gray taxis, yellow electric trams, and blue and white public buses. Personal cars were still somewhat rare in 1966, owing to a 100 percent import tax and a largely mom-and-pop economy. Greece was only twenty years removed from World War II and its Civil War. It would take another generation to create a real consumer society, not that that's necessarily an improvement.

I entered the American Community School two days after we arrived. I rode one of forty school buses eight kilometers to a dusty suburb called Halandri. The sunbaked ACS campus sat among modest houses, goats, chickens, and a small taverna where upperclassmen were allowed to buy sandwiches, Tam Tam (Greek imitation Coca-Cola), and cigarettes. ACS had two large rectangular two-story buildings serving grades 1–6 and 7–12, a gym, and a playing field that hated grass.

To settle my nerves before my first day of fifth grade at a new school, my dad had pointed out that he was a new kid, too. He'd be going to an office full of strangers. He suggested that we both do our best to make good first impressions. He advised me to listen to my teacher and if I had any questions, approach her after class. Got it.

The middle school principal escorted me to the door of Miss Andrews's classroom and introduced me as "Richard" (what happened to Rick?), the new boy with a cast on his wrist. I took a desk near the back. A few boys snickered, probably judging me as uncoordinated because of my cast. Miss Andrews, dark-haired, pretty, in her thirties, and with a sprayed-in-place bouffant hairdo, welcomed me and said, "There's only one rule in my class, Richard. When you raise your hand to answer a question, please keep your elbow on your desk. I don't want a sea of flailing arms." Seemed simple enough to me.

Later that morning during an easy lesson, every student but one threw their arms in the air hoping to get called on. Miss Andrews scanned the room and her eyes locked on the new kid. "Class! Look! This is Richard's first day and he's the ONLY one raising his hand the proper way!" I had scored with

Miss Andrews, but the kids, especially the boys, were pissed. The price of being good.

Recess saved me. I didn't know much about soccer, but I'd killed at kickball back in the States. When I drilled a soccer ball the length of the playground, all the boys yelled, "Richard's on OUR TEAM!" They tolerated the do-gooder after that.

My dad was a do-gooder, too. He made a point of refusing to accept bribes, primarily from Eastern European customers. His Greek staff told my dad, "The money is a gift. That's how business is done over here." Dad said, "Not anymore. We'll offer a good product at a fair price and see how things go." After about a year, the same guys who'd offered bribes were doing business with my dad on the up and up. My dad's cohorts were impressed, and probably a little shocked.

SUMMER OF '67

Six months after our arrival in Greece, our furniture finally arrived. My mom found us an affordable house ten miles north of Athens in an area called Kifissia (translates to "where the wind blows"). In 1966, my dad's American salary went a long way. Our house was like a Mediterranean villa. It had smooth, white, stucco walls and a classic red-tiled roof, five bedrooms, French doors onto a red-tiled patio, and a huge rose garden. We each had a bedroom to ourselves, and Mom was beside herself because the house came with a maid. The rent was $500 per month. We'd liked New Jersey, but Greece was another world.

I continued to hear original songs in my head. I could write down lyrics, of course, but I couldn't translate what I was hearing in my head to the guitar. It was frustrating. Guitar chords were a mystery, and I also wasn't excited by the wimpy sound of my nylon-stringed, hard-to-play, Lori acoustic guitar. Then, a miracle occurred. In the summer of 1967, my mom took a solo trip to the States. She came back with toiletries, clothes, household goods, and other staples that were difficult to find in mid-'60s Athens. But that wasn't all she brought back. I can still see her presenting me and my brothers with two stunning artifacts: a brand-new red Fender Mustang guitar and a pre-CBS Fender Deluxe Reverb amp.[3] She may as well have brought us Abe Lincoln's cabin or a spaceship. We wouldn't have been more shocked.

My mom's Olympian generosity changed everything. Although she rarely inquired about my interest in music, her actions said everything: here are the

---

3 Music gear gospel says that after Fender was purchased by CBS in 1965, quality plummeted.

tools you need. Have fun. We already had Chuck's set of Kent drums in the house. A guitar and an amp meant we could really make some music. All I had to do was learn how to play.

Mom arranged for me to take lessons from a Mr. Manitopoulos, an enterprising older Greek gentleman who taught guitar to all the American kids in our part of Athens. Conservatively dressed in a dark suit, white shirt, and tie, the balding Mr. M came to the house and bored me silly with his fingerpicking style on a nylon string guitar. I had my red Fender Mustang. I wanted to rock. I lasted just three lessons. (Part of me wishes I'd stuck with finger picking a little longer. To this day I cheat, using only my thumb and index finger. Don't tell anyone.)

About a mile's walk from my house alongside a dry river gully and past abandoned World War II bunkers was the American Club, a social center for ex-pat kids and adults. "The Club" was a five-story, late-nineteenth-century hotel complex, which had briefly served as Nazi headquarters and featured a restaurant, news stand, barbershop, swimming pool, basketball courts, and an outdoor movie theater. (Americans took care of their own.) Best of all, down in the basement away from the adults was the epicenter of my new Athenian universe: the American Youth Association, or AYA. The AYA had everything a pre-internet kid could want—pool tables, ping pong tables, pinball machines, a jukebox filled with rock 45s, and, most alluringly, a small "ballroom" with a low stage where bands performed at dances.

I couldn't believe my luck. Athens had real American rock bands! The most revered was the Zoo. They were so good they had a real 45 on the AYA jukebox, a minor-key number called "Six Miles From The Cage" (cool title). Other legit bands included the Web, featuring a skinny singer/guitarist named Rick Carlton, and the Blues Period, led by guitarist Mike Sadler, he of the herculean riffs. I snuck into teen dances every chance I got. The volume, the electricity, the snapping wires of sound drenched in reverb, the obvious joy and companionship that came from sharing a stage. A band looked to me like the greatest of gangs.

I was only eleven, but I managed to pick up some guitar tips. Whenever older kids brought their guitars to the AYA, I would gather my courage and ask them to show me how to play "Gloria" or "Hey Joe" or an "F" chord. Everyone knew me as Tim and Chuck's little brother, so if they were embarrassed to be seen with sub-teen me, they didn't show it.

By the time I was twelve, I knew most of the first position chords and was able to play a few dozen songs poorly, but well enough, I thought, to start a band. I found some guys who banged on guitars and drums, and after consulting a dictionary for cool words, we became the Vesperational Shirk. We were soon playing at parties. I'm sure we sounded awful, but I have a distinct memory of nailing three chords while singing "Satisfaction" and thinking *this is the greatest feeling in the world.* Thanks, Mick and Keith. Thanks, Mom.

BEHIND THE OLIVE CURTAIN

Despite the teen action at parties and the AYA, we ex-pats were behind the curve when it came to the rest of the world's exploding '60s youth culture. Greek record stores barely carried any rock music. Greek TV was a no-go, with just two channels, both controlled by the military government. Rock radio didn't exist. We may as well have been off the grid.

One summer, a group of hippie musicians from England parked their VW van on a dirt road behind the AYA. Scruffy, bearded, unbathed (our heroes!), Derek (flute) and Trevor (drums) formed a band with a guitarist and bassist from our high school. Derek and Trevor's van mate, Dave, came up with a crazy name that we all loved: *Monty Python's Flying Circus.* It was years before we realized Dave had nicked the name.

In June 1967, the Six-Day Arab-Israeli War broke out. Americans living in Lebanon, Egypt, Jordan, Syria, and Israel fled with their families to safer cities all over Europe, among them Athens. For my friends and I, the evacuation of Americans from the Middle East was less like war and more like Christmas. Cute girls and cool dudes flooded into town. We grilled them: "What albums do you have? Do you play guitar?" The Six-Day War led to at least two new Athens bands.

Not every refugee guitarist was cool. I recall one sunburned stoner who insisted he knew when a string was about to break. He aggressively pulled on my Mustang's strings, and before I could protest, broke three of them. He gloated, "See? They were about to go anyway." My jaw dropped in horror. My boneheaded guest had no idea how hard it was to find electric guitar strings in Greece. It's not like Bouzouki strings could cut it. The Mustang was unplayable for months.

Without access to record stores, touring bands, TV, or radio, the most reliable sources for new music were older siblings returning to Greece from college in the States. One summer Saturday in 1968, my twelve-year-old pal Chris Sand called me up and breathlessly said, "You've gotta come over! My brother just got back from the States, and he brought the coolest music you'll ever hear."

Chapter 7: Behind the Olive Curtain

Completely understanding the gravity of Chris's news, I bolted out the door and ran up my sidewalk past neat rows of olive trees and pollen-coated pines shading houses from the relentless Greek sun. Chris let me in to his modern stone and stucco house and led me upstairs where he carefully dropped the needle on Jimi Hendrix's "Purple Haze" from *Are You Experienced?* He handed me the album cover. The band had afros and crazy, colorful clothes. Next, he played "Sunshine Of Your Love" from *Disraeli Gears*. Cream's album cover was even more colorful, a fantastically complex pink and orange psychedelic collage. My twelve-year-old brain struggled to process these new sounds and images. Singers sang about things I didn't understand ("'xcuse me while I kiss the sky"), and guitars no longer sounded twangy. Cream's guitar sound was all fuzzy and bendy instead of bright and aggressive. Jimi Hendrix? His guitar howled like an injured animal. I couldn't imagine how he did it. In less than ten minutes, everything about music had moved beyond my understanding.

That same summer, my brother Tom arrived from LSU bearing precious gifts: *Fresh Cream*, the first two albums by the Doors, and Hendrix's *Axis: Bold As Love*. As a listener, I was in heaven. As a budding guitarist, I was wholly intimidated. This new music was so different and wild, so beyond simple barre chords, I doubted there was anyone in Greece who could play this stuff. How would we ever learn?

One of the best local bands, the Blues Period, led by guitarist extraordinaire Mike Sadler, rehearsed just up the hill from my house. One summer day, I was making a sandwich when Hendrix's "Crosstown Traffic" poured into the open kitchen window. Holy shit! The Blues Period had breached the forbidding wall of learning how to play Hendrix. Sadler gave this beginning guitarist a slim ray of hope. (And I do mean "slim." Fifty years later, Hendrix is still tough to get right.)

Even my dad smuggled new music behind the Olive Curtain. Returning home from a business trip to the States, he gifted me the Stevie Wonder masterpiece, *Talking Book*, and Emerson Lake and Palmer's debut album. Dad admitted, "I have no idea what these sound like, but the guy at Sam Goody's said they were good."

Finally, there was one other source of coveted rock info: newly serious rock magazines. I remember a huge spread in Crawdaddy from the early '70s titled, "Who Is Bruce Springsteen and Why Are We Saying All These Wonderful Things About Him?" The next time we visited the States, I bought his first album, *Greetings From Asbury Park*. I'm certain I was the only guy in

Greece who knew or cared about this guy. He seemed like someone to keep an eye on.

BASEBALL AND BLACK SABBATH

In New Jersey, my brothers and I had played baseball in local rec leagues. Greece, to my surprise, offered Official Little League and Pony League baseball. I pitched well and made the Athens All Stars in '67, '68, and '70, and each year travelled to Germany to compete in the Little League European Championship. We mostly got our asses kicked by more seasoned teams from Germany and Spain, but one year, we did manage to eke out a win over Holland.

On my third All Star trip, to Bremerhaven, Germany, one of my teammates, Pete, invited me on an adventure. A friend of his dad's picked us up in a Porsche and took us for a thrill ride on the Autobahn down to Bremen. Without a speed limit, we must've hit 120 mph at one stretch. Even more exciting, our host took us to a record store. We flipped through a few bins and Pete said, "Hold on, I'm gonna play you something." He led me to a listening station, placed the needle on an album and said, "Check this out." Sound of rain. Plaintive church bells. Crack of thunder. And then three notes of the scariest, coolest guitar sound I'd ever heard—a sweet blast of distortion aimed right at my teenaged brain. I didn't know it then, but I was hearing a root G, an octave G, and then a drop down to the devil's note, a tritone at C#. I'd just been baptized by the genius of Black Sabbath and guitarist Tony Iommi.

BAND LIFE

In seventh grade, I befriended a ninth-grader new to Athens who would influence my musical life for years to come. Matt Econopouly was clever, funny, and had an appealing, devil-may-care attitude that matched his mess of black curly hair and crooked smile. Matt would try anything for fun, from drugs to football to hanging out at police-patrolled Athens nightclubs. He was quick to abandon whatever bored him ("fuck football"). He was the kind of friend who kept you on your toes.

Crucially, Matt knew how to play "Hey Jude" on guitar. That was enough for us to form a band he called Officer Henry. We stormed the sub-teen dance circuit with our simplified but enthusiastic versions of "Land of A Thousand Dances," "Midnight Hour," "Hold On I'm Coming," "Slow Down," and other hits of the day. My first taste of rock 'n' roll debauchery came before an Officer Henry gig at the AYA. With our drummer Tim (a sixth grader), we had a pre-show dinner at a souvlaki shop and got plastered on cheap Greek beer. Drinking age? What's that? I loved the band life.

Officer Henry eventually ran out of steam, but Matt and I remained forever linked at the musical hip. He turned me on to artists like Velvet Underground, Golden Earring, the Stooges, MC5, Pretty Things, Free, and on and on. If Matt said a band was cool, they were cool. He was never wrong.

WHO THE HELL ARE THE MOVE?

Wandering around our high school during lunch one day, Matt and I entered a classroom where an extracurricular group was selling cool art posters. I glanced over the usual black-and-white prints by M.C. Escher and the bizarre triptych "Garden of Earthly Delights" with ice-skating penguins by Hieronymus Bosch. Matt called to me from across the room. "Hey! Come 'ere." I joined him in front of a huge black-and-white poster of an unknown rock band. Matt said, "Look at these guys..." His voice was tinged with awe. Five tough-looking, long-haired rockers with leather jackets, serious expressions, and attitude for days. It was an amazing photo, a perfect band shot. They had to be good.

"Who are they?" I wondered.

Matt said, "I don't know, but they are easily the coolest band I've ever seen."

I had to agree. I guess we'd simply missed 'em, being isolated in Greece. Then I noticed some tiny print on the corner of the poster. "Does it have their name down there?"

Matt leaned in and said, "Yeah! It says they're called...'the Move.'"

"The 'Move'? Who the hell are the Move?"

Matt got a faraway look in his eyes. "I don't know. But we're gonna find out."

BANDS BANNED

In April 1967, just six months after we arrived in Greece, a group of rightwing Colonels called the Junta drove tanks into Athens, sent King Constantine into exile, and took over the government in a coup d'etat. On top of the Junta's many more serious crimes, they hated rock 'n' roll and banned international artists from coming to Greece. Rock music was so squashed under the Junta that when the *Woodstock* movie opened in Athens in 1971, it was like Santana and Alvin Lee had parachuted into a forbidden no-man's land. Greek youth were so starved for live rock (or even a cinematic substitute), all showings quickly sold out. The unlucky fans without tickets went berserk and rioted, smashing glass doors and demanding to be let in to see their heroes. Now *that's* rock 'n' roll.

RECORDING STARS

One day in 1970, my dad came home from a business trip with a game-changing new gadget: a tape recorder one-tenth the size and price of a typical reel-to-reel machine. It was called a Sony Cassette-Corder. Instead of loose tape on messy reels, the cassette tape came enclosed in a small plastic case in configurations ranging from thirty minutes to two hours of recording time. All you had to do was plug in a small handheld mic and press two buttons, "Play" and "Record," and you were all set. (Okay, the above was a history lesson for readers younger than fifty.)

The Cassette-Corder enabled me and my friends to jam in my music room and listen back to what we'd done. Our recordings were mostly terrible, but, occasionally, our heads would all swivel—"Hey! Did you hear that? That part sounded pretty good!"

Cassette bands, with names like Rick Rock and the Flounders, Pancho's Army, and Captain Australia, were quickly all the rage among the twenty or so people at our school who could play music.

One cassette band soon rose in status above all others: CC Blues King. CCBK's tapes were less playful—they had an edge to them. The guitarist was my pal from Officer Henry, Matt, who had developed a primitive Stooges/Velvet Underground guitar style. Sibling lead vocalists Peter and Chris Christ couldn't sing all that well, but their impromptu lyrics convinced you they knew all about wild women, hard drugs, living in the city, and causing trouble without giving a fuck. (That wasn't far from the truth.) After creating a half dozen cassette albums, CC Blues King tipped the cassette world on its head by playing live in public.

For the live show, CC Blues King added me on guitar and a strange pair of stepbrothers on sax and drums. Our debut came at the Battle of the Bands in our high school gym. Anyone expecting recognizable songs was in for a long night. Matt—unshaven, long haired, dressed in ragged jeans and wrinkled button-down shirt—began each number by improvising a simple two- or three-chord pattern at maximum volume. The rest of us tumbled in behind Matt to increase the cacophony. Chris and Pete, handsome dark-haired brothers with jeans on and T-shirts off, vocalized whatever popped into their heads, occasionally pulling from themes previously captured on cassette. It was the closest I'd ever get to being in a grubby, down-tempo MC5 or Stooges.

Most of the crowd in the gym backed away, but a half dozen cool kids hugged the front of the stage and lapped up the noise and mayhem. We had fans!

Miraculously, CC Blues King were twice booked to play the American Youth Center. The first gig went so well we were offered the New Year's Eve dance, an actual paying gig. We took the money, but our horrendous racket drove the crowd out of the AYC a solid hour before midnight. Happy new year.

Our swan song was back on campus, the last day of school, June 1972. On a typically dry, sunny Athens afternoon, we set up our gear outdoors, in front of the music room. We were joined by our school's best drummer as well as a bassist (John Alex, who would acquire Greek Punk Scene notoriety a few years later). a first for us. Our music teacher even joined on electric piano. With a solid beat behind us for the first (and last) time, CC Blues King genuinely, incredibly, sounded *tight*. A crowd gathered, undoubtedly as surprised as we were by our sound. When CC Blues King finished its short set, we were met with wildly appreciative applause. We immediately retired.

I DIDN'T KNOW YOU COULD DO THAT

I loved being in loud bands and playing electric guitar, but the acoustic flip side to the cassette band scene appealed to me, too. Rick Carlton was five years my senior and a veteran of local Athens bands, including the Web and Soul Train (which featured a hot clarinetist, my brother Tim). Skinny as a popsicle stick and cocky to a fault, Rick wore prescription aviators, sang in tune, and played a beautiful sunburst Gibson Hummingbird acoustic guitar. Rick must've seen something in me because he bothered to teach me vocal harmony. We sang songs by Brewer & Shipley and a new band called the Eagles. He led me carefully through the harmonies of "Fifty States Of Freedom" and "Train Leaves Here This Morning," pointing out how the harmony vocal could shadow the main melody or do something completely on its own. With Rick's training, I was better able to hear the separate parts in tight harmony singing, a very useful skill.

Carlton was also talented enough to make songs sound whole with just his honeyed voice and the acoustic guitar. I loved that. It reminded me that the singer-songwriter approach offered a solitary environment to work on music and develop a singing voice away from band racket. I started writing songs in that style, mostly keeping them to myself and close friends. One was called "Plexiglass" featuring an early lyrical stab at "man in conflict with nature":

Looking through my plexiglass
And though I see green trees and grass
It don't seem right
Get inside my car and though I travel pretty far
It don't seem right

I spent a lot of solitary time writing songs that my teenaged brain felt were meaningful, or at least clever. It wasn't until a senior year music assembly in the school gym that my mom caught my singer-songwriter act. She was moved by my voice and lyrics. A little teary-eyed, she said, "I didn't know you could do that." I was proud to have her compliment my talent, and a little sad that I hadn't shared more of my music with her until that night.

A HELLAS OF AN ENDING

After eight years in Greece, it was time to find a college in the States. I applied to Michigan, UMass, UNC-Chapel Hill, and Boston University. UNC-Chapel Hill was my first choice, but I never heard back from them, so in December 1973, I accepted at UMass-Amherst. Then in May 1974, a dirty, beaten-up envelope with a single stamp arrived at our house in Athens. It looked like UNC had sent it by donkey. The letter announced, "We are delighted to accept your application to the University of North Carolina…" We called the UNC admissions office, and their offer was still good.

That summer, I traveled through Europe by Eurailpass with my pals Nanci Luehman, Betsy Neill, and Larry Frangias. We visited Pamplona's running bulls, got lost in Madrid, saw just how alive the hills were in Salzburg, Austria, and more. Our last stop together was Paris, France. On a rainy night at Notre Dame cathedral, a rich American couple took pity on us and offered a ride in their stretch limo, which we gladly accepted. They even gave us sixty francs to buy dinner and wine in the Latin Quarter. A great end to our trip.

Nanci, Betsy, and Larry were headed back to the States. I was going home to Greece via the port of Brindisi, Italy, like I had on my Eurail trip the year before. On that excursion I'd run into a cholera epidemic that had spread to Brindisi from Naples. I had to get an emergency inoculation from a panicked doctor in a municipal building, and then wait five days—with about $15 to my name—before boarding a ship to Greece.

This time, Summer of '74, all of Brindisi's ship schedules were delayed not by disease, but by war. Greece and Turkey were mobilizing for a fight over Cyprus. The Greeks had clumsily attempted a coup to unite Greece

Chapter 7: Behind the Olive Curtain

and Cyprus. When the coup went nowhere, Turkey's much superior forces invaded the island and divided it in two. Turkey claimed all the good parts and left the scraps to the Greeks. That's where things stand today.

So, Brindisi was once again chaotic as hell, but the adventure was definitely better this second time around. I spent a couple days in the port and on the ship to Greece with a kind, generous Danish girl who would take a souvenir home with her: my hopeless, know-nothing virginity. Thank you for being so patient, Christian.

(Editor's note: If that's what you call a sex story, let's just stick with the rock 'n' roll.)

CHAPTER 8

HOW TO ROCK

In August 1974, my mom accompanied me from Greece to North Carolina. We'll never forget the blanket of humidity that greeted us at Raleigh Durham Airport, or the first "y'all" we heard the next day at breakfast, courtesy of our drawling, incomprehensible waitress. We were a long way from the Greek accents of Athens.

My parents had paid the $1,800 out-of-state tuition on the assumption that I would study hard, pick a major, choose a career, and, after four years, get a job. That seemed fair, albeit somewhat fuzzy on the details and awfully distant in the future. I was fine with doing schoolwork, but the other kind of work where you did boring things under the thumb of a boss held no appeal. A whole career of it seemed beyond my imagination. (Can you imagine the Rick Hours I'd have to put in?) The only real job I'd ever held was a three-week stint at an Athens travel agency. I corralled luggage, counted bodies in bus seats, and imparted local knowledge for groups of American tourists. My favorite tourist question: "Is Greek rain hard or soft?" My expert answer: "It's wet." I was pretty sure I wouldn't go into tourism.

BACK IN THE USA

I loved music more than anything, but I had no illusions of pursuing music at UNC. In my mind, school and music were two different animals. School meant academic credentials, possibly in history, English, or journalism, which might help me finagle a job in one of those not-too-awful fields. Music was different. Writing songs, playing guitar, being in bands, recording—that was for me.

Other than my high school music teacher, I'd never known anyone who'd made a living from music. The idea of a music "job" or "career" had never occurred to me. Musicians who made money making records were magical, larger-than-life superhumans from places like London, Liverpool, Detroit, New York, Los Angeles, or even Asbury Park. I was pretty sure Jimi Hendrix,

Tony Iommi, Lou Reed, Iggy Pop, and Jimmy Page hadn't come from college towns like Chapel Hill, North Carolina.

Real musicians were on album covers. I was on the UNC meal plan.

And yet.

One day, at Buffalo Records, Chapel Hill's coolest local record store, I noticed a weirdly titled album, *Prolepsis*, displayed prominently alongside that week's other important new releases. *Prolepsis* was by a band I'd never heard of called Arrogance. I asked a clerk behind the counter, "Can you tell me what this album sounds like?"

She replied cheerily, "Sure! It's playing now." Oh! That answered my second question, "Who are we listening to?" I'd been trying to figure what band would steal a melody from "19th Nervous Breakdown," sing harmony like Brewer and Shipley, and come up with words about Santa killing his elves. "There'll be poison ivy hanging/where there once was mistletoe." It was jaunty and snarky and poured joyfully out of the speakers.

Intrigued, I asked her, "Do you know where these guys are from?"

She looked at me kind of surprised. "Yeah! They're from here. You didn't know that?"

Taken aback, I thought, *"You can have a big album and be from Chapel Hill?"*

I felt the earth tilt a little bit. I'd been dreaming away for eight years in a magical, sunbaked ancient land and lived through some amazing, life-changing experiences, but—back in the States—I didn't know shit from Shinola. I had a lot to learn.

I sought out live music at Chapel Hill's two best clubs, Town Hall and the Cat's Cradle. Touring bands loved playing Chapel Hill as it was the perfect extra gig midway between Atlanta and DC. In 1974, I caught, among others, the Dixie Dregs with soon-to-be Deep Purple's guitarist Steve Morse, and the Electromagnets with guitar virtuoso Eric Johnson. Morse and Johnson both flew around the frets with skills beyond my comprehension. Watching them play live was electrifying on the one hand and humbling on the other. I knew I would never play like them. Even the regional bands who came to town covering Led Zeppelin and Jethro Tull played at a skill level miles above mine. I wasn't even in the same league. I was eighteen, I'd written some good songs, I played and sang alright for being self-taught, but my isolated life in Greece hadn't prepared me for the level of musicianship in the States.

Hell, I could barely keep pace in my dorm. I became friends with a long-haired, beanpole guitarist from Richmond named Kevin who finger-picked circles around me. He had an original instrumental piece that was crazy gorgeous and frustratingly complex for me to accompany. He could also play the entire acoustic guitar opening of "Roundabout" by Yes, flawlessly. I countered with my four-chord song "Plexiglass," which Kevin learned in twelve seconds. Kevin played Joni Mitchell's "Help Me" in its weird tuning and made it look easy. I did "I Should've Known Better" by the Beatles and strummed its D and G chords with real feeling. I had miles to go.

THE NEW GREECE

I wasn't the only guy from Greece adjusting to life back in the States. My Officer Henry/CC Blues King buddy, Matt Econopouly, called me from Long Island and asked, "Is Chapel Hill near a place called Greensboro?"

"Yeah. About an hour."

Matt said, "Led Zeppelin's playing there in January. I tried to get tickets for their show at Madison Square Garden and it sold out in twenty minutes. If you get me a ticket for Greensboro, I'll come down and visit you."

We got Matt a ticket. Led Zeppelin (Gods from England, not some college town) played for two and a half hours. I was excited to be in the same room with them, but they couldn't match the sonic precision of their albums. Bathed in arena-verb, the songs were too often a washy mess. Still, they were a major notch on my concert belt, and now that I'd discovered the Greensboro Coliseum, I soon caught the Who, Jethro Tull, and Elton John, among others, all close to their mighty peaks.

After the Zeppelin show, Matt crashed in my dorm room during a stretch of perfect seventy-degree weather. A week turned into a month and, eventually, Matt found a place to live and never left Chapel Hill. He said, "This place is like Greece!" It wasn't really, but word spread, and soon my brother Chuck and his wife Julie moved to Chapel Hill, as did Matt's mom and sister. We'd started a migration and, eventually, fifteen of us from Greece had settled in the Southern Part of Heaven. Matt tipped his hat to our legacy while working at Chapel Hill's favorite late night food joint, Hectors. He created the Greek Grilled Cheese, a veggie masterpiece on grilled Pita bread that became legend to thousands of hungry, drunk, and stoned UNC students. Ask anybody who was there.

WORK?

Fortified by coffee, potato chips, and the occasional speed chaser, I spent freshman year grinding through ten liberal arts classes, none of which lit a fire beneath my career kindling. I even took a music course thinking I ought to learn how to read music. It didn't work. Notes on a staff still looked to me like birds on wires. It solidified my belief, mistaken or not, that reading music and creating it had nothing to do with each other.

When the freshman exams mercifully ended, I'd clawed my way onto the dean's list. Bravo for me, but General College felt like little more than factory work, and I had zero interest in doing it all over again in the fall. I decided to take a year off to follow a more personal agenda. I wanted to read some deep spiritual books, "find myself," write songs, fuck off for a year, and delay my career decision. I assured my worried parents it would just be one year and then I'd go back to school. They said, "Okay, but if you're not in school, we're not footing the bill."

Oh, right! *Money.* I'd forgotten about that.

My parents were temporarily living in Houston, Texas. I joined them there in summer (not Houston's showcase season) 1975. I found a job at a JC Penney gas station a few miles from my folks' apartment. I had no driver's license and no car, so getting to work took 45 minutes by bicycle. If you were sensibly cruising in an air-conditioned Buick in Houston that summer and saw a skinny long-haired kid sweating his balls off in a button-down shirt and reluctant khakis, it's good to see you again, too.

The gas station sat alone in a shopping mall's giant parking lot. You wouldn't mistake Houston's flat, suburbanized prairie for Mykonos. I told the manager I didn't know anything about cars. He showed me how to pump gas, check the oil, refill wiper fluid, and take money from the customers. Look at me. A year of college hadn't been a waste after all. I hated life.

On my third day, a twenty-five-foot JC Penney delivery truck rumbled into the station. I checked and changed the oil according to my boss's instructions. On the fourth day of my exciting new career, I spotted two guys in suits traversing the desert of concrete toward my gas station. I didn't know who they were, but my gut said they were coming for me.

They were. The suits confirmed I was the oil-change guy and then asked me to join them on a perp-walk to the mall. We entered a personality-less, fluorescent-lit office and took seats. The older of the two got right to it: "That truck you serviced yesterday had two quarts of oil in its radiator. The engine seized up and our driver was stuck in traffic on a busy highway."

Ohhhh, shiiiit.

"That engine will cost more than sixteen thousand dollars to repair."

Fuckety fuck! Sixteen million *dollars? Did I hear that right?*

I was scared. Did they really expect me to pay for the engine? I'd told my manager that I didn't know anything about...

"However, we are aware you didn't receive much training, so we realize that it may have been an honest mistake. We can't keep you at the station, though, so we'd like you to resign."

Yes! Oh, God, yes. I will resign.

Other than feeling bad about the truck, my three-and-a half-day career as a gas monkey had reached a dramatic, satisfying conclusion.

I spent the next three weeks at my parents' apartment complex, reading Krishnamurti alone by the pool, getting my spiritual shit together, and writing songs. My dad got his requested transfer from Houston to Atlanta, and I went with my folks to Georgia. For the remainder of the summer, I crashed at my parents' new house and worked a nightmarish dishwashing job at a multi-level restaurant/lounge called Daddy's Money. It was as bougie and gross as you'd imagine.

CALL OF THE WILD

When I wasn't elbow deep in grease at Daddy's Money or sleeping late to avoid thinking about Daddy's Money, I played guitar and wrote music. One day, my dad suggested I record one of my songs. Encouraged, and always pleased when my folks showed interest in my music, I went for it. I'd never set foot in a recording studio before.

The engineer placed me and my acoustic guitar on a stool in the live room. He positioned two large microphones, one in front of my guitar, the other inches from my mouth. In the expensive headphones, my voice, drenched in reverb, sounded magically huge, as if in a cathedral. The engineer returned to the control room. We could see each other through thick panes of sound-proof glass. He nodded in my direction, clicked on the talkback mic and said, "Whenever you're ready. Tape is rolling."

Tape is rolling. As in, this is the moment you record your music for eternity.

That seems a bit dramatic now, but that's how it felt. I was nineteen years old and in a real recording studio for the first time. The engineer's voice through my headphones sounded tinny, straight out of an Apollo mission. When I hit my strings, a device (I later learned it was called a compressor) made my guitar explode sweetly in my ears. I exhaled and began playing an original song, "The Call Of The Wild." The intro demanded rigorous strumming mixed with delicate harmonics. My guitar was in an alternate hippie tuning (DADAAD), so my left hand formed non-standard chord shapes. When the moment came, I sang the chorus with full open throat:

The call of the wild
Soon will come
To show me where we're from
I'll get there
When I try
And I'll see you when we die

The lyrics were supposed to convey something about our origins as souls, inspired by my recent spiritual search. At some point during the take, I made a mistake on the guitar and had to stop. "Sorry about that," my cathedral voice echoed. "I messed up."

Houston answered, "No problem. Take two, coming up."

I recorded "The Call Of The Wild" live, guitar and vocal performed at the same time, which is how I'd always played it at home and in my college dorm room, so why would the recording process be any different? When I was done, I sat in the control room, and we listened back. My song sounded kind of empty and lonely. The guitar playing was mostly fine but there were spots where I could detect uncertainty, moments where I lacked confidence to execute a passage properly. The reverb, instead of making my voice sound big, made it seem distant. The singing was okay, but when I reached for higher notes, my voice got a bit thin, and wasn't all that nice to listen to. I was not David Bowie. I was not Paul McCartney or Paul Rogers.

The engineer asked, "Do you want to do any overdubs? Do you have any more guitar parts or harmony vocals you'd like to add?"

"Nah, I don't think so." Overdubs had never occurred to me. "I think we're good."

"Okay, man. Nice job. Straight up live. I like it. Nice tune."

The session had lasted no more than an hour. I paid my $35 and got a cassette copy of my song for $5 more. I popped the tape into my car's player and drove home. I wasn't blown away. What had I expected? A masterpiece? I hadn't brought any ideas about how the recording should sound. No thoughts about overdubs. No vision. I'd shown up and played without really being prepared.

I told myself I wouldn't make that mistake again. Perhaps sensing my disappointment, the Universe offered me a gift.

CRAWDADDY WAS RIGHT

In August 1975, a month after my unsatisfying studio experience, little-known Bruce Springsteen was somehow on the covers of both *Time* and *Newsweek*. His third album, *Born To Run*, was getting the kind of national attention that had evaded his first two releases. Even more exciting, Springsteen was coming to Atlanta to play at Alex Cooley's Electric Ballroom, a small theater-sized club. When the day came, I figured it would be packed, so I got in line at 4pm for the 9pm show. I was surprised to find only half a dozen other fans loitering by the entrance. Feeling confident as the owner of all three albums, I asked one of the other early birds, a guy who looked to be in his thirties, "You know Bruce's stuff?"

He laughed and said, "Ohhhhhh, yeah." He motioned to the others in line. "All of us have been following Bruce down the coast from New York. We've seen every show."

Say what? Can you really do that? How much time and money does that require? "So, he's that good live, huh?" Wanting to establish my Bruce cred with this hardcore bunch, I asked, "Does he do 'Growin Up'?"

The others all smiled and looked at me with secret knowledge behind their eyes. "You just wait," the guy said. "Don't make me tell you anything. I don't wanna spoil it for you."

Five hours later, we early birds grabbed the best seats in the house, a front center table right beneath the lip of the stage. Springsteen would practically be in our laps. I felt an itchy anticipation as I was about to lay eyes and ears on the guy *Crawdaddy* had said all those wonderful things about. The lights went down. Skinny, scruffy-bearded, wearing a newsboy hat and a hoop earring, Bruce led the all-business E Street Band onto the stage. "Blinded By The Light," "Sandy," "Rosalita," and especially the new stuff from Born To Run like "Jungleland" and "Tenth Avenue Freeze-Out" came roaring off the stage with Springsteen screaming and whispering and beseeching and praying and shouting and testifying to the redemptive powers of rock 'n' roll. Skinny young Bruce, in leather jacket, torn jeans, and hi-tops, told quiet stories that would build into tempests of pent-up emotion, his band a tightly controlled tornado behind him. The power of the whole scene was almost too much to take, but I did my best to absorb and appreciate every thrilling second.

After an hour-and-a-half, the glorious Asbury Park tidal wave came crashing to an absolutely satisfying end. I popped off my seat and screamed and woooooo'd 'til I was hoarse. Bar none, it was the best rock show I'd ever seen in my young life. I looked forward to singing his songs all the way home.

I stopped clapping to pour the last of my beer down my throat as the E Street Band walked off the stage. Then Springsteen stepped to his mic and said, "Hey, alright. Thanks very much. We're gonna take a little break. We'll be back in about twenty minutes for the second half."

My body froze and my brain bellowed, "Second half?" I looked around the table. Bruce's traveling disciples were all smiling at me, thoroughly enjoying my dropped-jaw face. I'd been set up. Holy shit. No wonder they'd followed Springsteen from town to town. The most astounding, inspiring, moving, perfectly executed rock show I'd ever seen…had just reached Intermission. One of my tablemates, speaking for the group, asked, "So…did you enjoy the first half?"

THE SHOP

I returned to Chapel Hill in the fall of 1975 to begin my self-financed gap year. I rented a charmless apartment on the bypass road outside of town and secured a fine position at the Carolina Coffee Shop, a downtown Chapel Hill institution with dark wooden booths, black tables, low lights, classical music, and black-clad wait staff. All that darkness was rumored to prevent customers from getting too good a look at their food. I started on the kitchen cleanup crew and got acquainted with forty-pound plastic tubs of butter, overflowing trays of raw meat, frequent visits to the devilish walk-in freezer, and at the end of a shift, the coup de grace, a floppy, filthy mop. After just three days, the kitchen guys begged the owner to fire me for being too damned slow. Byron, the Shop's inscrutable piano-playing, chain-smoking owner, did so, but then inexplicably handed me six busboy shifts out on the restaurant floor. Busboy was my kind of job. No one cared that my hair fell below my shoulders, I didn't have to interact with customers beyond waving them to a clean table, and I was mostly free to think, daydream, and work on music in my head—a massive step up from destroying trucks at JC Penney in Houston and scrubbing nacho platters at Daddy's Money in Atlanta.

A NEW WAY OF LIFE

Once I settled in and became friendly with the staff, who were all a few years older than me, it struck me that nearly every person cooking, serving, and cleaning at the Carolina Coffee Shop lived a creative life on the side. A waiter named Mitch toiled in stop-action animation. A chef named Chip turned dinner napkins into abstract masterpieces with magic markers. (Chip became dean of the art department at University of Maryland.) A waiter named Steve with a law degree in his future designed crossword puzzles for *The New York Times*. (Steve became Director of North Carolina's Environmental Defense Fund.) One of our dishwashers was a pilot. The wait staff featured at least three screenwriters and filmmakers. When I mentioned that I played guitar and wrote songs, I was told, "Yeah, chef Eddie's a really good guitarist, too." Chef Eddie Ibarguen later dropped guitar and became Michael Jordan's golf coach.

The secretly ambitious Coffee Shop staff showed me, the naive ex-pat, that working a mindless job was the opposite of fucking off. It was a ticket to freeing your creative mind. My decision to take a year off from general college looked to be a better idea than I'd imagined.

I ditched my apartment on the bypass and rented an 8 x 10 single basement room in a boarding house three blocks from Franklin Street, Chapel Hill's main drag, where the Coffee Shop sat in the dead center of town. My room featured asbestos tile floors and grandma's busy floral wallpaper. It set me back $70 per month. It was the first time I'd lived alone, and I loved it.

When I wasn't cleaning tables, dreaming of finding a girlfriend, hanging out with Matt, or becoming a Carolina basketball fan, I obsessed over the sound of the band I wanted to build. The music I imagined in my head—elaborate chord sequences, delicious electric guitar sounds, stunning harmony vocals—was so good I remember wishing I had a helmet that could record my thoughts. It was thrilling to live in my concert hall head...but frustrating, too. Dreaming of game-changing music was easy. Assembling it with actual humans wasn't. How would I find musicians who could play what I was hearing? Hell, how could I bring my music to life if I wasn't skilled enough to play it myself?

My solution, if it deserves that lofty a title, was to trust that I would find a way. I wrote the best songs I could within my limitations as a singer and guitarist. Going as far back as the *Cristoforo Columbo*, I've possessed at least one musical superpower. I have an innate ability to know what works and what doesn't. I can spot a song's weakest bit a mile away. I know the difference between settling and reaching for something better. No song gets by me without becoming the best piece of music it can possibly be. I steadily built a batch of songs that earned my approval, recording them onto cassettes.

WHO ARE THESE GUYS?

I bussed tables at the Carolina Coffee Shop six days a week. Of all the Coffee Shop clientele, a pair of plaid-shirted, long-haired townies stood out. Even with a line of customers spilling out onto the sidewalk, Herb Bresky and Lee

Gildersleeve would waltz into the Shop and be seated in a prime booth in back. The entire wait staff would take turns stopping by their booth to banter back and forth, serve them eggs, sausage, pancakes, orange juice, bacon, unlimited coffee, more bacon, whatever they wanted—and then write them a check for two cups of coffee at twenty-five cents each. Wink, wink. I had to wonder, "Who are these guys?"

Herb was bashful, with thick black hair pulled back in a ponytail. He kept his head down, and always had a well-worn paperback handy in the left rear pocket of his jeans, usually a sword-and-sorcery novel. Herb had drawing skills, specializing in pen-and-ink fantasy scenes. He likely inherited the art bug from his father, a commercial artist whose original designs included the Marlboro box and the mint leaf logo for Breyers Ice Cream.

Lee Gildersleeve was the opposite of Herb, a loquacious bon vivant, popular with women, quick with a story and the owner of a cackling, trademark laugh. While Herb worked quietly as a bartender, Lee built houses and never let a day go by without blowing off steam after work with beers and good company at Chapel Hill watering holes like Tijuana Fats.

The glue that held this odd couple together appeared to be their mutual admiration of Robert E. Howard, creator of the Conan the Barbarian novels. That, and what came to be known as "The Movie." Herb and Lee had apparently been filming their own Super 8 sword-and-sorcery fantasy action film for years. Stories abounded about scandalous scenes and characters, but "The Movie" remained unfinished and unscreened, accumulating mystique with each passing year.

I was talking music with Herb once and he mentioned Lee had backed up Chuck Berry. I said, "Lee? He plays guitar?" Herb said, "You didn't know that? Yeah, I guess he doesn't talk about it much since he gave it up, but he was the best guitarist in town." I couldn't process this news. Why would the best guitarist in town quit playing guitar? I asked Lee about it once, but his explanation felt uncomfortable. He said he just gave it up and that was that. I sensed there was more to the story, but I didn't pry.

I showed Lee some of my songs. I also mentioned that I'd been offered an opening acoustic set at the Cat's Cradle and that I was thrilled but terrified. Lee must've liked what he heard because he volunteered to back me at the Cradle on bass guitar. I gratefully accepted. I figured it would calm my nerves to have someone on stage with me.

It didn't. On the night of my first ever solo show in Chapel Hill, I lost my voice halfway through my set. I couldn't have been more disappointed and embarrassed. Afterwards, Lee said to me in his Carolina drawl, "Aw, hey man, don't worry about it. You sounded good...until you didn't." He laughed and I tried my best to laugh with him.

Herb was among the small crowd at the show. He asked me, "How the hell did you get Lee to come out of retirement?"

I told Herb. "I didn't do anything. He volunteered." I'd seen my debut as half a disaster at best, but the bigger takeaway might've been that Lee saw something musical in me that rekindled something musical in him. It would be the first of our many times together on stage.

SNEAKERS, DIXON, AND TGS

I didn't get back into a recording studio after my dissatisfying Atlanta experience until I was nudged by my CC Blues King cohort, Matt. He'd written a song called "My Baby's M-M-Makin' Me Dance," a raucous rock 'n' roll throwback number Roy Wood might've appreciated. Matt wanted to finally leap the chasm from cassettes to real records. The problem? We didn't have any money. We also didn't know the first thing about studios in Chapel Hill, but once we started down the path, we were drawn, inexorably, like feta to Greek salads, to Don Dixon, the Godfather of North Carolina's recording scene.

Dixon was best known as the bassist/singer/co-songwriter in Arrogance, that local band with the popular album in the record stores. Live on stage, he sang and shouted with an agile, raspy Otis Redding kind of voice and abused his black Fender Precision bass guitar like it was his enemy. Dixon was handsome, dark haired, and entertaining to watch, and it was obvious, scanning a crowd, that women loved him.

A local band called Sneakers had a seven-inch EP in the stores on Franklin Street—yet another Chapel Hill band with a real record. The black-and-white cover photo made Sneakers look like junkies, so it was kind of a surprise when they showed up to play at Chapel Hill's family-oriented street fair, Apple Chill. With their gear set up near a pottery booth and a food tent, Sneakers plugged in and quickly ripped apart the artisanal festival air with a barbed, wiry, guitar-heavy attack. The singer, Chris Stamey, sounded like a smoother, higher-pitched Lou Reed. He wore a blazer like a young professor who'd write a thesis on his own band. Sneakers were a bit ragged, but in a cool, un-slick way. The drummer, Will Rigby, had the best "junkie look" of the bunch with his huge eyes and skinny arms pounding out face-slapping fills. Sneakers' songs were cleverly written and arranged with sharp, short, unexpected turns. *There's something great there* lit up like a neon sign in my brain. I bought the

EP. Sneakers, it turned out, had been produced by Don Dixon and a guy named Mitch Easter. It started to look like Dixon had a hand in everything that was cool in the local music scene.

Matt and I asked Dixon to produce two songs and he agreed. We budgeted the recording by borrowing a few hundred bucks from Matt's mom, an enormous sum we would happily pay back after we were rich and famous. Gaining momentum, Matt wrote a song for the "B" side called "Restless," a downtempo Free rip-off with acres of room for me to solo a la Paul Kossoff. Not wanting to repeat my underwhelming Atlanta session, I worked with Matt on the arrangements until we were convinced major labels would soon come calling on us as the new Free/Move.

Dixon arranged for Mitch Easter to be our drummer on the session and Matt claims we rehearsed with Mitch in his kitchen/studio along with Sneakers leader Chris Stamey on bass. Easter, who'd co-produced the Sneakers EP with Dixon, was a talented all-around musician and friendly guy with a puff of frizzy blond hair that made him look like an indie-rock Gene Wilder. For a guitarist, Easter was a surprisingly agile drummer. I was excited and impressed to be around guys who were skilled enough to be making records.

On the day of our session, Matt and I drove out to TGS Studio, a professional-sounding name for a freezing cold, thinly carpeted trailer in the leafless winter woods ten miles outside of Chapel Hill. Dixon, always armed with personality to spare, greeted us at the creaky, rusted door of the trailer with a sotto voce shout, "You guys ready to fucking rock?" Mitch arrived soon after and, after unloading his drums, generously revealed that he'd also brought a single pickup Les Paul Junior and his loud-as-hell Marshall amp for us to use. I would have some real oomph under my fingers.

Two challenges arose that we quickly resolved. First, Stamey didn't show up to play the parts we'd rehearsed. Dixon immediately volunteered to double up on bass and engineering. Second, when listening back to our take of "Restless," Matt decided he hated the lyrics for the third verse. We decided to mute the vocal on that verse and add the newly available terrain over to my guitar solo. I hadn't planned on soloing for nearly a minute and a half (eternity) but I loved it. With Mitch's Marshall amp literally shaking the trailer, I wailed on the Les Paul Junior, thrilled by the fat, distorted tone. I still wince at some of the string-bends that I pushed north of pitch, but overall, I passed muster. In fact, Dixon said the parts of the solo that weren't perfect were what made him like the solo even more.

"My Baby's M-M-Makin' Me Dance" and "Restless" came together painlessly. Dixon and Mitch merged their stylistic approaches effortlessly with ours. Matt's voice sounded surprisingly manly on tape—I hadn't realized he could sing like such a bluesy stud. Dixon gave us a quick mix of both songs, adding a nice touch to the start of "My Baby" with the sound of Mitch coughing. Matt and I were impressed by the session. We sounded like a real rock band. The sting of Atlanta lessened considerably. The only problem was, we were flat broke and didn't have the cash to press a single.

SCHOOL DAZE

I returned to UNC in the fall of '76 as I'd promised my parents. I knocked out my sophomore year of general college and, on the last day of school, declared for a journalism major. I decided if a job involved writing, I could live with it.

For one of my J-school assignments, I chose to interview Arrogance. The local heroes had just signed with Warner Curb Records. To my mind, signing with a major label was a dream come true, the be-all, end-all for any band. With Arrogance on a presumably heightened trajectory to fame and fortune, I expected an upbeat interview. Don Dixon's songwriting partner in Arrogance, Robert Kirkland, couldn't have been less impressed. "Signing a deal is like getting a job," Robert said with a derogatory emphasis on *job*. "For the time being, I've got a job with Warner Bros., and it probably won't last longer than any other fucking job I've ever had." He laughed, sardonically. I couldn't have been more shocked. How could Robert think of music as "work" or a "job"? Such a notion struck me as blasphemy. If anything, making music was the exact opposite of working a job.

I got another shock that same semester. I fell head over heels in love with an adorable freshman from Charlotte named Nancy. I'd had crushes before, but I'd never been in love. I floated around town and campus in a love-drunk stupor, convinced life was perfect in every way. Boring class? Think of holding hands with Nancy. Can't sleep? Think of kissing Nancy. Bussing tables at Coffee Shop? Picture Nancy walking through the front door. I loved her. She loved me. I'd nailed the secret to happiness, and nothing could possibly go wrong. The End.

THE BLAZERS

They weren't as cool as Sneakers or as popular as Arrogance, but Sherman and the Blazers had an album in stores and a following in the clubs. The Blazers played a few originals but mostly banged out covers by the Stones, Rodney

Crowell, Sleepy LaBeef, Elvis Costello...heady bar band stuff. Sherman Tate, a dark-haired, trim-bearded, friendly guy with an easy-going manner and a melodious North Carolina mountain accent, knew he wasn't an obscenely talented singer or guitarist, but he made the absolute most of what he had, and Chapel Hill loved him.

One day, at the Record Bar on Franklin Street, where he worked behind the counter, Sherman mentioned to me that two members of the Blazers, lead guitar and bass, were leaving town. He asked if I'd be interested in trying out for the band. I felt like it might be an odd fit, but I was flattered to be pursued.

Sherman came down to my boarding house to audition me. The leader of the Blazers quickly concluded I was the rock 'n' roll guitarist he was looking for. Late in the audition, Lee Gildersleeve arrived and told Sherman he played bass. Sherman suggested Lee could audition with the drummer, Ronnie Taylor. Lee, never lacking confidence, said, "No. Don't worry. You want me." The deal was done. I was in a band and Gildersleeve was officially un-retired.

Lee and I brought our talents to the Blazers at a fortuitous time. I'd been dumped by Nancy, the first true love of my life. My pain and self-pity had morphed into an album's worth of heartfelt, melodic, easy-to-play rock songs. Thank you, heartbreak and misery.

As the new lineup dove into rehearsals, the Blazers easily integrated my songs into the sets. When the reformed band emerged and began playing live, the Blazers were no longer just a covers act. Sherman relished the new sound of his band. He'd tell our audience, "Here's another song by Rick, I think y'all are gonna really love it. In fact, it's called 'I Can Love You.' How about that?"

The Blazers gave me my first taste of being a professional musician. We played Christmas parties for super-straight, white-collar companies and won over hairy tattooed warriors at biker bars thanks to our Lynyrd Skynyrd covers. On a good night, we'd each pocket a hundred bucks, real money. Four gigs a month would easily cover my overhead. I started working fewer shifts at the Coffee Shop.

The Blazers became regulars at the Cat's Cradle and Town Hall, Chapel Hill clubs where everybody went to dance and drink on Friday and Saturday nights. I was suddenly a part of the action in Chapel Hill. My tunes became crowd favorites, and Sherman and Lee's swaggering stage presences made us a fun band to watch.

UNC's *Daily Tarheel* gave the Blazers a glowing review. The fact that it was written by my journalism professor, Robert Friedman, takes nothing away from the praise, knowing his commitment to full objectivity, right?

> *(Miller's) effortless and fluid guitar work is as close as the group comes to out-and-out virtuosity... His compositions fit right in with the neo-British Invasion sound that, curiously, has become almost exclusively the province of Americans such as Tom Petty, Dwight Twilley, and Greg Kihn. The consistent quality and easy accessibility of Miller's songs are likely to interest some recording mogul soon.*

I'd never felt more "seen" than in Robert's review. At the very least, he convinced me I wasn't delusional about my talents.

Meanwhile, I was a UNC Senior and busting my ass to complete my degree. Journalism was a career I could stomach, if, heaven forbid, I ever had to get a real job. I felt an obligation to honor my parents' wishes that I pursue an honored vocation, but playing in a working band had shown me an alternate way forward. I was making money with the Blazers and playing music was a hell of a lot of fun. A song I brought to the Blazers, "Rock And Roll Must Be Right," revealed my feelings at the time:

> *Well, it don't take a college education*
> *To know how to deal with life*
> *Strap your guitars on, get your new shoes dirty*
> *And hang out with your friends every night*

Sorry, Mom and Dad.

HOW TO ROCK

After acing my last exam, I dutifully visited the J-school main office to see if any journalism jobs had been posted. There was one. A handwritten index card thumbtacked to the "Employment Opportunities" bulletin board announced, with as much gusto as capital letters could conjure, "AM RADIO STATION in WILSON, NC, needs NEWS REPORTER to join two-man NEWS TEAM. You'll cover City Council meetings, Police and Fire, etc." I half-heartedly imagined myself at a council meeting in Wilson, scribbling notes about new zoning regulations and plans to paint the high school. I thought, "Christ, no offense, Wilson, but I think I'll see if I can find something in Chapel Hill."

I knew right then I wasn't leaving town, and I wasn't going to pursue nine-to-five newspaper or radio work. I could survive on Blazers money and a part-time job or two.

That night, the Blazers opened for Arrogance at Town Hall. Since hearing *Prolepsis* five years earlier at Buffalo Records, I'd been a fan and had seen Arrogance play live more than any other band. It was a thrill to share a bill with them. During our sound check, I noticed Don Dixon listening to us from the back of the room. The Blazers played several of my songs, and, afterwards, Dixon approached me. He held his gesticulating hands in front of him a bit like a praying mantis, smiled and kind of shout-whispered to me, "You've got some good songs there, man! Really good."

"Thanks, Dixon. I appreciate that."

"How many of your songs do the Blazers currently play?"

"I think we do seven or eight so far.... Sherman's written some good stuff lately, too."

"Oh, gooood, good! Well, listen, there's a guy in town who's starting a label. He's calling it Moonlight Records. You know him, it's Dave Robert from the Cat's Cradle. He wants to start off with four artists, and I think you guys would be perfect. I think we should make a record." I told Dixon that sounded like a sensational idea. It wasn't like my journalism career would get in the way.

The band and Dixon chose ten songs for the record—six of my originals, two songs by Sherman, and two covers: "Oh, Pretty Woman" (the first record I ever owned) and "Rockin' Little Angel." Dixon booked the Blazers into TGS studios, no longer housed in a freezing trailer. TGS had moved into the high-ceilinged basement of owner Steve Gronback's modern log cabin home. A huge improvement. We would record for a solid week, my first session longer than a single day.

Dixon captained the recording process, handling the engineering and making suggestions as producer. Our basic tracks were done live, all four of us playing at once. The songs were simple, sturdy numbers we'd played in the clubs, and we stuck close to our arrangements. With Dixon steering the ship and Gildersleeve keeping us laughing, we settled into a good groove, getting keeper takes of several songs each day.

Lee anchored the band's bottom end and controlled tempo by playing purposefully simple parts on his Gibson EB-2 semi-hollowbody bass. Sherman covered the rhythm guitar parts, and I was free to add melodic lines and play all the guitar solos. I got some good tips from Lee for my solos.

On a song of mine called "Country Girl," we couldn't decide which solo we liked better. I suggested we let both solos play at the same time. Dixon was skeptical, but instead of a giant mess, the two solos complemented and answered each other in an interesting way. Dixon went along with it, and I felt like I'd won a small artistic skirmish.

I sang lead on seven of the ten songs. When I listened to my voice during playback, it rarely sounded how I'd imagined in my head. I wanted my voice to be a bit more powerful, a bit more agile, a bit more convincing. Hearing the truth takes some getting used to, but it's nice if your bandmates blow a little smoke. "Hey, man, you sound good, don't sweat it. It sounds like you." On Sherman's songs, he had only one directive: "Dixon, put some more fairy dust on my vocal!" That meant a dash of reverb and a rockabilly-style short echo.

At the end of the week, Gronback put rough mixes on cassettes for each of us. I must've listened to the album 50 times. I marveled at the professional sound of our band, the fullness of Ronnie's drums, the deep wooden tone of the bass, the metallic snap of my guitar solos. I'd never heard music I'd written sound so good. A declaration began to grow inside me. I felt like my songs announced, "This is who I really am, this is who I aspire to be, this is what I want people to know."

Apparently, I also wanted people to know that I had a horrible first-bloom mustache and that I drank Stroh's beer. Both were captured in the front cover photo for *The Blazers—How to Rock*. The back cover showed me leaping in the air, a gimmicky move that remains in my stage repertoire to this day.

EVERY MUSICIAN'S DREAM

I supplemented my Blazers income with part-time work at the local Chapel Hill newspaper, memorably called *The Chapel Hill Newspaper*. The publisher, Orville B. Campbell, was a legendary, imposing figure who had once been a record producer himself back in the 1940s. He recorded Andy Griffith's classic "What It Was, Was Football." In Chapel Hill, there's hardly a greater claim to fame.

My job was to paste up the editorial pages, Mr. Campbell's sacred terrain. I aligned Campbell's editorial copy perfectly on the page, ensured there were no typos, no extra air in the spacing. No one else at the paper wanted to be in Orville's firing line, but I didn't mind. I only worked from 11am to 1pm, fueled by cinnamon donuts and coffee. My college degree hard at work.

I worked in a large open newsroom with editors, reporters, photographers, and layout artists. We sat at desks or stood at tilted design tables, getting the paper ready for the presses while talking shit and cracking jokes. A beat-up portable radio in the corner was always on, usually to WQDR, the big rock station out of Raleigh.

One day during my shift, a radio deejay announced, "And here's some new music from a local band out of Chapel Hill. This is 'Top Of My World' by the Blazers."

Did I hear that right? I put down my X-acto knife as my song filled the room.

One year of love, one year of pain
I guess they balance out
'Cause I'm on top of my world again

The room grew quiet, and a couple of my closer acquaintances were all smiles, nodding their heads to my tune, looking my way and enjoying the moment with me. A writer who'd been buried in her work noticed the change in the room and looked up. She put two and two together, turned to me and said, "Wait. Is that you?"

Staff photographer Alex Webb answered for me, "Yeah, it's him! That's Rick singing!" An editor chimed in, "and playing guitar..."

It was one of the great moments in my life. WQDR likely had a couple hundred thousand listeners in cars, at home, on construction sites, in dentist's offices, at the pool, you name it. For the next three minutes, unless they changed the station, every listener was mine. It's a heady feeling to know your music is blanketing an entire region. I wish every musician could experience it. It's the absolute best.

On that day in 1980, when WQDR (the first "Superstars" station programmed by radio guru/free form radio destroyer Lee Abrams) played "Top Of My World" for three-plus minutes, I was on the same playing field as the Pretenders, Joe Jackson, Wings, Elvis Costello, Journey, the Romantics, Foreigner—pretty much everyone else getting airplay around that time. No, the Blazers were not even in light rotation, but airplay on a big FM station was a psychological milestone. What songwriter hasn't thought, "Hell, my stuff's as good as anything on the radio"? Well, now I had some evidence.

CHAPTER 9
THE WAITING ROOM

The summer after my graduation from UNC, Blazers bassist and world-champion party instigator, Lee Gildersleeve, informed me there was a room available in the house he shared with Herb Bresky at 404 Hillsborough Street. "Four-Oh-Four" was a known after-hours destination for those wanting to drink later than the state-mandated 2 a.m. I took my bachelor's degree and moved into the ultimate bachelor's pad.

A ten-minute walk from downtown Chapel Hill, 404 was a neglected rental house built in the 1940s, untouched by improvements. It was nestled in a bamboo grove at the end of a long, dirt driveway, famed for its chassis-destroying potholes the size of fishponds. The front door opened directly into a small kitchen with a sad linoleum floor worn thin and impossible to clean, not that we tried. Snakes roamed the warm dirt basement, and they might've had it better than us upstairs.

The first thing my new housemate Herb said to me with his slightly raspy voice was, "You're not one of those guys who's gonna come out of his room at three in the morning and tell people to be quiet, right?" Less than a month into my occupancy, I woke in the middle of the night to find a conga line of drunken strangers parading past my door in the hallway. The only person I recognized was a gentle and harmless street artist named Jim, Chapel Hill's best-loved acid casualty. Jim yelled, "Hey Ricky! Party's just getting started, man!" I thought, "I guess things are okay if Jim's here." I went back to sleep.

One day, I cooked eggs and sausage for breakfast. Herb shouted from his upstairs attic bedroom, "Hey, it smells good down there. What pan did you use?" Why would he ask? "Just a pan," I shouted back, taking a bite of egg. Herb responded, "You didn't use the wrought iron pan on the stove, did you?" referring to the heavy black skillet that, for reasons unknown, contained four large flat rocks. I yelled back, "No. It's filled with rocks." After a second, Herb said, "Okay, good." I shouted one last time, "Why is it filled with rocks?" Herb answered, laughing, "No one really knows. But we figured it's best to leave it in case there's an important reason."

The first time I showered at 404, I tiptoed into the filthy tub, prayed for hot water, and avoided touching the crusty, musty, never-washed towels hanging on the wall. I always took my own towel in with me to shower. If I forgot, I just dripped back to my room.

We rarely ventured into the tiny, dark living room except to warm ourselves in front of the fireplace in winter. One night, an after-hours bar crowd decided the living room was perfect for a dance party. The next day, we noticed the worn wooden floor had been danced downward about two inches and was no longer flush with the hearth of the brick fireplace. Miraculously, no one had fallen through the floor to the basement, which was good, because Lee still hadn't corralled all the snakes.

Our rent at 404 was $80 each per month. A few gigs with the Blazers and a couple of busboy shifts at the Coffee Shop ensured I could pay my share. We always made our rent, but sometimes the extra expense of heating oil caught us in arrears. One winter, we were a week late with oil money and 404 turned into a barely habitable icebox. When the oil truck, at last, negotiated our icy driveway and refilled the tank, we heard the beautiful sound of our cranky old heater firing up in the basement. Herb, Lee, and I, in hats and thick winter coats, gathered around the house's biggest heat vent, a metal grate on the kitchen floor. When the fan kicked in and we felt warm air in the house for the first time in days, we all moaned, "Ahhhhhhhhh" and rubbed our hands together with glee. We knew we were a ridiculous sight, three adults in a tight huddle over a heating vent, but, at that moment, life couldn't have felt any sweeter.

In summer, we migrated to the screened-in back porch with its hammock, wooden writing table, and thrift store chairs. Trees towered above the rear of the house and the land below sloped down to a creek. Lee noodled on guitar, Herb drew sword-and-sorcery scenes in pen and ink or read one of his ever-present paperbacks, while I created posters and calendars for the Cat's Cradle. A rough version of "halcyon" comes to mind.

LOOK, MOM, I'M USING MY DEGREE

The Raleigh-based *Spectator Magazine*, a weekly arts/politics/culture paper once described as the "*Village Voice* sprouting up in a tobacco field," debuted in 1978. The *Spectator* championed the Triangle area of Raleigh, Durham, and Chapel Hill (along with its three major universities in Carolina, Duke, and N.C. State) as a dynamic new cultural region, and its circulation grew quickly.

Chapter 9: The Waiting Room

I was excited when the *Spectator* ran a review of *The Blazers—How To Rock*, especially since they took pains to point out my impact on the Blazers' sound:

> The addition of Rick Miller's songs and voice gives the group an identity previously lacking. The more intriguing tracks are Miller's well-crafted tunes, strongly reminiscent of second-generation British and California pop of '65–'66.. not to attack Miller's writing as derivative, but rather to praise his ability to echo the classics so easily. The Beatles and the Byrds themselves captured our fancy by…joyously reflecting their influences. As an inheritor of this rock tradition, Miller makes pure references and has the chutzpah to concoct a snappy lyric or a catchy melody.

In 1981, an editor at *Spectator* with the fantastic name Godfrey Cheshire, solicited a gaggle of Triangle musicians to disclose the album or artist they felt had been criminally overlooked by the listening public. I chose the first three albums by my favorite under-the-radar act, Dwight Twilley. Beyond his debut single "I'm On Fire," Twilley hadn't made much noise, and deserved better. I made my case in two or three pages and sent it in. After *Spectator* ran my piece, Godfrey called saying he was impressed with my writing and offered me a weekly column as a music critic. *Spectator* would pay me pocket change, $30 per story, and whatd'ya know, I could claim to be using my degree.

I took my new role as a rock critic seriously. I vowed to be a journalist, not a huckster of hyperbole. The headline over my first review screamed, "Danny Gatton is God." So much for my anti-hyperbole crusade. Of course, if you know Danny Gatton's guitar playing, calling him God was kind of an understatement.

As *Spectator*'s music reviewer, I was waved through the door of every venue, large and small, in the Triangle. I didn't pay to see a live show for years. I liked most of the musicians I interviewed, and some made an especially lasting impression.

Iggy Pop. After performing the most intense show I'd ever seen, during which he implied that he had the artistic right to kill himself on stage, Iggy Pop happily reminisced in his dressing room about traveling south from Michigan to play golf in North Carolina with his parents when he was a young five handicap. It made my head spin. Insane rock show, and then, hmmm—nice guy and apparently a hell of a golfer. Iggy was still in stage clothes when he offered me the only seat in his small dressing room. As he stood chatting about some of his favorite golf courses, bands, and authors, commando Iggy changed his pants, literally, in my face. I'm available to answer whatever questions you may have about his manhood.

Roger McGuinn. I sat with the Byrds' founder in the top-floor restaurant of downtown Raleigh's circular Holiday Inn. It was off hours, and the room was empty but for us. We talked about the '60s LA music scene, Dylan, Roger's solo albums, his love affair with the Rickenbacker Twelve, the way Tom Petty echoed his style, and so on.

"Tom asked me what I thought was the hardest part about rock 'n' roll and I told him 'The waiting.'" (Ah ha!) That was cool to hear from the horse's mouth, but when McGuinn talked about his new wife and his acceptance of Christ as his Savior, our conversation reached a heightened level of intense sincerity. He said he'd been "struggling for years, doing drugs, not knowing which direction to go in, but at that moment of surrender, literally I felt like a hundred pounds lifted off my shoulders. I instantly felt great, and that weight has never returned." I believed him.

While McGuinn told me this very personal story, we noticed a plume of dark smoke outside, smudging the otherwise heavenly blue North Carolina sky. We went to the window, looked down and saw that a building was on fire just a block away. One of my heroes had just told me Christ had saved his life and now Raleigh was burning. Was this impressionable young writer supposed to take it as some sort of sign? It was dramatic, to say the least. When our interview concluded, I went to a nearby park, lay down on the grass and closed my eyes in the warm sun. My experience with Roger McGuinn had touched me. I hesitantly asked myself, "Am I supposed to surrender to Christ?" After a few minutes, my answer came. "Nah. Figure this shit out yourself." But I was happy for Roger.

Stiv Bators. I can't remember much about the former Dead Boy's show with his new band the Lords of the New Church, whom I found middling, but I'll never forget the soaking wet, black leather pants clinging to Stiv's skinny legs during our interview after the show. The aromatic combo of sweat, leather, beer, and whatever else he'd picked up on the road hung in the air with an acrid defiance. Stiv's pants took one look at my blue jeans and sneered, "Do you really expect to make it in rock 'n' roll looking like that?"

IN DEEP

I'm not a great hustler. Ninety-nine percent of my opportunities have come from people enjoying my work and asking me to do it for them, too. I created handmade posters for all the Blazers gigs. Cat's Cradle owner Dave Robert approached me and said, "Hey, I like your flyers. I'll pay you to make 'em for all the bands that play here." I happily made the jump from one or two flyers a month to twenty or more. Suddenly my "art" was plastered all over town and I had a few more nickels in my pocket.

More work came. I designed a detailed monthly calendar for the Cradle, pre-computer, all X-acto knife, magazine cutouts, and glue. Thousands were printed as full-color inserts in a local newspaper. That led to an eight-page insert I called Coffee and Cigarettes (also my diet) which combined stories about bands coming to the Cradle (Alex Chilton, T-Bone Burnett, Brave Combo, Jason & the Scorchers...) and goofy editorials and snarky guest columns from "Alan Cox-Allen" (Don Dixon) and "Pepsida DeWitt" (a witty writer named Arne Atwell). My efforts didn't add up to a real job, but I was doing my favorite kind of journalism.

BETTER LATE THAN NEVER

The two songs Matt Barrett and I had recorded in the freezing trailer but never pressed up, "My Baby's M-M-Makin' Me Dance" and "Restless," got paired with two more Matt originals and released by Moonlight Records as a four-song EP called *The Ruse*. Utilizing my flyer-honed graphic skills, I designed a ridiculous front cover using cutouts of a kangaroo playing a rare Ovation electric guitar in front of six Fender Showman amps. The EP featured "Six Pack," a devastatingly clever portrayal of alcoholism by Matt, later covered by Don Dixon on his album *The Nu-Look*. I played guitars and contributed background vocals on all four songs, but the EP was essentially a Matt solo record, as we didn't really have a band. That would finally change.

DADS SOCIAL CLUB

With a history going back to our pre-teen Officer Henry days in Greece, Matt and I knew what made us tick. Our sound landed on the rock side of folk. Matt was a strummer, with a steady right hand and good sense of time. He was never much good at single-note riffs and his child-like guitar solos had always been a source of amusement. It fell to me to embellish Matt's strumming with arpeggios, harmonic lines, and solos. Best of all, we sang well together. When we covered Beatles songs like "I Should Have Known Better" or "No Reply" at parties, we turned heads.

I'd once told Matt that, when I was done with college, we'd form a band. When I joined the Blazers, I know Matt wasn't thrilled. I never regarded the Blazers as "my" band, though. It belonged to Sherman and Ronnie, and the guitarist role had fallen in my lap. After three years with the Blazers, it felt like a good time to form a band truer to my taste in music.

Matt and I called our band the Dads. We stole the name from Gildersleeve, but it turned out Richmond, Virginia, had a Dads, Washington, D.C. had a Dads—for all we knew, every music scene in the country had a Dads.

We recruited a handsome, talented guitarist/singer recently arrived in Chapel Hill from California, Zoe Lagergren. He sported a David Bowie blond mullet and played guitar like Neal Schon. With Matt and I both on guitar, Zoe switched to bass. A friend of ours mentioned she was dating a drummer. We checked him out and Scott Swartzwelder became a Dad. Scott's day job was as a Duke University neuroscientist. Slacker.

The Dads' sound was crowded with differing agendas. Matt and I were Beatles-y, while Zoe and Scott could've easily anchored a Prog Band. A simpler rhythm section would've been a better fit for us, but Matt and I forged ahead, hogging most of the originals and adding songs to our set by the Move ("Down On The Bay"), Free ("Broad Daylight"), the Kinks ("Victoria"), and the Beatles ("Wait").

After a few rehearsals, we opened for Arrogance in Greenville, NC, and held our own before an alien crowd. Our early shows in Chapel Hill were jammed with curious locals, and it didn't take long to earn some coveted weekend slots. The Dads' calling card was punky pop music played relentlessly up-tempo, never more so than at a show in front of fifty sorority girls where we raced through every song ten times faster than usual.

The Dads' big brag was our association with Bad Brains, a legendary punk band from Washington, DC. Their first single, "Pay To Cum," had been produced by a guy from our high school, Jimmy Quidd (born Dimitri Hatzidimitriou). With his knack for networking, Matt befriended the Bad Brains and their DC-based manager, Mo Sussman. Matt arranged for the Bad Brains to play with the Dads in Carrboro, North Carolina, their first show in the South. They didn't disappoint.

Bad Brains were accomplished musicians who played so fast that audiences practically went into shock. Their special sauce was to mix in one or two slow, loping reggae songs, which made the fast ones hit with even more menace. In Carrboro, lead singer H.R., when he wasn't shouting incomprehensible rocket-speed lyrics, pulled off free-standing back flips and got himself and the crowd into such a fury that he spontaneously punched a hole in the wall next to the stage. Fortunately, he hit sheetrock and not a stud. Carrboro had never seen a band like Bad Brains. No one had. The Brains returned the favor and put the Dads on a bill with them at DC's famous Bayou club in Georgetown. We felt like we'd climbed to the pop punk mountaintop. DC was good to the Dads. We were even invited to perform at the prestigious Corcoran School of Art's graduation party in 1981. The previous year, the honor had gone to Talking Heads.

After our promising start, the Dads show gradually calcified. Rehearsals dissolved into chat sessions where we laughed a lot and solved mankind's problems with the aid of beer, wine, cigarettes, and pot. Instead of growing our set, we grew more interested in hanging out with our girlfriends. I'll admit, skinny dipping in a hidden pond and sleeping at my girlfriend Mary's country house with the windows open, crickets chirping, and the stars in the sky was enough to distract me from focusing on the band. It was as much my fault as anyone's that we didn't work harder to reach our potential. I regret that we never made proper recordings of our best material. We could've made a good album.

NOOOOO

On December 8, 1980, I was approaching the entrance to the Cat's Cradle when someone inside the club opened the door, saw me, and said, "Have you heard?" "No, what?" "John Lennon's been shot." I stood, shocked, and then turned around and walked home alone, trying to process the news. It felt like the world had tipped over.

The next day, I woke up early and raced to the record store to buy Lennon's new album, *Double Fantasy*. Listening to John sing love songs to Sean and Yoko broke my heart. The album was riddled with irony due to John's sudden, horrible death. The lyrics to "Beautiful Boy" included the mantra-like "every day, in every way, it's getting better and better." It certainly didn't feel like it that day. I did, however, recognize the phrase. It originated with a French psychologist named Emile Coue, who recommended its twice-daily repetition as an optimistic autosuggestion capable of reaching one's unconscious. The image of John chanting it for his kid was touching and, of course, tragic. I played the song repeatedly, crying my face off with every listen.

Just a few days after Lennon's shocking murder, the Dads were selected to participate in a memorial show at the Pier in Raleigh. We relied on the Beatles songs we already knew from our set, which included "Help!," "Wait," "Every Little Thing," and "Twist And Shout." On a moving night featuring the area's top bands, we gave one of our best performances.

AND YOUR BIRD CAN FREAK ME OUT

After performing at the Lennon Memorial concert, it was my job to write about it for the *Spectator*. I didn't want to waste ink on the fan-turned-assassin, Mark Chapman. I couldn't bear writing how much John meant to me personally. The story wasn't about me. Nor could I possibly summarize his effect on the world of music in one review. Everyone knew all that already. Searching for an opening to such a bleak story, I went back to John's love for his son, Sean, and Coue's mantra, "Every day in every way, it's getting better and better." It seemed preposterously contrary to the grim historical moment, but I decided to weave it into my story as a tribute to John's better angels.

Seconds after I committed to the idea for my story, a bird slammed into the large window next to my bed. I'd seen birds do that before, but instead of flying away, this bird kept slamming into the glass again and again and again, as if desperate to enter my room. The creature's wild insistence freaked me out a bit, to the point that I even moved across the room away from the window in case he managed to break through the glass. What the hell was going on? The odd thought occurred to me that maybe the bird was trying to tell me something. That's when it flew away.

When I finished my story, I attached a note to my editor, Godfrey, telling him about the bird. Godfrey called me back a few days later and mentioned that in many cultures, birds were commonly considered to be messengers from the dead. Whether such a thing is possible, as soon as Godfrey said it, it hit me like the truth. The bird had arrived right when I'd decided to take the high road in my story. Had it been sent to encourage me? To confirm I was on the right wavelength? Who the hell knows? But, if we're all free to believe a few spooky things, count me in as a believer in John Lennon's Free as a Bird Messenger Service.

GIRL OF MY DREAMS

When I was twenty-five, I dreamed I was seated at a heavy wooden tavern table. All was pitch dark except for a circle of light on my entwined hands resting on the table. From my right, a woman's smaller hands entered the circle of light, and took hold of mine. In the instant we touched, I thought, "This person knows everything about me." It shook me. Her face remained in shadow, but I could see she had long black hair. She was clearly important. When I awoke from the dream, the image of her hands on mine lingered. I wondered if I'd meet her someday.

A year later, she walked into my life. Hoisting a shoulder bag, an oversized purse, and a heavy rectangular cardboard box, a woman backed her way through the glass door of Chapel Hill's Universal Printing where I worked part-time in the evenings. She heaved the box onto the counter. I didn't recognize her right away from the dream, of course. She was just a customer. It didn't take long for my inner senses to wake up and pay attention. She was Asian American with long black hair nearly to her waist.

I asked, "What can I do for you?"

She nodded at the box and said, "Copy it. Carefully, please."

"Okay."

The box contained a stack of two hundred 20 x 17 sheets. Each featured a grid of light blue lines that wouldn't show up when photocopied. Printed blocks of type had been cut and pasted neatly onto the sheets. Tiny page numbers on minuscule paper squares had been carefully pasted in the corners. Some misspelled words in the body of the manuscript had been cut out and replaced with minute bits of correct letters. Each page was a delicate artifact.

I began copying, carefully. "What is this, by the way?" I asked, turning to face my customer.

Her colorless response was, "It's a book." I think she may've left out "you idiot."

As much as I'd always loved books, I'd never thought about how they were designed and put together. Apparently, it took a good eye, sticky wax, and a sharp X-acto knife. "Wow," I said. "It's amazing. Impressive."

"Thank you." This time she sounded less irritated by copy boy.

From our second-floor perch, Universal Printing's glass walls overlooked a parking lot and delivery entrances to shops on Franklin Street. Not exactly picturesque. But this evening, it was dusk, and the outside world was aglow in vibrant shades of purple and pink. My customer sat on a cushioned bench looking through the floor-to-ceiling windows with a million-mile stare. I don't know why, but the look on her face spoke volumes to me: I saw love, loss, pain, maybe even tragedy. But I didn't see defeat. She was a fighter.

It took an hour to copy the manuscript. My mystery customer waited patiently as I carefully lined up each page on the glass. We spoke a few times about the book, an academic tome from a small publisher in Durham. By the time she handed me a check, we had reached a cordial status. I glanced at the check as I put it in the cashbox. Her name was Anistatia Vassilopoulos. The Greek surname jumped out at me.

I met her eye with a slight smile. "You don't look Greek," I said.

Staring at me with the deadest, most disappointed eyes I've ever seen, she replied, "I used to be married to one."

"Ohhh…" I said. I smiled to myself. I loved Greece and the Greek people, but Greek men often carried a reputation for being terrible mama's boys—

spoiled, entitled, and incorrigible. "I lived in Greece for a while. I think I know what you mean."

She laughed. With her pleasantly husky low voice, she said, "Then I don't have to explain. Thanks for the copies. You did a good job. I'll be back with more. Have a good night."

I wanted her to come back soon. I was intrigued, big time. And just in case the mystery woman didn't return, I thought I'd better write down the phone number from her check. It wasn't cool, I knew, but I told myself I'd only call if I didn't see her again. If she DID come back, I'd get her phone number the proper way.

Anistatia Vassilopoulos came back. She said her friends called her "Stashe." After a few more tête-à-têtes at Universal Printing, we went next door to a bar and shared a drink. She told me her story, not in a casual, chatty way, but more like, "I want you to know who I am. Feel free to run away. I won't be offended." My intuition had been pretty spot on. Stashe was thirty-four, eight years older than me, originally from Chicago and more recently from San Francisco and New York. She designed best sellers as well as more prosaic academic books from university presses. She'd lost her husband and a child to cancer. Her rebound husband was a coked-up Greek mama's boy who cheated on her. She'd managed to get away from him when her book designer friends suggested she move to Chapel Hill: "We have FedEx now. You don't have to live in New York. Come to North Carolina."

She was like no one I'd ever known, which concerned me a bit, but I was fascinated. We went out. Our first date was on the Fourth of July. There were fireworks. On our second date, we went to her nearly furniture-less house outside Chapel Hill. Stashe spent the day in one room designing the layout of a book. In another room, I worked on my review of the LA band "X" for the *Spectator*. Every few hours, we'd meet in the kitchen for a cup of Stashe's killer espresso coffee. It was an eye-opening experience for young me. She quietly did her thing, I did mine. We didn't fill the day with stilted, getting-to-know-you chatter. She allowed me to truly be alone while in her presence. I hadn't known such an arrangement was possible. At the end of the night, she whipped up an incredible Chicken Kiev. The thought entered my mind that I was out of my depth.

Stashe asked to hear my songs, probably expecting to be disappointed. I played her some stuff on cassette and to her surprise and my delight, she said my songs were fantastic. She asked me what I was doing with my music. "Well, I'm putting together a new band and we're gonna make records and play clubs in Chapel Hill, Raleigh…" Stashe interrupted me. She said, with some steam in her voice, "No. I asked you, what are you doing with your music? How are you going to get noticed? Do you have a plan, or will you just play locally and eventually let your music rot away and die?" No one had ever spoken to me like that. It seemed a little harsh, but part of me knew she'd gone directly to the hidden insecurity of every musician: how do I make my dream come true? Maybe this mystery woman *did* know everything about me.

I'd never had a girlfriend like Stashe. She was older, wiser, more experienced, incredibly talented, hardworking, and quirkily intellectual. She knew more about life than me, and it made me uneasy. Things felt beyond my control. At times I struggled to commit to the relationship. I said to her, "What if I want to go to New Zealand for a couple years?" Stashe looked at me levelly and said, "Well, let me know when you're coming back so I can have dinner ready." See what I mean? You can't compete with that, can you?

Our relationship became more clearly defined by the roles we played for each other's benefit. My job was to slow her down, remind her there were nice people in the world, and convince her she wasn't crazy for leaving NYC and moving to relatively rural Chapel Hill. Stashe's job was to speed me up, get me organized, kick my musical ambitions into overdrive, and guide me to becoming a true professional.

When my brother Chuck mentioned that the house next door to where he lived with his wife Julie was for rent, Stashe and I moved in together at 107 Isley Street—a small, four-room brick house, a ten-minute walk from downtown Chapel Hill. It was as ordinary as you can imagine, but in good shape. Part of me hated to leave 404 Hillsborough St. In fact, I hated leaving so much, I kept paying my affordable rent for a few extra months in case I decided to move back.

I didn't move back.

RICK ROCK

I'd grown weary of musical democracies. The Blazers and Dads taught me a lot, but I was ready to try something new. I wanted to build a band where I would be sole songwriter and benign musical dictator. They say the brain is fully formed at age twenty-five, and at twenty-six, songs were pouring out of me. I was old enough to create a sound of my own, and young enough to think the world might give a shit.

I hand-picked two talented local guys, bassist Andy Church and drummer Chip Shelby, to join me. We jumped into learning my songs and hit it off immediately. I gave Chip and Andy lots of creative rope while reserving the final say on arrangements. It was a dream scenario for me.

I named us Rick Rock, echoing a high school gag by a friend also named Rick. (I was Rick Rock. He was Rick Roll.) We rehearsed for nine months and built a ninety-minute original set. Before we played a single note in public, we were tight.

We needed a 7-inch 45 rpm single to use as a calling card. I pulled together a whopping $400 and took the band into TGS studios, where I assumed the role of producer for the first time. Steve Gronback asked me, "Why aren't you using Dixon?" If Gronback was probing to see if I had a problem with Don, I didn't. I just said, "I think I can do it myself." With Gronback engineering, we recorded "Buddha, Buddha" and "(I'm Looking For A) Sputnik." Both songs were short, simple, direct, three-chord rock 'n' roll ditties with catchy parts. They were fun to play, and that joy came across in the recordings.

"Buddha, Buddha" announced what I'd decided my life's mission would be, which is hard to type with a straight face. I wanted to sing about love, or more specifically, Love, in as many sneaky ways as possible. All the spiritual books I'd read had the same conclusion: in this complicated, challenging, violent, often senseless world, love was the shit. Wiser thinkers have phrased it differently, but the message rang true to me. The lyrics of "Buddha, Buddha" said as much. I felt I was taking a real artistic stand by writing such embarrassingly personal lines:

Everything I do
Buddha did with love
And that's what I aspire to
Try to rise above the petty things I run into
I think of love when I do everything I do

Buddha, Buddha, Buddha
Fishing boats in the Greek blue sea go
Buddha, Buddha, Buddha
Enemy planes in the comic books go
Buddha, Buddha, Buddha
Young hearts when they fall in love go
Buddha, Buddha, Buddha

I wondered if listeners would call me out on that "I think of love when I do everything I do..." stuff. It just shows how little songwriters know about their audience. No one has *ever* commented on those lyrics. Not one word. But everyone who hears the song loves the repetitive, alliterative "Buddha-Buddha-Buddha" part. Because it's fun. I ought to try to remember that. Be fun.

LANDING A MARLIN

For Stashe, it was a short jump from designing books to record sleeves. She created a playful logo for our new imprint, Big Groovy Records, and an eye-catching black-and-white label for the 45. I couldn't have been prouder of my first self-released music. I felt like I had sole ownership of my craft for the first time.

As we were preparing to release "Buddha, Buddha" b/w "Sputnik," a new label called Dolphin Records sprang up in nearby Durham. Dolphin was affiliated with the Record Bar chain, giving Dolphin built-in regional distribution. Their first release would be a compilation album of "new North Carolina rock" called *Mondo Montage*. Dolphin put the word out that they were accepting submissions for the album. With my blessing, TGS studio owner Steve Gronback submitted both of my songs. As *Spectator*'s music critic, I was familiar with the area's original bands. There was a lot of competition, but I felt we stood a decent chance of being included. It would be ego crushing to be left out.

Gronback, Stashe, and I weren't sure if Dolphin would prefer "Buddha" or "Sputnik" or neither. Within a few weeks, Gronback called me with some good news. "You're on the album, Rick." I responded, "Oh, fantastic! Which song did they choose?" Gronback said, "Well, that's the thing. They couldn't decide which one they liked better, so they chose both." Wow. That was the opposite of ego crushing. I felt like king of the North Carolina hill.

Rick Rock was still in rehearsal stages and had yet to play in public. When *Mondo Montage* came out, the back cover of the album included bios of each band. Here's the blurb about Rick Rock:

> *Not much is known about these guys except that someone dropped their tapes off at the office and said they were a hit. We don't think they come from around here, but they do live here now. The combo is supposedly quite tight and exciting on stage, except no one has actually seen them play. Maybe by the time this record comes out something will have happened...*

That entry cracked me up. It couldn't have been more perfect.

Rolling Stone magazine reviewed *Mondo Montage* and raved about "Buddha, Buddha" and "Sputnik." Parke Puterbaugh's quote was, "You could land a marlin with these hooks!" The *Greensboro Record* declared "Buddha, Buddha" one of the Ten Best Records Ever Made in North Carolina. UNC's student radio station, WXYC, played it daily.

Rick Rock debuted at the Pier in Raleigh on a bill with three other bands from *Mondo Montage*. We grabbed the headliner spot on the strength of "Buddha" and "Sputnik" and perhaps the mystery factor surrounding our band. We went down a storm, and the crowd even forgave us taking the stage dressed completely in white, a gambit we'd come up with to set us apart even more. (My white T-shirt sported a Yin Yang symbol. It would haunt me when I saw *Spinal Tap*.)

ENCORES AND ONWARD

Stashe became our manager. She reached out to Triangle-area booking agents and, within months, we filled local clubs and began opening for national acts like Berlin, the Romantics, and R.E.M. We didn't mess around between songs or tell inside jokes. Our presentation was tight and professional. Opening for R.E.M. back at the 300-capacity Pier in Raleigh, we finished our set with "Buddha, Buddha" and the crowd went bonkers for us, chanting "RICK ROCK! RICK ROCK!" as we walked off. Chip, Andy, and I stood backstage, happy, sweaty, and wide-eyed, wondering if we should go back out. This was all new. When the chanting didn't stop, we looked at each other, shrugged, and returned to the stage. The thunderous applause went up another notch. Stashe stood watching from the wings. She told me later that R.E.M.'s Peter Buck had shouted at her, "Opening acts don't get encores!" Anistatia had turned to Peter and with her best Lauren Bacall voice said, "This one does."

Stashe found agents and promoters who loved our repertoire. They promised they could get tons of work for an all-original-music band. Chip and Andy quit their day jobs. Then, just as suddenly, dates vanished and agents asked, "Does the band do any covers?" Frustrated, Stashe cut out the middlemen. She called every original music club she could find and put together a tour herself. She routed us from Chapel Hill to Charlotte to Atlanta to Dallas to Indianapolis to Chicago to Lincoln to Minneapolis. Insanely ambitious, but I couldn't have been more excited.

Rick Rock hit the road in Chip's van. A friend of Andy's joined us as roadie. We ate fast food and crashed on friends' couches and at cheap hotels.

Chapter 9: The Waiting Room

Our crowds were small, but we consistently won them over. Rick Rock had something special. All I wanted was to stay on the road.

After an inspiring show for a smattering of college kids in Lincoln, Nebraska, we headed to Minneapolis where Stashe had booked us to play First Avenue, the club made famous by Prince. Before we got out of Nebraska, our van threw a rod. We were towed to a repair shop. I canceled the Minneapolis show. Drummer Chip put $895 for the repairs on his credit card and decided that was more financial pressure than he could bear. He solemnly announced he was returning to North Carolina to ask for his job back at the nuclear plant. Andy declared he would go home with Chip. And that was that. Rick Rock was roadkill.

Chip and Andy's mutiny crushed me. Our band had an "it" factor, something magical. I truly believed that, and I still do. I didn't want to listen to financial reason. I wanted to forge on, no matter what. I don't blame them if they saw me as obsessed or nuts or unreachable in my damn-the-torpedoes state of mind. I was a bit crazy, I'll admit. I'd gotten a taste of something bigger and exciting, and I liked it.

From Chicago, Stashe and I took a driveaway car out to San Francisco and spent a week with friends of hers in Marin County. We got our heads clear and then headed back to Chicago where we lived with her mom for a while. Stashe landed some design work with an old colleague. I began writing new songs. In December, when Chicago frighteningly morphed into a subzero, uninhabitable snowscape, we headed back to Chapel Hill.

Rick Rock had imploded, but Stashe and I had stuck together. We were a good team despite our ambitious failure of a tour. I wasn't sure of my next move, but I wanted Stashe at my side. In spring 1984, I invited her for a walk out in the woods near campus. I knew the location of a fire pit and brought hot dogs for cooking. I can't recall why I chose a weenie roast for the moment when I plucked up my courage to ask Stashe to marry me, but she said "yes," so maybe I knew what I was doing.

Our wedding that fall was a modest but boisterous affair in the side yard of our house on Isley Street in Chapel Hill. The ceremony managed to incorporate shots of ouzo with music from Prince ("Dearly beloved..."). My three brothers stood as best men, and Stashe and I exchanged vows in the company of just about every musician in the Triangle area. Scraping nickels together, we honeymooned on the beach in Delaware, and hung out in New York at a friend's house in the Bronx. *Exotic*. We splurged for Chicken Kiev at Manhattan's Russian Tea Room, our lone extravagance, and a nod to our memorable second date.

MUSI-CALL

Stashe and I were happy to be married, but we were broke. Rick Rock hadn't been the moneymaker that the Blazers were. My *Spectator* stories paid peanuts and I'd handed my poster business over to Matt while I was on tour. I took a job washing dishes at a Polish restaurant but chipped too many fancy plates and found myself gone. I'll never forget driving with Stashe to the A&P and buying $4.53 worth of chicken livers with the last of our money. That will challenge your confidence. Our bank account did a daily dance above and below $0.00. We wrote bad checks for amounts like $12.00 when we guessed wrong about our pathetic balance.

We fought our way out of debt by keeping our focus on music. We decided to create a directory for North Carolina musicians. It would list names, phone numbers, and instrumental expertise for as many North Carolina musicians as we could find, at no charge. To fund the book's publishing and pay our bills, we sold advertising. I crisscrossed the state and reached out to guitar stores, recording studios, P.A. companies, music clubs, record stores, management companies, graphic artists, newspapers, and so on. It turned out that I'd accrued some goodwill in the community as an artist and music critic. Nearly everyone I contacted jumped on board and wrote me a check for ad space. It was as close to an "It's a Wonderful Life" moment as I've ever had.

We named our directory *Musi-Call* and it succeeded because nothing like it existed. It took us eighteen months from conception to delivery, longer than we'd planned, but it was worth the effort. Delivering books to all the businesses who'd supported us was a very satisfying experience. I was grateful for their faith and proud to follow through. *Musi-Call* wasn't a big profit maker, but the ad revenue kept us afloat (no more chicken livers) while we labored away. It showed me there were alternative ways to make money without getting a normal job. Bye-bye dishwashing.

THE WAITING ROOM

All the momentum I'd created with Rick Rock was gone. I couldn't face starting another band from scratch, but I needed to do something to advance my cause. I longed to record without budget limitations, to work on a couple of songs until they were, if not perfect, at least the very best I could produce. I made a deal with Steve Gronback at TGS Studios. I proposed we record during his down hours when the studio wasn't busy. Whatever profit came of the songs, we'd share. Steve agreed.

Chapter 9: The Waiting Room

My best new songs were "Button" and "Dozers Away." "Button" was another non-traditional love song, a niche I determinedly mined. "Dozers Away" was one of a handful of songs I would write about Chapel Hill's vanishing charm as green fields gave way to shopping centers. (A famous producer in my future would say about "Dozers Away," "Great song. Too bad it's about bulldozers.")

As agreed, Gronback and I worked only during studio downtime. Our sessions were intermittent and few, but on the bright side, I had tons of time to conceptualize and fuss over my recordings. Gronback loaned me his Linn Drum, a top-of-the-line computer drum machine that allowed me to map out my songs down to the last bar and beat. It took six months to finish "Button" and "Dozers"—a recording eternity. But the results were as good as I'd imagined.

Stashe created cassette artwork and we confidently sent copies of "Button" and "Dozers Away" to a half-dozen major labels, unsolicited. If they didn't like my stuff, so be it. I couldn't do any better. To my great satisfaction, EMI and Island Records called me. I was told by both labels, "Your songs were everyone's favorite at this week's A&R meeting."

Yes! I will sign. What should we call the album?

Both labels asked, "Do you have other songs we can hear? Can you send us more demos?"

I just spent six months on those two songs. Do you really need to hear more?

I fudged, "Of course, yeah. We're working on more songs. We'll send them soon."

I called Gronback. He encouraged me to write a couple of good songs, quick. Soon after this incredible development, with not one but two major labels hot on my trail, I ran into Don Dixon near the Cat's Cradle on Rosemary Street in Chapel Hill. I was pumped to tell my longtime mentor the exciting news. "Dixon! EMI and Island called me. My songs were the favorites at their A&R meetings."

Dixon, rather than jumping up and down (like I was feeling inside), instead looked thoughtful and said, evenly, "Oh, good, man. That's good news."

"Yeah! I thought it was amazing news. I mean, two labels calling in one week was pretty incredible."

Dixon's expression didn't look like he thought it was incredible.

I said, "That's a good thing, right?"

Dixon said, "Oh, yeah. It's definitely good. It just means…now you're in the waiting room."

Waiting room? "What do you mean?"

"Well, kind of like it sounds," Dixon explained. "They know you're out there. So, you're in the waiting room."

I thought for a second. "Well, okay. How long do you usually have to stay in the waiting room?"

Dixon didn't hesitate. "About two years."

Two years? I was twenty-eight years old. Two years sounded like ten. I'd have to adjust my excitement level. Damn.

Dixon wasn't wrong. Those phone calls from Island and EMI initiated a courtship between me and the major labels that would last…two years. Speaking of courtship, don't ever meet with a major label A&R person unless you are accompanied by a manager, a lawyer, or at the least someone smarter than you. I took a meeting in New York with an A&R guy named John Mrvos at EMI. We plopped ourselves down in his office. John had dark long hair, and looked like an artist-friendly guy. He'd previously been in radio, at WXRT in Chicago, a cool station. John leaned back in his office chair and opened our conversation by saying, "So. What do you need?"

I played with the question in my head. What do I need? How the hell do I answer that? I should have asked, "What do you mean by what do I need?" Instead, I wanted to look knowledgeable, so I ran through the possibilities of what Mrvos could be referring to. Since I was sitting in the office of an A&R man in pursuit of a record deal, I deduced he meant, *"What do I need to make a record?"* I was somewhat fluent in album budgets of the time, so I said, "Oh, I'd guess a hundred grand."

Mrvos's face dropped with disappointment. He looked bummed out, like I'd completely failed his test. WTF? He didn't say anything like, "Oh, I'm sorry, let me make myself clear. What I meant was…" Nothing like that. Our meeting was pretty much over. Ugh. I hope we get some do-overs in the afterlife. To this day I still don't have a great answer for Mrvos's question. There are lots of possibilities. A record deal. A career. A backing band. A new van. A recording studio. A better guitar and amp. A cool haircut. How about someone to tell me what you mean by the question?

Island Records came to the rescue. They liked my music enough to put up $2,000 in demo money for Gronback and me to record two new songs. We chose "Pages Of Love" and "Something In My Heart Stopped." On "Heart Stopped," we brought in keyboardist Dave Adams from Raleigh band Glass

Moon. He came up with a beautiful intro and added much needed spice to the track. I thought we had something special with "Heart Stopped," namely an undeniably catchy chorus:

Something in my heart stopped when you walked by
San Francisco Bay went completely dry
Verrazano Narrows grew too wide
Cerebellum breakdown when you said hi
Something in my heart stopped when you walked by

Steve and I took my new songs to Island in LA. Our A&R contact had been Iain Matthews, who, after a long career as a recording artist (Matthews Southern Comfort), had taken a job on the business side. Unfortunately, by the time we finished our demos, Iain was no longer at the label, so we met with Lionel Conway, a well-traveled music exec who had worked with the Beatles, Traffic, Free, Jethro Tull, and whatd'ya know—the Move—among many other bands. Lionel was something of a music business legend, but I was sadly ignorant of his rock history cred in pre-Google 1984.

No matter how cordial meetings like this can appear to be, for artists they are fraught with anxiety. Watching music execs listen to, and judge, your precious, personally meaningful music is nothing less than torture. You can't help but scan their expressions as your song plays. You think, "Here's the big chorus... and...no reaction? Fu-u-u-ck!" Three-and-a-half minutes can't go any slower.

Lionel listened to both songs he'd paid for and wasn't knocked out. He said, "I think I still prefer the first two songs we heard from you, Rick. These are fine, but they don't nudge me any closer to offering you a deal. Do you have anything else I could hear?" Sigh. The ol' "anything else" question. Trying to lighten the mood, I decided to throw a joker on the pile. "Well, I have a song that's kind of psychedelic called 'Psychic Waitress.'" Recorded on cassette four-track, "Psychic Waitress" sounded something like the Move's "Here We Go Round the Lemon Tree." The lyrics were tongue in cheek:

4:00 am and I can't wait
Hash browns, eggs, and toast
Try to order, it's too late
She already knows
Psychic waitress, always knows what I want

My gamble bombed. I'll never forget Lionel Conway's professional assessment: "Is this some kind of a joke?" I took that to indicate Lionel and I were not on the same page. I was either an idiot or simply not Lionel Conway's type of artist. Let's just say both. I felt like a fool. I was clearly unable to understand what made A&R guys tick. To my ears, "Something In My Heart Stopped" had all the ingredients of a hit, but it had not landed with Conway at all. I could feel a divide widening between my understanding of music and my comprehension of the music business. Maybe I just didn't have the goods. Sigh.

I was still stuck in the infamous waiting room, but our meeting with Island wasn't a total loss. Lionel Conway liked Gronback's production work on my stuff, and not long after our meeting, the LA "psych revival" band (and Island Records artist) Rain Parade were camped out at TGS studios in Chapel Hill, being produced by Steve Gronback. The resulting album *Crashing Dream* came out later that year. I hope Steve made some dough. Other than our demo money, he wasn't making much working with me.

UNFORGETTABLE

Back in Chapel Hill after my thud in Los Angeles, I was feeling pretty low, so I dropped into Tijuana Fats, a Mexican restaurant/bar and dependable spot for finding friends and maybe a drink or four. I saw no one I knew, so I turned to leave. On my way out, I overheard the hostess say to someone, "Do you know who that was? Rick Miller. He's an amazing songwriter." She couldn't have said it at a better time. I needed it. Thanks, stranger.

I was hanging out in front of the Cat's Cradle with an up-and-coming alt-country punk guitarist named Alejandro Escovedo. We were taking turns showing each other stuff on his acoustic guitar, and I played him the fastest blues lick in my repertoire. His eyes opened wide, and he shouted, "WHAT A RIFF!" I was delighted to impress Alejandro, a nice guy who's gone on to have a remarkable, highly respected career. Funny how praise is so memorable.

So is admonishment. In my role of *Spectator* music critic, I reviewed an Alex Chilton show at the Cradle and quoted Chilton's bassist as saying something along the lines of, "Yeah, the band is pretty wobbly and under-rehearsed at times." When Chilton returned to the Cradle months later, the bassist came straight at me and said my story got him in deep shit with Alex. "I was speaking to you off the record! Only an asshole writer would publish that kind of shit." I felt terrible. I'd found the quote to be honest, accurate, and not an insult to anyone. But I should've made sure the bassist was comfortable with me using it. Bad form on my part.

ME & DIXON

While my major label pursuit was stuck in the waiting room, Don Dixon asked if I'd do some touring with him on guitar and vocals. I missed playing live after Rick Rock's disintegration and jumped at the chance to get back on stage. Dixon covered bass and lead vocals, a lanky, teenaged hotshot named Rob Ladd from local stars the Pressure Boys delivered punishing drums, and I would cover guitar and vocals. My rig at the time was a '60s Fender Jazzmaster through two Fender Deluxe Reverb amps. Classic, right? Yes, until I admit that I ran my signal through a Rockman, Tom Schultz's guitar processor with a belt clip. Oh, 1980s, we had fun, didn't we?

We called the band Me & Dixon and quickly assembled two sets of music. The first featured the best of Rick Rock plus a bunch of my newer songs. The second set spotlighted Dixon's latest music from his solo albums as well as some classic Arrogance favorites. I was flattered that Dixon split the show between his and my repertoires. Ever since I'd heard Arrogance in Buffalo Records when I first arrived in Chapel Hill, Dixon had been something of a North Star on my otherwise zig-zagging path to a music career. To ascend from fan to bandmate was a significant milestone.

Me & Dixon rolled through the southeast. I initially relied on Dixon's star power to carry the show, but once my guitar parts solidified, I played with more confidence and swagger. Same with Rob. He picked his moments to blow minds, and Dixon and I learned to get out of his way. Our loud little trio played packed clubs in Winston-Salem, Columbus, Savannah, Athens, Atlanta, and more. By the time we finished our run with a memorable home show at Chapel Hill's Cat's Cradle, we were road hot. A roaring crowd came to cheer on their local "all-star band" as we were dubbed by *Spectator Magazine*'s Jonathan Mudd. I felt like the king of Chapel Hill.

We followed the southern leg with a run to Baltimore, New York, Hoboken, Providence, Boston, and Haverford, Pennsylvania. That northern circuit featured Mitch Easter's Let's Active and power pop kingpin Tommy Keene, two bands I would've paid to see. The money I made was mostly maintenance level, but the Dixon tours made me feel like a proper working musician. We were playing great clubs, living in hotels, laughing our asses off as we drove from city to city, eating breakfast at midnight, all the stuff that makes being in a band so much fun. I noted, too, that Dixon's way of doing things was the opposite of what I'd done in Rick Rock. He had a loose approach to playing live that could be just as effective as detailed overkill. It helps, of course, when your leader sings like Otis Redding and your drummer kicks ass.

CHAPTER 10

GUY IN BAND

Stashe and I became friendly with an act from Florida that was recording with Steve Gronback at TGS. Jeanne and Shelby Creagh were a handsome wife and husband team doing synth-pop, stylistically on point for the mid-1980s. They called themselves Head For Tall Trees. Jeanne, a vivacious ball of energy with blonde curly hair piled high on her head, and Shelby, with his dark shoulder-length hair and good looks, seemed ripe for success. Like other pop bands of the time, they pulled their sound largely from synthesizers and drum machines. Gronback, who worshipped Roxy Music and Peter Gabriel, applied the perfect glossy touch to their demos. With three songs in the can, Jeanne dubbed up fifty cassettes. She mailed one to every record label she could find, kissing the envelopes and saying a little wish. Jeanne's prayers and their three-song demo were good enough to land Head For Tall Trees a deal with Chrysalis Records. The label was so excited about their new act that they moved Jeanne and Shelby into a New York apartment and gave them $50,000 to buy home studio equipment.

Stashe and I felt like we, too, ought to be in New York, in the middle of the action, better able to move my music forward and to get Stashe's design career back on track. As much as I loved Chapel Hill, I agreed it was time for new opportunities and experiences. We packed up our two Maine Coon cats, art portfolios, word processors, my Fender amp, acoustic and electric guitars, and, on January 19, 1986, my thirtieth birthday, we drove north and moved all our stuff into one room on Bethune Street in Manhattan's West Village for $750 per month.

PARTHENON HUXLEY

My address wasn't the only thing that changed on my thirtieth birthday. I also decided to call myself Parthenon Huxley. Why do such a thing? I didn't hate "Rick Miller" and I wasn't mad at my family lineage. I wasn't even overly concerned that a guitarist/singer also named Rick Miller had moved to Chapel Hill and formed a band called Southern Culture on the Skids.

I tell people I changed my name because I thought it would be fun to be known by a ridiculous but meaningful moniker. "Parthenon" acknowledged my boyhood in Greece and "Huxley" had a nice ring to it while doubling as a shout out to English author Aldous Huxley (I didn't love *Brave New World,* but his novel *Island* had rung my bell in college). It may also have been an attempt to anoint myself an adult artist, committed to music. I was thirty years old, long overdue to declare once and for all that the go-to-school-and-get-a-job model had fizzled from lack of interest.

My name change may also have been nudged by a rejection letter I'd received from Steve Ralbovsky, the Columbia Records East Coast Artists and Repertoire Director of Talent Acquisitions. Roughly a year before I moved to New York, Mr. Ralbovsky thoughtfully wrote, "Might I suggest that you call yourself something else. In my opinion the name (Rick Rock) takes away from the quality of the writing." If I ever run into Ralbovsky, I'll ask him how I did.

I wasn't the first guy in my family to adopt a stage name. My dad had done it twice. As a strapping 130-pound teenager getting into amateur boxing in Michigan's Upper Peninsula, George Miller felt he needed a tougher sounding name and went with "Joey Morgan." He won a few, lost a few—who knows if the name helped? Then, when he retired from the corporate world, he took up painting in a primitive art style and signed his paintings "Joe M." I was in good company.

THE M-WORD

Long past its prime as the site of Bob Dylan's New York City debut, Gerde's Folk City in Greenwich Village held open mic hootenannies on Monday nights. I caught an artist named Bianca Bob Miller, who sang, "I'll be your pilot fish/I'll suck the scum off your skin any time." Hearing that, I had to introduce myself. It turned out Bianca Bob knew Peter Holsapple of the dB's, a band from North Carolina I admired. Bob, an eccentric native New Yorker with a riot of dark curly hair, took me along to her favorite haunts for weird poetry readings and acoustic shows. Her local knowledge and easy friendship made New York a more welcoming place.

I filed stories for the *Spectator* from New York, but the more I wrote about other artists and their successes, the more frustrated I grew with my own musical trajectory. I called my editor, Godfrey Cheshire, and told him I didn't want to write another piece for *Spectator* until I had landed a record deal myself. He was fine with that, and probably relieved, since I was notorious for missing my deadline.

Stashe and I hung out often with Head For Tall Trees at their apartment on 8th Street and 5th Avenue. We listened to their new music, and I played them my latest demos. Jeanne mentioned they were scheduled to meet with Mark Goldenberg, a producer from LA who'd written some very successful songs for Linda Ronstadt and worked with producer Peter Asher. Goldenberg arrived in New York accompanied by his manager, Michael Solomon. Jeanne called me and said, "We really like these guys, Parthenon. You should come over and meet Mark's manager, Michael. He's a cool guy. You need to give him your demo tape."

I could've kissed Jeanne for her thoughtfulness. I met briefly with Solomon and handed him a tape with "Buddha, Buddha," "Button," "Something In My Heart Stopped," and four other songs. Solomon called me later that evening and said, "Can we meet for breakfast?"

Michael was a neatly dressed, dark-haired, very engaging guy with good energy, fun stories, and expensive round tortoiseshell glasses. He told me he'd worked with Harry Chapin, Tom Waits, and other interesting artists. That had led him to form a small, wryly named management company, The M-Word, to which he'd signed several clients, including Goldenberg and singer/songwriter Karla Bonoff.

Michael said, "So I listened to your tape. I really like your songwriting."

I really liked Michael Solomon's taste in music.

"How would you feel if I took your tape out to Los Angeles and pitched it?" I assumed he didn't mean "into the Pacific Ocean" and said, "That sounds great." I didn't know how connected or capable Michael was, but I liked him, and he liked my music. Win, win. He and Goldenberg returned to LA with my demo tape, and possibly my future, in Michael's hands. I called Jeanne to thank her again. Fingers crossed.

STAR SEARCH

LA hadn't been on my radar, but it suddenly seemed like an intriguing option. I'd been there once before and loved it. In 1984, on assignment for *Spectator*, I'd written a feature piece on Arrogance guitarist Rod Dash and his opportunity to compete on *Star Search*, the corny predecessor to *American Idol* and *The Voice*. My angle was Rod's conflict about competing on a show he'd normally be embarrassed to watch. Conflicted or not, Rod got a free trip to LA out of *Star Search*, and he made the most of it. After checking in at our hotel, Rod drove his band and me up to the secluded Laurel Canyon home of his friend, Doors producer, Paul Rothchild. Paul welcomed us into his hillside stained-glass-windowed house, treated us to Corona beers and shared tales of working with Jim Morrison and Janis Joplin. Rothchild made the music business sound groovy but ambitious, like hippies ran the world. I couldn't have felt more at home. It didn't hurt that Laurel Canyon's Mediterranean topography under the bright blue LA sky thrillingly reminded me of Greece.

Late in our visit, Paul's seventeen-year-old son Dan arrived. We had a fun back-and-forth chat about the kinds of music we liked, and Dan flattered me by asking for a tape of my demos. Not knowing if I'd ever see Dan Rothchild again, I handed one over.

Now, two years later, in New York, I'd handed a demo tape to another LA guy, Michael Solomon. I was hoping to see a lot of Michael.

THE SOUND OF SILENCE

Stashe and I moved from our 12 foot by 10 foot cubicle in the West Village to a roomier, but gloomier, loft apartment at 144 Stanton Street in the down-on-its-luck Lower East Side. In 1986, Stanton was the kind of street I would normally fear to walk, much less inhabit. Most days, a one-eyed drug dealer sat on our narrow stoop, begrudgingly lifting his haunches to let us enter our home. I heart New York.

Head For Tall Trees prepared to record their album in LA with Goldenberg. Working on songs at home on their twelve-track Akai machine, they employed a handsome, dark-haired bass player named Robert to play on their demos. Robert had been plugging away in bands for years without much to show for it. Despite his talent as a musician and his gig with Head For Tall Trees, he was frustrated with the music business and ready to hang it up. He wasn't shy about warning Jeanne and Shelby of the pitfalls possibly awaiting them in LA. Perhaps weary of Robert's negativity, Stashe offered to teach him graphic design. He didn't need to hear the offer twice. Robert jumped at the opportunity to apprentice in a new trade.

Stashe brought Robert to our loft and was immediately impressed by his abilities. I liked Robert, but his apprenticeship ballooned a bit too quickly for my comfort. I wasn't super-thrilled to have him in my apartment for eight hours every day, side by side at a drafting table with my wife. There was nothing technically wrong going on, but he became something of a perfectly friendly wedge between Stashe and me. I wound up leaving the apartment a lot, seeking the company of Bianca Bob and other acquaintances. I wasn't mature or brave enough to express my true feelings directly to Stashe or Robert. Perhaps I was afraid of how they might respond. I just kept quiet, telling myself I was being cool and reasonable. Right.

It was quiet on the music front, too. I hadn't heard back from Solomon. The buzz from our meeting calmed down. I decided to do what I loved best and began putting together a band. I found a capable drummer and a singer/keyboardist/violinist named Mindy Jostyn. The drummer had access to a soundproof room, and the three of us managed to drag our gear across Manhattan to play together. Mindy was talented, with a bright, eager personality. She loved my songs and nailed her parts quickly. The drummer, with a thick patch of blond hair and sideburns, locked in as well. We had the makings of a nice band, but our momentum was derailed when paying opportunities took the three of us in separate directions.

When our nascent band fell apart, I was sorry to lose track of Mindy Jostyn. I found out years later that she'd gone on to play with Billy Joel, John Mellencamp, the Hooters, Carly Simon, and many others. I'd assessed her talent correctly and was belatedly thrilled for her great success. I never got to congratulate her. Sadly, Mindy passed away from cancer far too young in 2005.

HEY, HEY, VE'RE DON DIXON BAND (WITH NORWEGIAN ACCENT)

As the LA possibility lingered and our apartment remained crowded during the summer of '86, I got a call from Don Dixon. He asked if I'd like to tour Europe with—"Yes," I said, before he could finish his question. Touring Europe sounded like the perfect getaway. Dixon and I were joined by two of North Carolina's best musicians and funniest people, drummer/singer/songwriter Terry Anderson ("Battleship Chains," "I Love You Period") and Dixon's Arrogance bandmate (and *Star Search* contestant) Rod Dash, who sang and played keyboards and guitar. A true North Carolina all-star band.

Dixon's album *Most of the Girls Like to Dance But Only Some of the Boys Like To* on Demon Records (Elvis Costello's label) had apparently done good business in Europe, particularly a song called "Praying Mantis." The four of us flew to Brussels and stuffed our jet-lagged bodies and gear into a rental van. Phillip, our amiable Belgian driver with a wavy mullet, took us to an Indonesian restaurant named Mancock. I said, "That sounds like a great nickname for somebody in this van." The four of us pointed at Phillip, and from that moment on, "Mancock" Phillip would be.

We had just one night to rehearse. Mancock drove us through dark countryside to a loft space in a farmhouse. We ran through the set, and any concerns about song arrangements were met with Dixon's typical lack of alarm. He chuckled in his raspy way, "It'll be fine. Don't worry too much about any of this stuff." Alright, I thought. You're the boss. I gave Rod a look. "Do you know what you're doing on this song, Rod?" He said, "Not really, but I guess I'll figure it out onstage." We laughed. Terry, employing his favorite aggravated redneck voice, said, "You guys must really suck. I know exactly what the fuck I'm doing."

The next morning, we filmed a segment for a Belgian Pop TV show—a great sign. If your record's making enough noise to justify a TV appearance, things are going well. We did our best to accurately lip-sync "Most of the Girls Like to Dance" while fighting off the brainless fog of jet lag. The best thing about faking it on TV is you can't make mistakes. We nailed it.

That night, things got a lot more real. Mancock drove us to the city of Leuven, where Dixon was the penultimate act on a three-day festival headlined by Graham Parker. On a warm summer night, 15,000 fans packed into Leuven's dramatically lit medieval city square. Offstage just before the show, I clinked glasses with Dixon and we each threw back a shot of promoter-provided whiskey. We felt the burn and Dixon shouted, "Good for the throat!" The concert emcee was shouting at the crowd in indecipherable Flemish, but, at last, he said something that sounded like "Don Dixon!" I crossed the huge festival stage to my amp, plugged in, and pretended I wasn't scared to death. We jumped into our little quartet's under-rehearsed versions of Dixon's tunes and the heaving sea of music-loving beer drinkers roared their approval. During "Praying Mantis," the crowd sang all the words back to us louder than the PA. My confidence increased. I wasn't sure what I'd expected from the show, but I hadn't expected that. At one point, I wandered over to center stage and shouted in our leader's ear, "Holy crap, Dixon! You're huge in Belgium!"

Each show got better and tighter as Dixon's tour took us to an outdoor festival in Groningen, Holland; an opening slot at 6,000-capacity Club Ahoy before UK act Talk Talk in Rotterdam; a club in a former bomb shelter in Bergen, Norway; the Mean Fiddler pub in London, England; and a canal-side club in Utrecht, Holland.

The venue I was most excited to play with Dixon was the famous Paradiso in Amsterdam. I had some history there.

BE MORE CAREFUL NEXT TIME

Twelve years earlier, in 1973, I'd been a seventeen-year-old wanna-be hippie on a Eurail trip. In Amsterdam I'd bumped into an acquaintance from my Athens high school. We found a shady spot in Vondel Park where we could sit and sample the local plant life. Shortly, two Dutch policemen sauntered up behind us and asked to see our passports. I felt my body go heavy with dread as my young life flashed before my eyes. More accurately, my young life splashed down the toilet.

I handed over my passport and tried not to freak out. One of the cops pointed to our joints. "What is this?"

"Hash," I replied.

He asked, "Where did you get it?"

"Somewhere by the square."

"Do you have more?" I did. I handed it over. After a couple minutes of slowly flipping through the pages of my passport, the cop who was about to ruin my life, forever alter my relationship with my parents, possibly put me in jail or expel me from Holland...handed me back my passport...handed me back my *hash*...and inexplicably said, "Be more careful next time." And that was that. They walked away.

My life popped out of the toilet and landed back in leafy, sunny Vondel Park. I looked at my acquaintance, who was as stunned as I was. We couldn't believe our luck. We looked around. The cops were gone. Everything was really okay. We laughed like maniacs and decided we should see Commander Cody and His Lost Planet Airmen at Paradiso to celebrate. We lined up for the show where several patrons generously shared their smoky wares. By the time we were inside watching guitarist Bill Kirchen rip through "Hot Rod Lincoln," I was on a memorable, deliriously happy musical ride. Now twelve years later in 1985, I was not only back at Paradiso, I was performing at the legendary club's grand reopening.

(Editor's note: Finally! A drug story in this alleged "rock memoir." That's one lame sex story, an okay drug story, and 300 pages of Rock 'n' Roll.)

The Don Dixon Band (a utilitarian name Dixon would never use in the States, and which we always pronounced in the local accent), was riding a good groove by that point in the tour. All the crucial details, like harmonies, syncopations, and solos, had been nailed down, and we were *performing* the songs, not just remembering how they went. At the end of our two-hour show, the SRO crowd would not let us leave. We went back out for one, two, three, four, five encores, and the Amsterdammers still demanded a sixth. I'll never forget Don, Rod, Terry, and me catching our breath backstage, soaked in sweat, and laughing our asses off at the absurdity of the crowd's desire. Terry said, "Dixon! What the hell are we gonna play? We've already done everything we know plus everything we don't know." Dixon laughed and said, "Fuck it.

Let's do Mustang Sally!" Out we went for encore number six. Wilson Pickett had the last laugh in Amsterdam.

I was grateful to Dixon for bringing me to Europe. From my perch as sideman, I watched how he treated his audience, the label reps, journalists, sound crew, van drivers, and fans equally well. People liked working with him (including me) and everyone enjoyed Dixon's company. He was the star of the tour, but he wasn't at all pretentious or impressed with himself. That seemed like a good way to go.

WHAT'S THAT?

Back in New York, nothing changed in my Stanton Street apartment until I answered a long-awaited call from Michael Solomon. Michael said, "Sorry it's taken so long to get back to you, but I think you'll be happy to hear what I have to say. How would you feel about a publishing deal?"

I remember my response clearly. "What's that?" I thought guys like me were only interested in record deals.

Michael said, "Well, it's not a record deal, but it could be a really good thing for you. The company is MCA Music Publishing. I have a good friend there named Rick Shoemaker. He's the VP. I snuck into his office and put your tape on his desk where he couldn't miss it. A few days later he called me and said, 'Who the hell is Parthenon Huxley? I love these songs!'" Funny how much I already liked Rick Shoemaker. I also loved that Solomon snuck into his office on my behalf.

As Solomon spoke to me from Los Angeles, I gazed through one of the two windows of our Lower East Side apartment. Our view was of a sunless, mossy, trash-strewn, inner courtyard where humans never tread. I imagined Solomon in sunny LA. A good feeling was starting to buzz up my spine. Michael went on, "It would be a co-publishing deal, which means you'd split the ownership of your songs with MCA while retaining 100 percent of your writer share. In return, you'd get a monthly advance and access to MCA's recording studio here in LA where you can record whenever you want."

Jesus.

"Also, if you sign with MCA, they will help you get a record deal. They know everyone at the labels and, with MCA behind you, it would make a big difference."

This was getting very exciting.

Finally, Michael said, "If we pursue this, it also means that I'll be your manager. We hadn't really talked about that in any detail, I realize, but that's what I'd like to happen."

"Okay. Be my manager."

Michael laughed. "Alright! I will!"

Solomon had pulled off a miracle. His call couldn't have been more exciting. I felt like all the work I'd put into my demos had begun to build something after all.

I spoke with Michael again a few days later. Rick Shoemaker, along with MCA's VP of Film and TV, Scott James, were coming to New York. Michael said they wanted to meet with me and hang out, go to dinner, and get to know me. "I think you'll like Rick and I think he'll like you. Just be yourself and have a good time. Make a good impression."

My look in the '80s: shoulder-length hair on the right side of my head, short hair on the left. Chuck Taylor high tops, one black, one turquoise. Skinny black jeans (trend setter) and button-up dress shirts offset by turquoise suspenders (New Romantic nerd). I was a vision. Clearly, I'd have to impress Rick Shoemaker with something other than my look.

Rick and Scott took me out to dinner at a West Village restaurant I'd recommended called The Black Sheep (I could never have afforded it on my own). Shoemaker was an engaging guy with an in-the-know West Coast vibe, a salt-and-pepper beard, and a bit of playful mischief behind his bright eyes. He easily moved between friend mode and business mode. Scott James, MCA's film and television head, must've been in his thirties, but looked like a high school senior. He smiled and laughed easily and couldn't have acted less like a hard-ass music executive. The three of us chatted like pals and enjoyed a delicious, expensive dinner, courtesy of Rick's MCA American Express card—my first "industry meal." I thought, "This is way better than an A&R meeting."

We then piled into a chauffeured black town car and headed to a downtown club. Rick, perhaps emboldened by the wine from dinner, began singing silly lyrics to Beatles songs: "Heyyy Duuuude...don't make it rad..." Scott gamely gave it a try and we were all laughing. Then Rick put on his best Thurston Howell III impression and swaggeringly intoned, "Your turn, if you please, Mr. Huxley..." Without missing a beat, I sang to the tune of "Eleanor Rigby": "Parthenon Huxley/rides in a car with his buddies from M C A...they came from LA-ay..." Rick's eyes lit up and he shouted, "I LOVE this guy!"

And that's how you secure a publishing deal.

After my evening with Rick and Scott, I visited MCA's New York office and met with VP Danny Strick. I wasn't sure what made Strick tick, but we bonded on an artist from the late '60s named Emmitt Rhodes and, from then on, hit it off fine. Strick sent a positive report to Shoemaker in LA.

Michael Solomon called me soon after and announced that a deal with MCA had been drawn up. He arranged for me to meet with a music biz attorney named Evan Medow. I found him in the towering, marble-columned lobby of Evan's hotel in Manhattan, and we sat together at a small table. Evan sported a monk's sidecar of brown hair around his balding pate. His slightly cock-eyed expression made it appear he was always thinking of a joke. Maybe he was. I liked him.

Evan arranged a stack of paper on the table and ceremoniously placed a pen on top. My contract. He chuckled and said, "You ready to do this?" I looked at the document. Atop page one were the words "Music Corporation of America." Wow. I thought, "It doesn't get any less indie than that." Evan walked me through some of the provisions. He said, "The first year, you'll get an advance of $10,000. If things work out and they keep you around, it goes up to $15,000 in year two, $20,000 in year three, $30,000 in year four, and so on. There are also bonuses. If you sign a record deal with a major label, MCA will pay you a bonus of $5,000. If your major label record then gets released, there's another bonus of $10,000. Sound good?"

I said, "Yeah. I think so." Trying to appear knowledgeable, I asked, "This isn't a big publishing deal, is it?"

Evan smiled and shrugged. "There are bigger deals, sure. But—is anyone else paying you $10,000 to write songs this year?"

I reached for the pen.

A year earlier in Chapel Hill, Don Dixon had warned me that even if the major labels knew you were out there, it could still take years to land a record deal. With MCA as my partner, I felt I'd moved to a much better seat in the waiting room. Signing with a major seemed less like an elusive dream and more like an inevitability thanks to Solomon and Shoemaker's stunning belief in my talent. My career was suddenly more alive than ever, and I would be paid for doing the thing I loved most. How crazy was that?

A FORK

Beckoning me to LA was my new champion Rick Shoemaker, a sixteen-track recording studio in MCA's basement, and my manager, Michael Solomon. I was headed West. Stashe chose to stay in New York. I wasn't surprised. She and her apprentice Robert were working away on design projects that were pouring in now that New York vendors knew Stashe was back for good. It made sense for her to be where the work was. I was in the same boat, but my dock was on the other coast. About Robert, Stashe said, "I think he needs me." I interpreted that to mean she'd essentially moved on to her next reclamation project.

As friends and business partners, Stashe and I had been great for each other. Our roles as husband and wife were trickier. Our marriage was stuck in neutral at best. We'd grown less close but stayed cordial, choosing to avoid any unpleasantness about our living situation. I respected Stashe and appreciated all she'd done for me, but for months I'd felt like a stranger in my own home. I wasn't happy. Worse, I was lonely. I'd even struck up a platonic relationship (I told myself) with a pretty East European friend of a friend. We'd gone out for drinks a few times. One night we were listening to a band in a typically tiny New York club. I was enjoying myself and looked around the room, checking out the audience. With a jolt I spotted Stashe and Robert seated at a table. Stashe caught my eye and raised her drink to me. I raised mine back. That was the extent of our communication that night. No questions, no funny looks. No nothing. Neutral.

It was odd, no doubt. Surely not how married people behaved. But no matter how strained things became around that time in New York, Stashe and I had forged a deep connection. In a few short years, we'd changed each other's lives. I knew that, at the very least, we would always cheer each other on. That was our way of loving one another. We wanted the best for us both. (We still do.) But. Part of me also felt confused and sad as hell. Before I left, Stashe and I rented a storage unit. What I wasn't taking to LA, I stuffed into cardboard boxes and stacked up in a cage somewhere in Queens. I wasn't completely gone.

I LOVE LA

As odd as things felt in New York, I was excited to move to California. I would arrive with a paying job waiting for me, and not just any job. I would be an Artist/Staff Songwriter at Music Corporation of America. Work and music had officially become the same thing. Twains did meet. Music had always been my personal and private domain. For at least the next year, my songs would be judged by my employers and half-owned by a corporation. Could I do it?

In advance of my move, I wrote down a short list of personal directives:

1. The world owes you nothing.

2. Do not panic.
4. Express your genius through your work.
3. You are not a slave.
5. Be polite.

Mark Twain is said to be the source of #1. The full quote is "The world owes you nothing. It was here first." I've always agreed with that, and probably wrote it down to remind myself that signing with MCA didn't mean squat unless I worked hard, wrote great songs, and earned my place in the business. #2 is the antidote to #1. I have no idea why #4 came next, but its message is my motto. If your work makes you look like a genius, it relieves you of having to *tell* people you're a genius. #3, this odd note about not being a slave, was a reminder that signing with MCA didn't bind me to doing work I might not believe in. Look at me—taking a stance against the overlords at my new job before I even started. #5 is a nod to my upbringing, an echo of my dad's advice to me before my first day in fifth grade in Athens. I felt like Los Angeles was something of a loose sin city, a place without typical social restraints or norms. It seemed like a good idea to hang on to one's civility if possible. Was I a wild man or what?

My flight from Newark reached the eastern edge of Southern California at night. I peered out my window. The city below shimmered with millions of gold and white lights, unending except where dark mountain ranges rose too high for civilization to climb. For some reason, I took comfort from seeing baseball fields, clustered together like green four-leaf clovers. Maybe they reassured me that not everything in my life was new and foreign. I straightened the back of my seat and tightened my seat belt, ready to land. An hour later, it dawned on me that I was still waiting to land. I thought, "Holy shit this place is big."

Michael Solomon lived in a charming, but tiny, Venice Beach bungalow. He had me crash on a spare futon for a week until I found a bigger sofa at the home of Solomon's client, and Head For Tall Trees producer, Mark Goldenberg. Mark and his wife, Jennifer Condos, lived in the Valley, just south of Ventura Boulevard in Van Nuys. If you've seen Tom Petty's video for "Free Fallin'" with the Cadillac dealership and the hot dog stand, that's the neighborhood. Like Mark, Jen Condos was a working musician, a skilled bass player, whose career would include stints with Don Henley, Stevie Nicks, Ray LaMontagne, and many others. They were incredibly kind to let me crash at their place while I looked for a landing spot of my own.

Chapter 10: Guy in Band

One day, I was alone in their house and the phone rang. I picked up. A voice said, "Hi. Is Mark there?"

"I'm sorry, he's not. Can I take a message?"

"Yes, tell him Eddie Kramer called, please."

"Sure. Can I tell him what it's about?"

"Yeah, tell him I want to talk to him about an artist I'm producing."

"Oh, okay," I said. "So, you're a producer? Cool. Anything I've heard of?"

Eddie Kramer said, "Yeah, I've made a few records."

The above is so painful to write. I truly wonder about me sometimes. The only excuse I have is that, when I was growing up and looking at credits on album covers, I was always more interested in the musicians than the engineers or producers. Had I paid attention to producer credits, perhaps I would've noticed Eddie Kramer's name on Jimi Hendrix *Are You Experienced*, Jimi Hendrix *Axis: Bold As Love*, Led Zeppelin II, Led Zeppelin *Houses of the Holy*...you know, "a few records." Not that a phone call would've led me to become pals with Eddie Kramer, but, Christ, it would've been nice to acknowledge the years of listening pleasure he'd given me. Thank you, Eddie.

I loved discovering Los Angeles. There was a lot to take in: perfect weather, impressive mountain ranges, beaches, endless places to eat, tons of talented and fun-loving musicians. More so than anywhere I'd ever been, Los Angeles pulsed with a palpable current that intimated possibilities and opportunities. It felt like everyone I met was plugged into the business. "She's a backup vocalist for Madonna." "He plays guitar with Linda Ronstadt." "She sings with Stevie Wonder." "He's worked with Michael Jackson." If I was gonna live in a company town, LA was a great choice. Industry gossip and juicy stories about stars, important business players, record labels, and so on were the coin of the realm. I was a business-naive newcomer, but I felt like I'd pulled my chair up to an endlessly exciting table.

GUY IN BAND

Hollywood threw me some low-hanging fruit. Like a cliché in a bad movie, I was the new guy in town who immediately lands TV and movie roles without even trying. A fellow MCA staffer named Tena Clark was Musical Director for *Throb*, a TV situation comedy set at a record label. Tena thought my "look" would work well for an upcoming episode. I made my first trip to a television lot, not far from Gower Gulch, the site of Hollywood's earliest film studio. The guard at the gate found my name on his clipboard and waved me through security. I felt like I was "somebody." Tena kindly met me at my car and guided me down wide lanes that ran between tan buildings the size of airplane hangars. The lot hummed with activity, and I noticed how all the workers looked like my artist friends from Chapel Hill: painters and carpenters in spattered jeans and work boots. It dawned on me that LA was a city where artists had jobs doing what they loved. I felt right at home.

Tena took me to the set, where I was introduced to a group of guys my age with leather jackets, mounds of hair, and skinny legs in black jeans. Got it. We'd be playing a band. I volunteered for the role of "drummer." I know. I was really stretching my acting chops. We didn't mingle with the real actors like Jane Leeves, who would one day upgrade to *Frasier*. Until it was time for our scene, we stood on the periphery and watched the pros work. It was fascinating to observe a talented cast, a focused director, and a no-nonsense crew working so diligently and professionally on a show that was so corny. I was reminded of a phrase attributed to Martin Mull: "Hollywood is like high school with money." *Throb* wasn't much better than a show you'd catch in a high school gymnasium, but I would get paid real money for my two minutes of drumming. I thanked Tena for bringing me on. She said I'd done great, and in fact, *Throb* brought me back a few weeks later for another episode where I played "guy in band." And that's how typecasting begins.

BUT THE BEST WAS...

One evening early in my new life in LA, I stopped by a bar on Sunset Boulevard. Two women sang and played acoustic guitars on a small stage, ignored by half of the small audience. Too bad, because one of them had a sensational voice, full of character with a huge range. I greedily thought she might be interested in singing on my demos at MCA. When her set was finished, I introduced myself and praised her voice profusely. She had straight blonde hair with bangs, pink lipstick, and bright, striking eyes.

"Oh! That's nice of you to say," she said, acting surprised someone noticed. "We're just up there having fun. What's your name?"

"I'm Parthenon."

"Woah." She laughed, taking a step back. "That's quite a name there, Parthenon. Parthenon what?"

"Huxley."

"Even better. Well, I'm just Robin."

"What's your last name, Robin?"

"Lane," she said.

I froze. "You're *just* Robin Lane? Oh, Jesus. Really?"

She laughed. "Why do you say that, Parthenon?"

"You're Robin Lane for Christ sakes. I saw you play at the Pier in Raleigh, North Carolina. I wrote a review of your show."

"I hope you wrote nice things," just Robin Lane said, still laughing her easy laugh.

"I did."

I marveled that LA was the kind of town where you could hear Warner Brothers recording artist Robin Lane singing at a random noisy bar on a Tuesday night—the same Robin Lane who sang with Neil Young on "Round And Round" from his album *Everybody Knows This Is Nowhere*. It was the kind of wacky town where Robin and I would become great friends, she would sing on my demos at MCA, and she'd take me backstage after a U2 concert where I would play a game of pool with The Edge.

HARMONY SANDWICH

Michael Solomon's client, Karla Bonoff, was selected to showcase two of her songs at an annual concert thrown by the National Academy of Songwriters. The show would take place at the prestigious Wiltern Theater, and Michael asked if I would play guitar and sing backup for Karla, alongside Karla's good friend Linda Ronstadt. Yes, please.

Rehearsals took me to a classic '70s recording complex, Alley Studios, in the Valley on Lankershim Boulevard. Off a dark hallway, I found a large room with a dozen musicians breaking down their gear, about to vacate so the next rehearsal could begin. I entered, and a tall man in a loose button-down shirt extended his hand toward me as he headed out. We shook. "Hi! I'm Brian," said Brian Wilson. "Hi, Brian, I'm Parthenon Huxley." "Nice to meet you, Huxley," and out the door he went.

Well, that was delightfully weird, I thought. I just shook hands with one of the greatest songwriters in rock history. Why would he shake hands with me? Years later, I learned our interaction had come during a particular phase of Brian's treatment by the infamous Dr. Eugene Landy. Landy had encouraged Wilson to introduce himself to people as an exercise in social normalcy. Reportedly, and I hope this story is apocryphal, he once introduced himself to a woman backstage at a concert, saying as instructed, "Hi. I'm Brian." The woman's response was, "I know, Dad."

Karla arrived and introduced me to her friend Linda. Normal, right? We ran through the songs with a back-up band, and all went well. Afterwards, the three of us found a small room upstairs in the Alley Studios complex and rehearsed our vocal parts. Tucking my voice into a Bonoff/Ronstadt harmony sandwich was this singer's nirvana, and when Linda said, "Hey, that sounds really good, guys!" I felt like I'd joined a special club.

Our short performance at the Wiltern went by in a blur, but I did my professional best to act as if Linda and I sang together all the time. Bonoff was great to work with, and the whole experience was made easier by Ronstadt, who, beyond owning that spectacular voice, was easygoing and likably goofy. Waiting to go on, we had a fun talk about raising kids, even though neither of us were parents and Linda had never married. "I'll definitely home school my kids if I ever have any." (She adopted a girl and a boy just a few years later. Not sure about their schooling.)

After the show, there ensued the usual high-spirited hubbub backstage where performers, buzzed on adrenaline and relief, were on their best behavior. In a room loaded with songwriters, I was introduced to Chicago's smartly dressed and young-looking Robert Lamm, composer of "Saturday in the Park," "Does Anybody Really Know What Time It Is," "25 or 6 to 4," and more. Robert and I got into a nice long chat, and when it came time to empty the theater, Michael offered to send Lamm a cassette of my music. Robert was kind enough to act interested. I never expected to hear from him.

IS THIS YOUR FIRST TIME?

As long as friends didn't mind me on their couch, I was happy to live out of a suitcase. I enjoyed being unburdened of household stuff. My only big purchase was a perfectly preserved cactus-green 1966 Dodge Coronet, with black bench seats and a V-8 engine. I was mobile, and free to go anywhere and do anything I wanted. I didn't need an office to write songs, which I did in my head all day anyway. I had a thousand dollars in my bank account, and it felt like a million.

One of the first persons I looked up in LA was a friend from North Carolina who'd worked at Record Bar. Carla Lockhart, a classic native Californian with a zest for fun, welcomed me to town and offered her place on 6th Street as yet another temporary crash pad. The first night we got together, she generously handed me tickets to see a show at the Palace Theater in Hollywood. I'd never heard of "Chris Isaak," but he turned out to be pretty good. In LA, that's just a Tuesday night.

Carla introduced me to her friend Virginia Lee Hunter. A photographer, Lee wound up creating a cool headshot for me, featuring a unique foreground of wooden figurines casting shadows. It's still posted on my Allmusic entry all these years later.

Chapter 10: Guy in Band

I was walking with Lee to her bungalow one day when she spotted her neighbor leaning out of an upstairs window. Lee shouted, "Tom, this is my friend Parthenon. He's managed by Michael Solomon." Tom Waits shouted back, "Nice to meet you, Parthenon. Tell Solomon I said 'hey.'" I quickly learned that LA's unwritten code said *stars have to live somewhere, so don't act surprised when you see one.* I still got a huge kick out of being introduced to Tom Waits.

Carla Lockhart also introduced me to her friend Shalini Waran. Shalini was a diminutive, fearless, chatty firecracker from England who worked for a film director named Roger Donaldson. She was outspoken, the life of the party, and when she told me she'd been one of the screaming teenaged girls in *A Hard Day's Night*, I was in awe. Shalini was working on a movie called *No Way Out*, starring an up-and-coming actor named Kevin Costner. One night, as she was leaving a party at Carla's house, she handed me a key to her apartment. In her London drawl, she said, "I like you, Parthenon. You can't stay on Carla's couch forever, so here's a key to my apartment in the Valley." I started to protest. Shalini went on, "Oh, shut-tup already. I have a spare bedroom that's just sitting there. You can use it as long as you like, rent-free. I don't need the money. I assume I'll see you soon. Goodnight." Shalini pivoted flamboyantly and left. Her apartment was a mile from MCA. I accepted her incredibly kind gesture and lived in that spare bedroom for six months.

One morning, early in my stay at Shalini's, I was startled awake and found the entire apartment shaking violently. It didn't seem logical that a giant garbage truck would idle in the courtyard outside my window. I then realized: earthquake! I had slept naked, so in a panic I wrapped a sheet around me and ran out of my room shouting, "Where do we go? Where do we go?" I'd read something about getting under a doorway. I opened the front door and saw all our neighbors running out into the courtyard. I was in a sheet, so I hesitated. I then saw Shalini sauntering out of her bedroom like she hadn't a care in the world. "Oh, for God's sake, relax, Parthenon. It'll be over in a few seconds." As reassuring as that sounded, I found it hard to relax when the entire world was moving in violent rhythms like a thrill ride. I stood in the doorway as the quake continued for twenty more terrifying seconds and yelled, "Holy shit, this is insane!" Shalini stood with me in the door, calmly lighting a cigarette. "Oh, is this your first time?"

CHAPTER 11

WEIRDEST A&R MEETING EVER

My boss Rick Shoemaker wanted MCA Music Publishing to feel like the Brill Building, New York's legendary song factory from the '50s and '60s. Shoemaker told me, "Our offices are up on the fourth floor. We'll never go down to the studio unless we're invited. We want you guys to do your thing, make magic, and when you're ready for us to listen, bring a mix upstairs so we can hear it." MCA's sixteen-track 2" tape recording studio, a fully outfitted audio playground available to all staff writers and artists, hid behind two black metal doors in the parking garage's elevator lobby. It would become my new home. I couldn't have landed at a more supportive place.

I developed working relationships with MCA's audio engineers. In addition to staff engineer Mike "Fen Man" Fenell, guys like Barry Rudolph, Mikal Reid, Ernie Sheesley, Ryan Greene, and others were pro engineers who moonlighted at MCA, bringing years of experience and expertise to what was technically a demo studio. I quickly learned to trust their ears. During an early session, blond, easy-going, coulda-been-a-surfer Ernie Sheesley told me, "You're a little flat on the second line of the first verse, so let's punch that in, okay?"

I said, "Uhh, are you sure, Ernie? It felt pretty good. Can we hear it back?"

"Yup. Coming up now."

I listened intently. The second line was indeed flat, not up to the correct pitch. I'd been schooled, kindly and patiently.

"Well, whatd'ya know. It's flat. Okay, let's do it again."

When I began working at MCA, I was already thirty-one years old and a reasonably accomplished guitarist, singer, and songwriter. I'd been at it for twenty years. My studio work, however, had been limited. The Blazers album, the Ruse EP, "Buddha, Buddha," "Sputnik," and my major label demos were my only pro recordings. Thanks to MCA's engineers and the LA musicians who played on my new songs, my studio chops quickly improved.

For instance, a common guitar-player problem is a tendency to "rush," meaning we hit the strings just slightly ahead of the beat, thinking we're adding excitement or energy. In fact, rushing makes a recording sound disjointed. The groove goes away. A skilled listener can hear when this happens, even for a moment or two. I got used to MCA's engineers telling me to "lay back," "pull back," or "sit back" with my guitar parts. Okay, so how does a guitarist learn to lay back? Next time you see a live band, note how the guitarist (or bassist) will often steal looks in the drummer's direction. They're not seeking eye contact—they're watching for the exact moment when the drummer's stick hits the snare. The guitarist will make sure he's hitting his strings precisely in time, with the drummer's snare, and not a millisecond sooner.

The same process applies to recording. I had to learn how to really listen as I played my parts, to match my right hand (the one with the pick) to the tempo set by the drummer. Few things will drag a recording session down faster than a musician who doesn't play in time. I got better quickly.

Studio shifts at MCA were strictly eight hours. We writers were expected to arrive on time and depart on time. That said, we all recognized that if a mix was in progress at the end of a preceding session, courtesy demanded that the next group wait out by the coffee machine until the mix was done. Only then could you start hurling good-natured insults at the time-hogging, grossly inconsiderate, holier-than-thou, self-important, delusional hot shot who thought his session was so much more important than everyone else's and so on. Standard musician abuse.

The nice thing about a preceding shift running long was that it gave me a chance to hear other writers' songs and watch them work, if only for a few minutes. Two of the better known MCA writers were Glen Ballard (Alanis Morissette, Michael Jackson) and Robbie Nevil (his single "C'est La Vie" reached Billboard #2). Robbie was a talented guitarist and singer, and Glen was known as the hardest-working writer of us all, an obsessive who would've been in the studio all day every day if allowed.

Most of MCA's writers labored in a pop R&B direction, so I was a bit of an outlier in the writer/artist department. Whenever I visited the fourth floor, nearly all the music blaring out of the offices of creative directors was saturated with bell-like Yamaha DX-7 pianos, chorused Stratocaster guitars, drum machines, and over-the-top singing: classic '80s pop R&B. I knew that stuff was hot, and a smarter writer might've tried to get in on the action, but I just couldn't relate. I didn't hear that kind of music in my head. I was a guitar-based, '60s and '70s band-guy type of songwriter. That was my True North and I've had to live and die by it my whole professional life.

Fortunately, I had Rick Shoemaker's ear, and his confidence in me meant everything. Whenever I'd walk into his office at MCA, Rick would shout, "P-Man! Buddy! How's my favorite writer?" (Every writer was Rick's favorite writer.) He just wanted to hear that I was happy with my situation and that I was making magic downstairs. He was also praying I'd write some hits and justify his signing me.

One of the first songs I recorded, with co-production help from fellow staff writer Tommy Faragher, was "Double Our Numbers," a song from my Rick Rock days that I thought was one of my best. Another was "Chance To Be Loved." "Chance" started out in my head as kind of a breezy Smokey Robinson number (not my forte), but I ended up producing it like an epic Beach Boys mini symphony. Both songs were on point, lyrically, following my "Buddha, Buddha" model of singing about love in as many new and different ways as possible.

MCA and Solomon began taking my stuff around town to the record labels. Their pitch was, "We believe in this guy and have already signed his publishing. We want to partner with a label and, together, take it all the way." At a meeting with Columbia, an A&R man named Jamie Cohen noticed "Button" on my demo tape. He asked, "Isn't 'Button' a song by Rick Rock? Is Rick Rock now Parthenon Huxley? I'm intrigued!"

Jamie Cohen was a cigarette-thin, fashionably bespectacled, hyper, animated guy who spoke in his own kind of jazz lingo. He'd grown up in Cleveland, the son of a record distributor, destined to be in the business. Jamie became my champion at Columbia. We met in his office in West LA just to hang out and get to know each other. It turned out he'd heard about me while scouting a band in Chapel Hill. Jamie talked quickly and jumped from subject to subject a lot. He asked me, "Do you like the Smiths?"

"They're okay," I said, although I hadn't heard a lot of their stuff.

Jamie asked, "Have you heard 'Girlfriend In A Coma'?" and put the record on, loud. I was impressed that Cohen was a record exec who loved cool music and who'd guessed correctly that I would appreciate a song as melodically sweet and lyrically macabre as "Coma." It may've been the best A&R meeting I'd ever had.

Hoping to build momentum at Columbia, Solomon and MCA got my tape to Staff Producer David Kahne. Kahne had produced one of 1987's biggest albums, *A Different Light* by the Bangles. The record had gone triple platinum, riding the success of singles like "Manic Monday" and "Walk Like an Egyptian." It would be good to get somebody like Kahne on our side.

PICTURE A SPHERE

When I wasn't crashing on couches or in spare bedrooms in LA, I was returning to New York to check in on Stashe and grab more of my belongings from our storage space. During one of my trips to New York, Michael Solomon called and excitedly informed me that David Kahne wanted to meet with me. Since I wasn't officially living anywhere, Columbia agreed to put me up at the Hollywood Roosevelt Hotel for a couple days. I flew back to LA and checked into a brightly colored room close by the sunlit pool. A perfect setting for a big LA moment. Major label, here I come.

As arranged, Kahne arrived at the Roosevelt so we could get acquainted and discuss recording for Columbia. Kahne did not look like your typical record company producer. His brown hair was neatly cut short, he wore plain blue jeans, a blue button-down shirt, and sensible shoes. For an LA-based guy, he was pristinely free of typical rock 'n' roll trappings like tats and long hair. Kahne's plain wrapper exterior was the perfect front for what I'd soon learn was a complex, imaginative mind. Kahne sat by a small table, I sat on the edge of my bed. Outside my room, young revelers were drinking beer and laughing by the hotel pool, enjoying a Hollywood weekday afternoon. It was 70 degrees in January. This is so rock 'n' roll, I thought.

"So," Kahne began, "Columbia Records."

"Columbia Records," I echoed back. I smiled a little nervously. He was probably about to tell me the amazing history of the label and its genre-shattering artists like Bob Dylan, Bruce Springsteen, Billy Holiday, and on and on. This was going to be fun.

Kahne said, "I'd like you to picture a sphere."

"Okay," I said.

"On the outside of the sphere," Kahne continued, shaping a globe with his hands, "you can see Bruce and Barbara." He looked at me.

"Springsteen and Streisand…?" I guessed.

"That's right. Now, on the inside of the sphere, there's nothing but a bottomless black hole."

I thought, "That's a weird thing to say about the label you work for." I waited a beat. Then another. Kahne didn't speak. He just looked at me. Apparently, David Kahne had just wrapped up his amazing pitch for Columbia Records. The inside of my head felt kind of muddy. Why did this highly anticipated meeting about my future with Columbia Records suddenly curl up on the faux shag carpet and die? What exactly was Kahne doing here? After an agonizingly awkward twenty seconds, I took a stab at a response to his black hole scenario. "David, are you saying I shouldn't sign with Columbia?"

Kahne smiled. "I'm not saying that."

I thought, "Ok. Good. I mean, I think it's good. Hard to tell." He sure wasn't sugarcoating anything or overloading me with info. I exhaled. I then simply decided that whatever Kahne was warning me about, however scary a picture he was painting of Columbia Records, the opposite reality—not being on a major label—was, in my mind, at age thirty-one, worse than his bottomless black hole. I wanted to be on a major. Maybe it was sentimental or pie-eyed, but that was the dream. I wanted to be on a real record label, one that meant something to me when I was growing up. Reprise meant Jimi Hendrix, the Kinks, and Neil Young. Capitol meant the Beatles, Raspberries, and Grand Funk. Island had Free and Bob Marley. Atlantic was Led Zeppelin and Buffalo Springfield. Columbia meant Springsteen, Dylan, Chicago and Santana.

I said, "I still wanna do it."

David clapped his hands and said, "Great!" He laughed a little laugh, like this meeting had been fun. I just shook my head. (Kahne is fond of Eastern philosophy. I imagine his "sphere" analogy may've been his attempt to reduce Columbia to its simplest form. He did pretty well.)

Kahne told me we'd start by recording two songs for $5,000. (Sigh, another demo deal....) Then he added, with a touch of inevitability, "If it goes well, which I think it will, we'll make it official and do a full deal." We shook on that, and he left. Move over Lionel Conway at Island and John Mrvos at EMI, who had granted me those earlier audiences. I had a new champion for the weirdest A&R meeting ever.

Kahne and I got to work on two songs in accordance with the demo deal, or should I say, I got to work and took the demos to Kahne for his feedback. One, a song called "Love For Nothing," which I'd co-written with an MCA writer named Brock Walsh, turned into a proving ground for me and Kahne. Upon first listen in his office at Columbia's West LA headquarters, Kahne was dissatisfied with the "lift" of the chorus. He'd hold his hands palms up, waist high, and rise on his toes to, I think, demonstrate what he meant by "lift." "I just wish it would lift more when the chorus hits. What if you tried a different sequence of chords at the end of the pre-chorus?"

"I can try something...", I said.

"Okay!" Kahne replied, smiling. "Great."

I dutifully spent the next few days working on the pre-chorus, looking for something that might give the chorus more lift. Personally, I thought the existing chord sequence was the perfect lift into the chorus, but I was willing to experiment. I made a change, thought it was okay, and brought the song back to Kahne.

He said, "I see what you did and why you thought it might work, but it still doesn't do what I'm looking for. Can you maybe try something else?"

I was dying a bit inside, but Kahne was the producer of Billboard's Song of the Year ("Walk Like An Egyptian"), so what did I know?

"Sure."

"Great!" Again, the Kahne smile of appreciation. I liked David Kahne, but I wasn't sure why.

I produced three iterations of "Love For Nothing." After Kahne listened to my third attempt at a better "lift," he ejected the cassette out of the player behind his desk and walked over to a different stack of cassettes. He grabbed my original demo, popped it in the cassette player, and listened. The pre-chorus lifted quite nicely into the chorus.

Kahne looked at me. "It sounds best the original way, doesn't it?"

"I always thought so," I said.

"Yeah, I guess you did," Kahne said with his customary chuckle.

And that signaled the end of our "lift" search. I still don't know if Kahne really believed there was a better way to get to the chorus, or if he'd just been testing my patience to see how we'd work together. Either way, I felt like we ended up respecting each other. We were each willing to bend. Win, win.

NOBODY KNOWS WHO I AM

Next door to Shalini's apartment complex on Moorpark Drive in the Valley was a park with a basketball court. I'd made it a habit to get some exercise each day by shooting baskets. One day MCA VP and Laker fan Betsy Anthony joined me for a shootaround during her lunch hour. As we hoisted shots and pretended to be James Worthy, I suddenly spotted Michael Solomon and my former couch provider/current bass player Jen Condos walking under shade trees toward us on the court. Michael and Jen were fully dressed for business. I didn't think they were coming for a game of two on two.

Michael, smiling broadly, walked onto the court and shook my hand. He said, "Congratulations. You got the deal. You're a Columbia recording artist."

Wow! It had happened.

Solomon said, "I just spoke with Kahne. He's very happy. He thinks you guys will work great together."

"Congratulations, P-Man!" Betsy said, smiling brightly and using my unofficial MCA moniker. Jen gave me a hug.

Solomon said, "This deserves a celebration. How about I call Shoemaker and a few other people and organize a dinner for this weekend?" Sounded good to me. We chatted for a few minutes and then Jen and Michael left, and Betsy went back to work. It had been thoughtful and sweet of them to find me and give me the good news in person.

I went back to shooting hoops with a lightness in my step and a little more air under my free throws. I'd made it! I'd reached the top of the hill. A major label deal was officially mine and it was with Columbia Records, arguably the leading record label in the world. I imagined my name on the charts, my songs on the radio, my face in magazines, my words in quotes. This was fun, and it was really happening. Bruce, Barbara...and Parthenon Huxley, right? I couldn't wait to share the life-changing news with friends and family.

I called Godfrey Cheshire at the *Spectator*. "I'm clear to write again, Godfrey." Godfrey laughed, "Well, well! Does that mean you're signed? Congratulations! Do you want to write a story about it?" I did. *Spectator* called my feature story "Fast Break in LA/Tar Heel Rocker Scores at CBS." Basketball metaphors go down easy in North Carolina.

A week after signing with Columbia Records, I awoke one morning and, excited by my incredible good fortune, began playing out fantasies like performing on *Letterman*. Suddenly I thought, "Nobody knows who I am." My fantasies stopped, replaced by hard realizations. I had no band. I wasn't pulling hundreds of fans into clubs across the country. I had no history of radio play outside of North Carolina. I wasn't the son of a famous person. I had no relatives in the music industry who might nudge me up the ladder. I was no one, and yet I was making a record for CBS? Suddenly, it didn't add up. All I had were my songs—thank God I was confident they were good. I thought they carried some weight in the big-spiritual-picture department while still being catchy and singable. "Chance To Be Loved" was an anthem to Love, "Double Our Numbers" was a three-verse mini novella about Love, and even "Saving the Planets," a song that referenced an arcane book about the nature of reality ("The Seth Material") had a sing-along chorus. It seemed like my only chance for success was dependent on making a kickass album. Fortunately, I knew I could do it.

DIGITAL?

David Kahne explained his production plan for my record. He felt it would be a waste of time to re-record the stuff I'd done at MCA. "Your demos are really more like masters. They're well recorded, and we should keep what you have. What I want to do is transfer your sixteen-track demo/masters from analog tape to a thirty-two-track Sony digital recorder. That'll give us sixteen more tracks to add overdubs."

I didn't know what Kahne meant by a digital recorder. He said, "It's a new kind of recorder that doesn't use magnetic tape, so you can't wear the tape out." Oh. Okay. I still didn't know what digital meant (it was 1987).

Kahne added, "Our budget is $70,000. By using your MCA recordings instead of starting from scratch, the album will be a lot cheaper to make. I think we can do it for fifty grand. I'd like you to pocket $20,000 off the top if possible." Sold. That was very thoughtful of David. Maybe he wanted me to have some spending money if I plummeted into the bottomless black hole.

Kahne and I chose ten songs. Six were carryovers from Chapel Hill and New York and four were newly written in LA. My Columbia album, which I called *Sunny Nights*, would be a "best of" my recent past.

Whenever David Kahne needed guitar on a session, he called Rusty Anderson. Rusty was a friendly, long-haired dude with an easy smile and a blistering style of guitar playing that had turned heads in Southern California since Rusty began playing in bands as a teenager. I met him at a session he was doing with Kahne for an artist called Natalie Archangel. Rusty put down some relatively simple, straightforward parts as requested by Kahne, but in between takes, like most guitarists, he fiddled with his effects pedals and fired off random riffs to check his sound. My ears went on alert. Rusty's throwaway stuff was better than most players' greatest riffs. The guy had a beautiful, distorted tone and huge Rachmaninoff hands that seemed capable of playing anything. I thought, "I gotta get this guy in my band."

With Kahne co-producing *Sunny Nights*, it was inevitable Rusty would be brought in to play on my album. Conveniently, I'd written a new song called "Guest Host For The Holy Ghost," which was a perfect vehicle for Rusty's slash-and-burn style. Along with Jen Condos on bass and Rob Ladd (from Me & Dixon, visiting LA) on drums, we ran through the arrangement at MCA a few times and then captured "Guest Host" in one take, a beautiful piece of live recording. Rusty's aggressive, exciting performance perfectly complimented my cynical lyrics about a Christian televangelist.

He will be my main man
'Cause no one draws a crowd like He can
I'll use His halo as my logo
On my business cards and TV show

Kahne transferred my MCA recordings to his futuristic new digital machine, and we spent a week at Sunset Sound Factory perfecting some of my lead vocals and overdubbing new parts. Rusty added beefy guitars to a waltz called "Shoebox," a Blazers-era tune called "Don't Worry," and "Something In My Heart Stopped." Kahne added some very creative keyboard/synthesizer parts to several songs. His ideas were always valid, but the preponderance of synth parts steered *Sunny Nights* away from guitar, my prime instrument. The album became a bit kitchen-sinky, with perhaps a few too many ideas fighting for the listener's attention. Not unlike ELO, actually. But overall, I was on board with the sounds we were getting, maybe just because it was so exciting to make a record.

MY COFFEE'S ON FIRE

My concept for the album artwork was a Dadaist photo of me sitting at a floating boomerang-shaped table on which would be placed a flaming cup of coffee and a newspaper with the headline "DON'T WORRY EVERYTHING'S GOING TO BE JUST FINE." In the background would be a TV cabinet filled with books and a large picture frame holding nothing. I had drawn the whole thing out and presented it to Columbia's art department. I got the feeling they weren't accustomed to artists butting into their business, but they liked my idea and agreed to go with it.

One advantage to being on a major label is budget. Columbia's art department hired a fabulous photographer named Dennis Keeley to shoot my album cover. Dennis's portfolio was loaded with stunning photos of Tom Petty, Frank Zappa, Crowded House, Tom Waits, and others. Sold. The photo studio was in a small, Spanish-style building on Melrose Avenue, half hidden by overgrown bougainvillea. I climbed outdoor stairs to the second-floor studio and stepped inside. Woah! The pencil drawing I'd done of my album cover had, literally, sprung into existence. In the center of the room was a '60s boomerang table suspended from the ceiling by nearly invisible fishing line. A TV filled with books sat beneath a sunlit window with a full moon. An authentic-looking newspaper (*The New Angeles Times*) rested on the table with my "Don't Worry" headline. Best of all, a gigantic coffee cup rested on the table next to a small bottle of industrial flame fluid.

An energetic, red-haired set decorator in overalls saw me taking it all in. "What do you think?" he asked. "Did we get everything right?"

"It's amazing!" I said, "I can't believe it. You even found the boomerang table."

"Yeah, that took a little digging, but I knew I could get one," he said, chuckling.

"Are we gonna have fire in that coffee cup?" I asked.

He laughed. "Oh, yeah. Just wait 'til you see the fire. I'd be very careful around that coffee cup if I were you!"

I changed into black jeans and a gray blazer, surrendered to the hair and make-up person until they were satisfied, and then pulled up a chair to the suspended table. The tricky element was the fire. The set decorator filled the coffee cup with a special fluid that, when lit, would create a three-foot tall plume for several seconds. I would sit casually, holding a bowler hat, while flames jumped into the air a foot or two from my head (and hair). With each lighting of the cup, Dennis Keeley would fire away with his camera. We shot the scene for about twenty minutes. It felt like we were creating something special.

After Dennis was satisfied that he'd captured the shot, he said, "I have several rolls of film left. Why don't you stand in different parts of the room, and I'll see if I can get some good extra shots. You never know what Columbia might use them for."

At one point, I stood in an arched doorway with my back to the camera, holding my guitar with the neck pointed at the ground. I didn't overthink what I was doing, I was just hitting poses that Dennis thought were interesting.

The next week, I visited Columbia's art department. Several of the fire shots were circled on a color proof sheet. We landed on the one that we thought looked best. The fire in the coffee cup was tall, my expression and posture were casual. Great. Just what we were going for. Then Art Director Nancy Donald said, "So Parthenon, we know you love this concept, and we do, too, but there's a photo we want to show you. It's one that Dennis took at the end of the session." Nancy pulled out a color proof sheet with a single photo circled in red. As soon as I saw it, I knew where she was going. I said, "You think that should be the front cover, don't you?" Nancy looked up at me with a little smile on her face, probably relieved that I'd said it myself. She said, "I mean, look at it, Parthenon. It's such a great shot."

It was the photo of me standing in the arched doorway, my back to the camera. It had an inexplicable "X" factor. Something in my posture and the empty space around me drew the eyes in. Funny how, after all the thought I'd put into the Dadaist cover for the oxymoronic *Sunny Nights*, I, too, could instantly see that this offhanded photo by Dennis Keeley would make a better cover.

"Can we use the flaming coffee cup on the back?" I asked.

"Absolutely. You'll have your concept on the cover, it just won't be the front."

NOT WENDY

One day at MCA, the bassist I'd hired for my session reached into his oversized Army parka and dug out a cassette tape. Kevin McCormick handed it to me and said, "You should check these guys out. Listen to 'Rich Man's War.' I think you'll like it." The tape was by AKA Graffiti Man, a band featuring the Native American poet John Trudell and guitarist Jesse Ed Davis. I didn't know Trudell, but Davis had played with John Lennon, Eric Clapton, George Harrison, Taj Mahal, and a myriad of other '60s titans. I was intrigued.

"Thanks, Kevin."

"Rich Man's War" was a poetry/blues mashup with Trudell's narration and Davis playing slide guitar. Not my usual cup of tea, but cool. Not long after Kevin gave me the tape, I saw that AKA Grafitti Man were playing in town at Club Lingerie, a misleadingly named, standard-issue rock club in Hollywood. After a *Sunny Nights* recording session at Sunset Sound Factory with Kahne, I walked the few blocks through Hollywood to Club Lingerie and took a position at the bar with good sight lines. As I waited for the band to come on, I noticed a woman seated with her friends at a crowded table. She sported a cumulus cloud of curly auburn hair above a striking, pretty face. I thought I recognized her as Prince's former guitarist, Wendy Melvoin, from the band Wendy and Lisa. Wendy and Lisa were signed to Columbia Records, as was I. A plausible scenario developed in my head: I could introduce myself as a label mate and we'd talk about all kinds of interesting musical things. Great idea. What did I have to lose?

AKA Grafitti Man put on a fine show, but truth be told, I'd spent much of their set distractedly running through a dozen possible conversations with Wendy. When the band wrapped things up and Club Lingerie grew quieter, I was all set to make my approach. This was going to be fun. I headed over to where she was seated.

"Excuse me. Hi. Are you Wendy?"

"No," said the person who was suddenly not Wendy.

"Oh," I said. I stood frozen. My plan hadn't allowed for this startling development.

Not Wendy asked, "Are you looking for someone named Wendy?"

"No," I replied honestly.

"Well, it was a nice try."

When Not Wendy said, "It was a nice try," she was trying to get rid of me. However, I, in my role of Not Perceptive, took it as a positive.

I asked, "Well, what *is* your name, if you don't mind me asking?" She was not interested in talking to the clown with long hair on one side of his head and two different colored shoes, but she was too polite not to answer. Not Wendy turned out to be screenwriter Janet Heaney. She was a screenwriter working on a Native American political/buddy film called *Powwow Highway*. Her producer was Handmade Films, George Harrison's company. Janet was checking out John Trudell as a possible collaborator on the *Powwow Highway* soundtrack. The clown with long hair on one side of his head told the screenwriter he was musician Parthenon Huxley, a guitarist, singer, and songwriter working on his debut album for Columbia Records.

With our bios revealed, we smiled at each other, acknowledging our somewhat parallel career arcs. "Well," our eyes said to each other, "aren't we talented and on the rise?" The next band started their set. It was loud. I asked Janet the screenwriter if she'd like to continue our conversation outside. She said, "Okay."

We stood in front of Club Lingerie on uneven concrete slabs of sidewalk buckled by the roots of a Ficus tree. For the next twenty minutes, Janet and I had one of *those* talks. We opined on movies and music and siblings, and LA. We made each other laugh. We locked eyes and blushed. We divulged things too personal for a first talk. We enjoyed every second with each other right up to the point where she had to go back into the club.

"My friends will be wondering where I've been."

"Okay."

She gave me a business card with her phone number. No disrespect to real Wendy, but Not Wendy had blown me away. Janet told me later that her friends, in particular, her boyfriend, had known exactly where she'd been. When she settled into the passenger seat of her boyfriend's car, he'd immediately asked, "Who was that guy you were talking to for such a long time?" Without hesitation, Janet said, "That was Parthenon Huxley." Janet told me later that, after she voiced my name, it hung in the air like a little neon sign for their entire ride home to Santa Monica.

Janet rebuffed my first two or three attempts to ask her out, but she finally agreed to meet me for a late afternoon lunch at the Rose Café, a casual LA hotspot five blocks from the beach in Venice. I knew that lunch meant "not a date." She also told me she had to attend a screening that evening and couldn't stay too long. She was hedging her bets and giving herself an out. I didn't care. I arrived at the Rose Café and found her browsing in the café gift shop. When our eyes met, Janet smiled and said, "Hello, Mr. Huxley." I could've passed out. I found her dazzling. On the breezy outdoor patio, we settled in for another of our talks, this time for two hours non-stop. Janet was a confident, stunning beauty with a professor's vocabulary, an artist's vision, and a wicked sense of humor. When I covertly dropped her off a few blocks from her apartment building in Santa Monica, she slid across the front bench seat of my 1966 Dodge Coronet and kissed me on the cheek. I was a goner.

TRUST ME

One day, at Sunset Sound Factory, David Kahne informed me that he would be bringing in a session drummer to replace the drum machine tracks on five songs I'd recorded at MCA. That night, I sat at Shalini's kitchen table and mapped out a drum arrangement for one of the selected songs, "Saving The Planets." I didn't (and don't) know how to write music on a staff, so I taped together three 8 x 11 sheets of unlined paper and created my own version of a cue sheet. After a couple hours of careful crafting, it looked like an engineering diagram from Star Trek. I brought it in the next day and showed it to Kahne.

He gazed at my chart with a slightly horrified expression on his face. "Uh, this is impressive, but there's no way anyone could possibly follow it." He handed it back to me with a look that said, "end of story." I was crestfallen, but also admitted to myself that my scribbles likely only made sense to me.

"Well," I said, searching for options, "will you be writing charts for the drummer?"

Kahne said, "No."

"Okay, will you send him a tape of the songs so he can get familiar with them before he shows up?"

"No."

"So, he's gonna come in to play on my songs without having heard them?"

"Yes."

I was almost pleading by this time. My songs represented years of blood and guts for me. In my mind, they were nuanced, intricate marvels. I couldn't imagine a drummer just showing up and playing them correctly. "How is that gonna work?" I asked.

"Trust me," Kahne said.

Carlos Vega was a dark-haired, friendly guy with a confident stride and good energy. He had "pro" written all over him, and some of my "precious songs" apprehension began to ease. After some chitchat and a little catching up on things with Kahne, Carlos said, "Okay, can I hear the first one?" We stood in the control room and listened to "Shoebox." Carlos looked at me and said, "Nice song, man. Really nice." When "Shoebox" was over he said, "Okay, I think I got it." Carlos went into the recording room, sat behind his kit, made some minor adjustments to a cymbal's positioning, and was ready to go. Kahne rolled tape and pressed "Record."

I noticed right away that Carlos Vega wasn't really playing my waltz-time ballad, he was consuming it. He enveloped the rhythm of "Shoebox" with his years of experience, his bottomless knowledge of feel and timing, and began to own it on his first pass. Kahne and I stood at the console in the control room, listening to the loud and clear studio monitors and watching Carlos focus on his task through the double-paned soundproof glass. About two-thirds through the song, I gave Kahne a quick wide-eyes-and-lifted-eyebrows look. He nodded his head once, smiled, and went back to enjoying the experience of watching a real pro at work.

When "Shoebox" reached its end, Carlos asked, "What do you think? Something like that?" Kahne hit the talk-back button and laughed, "Yeah, something like that will be fine, Carlos." Mr. Vega gave us five outstanding drum tracks in one afternoon. Amazing. The next day, Fish, the charismatic drummer of Fishbone, came into the studio and played drums on "Don't Worry." I didn't draw up a chart. Somehow Fish nailed it all on his own. I was learning.

ECHO PARK

Shalini kindly insisted I could stay in her extra bedroom for as long as I wanted, but my relationship with Janet was moving forward, and it was time to end my couch-surfing phase. I rented the lower-level single apartment in a hillside house in Echo Park for $400 a month and moved in with my meager belongings. My new home sat close to the top of LA's second steepest street, Ewing. At the bottom of the hill, I'd rev the V8 of my Coronet and bomb up the 32 percent grade until I was even with my driveway on the left. I'd ease off the gas, turn left, and let momentum swing me into my parking spot. It was always a thrill.

After the Rose Café, my liaisons with Janet remained covert, as she was still negotiating an exit from her previous relationship. Perhaps to ease any guilt I might feel, she said she'd been ready to move on before we'd met. Echo Park became our hideaway. I would listen for Janet as she flew down the steps to my open door and into my arms. I guess I wasn't the only goner. Our connection was electric. I couldn't believe my life.

We only had a short time before Janet would leave for South Dakota to be writer-on-set for *Powwow Highway*. Besides our liaisons in Echo Park, Janet and I met discretely for a drink during sunset on the Santa Monica Pier. We loved the romance of magic hour and watched workers assemble a tent on the beach for something called "Cirque de Soleil." Another secret rendezvous was on the mountaintop movie set of *Rock 'n' Roll Mom*, a Disney TV movie starring Dyan Cannon. I had a small part as "guy in band." Typecasting! Janet the screenwriter got a kick out of seeing me in my absurd heavy metal makeup. For Janet and me, LA had become nothing less than a Hollywood playground for two starry-eyed lovers in the discovery stages of a breathless romance. Even Janet's pending departure seemed like a plot device to make our love burn brighter in absentia. True to our story, Janet the writer sent me a letter or package every single day she was gone.

TRICKY

David Leonard (*Purple Rain, 1999*, Bangles, KD Lang) mixed *Sunny Nights* at Craig Huxley's Enterprise Studios in Burbank. Every day, I parked my '66 Coronet next to a Rolls Royce with RTB on the license plate. The Rolls belonged to Queen producer Roy Thomas Baker, just one of those LA reminders of where you stand in the rock 'n' roll pecking order.

As *Sunny Nights* approached release, I was taken to lunch by Columbia's marketing department. The seven of us—six women and I—chatted a bit awkwardly at a large round table in a restaurant close to the CBS offices in Century City. The head of marketing asked, "So, Parthenon. Who do you want to be?" I turned to her as I swallowed a bite of food. What did she mean by that? It sounded like another one of those tricky record business questions. Maybe I was supposed to say something edgy like, "I'm the bastard son of John Lennon and David Bowie" or "I'd like my songs to revive the Love Generation and make it cool to love each other again." I don't know whether the head of marketing would've taken me seriously or spat in her soup. All I could honestly say was, "I'm the guy who wrote these songs." As in, my identity is fully embedded in my music. She nodded and went back to her soup.

GENIUS OR CLUELESS

My champion at MCA, Rick Shoemaker, left a message on my answering machine in his usual game-show voice. "P-Man! It is I, the Publisher of Love. I've just listened to the final mixes of *Sunny Nights*. I absolutely love it. I can't believe how great it sounds, not that I didn't think it would be great. You and Kahne have done an amazing job, and I couldn't be happier. It's up to Columbia now and we'll see what happens. We're either geniuses or we haven't got a clue."

It felt great to please my boss. I loved Rick's enthusiasm, especially that last line, which gave me an idea. I called up Kahne and asked if we could add one little thing at the end of the album. He said, "Well, we're mastering in a few days, so we need to do it quick. What do you want to add?" I met with Kahne and brought my voice message cassette. We grabbed Shoemaker saying, "We're either geniuses or we haven't got a clue," ran it backwards and put it at the very end of *Sunny Nights*. It's the last thing you hear before the needle falls into the runout grooves. Geniuses or clueless. We'd soon find out.

MY CHANCE TO BE LOVED

Columbia chose "Chance to Be Loved" as my first single. I thought it was an odd choice. "Double Our Numbers" was more up-tempo and representative of my guitar-leaning sound. "Chance" had a lovely, simple message ("Everybody gets a chance to be loved"), but that message was delivered over a complex, mini-orchestral pop arrangement. A backbeat didn't arrive until the song was nearly over. Also, it was the '80s—when musicians first had access to synthesizers—and David Kahne and I had greased the track up with so many synthy pads, bells, and whistles that we nearly buried the core arrangement. Still, I did write it, and I liked the weirdness of it. At first, it looked like Columbia knew what they were doing, judging by the reactions from radio programmers.

Sky Daniels from San Francisco station KFOG: "Its compelling production, surreal arrangement, and the advance word from Columbia A&R aces Jamie Cohen and John Mrvos had me ready from listen one. The first time I played it, I got immediate phones asking 'What is it? It's great.'"

Bob Jefferies from Medford, Oregon's KBOY: "There is a uniqueness about this record that is unlike anything I'd had the privilege of hearing in years…cinematic in feel…lyrically dynamic…. Huxley crosses musical genres, and that ride from the loop in Chicago to the freeways of LA packs a musically exhilarating wallop."

Jeff Riedel from KKDJ in Fresno, California: "Crystal clear production…. The song draws you in and takes you where he's coming from. 'Chance to Be Loved' provides your listeners with innovative relief from four-chord banality. Don't blow your chance."

Kim Alexander from WHCN in Hartford, Connecticut: "Compelling and cinematic. Dare to be different—play 'Chance to Be Loved.'"

Michael Hughes, WRDU in Raleigh, North Carolina: "Parthenon Huxley. It's rock 'n' roll for people who read."

Here's one of my favorites.

The Hard Report: "…the Association on Acid. From a compositional standpoint, 'Chance to Be Loved' sounds, at first, like a tone poem, but a few more listens will unveil a perfectly preserved chunk of neo-psychedelic pop à la Dream Academy, only more angular and sophisticated. Undoubtedly, the most unusual offering of the week—and possibly one of the most reactive."

The rock press joined in.

Creative Loafing: "Parthenon Huxley is a name not to forget. Do albums wear out? I hope not. (#1 Album of the Year)."

Cashbox: "The lyrics touch upon fundamental questions of identity without ever lapsing into cliché."

Rolling Stone: "Overflowing with songwriting smarts, good guitar work, and a big beat, *Sunny Nights* is a monumental debut." (*Rolling Stone*'s reviewer, Parke Puterbaugh, gave my album four stars. His editor knocked it down to three stars, perhaps out of deference to Patti Smith, whose album was also awarded four stars.)

Shoemaker, Solomon, and I pored over the weekly radio reports to see how "Chance to Be Loved" fared. We got plenty of "adds" on stations scattered around the country, meaning "Chance" had been added to a station's overall playlist. The trick was to get increased spins based on listener calls and move into higher and higher rotations, the promised land being "Heavy Rotation" in Los Angeles and New York, the two most influential radio markets.

As the weeks went by, "Chance to Be Loved" picked up plays in Chicago, San Francisco, Atlanta, Dallas, and New Jersey, but it didn't leap onto any "Most Added Tracks" lists and it didn't get a chance to be loved in New York and LA. Barring a miracle, my first single was about to peter out after just four weeks. It would not climb the charts, it would not put me on *Letterman*, it would not be a hit.

GLUB, GLUB, GLUB

The most telling anecdote regarding the fate of *Sunny Nights* came from Michael Hughes, the Music Director in Raleigh, North Carolina, who'd come up with "Parthenon Huxley. It's rock 'n' roll for people who read." He pulled me aside after a show at Raleigh's Rialto Theater, where my band had played a sold-out show opening for Don Dixon and Marti Jones. Michael asked me with a sense of urgency, "Do you know what Columbia's doing to your record?"

Pray tell.

Michael said, "We asked the Columbia rep what song from *Sunny Nights* would be the follow-up single to 'Chance to Be Loved.' We told him we thought 'Double Our Numbers' was a hit. You know what he said?"

Hit me.

"He said, 'Oh, play whatever you want from *Sunny Nights*. We want you to push *Billy Joel Live in Russia*.'"

There it was. I was officially not a priority on Columbia. There would be no push on a second single. They threw "Chance to Be Loved" against the wall and it didn't stick. End of story. When the Dixon tour reached New York, Michael Solomon and I went to the Columbia offices to see if there was any hope of drumming up support for *Sunny Nights*. We entered Black Rock, CBS headquarters at 51 West 52nd street, and took the elevator up to Columbia Records. A bored, expressionless receptionist asked, "May I help you?"

I said, "Michael Solomon and Parthenon Huxley are here to see (Columbia Publicity Guy)."

"Who are you with?"

I paused for a second. "I'm a recording artist on Columbia."

"Just a second." The receptionist had no inkling of her unintentional insult. I was really feeling the major label love. A few minutes later, we were ushered into a huge corner office. The Columbia Publicity guy was on the phone and signaled for us to have a seat on his couch. He spoke into the receiver: "Well, how do you lose something that big?" Michael and I looked at each other, eyebrows raised. "Okay," he continued, "just keep me updated. Let me know." He hung up the phone and saw our curious expressions. He explained, "They can't find Pink Floyd's pig." Michael and I snorted.

Chapter 11: Weirdest A&R Meeting Ever

Pink Floyd losing their giant inflatable pig was by far the most interesting part of our meeting, which went nowhere. Publicity Guy was sympathetic to our cause but told us in so many words that our fate was out of his hands. If the higher-ups wouldn't push a second single on *Sunny Nights*, my dying record could not be helped by anyone at Columbia in New York.

We were wasting our time. It was a familiar feeling. Even when I was on a major label, my meetings didn't go well.

I look back at that juncture—the month or two that "Chance to Be Loved" was alive on radio—as a pivotal point in my musical career. A Columbia Records release of a Parthenon Huxley single was as close as I would get to becoming a widely known artist. Had Columbia pushed harder, had "Chance to Be Loved" captured the ears of an influential station in New York or Los Angeles, had the label gone hard with "Double Our Numbers" as a second single, my career and the arc of this book might have been very different.

I lecture at a recording school in Rockville, Maryland. Many of my students dream of becoming a star. I try to paint them a picture of the odds they face. I suggest that, if all the world's musicians filled a six-mile-deep ocean, the biggest stars—the artists everyone has heard of—would be just a thin layer bobbing on the surface. That's it. One thin layer of musicians on an ocean six miles deep. I tell them that when "Chance" was released and buoyed by solid industry buzz, I felt like I'd risen to just beneath the surface of that ocean full of musicians. There I was, looking up at the bobbing butts of the biggest acts in the business, thinking, "Almost there. Please let 'Chance' be a hit. I'm so close..."

Glub, glub, glub. I never broke the surface.

Sunny Nights broke my heart a little bit. I thought it deserved better. I was astounded that Columbia let it die so quickly and with so little bother. As a last gasp, Solomon and I put together a college-radio campaign, but were told by Columbia's marketing department we needn't have bothered. My record was dead, and my eight-album deal was nothing but contractual eye candy. The "Second LP" in my contract was Columbia's "option" to pick up.

I went through the motions of submitting new song demos and even performed a showcase for Columbia execs at Hully Gully rehearsal studios in Silverlake. My band sounded amazing, we killed the showcase, and I think the Columbia execs, who knew they were going to pass, were jolted by how much they enjoyed the show. Nevertheless, I was a dead man walking. To no one's surprise, Columbia dropped me. David Kahne had warned me about the bottomless black hole, and down I went.

Despite my failure, I was proud of the slab of vinyl with my name on the red Columbia Records label, the same label I'd stared at as a kid while listening to Springsteen, CTA, Dylan, and Santana. That was a victory. I would always be Parthenon Huxley, Columbia Recording Artist. I can't tell you how many musician friends of mine have signed with a major, made an expensive album, and watched their work go unreleased. Jeanne and Shelby, my friends in Head For Tall Trees, made their Chrysalis record for $300,000, yet only promo copies were ever pressed. All their hard work and dreams of success fell through the cracks because of an inexplicable in-house rivalry between execs at the label. Jeanne and Shelby were devastated and wound up selling their recording gear to buy drugs. Their bottomless black hole was way more real than mine.

A TITCH SAD

My major label deal was officially over, and so was my marriage. Stashe came out to LA. We met on a weeknight at the Starlite Lounge, a low-key bar in the Valley. Amidst an old-school ambience of cigarette smoke, pool tables, and a jukebox, we ordered drinks and settled in at the bar. We were glad to see each other, despite the evening's agenda. We caught up on all our news, good and bad. Eventually, tearing up a bit, we acknowledged the separate paths our lives had taken. "So," Stashe said, "shall we make it official?" We clinked glasses. I said, "To the most amicable divorce ever." She seconded my motion and added, "I'm still going to harass you, you know? That will never stop." By harass, Stashe meant egg me on as an artist. I smiled. "Good."

Despite our inevitable decision to finalize our divorce, I didn't feel like we had failed one another. Stashe had done wonders for my confidence and scale of ambition. I would always be grateful. And Stashe was happy in New York. She was in a new relationship and better off, I think, for having met me in Chapel Hill. She was still close with my parents, my dad particularly, and she even kept my original family name as her own. She would stay Anistatia Miller. As far as divorces go, ours was a titch sad, but it didn't end our bond or our friendship.

CHAPTER 12

MY EXPANDING PORTFOLIO

Columbia Records had given up on *Sunny Nights*, but a Columbia recording artist loved it. Chicago's Robert Lamm called me up, praised my album, and asked if I'd like to write with him. I drove out to Robert's stunning house in Beverly Hills, and we went to work in his music room. Robert showed me a propulsive, punchy riff in a 6/4 time signature and some lyrics about split personalities. I went along for the ride and came up with a bi-polar chorus lyric that made him laugh: "Shut your mouth or I will have to kill us/There's only room for one of you in me." Robert went for it and our song "Schitzoid" appeared on his *Too Many Voices* album. Another song of ours, the considerably less weird "You're My Sunshine Everyday," made it onto Robert's *Subtlety and Passion* album. It was a thrill to work with Robert, a true artist with a massive musical vocabulary and a voice I've always admired.

THE HANDMADE TALE

Janet left her Santa Monica apartment and rented a hillside bungalow a mile from me in Echo Park. The property included a small office/guesthouse with striking horizontal wood paneling salvaged from the Spruce Goose, Howard Hughes's legendary transport plane. It became Janet's writing room.

Janet's split from her boyfriend Carl had been bumpy, but they'd managed to cordially stay on professional terms. They would continue to work together during the promotion of *Powwow Highway*, set for release in early 1989.

In December '88, Handmade Films hosted a pre-release cast and crew screening at the Directors Guild on Sunset Boulevard. We were excited to see Janet's work on the big screen for the first time. Before the show, we mingled in the crowded lobby, and Janet happily reconnected with all the actors and crew she'd met on set in South Dakota and New Mexico. At one point, Janet, along with Carl and her co-writer Jean Stawarz, were ushered into a private room off the lobby to meet with executives from Handmade Films. I wasn't invited, so I got a drink and waited for Janet to reappear.

When she came out of the meeting, Janet's face was lit up and she was laughing with Carl and Jean. I asked, "What happened?" Janet said they'd stood in a line to speak with each of the executive producers from Handmade, who were, of course, all British. Janet had asked one of them, "What got you interested in a story involving Native Americans?"

The Handmade executive with the Liverpool accent answered, "I've always loved the American West," and then George Harrison added for context, "I'm not from America, you know."

Janet had found that hilarious and thought, "No shit, Sherlock." We cracked up, relishing her private chat with a Beatle. How nice to meet George Harrison on the night your movie debuts. My new girlfriend couldn't have been happier. The crowd migrated into the Director's Guild theater. When Janet and Jean's screenplay credits came up, we all yelled and clapped like it was the best part of the movie. To a writer with dreams like Janet, maybe it was.

A month later, I accompanied Janet to the Sundance Film Festival in Park City, Utah. A successful reception at Sundance would bode well for her movie's chances at the box office. The theater on Park City's steep main drag was packed for *Powwow*. The crowd laughed and gasped at all the right places. Afterwards, Janet, Jean, and Carl gave thoughtful answers to questions from the industry-savvy audience. I loved watching Janet address the crowd. She was the kind of person who spoke in fully coherent paragraphs without once saying "uh" or "um."

The crowd showed *Powwow* a lot of love, especially the performance by Gary Farmer, a large, loveable Native Canadian who stole the movie. There was a buzz in the room, and I began to think *Powwow* might have enough charm and pizzazz to be popular at the box office.

At another screening later that day, we watched a festival entry called *Sex, Lies & Videotape*. The second it was over, the crowd went nuts. The rookie director, Steven Soderbergh, bathed in the applause and fielded questions for a solid hour until we all got booted out of the theater. It was obvious that Soderbergh would be the hot new director to emerge from Sundance and that *Sex, Lies & Videotape* would be a hit. "Ohhhh," I thought. "That's what it looks like when people are truly excited about a movie." *Sex, Lies & Videotape* would not only be a hit, but it would also make Soderbergh a star and help put Sundance on the map as a viable commercial gateway for indie films.

Powwow Highway won the Filmmakers Trophy at Sundance, a nice achievement, but only managed to secure a limited release through Warner Brothers Distribution. Janet's film would play on just twelve screens, all indie art houses scattered around the country. Despite good reviews, a loveable lead character, a Beatles producer, and a soundtrack featuring U2 and Robbie Robertson, *Powwow Highway* barely dented the box office. It quickly retired to videotape.

Although it failed to connect with a wide audience, *Powwow Highway* lived on in other ways. It would rightfully earn a revered place in the Native American community. It's one of a small handful of movies to feature Native actors in Native roles and paint an honest portrait of life on the reservation. It was no small achievement.

Janet and I had met during the exciting pre-release phase of our big breaks. Like every artist or writer, we had fantasized about success before the public had a chance to hear or see our work. Now we were on the other side. *Sunny Nights* had tanked, and *Powwow Highway* had sputtered. Did we have any other tricks up our sleeves?

NEXT

Janet had most of a screenplay written for a film she called *Running Out*. The pitch: a doddering grandmother seeking to retain custody of her orphaned grandson goes on the run from social services. She envisioned it as an indie film, another notch on her belt as an up-and-coming screenwriter and filmmaker. She readily acquired an agent, who began pitching *Running Out* around Hollywood.

THE WRONG LORD-ALGE

In my case, MCA Publishing had a plan. "Fuck Columbia," MCA Music President Leeds Levy said. "We have a studio in the basement. We'll make another record here and find a home for it when it's finished." MCA ponied up a $55,000 budget (an amount I would have to recoup), which was more than the $50,000 Kahne spent on *Sunny Nights*. I was blown away by MCA's faith in me.

Budget in hand, Michael Solomon began searching for a producer. I should've said, "Hold on. I need to write the album first." I write songs constantly, but it takes time for the best ones to rise to the top. The songs on *Sunny Nights* were cherry-picked from a huge pile of unreleased songs. I'd written new tunes since coming to MCA, but, for whatever reason—perhaps leaving bucolic Chapel Hill for 1980s New York and LA—my lyrics had taken on a socially critical, even preachy tone. Bob Dylan's description of songs like these is "finger-pointin' songs." That's not where I wanted to live as an artist.

There's a weird color in the LA air tonight
It's slightly foreboding, like something isn't right
Yeah, we breathe a forest fire in a city with no trees
Oh, what we'd do to feel a breeze come and blow it all away
("Mile High Fan")

After a while it seems pointless to smile on the street
We wonder why it's so hard for two strangers to meet
Your face is concrete
("Mr. Stoneface")

Ronald McDonald is the Satan of taste
Tempts me with sugar fat and grease on a styrofoam plate
Burn down the Amazon gotta make more room for meat
("New Age")

Stalin's uncool in Soviet school
Africa's a landfill, Sony bought Brazil
Will change make us better when we're changing faster still?
("R.E.D.")

Sunny Nights brimmed with high-brow optimism and Love, and I'd wanted that to be my calling card. With my new songs, I was being my own worst enemy. If I'd had my head on straight, I would've met with MCA and Solomon and discussed expectations for the second record. How much time could I have to write new material? Do we want it to sound like *Sunny Nights*? Is making a record right away without a label really the best option?

Instead of taking a step back to plan, I got caught up in finding a producer. The first name on my list was, Englishman, John Leckie, who'd worked with one of my all-time favorite bands, XTC. We reached out and Leckie came back asking for a fee of $25,000, or nearly half our budget. We had to say no thanks.

Next, Solomon took me to meet Bob Bortnick, a former guitarist and singer for a band called Dancing Hoods. Bortnick was now managing producers, including a recording engineer named Jeff Lord-Alge. Jeff was a skinny, brash, New Jersey dude with dark, thinning, shoulder-length hair. His older brothers, Chris and Tom, were very successful mix engineers and

Grammy winners. Jeff was a good talker and claimed he was ready to make the step from engineer to producer.

Even after *Sunny Nights* bombed, I continued to perform around LA and up the California coast. A friend from Greece, Steve Vagnini, booked us into San Jose, Santa Cruz, San Francisco, and his adopted home of Monterey. Steve did loads of promotional work and helped make Monterey my band's second home. We loved playing there because of him.

My band was talent rich. At any point during my show, Rusty Anderson might crank out the greatest guitar solo anyone had ever heard. Jen Condos and Rob Ladd were a dream rhythm section who would go on to play with Don Henley and Roger Daltrey, among others. Rusty, of course, has been with McCartney for more than two decades.

I wasn't worried about impressing Jeff Lord-Alge. We could've played all covers and gone over great. Our sound was all there. It was my new material that needed examining. Solomon invited Jeff to hear my band at an LA club. Jeff came backstage after our set. He was excited and couldn't wait to get into the studio with us. I said, "Great. Well, first, we'll do some pre-production and figure out which songs should make the album." Jeff insisted that wasn't necessary. "We'll just record the songs from your show, you'll see, it'll be great. Wait 'til you hear the kinds of sounds I get in the studio."

At that moment, I should've told Jeff goodbye. He wasn't ready to be a producer. He wasn't interested in getting to know me or discovering what kind of album I wanted to make. A producer's job is to capture an artist's vision, not a random live set. Jeff was banking on his engineering skills to win the day. I was uncomfortable with his approach and should've told him so. Instead, I decided to go along to get along. I agreed to give him a shot.

Jeff was a good engineer. As he'd promised, my band sounded huge in the headphones as we cut a couple of songs live in the studio. The drums were big, the guitars meaty and powerful, and the vocals were up front and wide. The first session went well enough to create some momentum, and before I knew it, the project was underway with us working together. I was going against my gut, but hoping for the best, surmising that maybe if I got out of the way and let things happen organically, something magical would happen.

It didn't. We ended up making an album that I didn't particularly care for. The so-so songs from our live set didn't get any better because of Jeff's capable engineering. If we'd had a pre-production phase, I could've weeded out the weaker songs and written better ones. The album had some tremendous moments, but the peaks were adjacent to forgettable valleys. For instance, a song called "New Age" really took off during Rusty's beautifully composed guitar solo, but it crashed to earth during my obnoxiously strident vocal about "burning down the Amazon to make more room for meat." The lyric wasn't wrong about the issue, but the song wasn't right for my mission.

I have one rule regarding my recordings. I need to be happy with every single moment of a song from start to finish. Period. I couldn't make that happen with the Jeff Lord-Alge recordings. My band played great—that was not the problem. It was my songs, my lyrics, my arrangements that fell flat. The album didn't find a label, and it never got released. Jeff Lord-Alge got a new jeep.

I've never worked with an outside producer since.

WORKIN' FOR MCA

One of my directives before arriving in LA had been "I will show my genius through my work." Unfortunately, my work had shown not my genius, but rather my indecisiveness and lack of vision. Literally *no one* loved the Jeff Lord-Alge album. The music hadn't come from my heart. I'd fucked up.

MCA, of course, wasn't thrilled. Their investment in me was now well into six figures. We had a sober meeting on the fourth floor, where it was spelled out that, after two unsuccessful albums, MCA would need me to pursue other avenues to earn some money and recoup my advances. They asked me, "Have you done much co-writing?" I said, "Sure. Yeah." I hadn't really, but that's where my music career went next: co-writer. Writing songs for other artists. Plan B. Sigh.

I was disappointed by my demotion from "Artist" to "Writer" at MCA, but it could've been worse. They could've dropped me and cut their losses. Instead, Rick Shoemaker, Leeds Levy, Carol Ware, Betsy Anthony, Sherri Orson, and the whole executive crew at MCA continued to invest in me and my songwriting abilities. I was buoyed by their faith.

My job was to write hits, or at least singles. Over the next three years, I would collaborate with classic rock act Foreigner, indie downer darling Mark Everett, former child actress Danielle Brisebois, southern rock hero Damon Johnson of Brother Cane, Rod Stewart guitarist Stevie Salas, UK ska champion Dave Wakeling of the English Beat and General Public, king of the major seventh chord Marshall Crenshaw, Keel guitarist Marc Ferrari, and more. My co-written songs would be good enough to land on various Billboard charts, a greatest hits collection, and albums released by Island, Mercury, Polydor, IRS Records, Atlantic, and more.

MCA's plan very nearly worked.

Chapter 12: My Expanding Portfolio

A JOB CALLED E

MCA Creative Director Betsy Anthony matched me with a young artist from Virginia. He lived in an apartment over a garage in Atwater Village, a sunbaked neighborhood a few miles east of Hollywood across the LA River. His name was Mark Everett, but he called himself E. He recorded demos on four-track cassette, and despite that low-fi medium, E's personality jumped off the tape. His songs were simple, poignant, romantic, a bit downbeat but with a dash of hopeful. He played all the instruments on his demos and sang in an appealing, gravelly voice. He was managed by a guy named Carter, a colorful and insightful music industry veteran who'd landed E a record deal with Polydor. Carter thought co-writing might broaden E's palette a bit.

I was still living in the Echo Park hills, but I'd moved one street over from my single apartment on Ewing to a small house on Baxter, officially the steepest street in Los Angeles. Baxter slopes at a gravity-heavy 32 percent grade and has its own place in Hollywood history. The Little Rascals plummeted down Baxter in their homemade fire engine, the Beastie Boys flew over Baxter's intersection with Alvarado Street in their "Savatage" video, and O.J. Simpson's dummy rolled down Baxter on an auto mechanic's creeper in *Naked Gun II*. In 2022, a viral video showed a rented Tesla going airborne over the intersection of Baxter and Alvarado and crashing into two parked cars. I screamed up and down Baxter every time I left my house.

E arrived for our first songwriting session and said, "My truck almost flipped over when I turned into your driveway." (What else is new on Baxter?) E looked a bit like Charlie Chaplin's Little Tramp: short dark hair, unshaven, hunched shoulders. He could play a good loner. Speaking of appearances, look who's talking—I sported a beard on half of my face, opposite the half of my head that had shoulder length hair. Did I think I was Man Ray? What the fuck was wrong with me? E and I made a real pair. Luckily we made each other laugh.

I welcomed E into my house. He chuckled at the turquoise 1950s hairdryer chair in my entrance foyer, and we settled onto opposing futons in the living room. Through a south-facing window, LA's downtown skyline loomed ghostlike in the smog. I tuned an acoustic guitar and strummed an E chord followed by F# minor.

"What's that?" E asked.

"Oh, nothing. Just messing around."

"Play what you just played again," E said. I did. "Okay, that's the start of the verse." E was excited. I picked up his energy and we were off.

I was the guitar parts generator. E was the song shaper. He quickly heard something coming together in his head. When he wanted a new part, I'd try a few things until he'd say, "That's it. Go with that." E sang a melody over what we were creating, and I'd pitch in with alterations or complimentary ideas. When we had our first song sketched out, E said, "Okay, I'm gonna go in the other room and write the words. I'll be back in a little bit." I made coffee and a half hour later, E had the whole song finished. Speaking as a writer who can mull over lyrics for months, I was impressed.

Our first collaboration on Baxter Street was called "Hello Cruel World." In line with E's other songs, the lyrics were skeptical, sad, and a smidge hopeful all at once.

Hello cruel world, so this is you
A broken heart, but with a view
I'm looking out to face another day
Norman Rockwell colors fade
All my favorite things have changed
But what the hell, hello cruel world

I took E to MCA and we recorded "Hello Cruel World" on two-inch sixteen-track tape, a significant upgrade from E's four-track cassettes. E's manager Carter and Polydor President Davitt Sigersson heard the result and got very excited. Sigersson said, "This is E working with Parthenon? It sounds amazing! They should co-produce the album together." I was paid $5,000 to co-produce E's major label debut. My resume now read Artist/Guitarist/Singer/Songwriter/Co-Writer/Co-Producer. My portfolio was expanding, and that was good. I just didn't want to move too far down the chain from my original job as Artist.

We recorded *A Man Called E* at a home studio directly across the street from my house on Baxter. My neighbor, Jim Lang, was a convivial composer/musician/engineer with a handsome bald head and a ready laugh. He was also a former touring keyboardist for Todd Rundgren and Joe Cocker and had the silver boots with four-inch heels to prove it. He'd more recently begun creating music for animated shows like Nickelodeon's *Hey Arnold!* He called his basement operation Knobworld.

Every morning, coffee in hand, I crossed Baxter Street and ducked into the studio (also nicknamed The Submarine due to its low ceilings) to get to work with Jim and E. Our budget was small, so we used mostly drum machines and electric pianos instead of costly human drummers and grand pianos. I played acoustic and electric guitars and sang harmony vocals. E did everything else. The three of us made a good team. When we weren't laughing our asses off at dumb jokes, bad vocal takes, or the dozens of cartoons I drew of E, we made an honest, charming album released as *A Man Called E*. "Hello Cruel World" was selected to be the first single. Another E/Huxley collaboration, "Nowheresville," would be the follow-up.

Like me, when I was on Columbia, E was a total unknown with a single coming out on a major label. This time, it worked. Polydor saw "Hello Cruel World" climb to #6 on the Billboard Alternative Charts and our little album got a lot of attention on radio and glowing reviews in the rock press. Critics were consistently drawn to the contrast between E's catchy music and his morose, downtrodden lyrics, which gave the listener the unusual feeling of being romanced by a troubled loser. In real life, E gamely faced down the troubling parts of his past by being funny as hell, fearless, and supremely confident in his craft.

The same contrast manifested in our live show. After just a few rehearsals and warm-up gigs in San Luis Obispo and Santa Barbara, we toured the country, playing twenty-five cities as the opening act for rising star Tori Amos. E and I did our thing on piano and guitars, and Carter found a shaggy blond bespectacled bassist from Santana's band named Chris Solberg, completing the trio. During the breaks between E's woe-is-me songs like "I've Been Kicked Around," "Fitting in with the Misfits," and "Nowheresville," E and I engaged in silly stage talk like a TV host and sidekick.

"Parmesan...?" E would say.

"Yes, F?"

"I'm getting the distinct feeling that, compared to last night, this East Lansing crowd is kicking some Indianapolis ass, don't you think?"

"I couldn't agree more, sir!"

Audiences ate up our gratuitous patter and as the tour went on, our sad/not-sad dog and pony show began to receive standing ovations. We were as delighted as we were surprised. I was paid about $500/week to tour, which seemed like easy money. I also noted that my job portfolio had expanded to include Touring Sideman. I was pleasantly shocked at how successful our co-writing partnership had become.

Back in Los Angeles after the tour, E moved into a house not far from me in Echo Park and began dating my girlfriend Janet's sister, Jocelyn. Despite our successful partnership and growing family ties, when it came time to make the follow-up to *A Man Called E*, Mark (E's real first name) kicked me to the curb. He hired Michael Koppelman, an engineer from Minnesota, to be his co-producer. My role was reduced to co-writer, and I delivered the album's two singles, "Shine It All On" and "The Only Thing I Care About" as well as an album track that I loved called "My Old Raincoat." With Mark and Koppelman behind glass in the control room, I sat out in the live room and recorded guitar parts on my three songs. When I'd finished my overdubs, Mark spoke into the studio talkback mic and said, "Pack your bags, Huxley." My contributions to E's second album, *Broken Toy Shop*, were over. That stung.

I never got a good explanation from E about the dissolution of our successful partnership. Years later, on a phone call, he said, "Yeah, I could've handled that differently." Although he technically owed me nothing—I fully support artistic control for all artists—we were practically family. I felt I deserved better. That said, right when E's album came out, Polydor Records folded, radio and tour support vanished, and *Broken Toy Shop* was dead in the water. So, I didn't miss out on much. E's eventual career revival was engineered by his manager Carter, who recognized that the artist called E was no longer viable. He told E to start a band called eels, surmising that an eels record would directly follow E albums in record store racks. Carter's plan worked, and eels signed with Dreamworks.

THE OTHER CBS

While I wrote, recorded, and toured with E in my Plan B role as collaborator, Janet received interest in her screenplay, *Running Out*. Unfortunately, it wasn't the kind of interest she was interested in. Instead of an indie production company, it was CBS TV that came calling. Janet thought of herself as a filmmaker, not a writer of TV movies. Her agent understood the artistic divide between film and 1990s network television, but pointed out the six-figure fee Janet would receive.

Janet went along begrudgingly with her agent's advice. The money was nice, but piece by piece she had to relinquish artistic control of *Running Out*. She'd intended her story of an older woman fighting dementia to be realistic and a tad gritty. CBS wanted something softer, and a CBS creative VP even changed Janet's title to *Mrs. Lambert Remembers Love*, which made Janet want to puke. On the bright side, the network landed living legends Walter Matthau and Ellen Burstyn in the lead roles, with Walter's son Charles directing.

I joined Janet on set in San Francisco, and I got to watch Walter Matthau offer four takes of a simple scene involving a conversation at a restaurant. He gave each take a uniquely nuanced spin while still delivering the essential lines. I was mesmerized. It was the first time I'd seen acting on that level. I could see how Matthau was providing the editor all sorts of wiggle room to connect the current scene with the action preceding and following. Simple, but brilliant.

Another perk of the unfortunately titled *Mrs. Lambert* TV movie was an invite to dinner at the Matthau's house in Pacific Palisades after the conclusion of shooting. The fifteen or so people seated at dinner included Walter, of course, his director son Charles, and Walter's great pal Jack Lemmon. We're supposed to behave ourselves in Hollywood and not gawk at stars, but, that night, it was tough to be nonchalant. I spent most of dinner having a great talk with William Schallert, a remarkable character actor who'd appeared on *Star Trek, Patty Duke, Bonanza, Gunsmoke, The Rifleman, Dobie Gillis, Father Knows Best,* and just about every other TV show made since the '50s. He struck me as a kind, easygoing man.

FOREIGNER POLICY

After my successful pairing with E, MCA's search for Huxley-generated income led to another interesting assignment. Mick Jones of Foreigner was holed up in an LA rehearsal studio with a singer named Johnny Edwards, who'd been picked to replace the recently departed Lou Gramm, Foreigner's original singer. Mick and Johnny were writing songs for a new album, and would I like to get involved? How do these things happen? I suppose it's possible Mick heard something he liked on *Sunny Nights*.

I drove out to an innocuous industrial park in the Valley to join the songwriting party. The huge rehearsal room was a typically sparse, functional space. In the center of the room were road cases, a few chairs, and several guitar amps and vocal mics ready to go. Mick Jones stood waiting with his trademark Fender Stratocaster plugged into a Marshall stack. I was a fan of his work and excited to hear him play. His solo on "Hot Blooded" with its wild Jimmy Page-esque flailing was a classic rock landmark. Mick, a soft-spoken Englishman, politely welcomed me. He seemed somewhat reserved at first. Johnny Edwards, on the other hand, was an easygoing, friendly American with a soft Kentucky drawl. He had shoulder-length shaggy brown hair and a big rock voice with acres of range.

The three of us convened each day for a week. We faced one another playing guitars, exchanging ideas, and piecing together parts for half a dozen songs. I felt like we were creating some good stuff. It was, principally, Johnny's job to write lyrics, but I jumped in with ideas when I thought I had something that would work. Mick, of course, had authored classic rock perennials like "Double Vision," "Cold as Ice," and "I Wanna Know What Love Is," so I readily deferred to him when it came to judging whether a part would stick or not. Foreigner was his band, after all. After a good week of work, I went home for the weekend, looking forward to coming back and finishing the songs we'd started. I was excited by our progress and enjoying the relaxed vibe in the room.

The writing sessions ceased without explanation. I couldn't conjure a reason. No one at MCA knew anything. There was simply radio silence from the Foreigner camp. I thought, "What did I do wrong?"

A *year* later I got a phone call. "Oh, hullo, Parthenon, this is Kevin Jones, Mick's brother. The guys are putting out a greatest hits album with three new songs, and we think you may've contributed to one of the new songs."

I said, "A greatest hits album? What happened to the new album with Johnny Edwards singing?"

"Uh, well, Johnny's no longer with the band. A funny thing happened. Mick and Lou Gramm were both staying at the Sunset Marquis in LA when the riots broke out. They were stuck in the hotel for a few days, and they ended up talking and working things out. So, Lou's back in the band."

I felt bad for Johnny Edwards. I recalled him mentioning he'd bought a house when he got his big break and joined Foreigner. *Oops.*

"Anyway," Kevin continued in his mid-Atlantic English accent, "if you wouldn't mind, we'd like you to come down to the office and have a listen to the song to see if you can confirm your contribution."

I met Kevin at an office in Hollywood where he had a small sound system set up. I sat between the speakers and as soon as he hit "Play" I said, "Oh! It's 'Golden Boy'! I always liked that one." A year earlier, Mick had explained to me that "Golden Boy" was dedicated to his youngest child. Mick had spent most of his parenting years on the road and "Golden Boy" was an attempt to explain to his kid that even though he was often away, he loved his son and wished he could be with him. I thought it was a lovely idea, and a nice contrast to Foreigner's cock-rock like "Hot Blooded."

Kevin corrected me. "Oh, sorry, no, it's not called 'Golden Boy' anymore."

I turned to face Kevin. "Oh? Why not?"

He said, "Some thought it sounded too gay."

Ouch. I turned back toward the speakers. That was a shame. I asked Kevin, "So what's it called now?"

"The new title is 'With Heaven On Our Side.'"

Bland. I listened on. The lyrics were perfunctory. They could've been about anything or anybody. I felt strongly that the song would've been way better as "Golden Boy," not that anyone was asking for my opinion. Nevertheless, when the section I'd written came on, I recognized it and pointed it out to Kevin. "That's my bit there."

"Okay, great. We thought that was the case. The band will be at the studio finishing the recording next week. They may want to make some changes. Could you make yourself available to work on it?"

"Sure thing." I had to hand it to Foreigner. I didn't like the new title and lyric direction, but it was extremely thoughtful of them to track me down after a year and include me in the creative process. I'm not sure many bands would do that.

I met Mick and Lou at Alley studios in the Valley, the same studio where Brian Wilson had introduced himself. Mick, Lou, and I took over the same small upstairs room where I'd had a heavenly vocal rehearsal with Karla Bonoff and Linda Ronstadt. I sat with a blank notebook ready to help with lyrics if necessary. Skinny, leather-jacketed Lou Gramm stood, singing and trying out lyric ideas. It's exciting when a voice you've heard on the radio for twenty years is suddenly pouring out of a guy's throat a few feet away. Pretty cool.

As we worked our way through the song, Mick and Lou were having trouble with a couple lines in the pre-chorus. I saw an opening and made a few suggestions. As I sometimes did when discussing lyrics, I explained my thinking behind the lines I'd offered, hoping to add context. "It seems like the singer is still undecided about where he stands in this relationship, so if he gets a little desperate in the pre-chorus, it will make emotional sense."

Mick said to Lou, "See what I mean? He's different, isn't he?"

Lou chuckled, "Yeah."

I assumed Mick was referring to me (I was right there) but I didn't feel like I was expected to respond or acknowledge the remark. I hoped it was a compliment. We ended up using my lyric suggestion, so maybe it was. The weird thing about working with famous artists is that you're just there to work, not become friends or even become too friendly, not that that can't happen. Co-writing can feel like a business meeting, which I guess, in a way, it is. "With Heaven On Our Side" appeared on Foreigner's *The Very Best and Beyond...* in the *Beyond* part. Released as a single, it made it onto Billboard's Hot AC Top 20, but didn't do much damage. (I wish they'd stuck with "Golden Boy"!)

I WANT 62.5%

My next MCA co-writing assignment paired me with Dave Wakeling, the blond, left-handed, Vox Teardrop guitar-playing singer from the English Beat and General Public. Dave's bands were best known for "Mirror In The Bathroom" and "Tenderness." We spent an afternoon working on a new song for Dave's I.R.S. Records solo album called *I Want More*. He'd come to our writing session saying he was interested in doing something in the vein of "I'm Waiting For The Man" by the Velvet Underground. Great. Let's do it. As when I worked with Lou Gramm, I loved hearing Dave's voice up close, in person. He had an appealing, sandpapery, recognizable tone, perfectly suited for pop records. This was gonna be fun.

After about three hours of plugging away at lyrics and music, Dave said to me, "Okay, Parthenon, just so you know, at this point I've got you down as responsible for 37.5 percent of the song." I chuckled and said, "Oh, okay." I assumed he was kidding. When it was clear he wasn't, I nearly fell off my futon. Starting a song from scratch suggested, to me, a 50/50 arrangement. That way, both writers are at ease in pursuing a common goal, which is the best song you can conjure, no matter whose ideas win out. I tried not to let on, but Dave's accountant-like approach to our creative process sucked the energy right out of the room. Going forward, any new ideas I offered could be construed as an effort to raise my percentage rather than improve the song.

"I Want More" rose to the lead track position on Dave's album, *No Warning*. A few years ago, I checked the song's registration with BMI. I was curious if I'd held on to my percentage. Dang it! He dropped me down to 25 percent! I should've known. The song was called "I Want More."

HOT SHOT

Sunny Nights hadn't set the world on fire, but it had fans. One admirer was a hotshot guitarist from San Diego named Stevie Salas. We met through Jamie Cohen, my Columbia A&R man. Stevie was brash, confident, talented, and funny as hell. His big break had been a year on the road as Rod Stewart's guitarist and he never let anyone forget it. He had his eye on stardom, and it looked like he was on his way when Island signed Stevie's power trio to a record deal.

Beneath Stevie's feverish, hustling personality was an artist who really wanted to do good work. Stevie wrote muscular, guitar-heavy funk rock and played the shit out of his guitar. The only thing slowing him down was his backlog of unfinished lyrics. He knew what he wanted to say but needed help saying it. He was a fan of my lyrics on *Sunny Nights* and asked me to help him out.

We'd pick up food from Paquito Mas and hunker down at Stevie's hillside house overlooking Universal City. When I threw lyric ideas at him, Stevie's reaction was always perfectly clear—yay or nay. He knew what he wanted and didn't waste time. Our collaboration worked smoothly, and I wrote about half the lyrics on his 1990 album *Stevie Salas Colorcode*, including "Blind" and "Two Bullets And A Gun." That album, produced with Bill Laswell, didn't set the States on fire, but it opened the door for Stevie in Europe and Japan, where he has toured ever since. As a bonus, Stevie's bass player CJ deVillar and drummer Winston Watson both become great friends of mine as well as future collaborators.

PURGATORY FALLS, THE FARM

Four years after our talk at Club Lingerie, Janet and I married in September 1991. Janet's dream had always been to get hitched in the woods behind her family's Purgatory Falls Farm in southern New Hampshire, where she'd ridden horses on trails as a teen. For the site of the ceremony, Janet chose a clearing surrounded by towering pines, a kind of natural cathedral. A volunteer army of Janet's brothers and cousins, plus my best man, Dads drummer Scott Swartzwelder, hung speakers from trees, cleared low-hanging branches from horse trails, and built a wooden walkway over muddy terrain that stretched from the Heaney house to the wedding site. My ambitious bride oversaw the entire production, which included horse-drawn carriages, hand-hewn log benches for the ceremony, and dinner for 150 family members and guests under a massive tent set up in a field next to the farm. I told the gathering I was forever grateful to have mistaken Janet for Wendy from Prince's band.

RENT-A-KID

Happily married and back in LA, Janet and I weren't especially anxious to move in together. We each liked our little houses, which suited our work-at-home lives. We spent every night together at one house or the other, so for the price of an extra toothbrush, we had the best of both worlds—commitment and creative solitude.

One day, Janet found an index card wedged into her gate on Lucretia Street. It read, "Rent-A-Kid. I will walk your dog. Rake your yard. Call Alain." Janet thought "Rent-A-Kid" was clever and called the number. An enterprising twelve-year-old named Alain Romero lived at the bottom of

Janet's Street with his two younger brothers and nearly blind Albino mother, Milagro, who was unable to work. Alain helped Janet with her cats and yardwork, and a friendship blossomed. We began taking the three Romero boys to Dodger games, movies, and picnics. They'd never experienced such things and their genuine appreciation was heartwarming.

SENSES WORKING OVERTIME

In 1989, Michael Solomon phoned me with head-spinning news: our friend Paul Fox was producing the next album by XTC, one of my all-time favorite bands. Paul kindly invited me down to the studio to meet the guys. I bee-lined it to Ocean Way, one of LA's revered studios, where XTC were finishing basic tracks. Paul welcomed me and I took a seat in a conference room, waiting for the band to finish a take. Andy Partridge, writer of exquisite, poetic, amazing music and lyrics, soon barreled into the room. Paul said, "Andy, meet my friend, Parthenon." Right on cue, Andy put out his hand and said, "Well that's a monumental name!"

I'd arrived at dinnertime, and Paul collegially invited me to join him and the band at a Hollywood restaurant where they'd be meeting up with an old friend. The old friend turned out to be David Byrne. Despite Partridge's name, it was Byrne who was more bird-like, sitting at attention with nearly unblinking eyes, enjoying his old friend Andy's animated stories. I couldn't imagine two more different people. I asked, "How do you guys know each other?"

Andy turned to me and said, "We know David from the days when our bands played all that *scratchy music*." I loved that description of both bands' aggressive, syncopated strumming of electric guitars. XTC had brought Talking Heads to Europe and the Heads returned the favor by inviting XTC to tour the States. I wish I'd seen both tours.

After dinner, XTC returned to Ocean Way to overdub some percussion on "Cynical Days," a song by XTC's reserved bassist Colin Moulding. Paul Fox recruited me and XTC guitarist Dave Gregory to join Pat Mastellato (moonlighting from his gig with Mister Mister) on tambourines. The goofing off started immediately and soon we had christened ourselves The Three Tambourines. When we weren't laughing, we gave Paul Fox some acceptable takes and just like that, I had played on the new XTC album. I'll make a note to add "professional tambourinist" to my portfolio.

VEG IS A BUZZWORD

MCA paid me advances against royalties to co-write with other artists. As a real job, I could hardly complain. Still, I missed the freedom and creativity of playing with a band. I'd met drummer Winston Watson and bassist Paul Martinez when I was working on the *Colorcode* album with Stevie Salas. Seeking refuge from the Hollywood hustle, Paul, Winston, and I began jamming regularly in my basement just for our own pleasure.

I taped our jams on cassette and eventually began assembling the best parts into proper songs. We recorded a few things at MCA and immediately knew we were onto something special. Much as we wanted to keep our little three-piece to ourselves, we were doing a terrible job of avoiding momentum. Our engineer pal CJ deVillar snuck us into Conway Studios, one of LA's best rooms, and captured two more tracks that blew our hair back. Suddenly, we had a demo reel that revealed us to be a kind of Cream/Black Sabbath/Beatles hybrid. We first called ourselves the Buzzwords and eventually VeG. We debuted live in San Francisco at an outdoor animal rights concert by City Hall. None other than Grace Slick introduced us and you can't get more San Francisco than that. Next was a showcase in Portland, Oregan, at the NXNW festival, where a critic was "blindsided by brilliance" and singled me out as a "pop visionary." VeG performed at ASCAP's "LA's Best Kept Secrets" showcase at Hollywood's Coconut Teaszer Club. The guitarist from the band following us said he caught our show and loved it. His name was Tom Morello, and his band was called Rage Against the Machine. They wouldn't be a Best Kept Secret much longer.

Winston got us hired to be the studio backing band for Paula Jean Brown of Giant Sand and the Go-Go's. The studio owner/engineer, Harvey Moltz, was floored by our sound and insisted we make a VeG album when Paula's was finished. Isolated in the hills above Tucson, Harvey's studio was serene and creative-friendly. With no managers, lawyers, publishers, or labels involved, the VeG studio experience was magical and musical to the core. It was one of the few times I've recorded away from home, with a single mission receiving all my focus, all day long. A fantastic way to work. We completed the album in Tucson and mixed back in LA.

Mojo Magazine called our self-released VeG album "marvelous stuff" and called me "a major talent, with a gold-dust voice." The *Arizona Daily Star* said, "Infectious melodies, guitar hooks that won't leave your brain." All the great things that happened to VeG resulted from the three of us playing freely together, for fun. We wouldn't have had it any other way.

The VeG story might've had a few more chapters, but opportunity called for Winston. He was offered the job of a lifetime, playing drums with Bob Dylan, and it kept him on the road for the next five years. VeG, with its promise of artistic freedom and fun, went into hibernation. But you never know. Some gardens spring back to life.

BIRMINGHAM AMERICAN STYLE

MCA found me a co-writing assignment I could sink my teeth into. Birmingham, Alabama's Damon Johnson was tall, rail thin, long-haired, skilled on his Les Paul, and in a real pickle. Growing up playing in bands, he'd always stuck to guitar and left the singing to others. Now he'd formed Brother Cane and found himself center stage as lead guitarist *and* lead singer. On top of that, Brother Cane was signed to Mercury Records and the label expected Damon to write a hit album.

Damon spoke on the phone from Alabama, his voice infused with an appealing Southern drawl. "Parthenon, man, I've always had a lot of confidence in myself, and this is what I've been working toward all my life, but…", he said with an ironic laugh, "when it comes to songwriting and creating lyrics that I'm gonna have to sing, I just, I just don't know how to *do* this, you know what I'm sayin'?"

I was disarmed by Damon immediately. He was thoughtful, genuine, and not afraid to admit what he didn't know. I said, "Damon. Here's what we'll do. We're gonna write about stuff that you know. That you feel is true. You don't have to create some rock 'n' roll fantasy-world bullshit and pretend you're someone you're not. We're gonna figure out what's important to you and put it down in a way that when you sing it, you'll feel it—because you'll mean it. Does that sound like a plan?"

I could hear Damon exhale on the other end of the line. "Yeah, Parthenon. Thank you. That sounds like a great plan."

I based myself at my oldest brother Tom's townhouse in Birmingham. Brother Cane's front man met me there, fearlessly sporting knee-length blue-and-white tie-dyed shorts. I didn't care what Damon wore, but I wagered his look would not hold up for longer than a week once he began recording in everyone-wears-black Los Angeles. (I'm not one to talk about late '80s fashion. One night in Hollywood, Stevie Salas and I ran into his former employer, Rod Stewart. I was sporting sweatpants that Patrick Nagel might've vomited. Rod told Stevie, "Tell your friend never to wear those pants again." You know you're in trouble when a rooster like Rod Stewart offers fashion advice.)

Damon and I discussed the kinds of songs he wanted to write for Brother Cane. We agreed that "Babe I'm Gonna Leave You," "Stairway To Heaven," and a few others had pulled off a nice trick by starting mellow and ending with a bang. We agreed that concept could work for a song we called "Woman." I devised some dramatic acoustic guitar sequences, which slowly built to an aggressive electric guitar pattern from Damon. Even playing through a practice amp, Damon had impressive tone and attack. He was one of those guitarists—guys with skilled hands—who could make any gear sound great.

The lyric in the quieter opening section came directly from our plan to write about Damon's truth—in this case, his trepidation about fronting a band and trying to hit a homerun for a major label.

I used to know better
Now I don't know what's worse
Having it all, maybe
Or having nothing for sure

Damon needn't have worried. He turned out to be a natural front man. "Woman" became a fan favorite on Brother Cane's Mercury debut and Damon went on to make three Brother Cane albums and place a #1 song on Billboard's Hard Rock chart. He's had stints with Alice Cooper, Thin Lizzy, and Lynyrd Skynyrd on top of a successful solo career. I'm proud to have played a small part in his story.

GOIN' TO THE GO-GO

MCA signed Go-Go's drummer Gina Schock to the writing staff. She was a plain-spoken, no bullshit gal from Baltimore with short, dyed hair who was as comfortable in a sweatshirt as she was onstage with the world's most successful female rock band. We got along well and managed to write a couple songs when she wasn't consumed with Go-Go's business. When it was time to record, we hunkered down in MCA's basement studio.

Hanging out at the MCA sessions was a songwriting partner of Gina's, a guy with short blond hair and wire-rimmed glasses named Jim Jacobsen. Jim was pretty low key and didn't speak much during the session, but as we were packing up to leave, he approached me and said, "Hey, I really like the way you play guitar. I wonder if you'd come over to my house next week to do some recording?" As any musician would, I said I'd be happy to. Jim's accent, while softened by LA, still had a trace of the Midwest. I didn't know it, but he'd studied music composition at the Wisconsin Conservatory of Music, the University of Chicago, and Stanford. He was one of those musicians who knew what he was doing.

Jim shared a house with his architect boyfriend high in the residential hills above LA. As I knocked on his front door, a whiff of night jasmine from a flower pot rocketed me back to Greece. I took it as a good sign. Jim helped me carry my seventy-pound Vox AC30 amp and a Fender Stratocaster into his basement studio. Once I'd dialed up a sufficiently aggressive guitar sound, he hit "Record." All I heard was a click track at about 110 BPM (beats per minute). There were no other instruments for me to play along with. Just "tick, tick, tick…"

Jim, sitting at his recording console, looked at me with a cockeyed smile and said, "Whenever you're ready, start playing."

I asked, "Play what?"

"Whatever you like."

"Really? Alright. Start the click over and I'll go."

I instinctively struck an A power-chord and let it ring for a few beats. I followed it with a quick D and G, took a left turn to an E minor, and then back to A. I changed my rhythmic attack, keeping in time with the click, but with a muted strumming. As my ad hoc guitar track took shape, I improvised other sequences of chords that I knew would eventually lead me neatly back to the first pattern. After about two minutes, I arrived at what sounded like an ending and stopped.

"That was great," Jim said. "Do something like that again."

He started the click track again and I played another two minutes of random rock. This was a highly unorthodox session, but I was enjoying myself. With no apparent rules, what could go wrong? Jim said, "Okay, now play a solo over the first pass you did." I obliged. I wasn't wild about my first solo attempt, so I insisted on giving him two or three more to choose from. I did the same over the second track.

After a half hour, my new friend Jim said, "You did really well. I'd like you to come back next week and do it again." He then handed me a check for $200. I thanked Jim for the check, and was delighted to be making $400 an hour, but I still had to ask, "Do *what* again? What exactly did we just do?"

"You'll see when you come back next week."

The next week, I set up my amp, got my guitar sound again, and sat ready for whatever it was we were doing. This time Jim hit "Play" on his console, and I heard a finished, fully mixed instrumental track with keyboards, drums, bass, strings, and bits of guitar. It was vaguely Steely Dan-ish and sounded nothing like the more aggressive rock music I'd created the week before. I listened carefully to the guitars to see if I recognized any of my parts. I can't say I did.

"What do you think?" Jim asked.

"Are those my guitar parts?"

"Yeah."

"Really? It doesn't sound like what I did."

Jim said, "Well, I've manipulated your tracks pretty heavily."

Huh?

This was my first taste of modern digital recording. Unlike the digital tape machine David Kahne used in 1988 on the *Sunny Nights* sessions, digital recorders by the early '90s were essentially computers, no tape required. Guitars, vocals, violins, drums, handclaps, street noise, any sound that could be recorded by a mic, was no longer stuck on a piece of tape in the sequence it was recorded. Instead, all recorded sounds were turned into ones and zeros (digitized) and stored on a hard drive, where they could be copied, moved around, and pasted anywhere in the song. In my case, Jim had listened to my guitar performances, isolated the bits he liked best, and pieced them together as entirely new parts to fit his song. A real Frankenstein guitar job.

I know, I know. In today's world, this is *duh!* stuff. The software behind TikTok would outperform an early digital recording system. In 1992, though, the possibilities were mind blowing. I felt like I was standing in one century and looking into the next.

I recognized that Jim was performing digital wizardry, but I still didn't understand what kind of music we were making. It seemed completely random. Jim explained. "It's called Production Music, or Library Music. I work for a Danish guy named Olie. He puts my music into TV, movies, trailers, wherever instrumental music is needed. I've been doing it for about ten years. You wouldn't know it, but you've heard my music in commercials and all over TV. Movies, too. I had twenty-two minutes of music in *Pulp Fiction*." That got my attention.

Jim and I created instrumental tracks in tons of styles—rockabilly, acoustic pop, boy band ballads, dramatic movie themes, hard rock, metal, Southern rock, pretty much every kind of music I never did as an artist. The music was all "work for hire," and I felt free to create tracks without second-guessing my choices or agonizing over content. Whenever Jim and I created a piece of music that made our hair stand up (in a good way), we'd be tempted to keep it for ourselves, but we never did. We had a rule, which Jim would shout in his best Hollywood producer voice: "Always give 'em the 'A' licks, kid!"

After working with Jim for a few months, it dawned on me that we never argued over anything, musical or otherwise. We hadn't even raised our voices. We did our jobs, and everything worked out. That's rare in the subjective world of co-creating. A thought occurred to me, and one day in his studio I asked Jim on a hunch, "What's your birthday?"

"January 15, 1956."

So that was it. I was January 19. We were born four days apart. I said, "No wonder I never argue with you. You're me. Well, to be more precise, you're the gay me."

Jim laughed, "Let's make sure we keep that part straight."

One of my favorite projects was handling all the guitars and vocals on Jim's hypersonic theme song for *The Downer Channel*, an NBC sketch comedy show executive-produced by Steve Martin and featuring comedians like Wanda Sykes. Jim's song was a galloping thirty-second speed bomb packed with hooks. You can hear it on YouTube. Unfortunately, even Steve Martin can't win 'em all. The show tanked. I'm convinced *The Downer Channel* was ahead of its time and would work perfectly in this age of memes and internet griping. Timing. Is. Everything.

OVER AND OUT

In 1992, I was in my fifth year at MCA Music Publishing. I was a classic close-but-no-cigar songwriter. My songs reached the AC, Alternative, Album Rock, Modern Rock, and even college charts, but not the Billboard Hot 100, the only chart that mattered. My co-write with Mark Ferrari, "Kiss The Ground You Walk On," narrowly missed inclusion on the *Bodyguard* soundtrack (so I heard), where it would've likely made me half a million dollars. As a consolation prize, "Kiss The Ground" appeared on a posthumous LP by the amazing blind lap steel guitarist Jeff Healey. I wrote lyrics for Marshall Crenshaw that he couldn't imagine singing. Wilson Phillips demo'd a song I wrote with Gina Schock but didn't put it on an album. Columbia might've had a hit with "Double Our Numbers" if they had pushed a second single. And so the story goes.

Rick Shoemaker, my biggest supporter at MCA, took a senior vice president job at a competing publishing company, Warner/Chappell Music. I still had supporters at MCA, notably Betsy Anthony (who'd introduced me to E) and Sherri Orson, who always believed in my talent, but the truth was, I wasn't making enough money for MCA to justify keeping me on staff. My hits weren't HITS. MCA let me go in 1993. I would no longer be paid to write songs. Amazing job, but a tough business.

As a parting gift, the Universe bookended my stay at MCA with two more movie roles. I landed in *Dragon: The Bruce Lee Story* as, wait for it, "guy in band." This time, my fake movie combo performed "California Dreamin'" on the veranda of a Malibu mansion with Bruce Lee's real-life daughter singing lead. We got a brief on-set visit by Buddy Hackett, a friend of "Dragon" star Robert Wagner. Hackett's brown jumpsuit made him look like a giant chocolate tick. LA knows how to entertain.

Gina Schock got me my final movie gig, *The Flintstones Movie*. You can briefly see me behind a boogaloo-ing John Goodman in my role as "guy in band" (surprise) playing bass with the cutely renamed BC-52s. I begged the show dresser to let me keep my leopard print Fred-smock, but she laughed and said, "No way. Sorry." No more co-writing, no more acting.

CHAPTER 13

THE EASIEST ALBUM EVER MADE

For the first time in five years, songwriting wasn't a job anymore. MCA no longer dictated my agenda or paid me advances. I reverted to writing songs to please myself, the unpaid artist. I was less financially secure, but I felt liberated.

Janet's career had similarly devolved away from her dream job of indie filmmaker. When CBS Television produced *Mrs. Lambert Remembers Love*, it led to Janet getting more work in TV movies. She rewrote a script for ABC called *Lies and Lullabies* starring Susan Dey as a cocaine-addicted mother battling for child custody. The money was great, but the story wasn't Janet's original work. She was a hired gun working within the strict parameters of network television. She wasn't on a path to artistic satisfaction. The network interference on one project, a re-write of a TV movie called *A Mother's Right: The Elizabeth Morgan Story*, left Janet so frustrated she changed her screen credit from Janet Heaney to "Lucretia Baxter," a mash-up of our street addresses. She eventually bit the bullet, bailed on television, and began work on a spec script with a friend.

NOW WITH EVEN LESS CRUELTY

Janet also devoted time to animal care and animal rights. She'd grown up on a farm, and, being Janet, she dove in headfirst. She joined animal rights groups, became a vegetarian, rose to president of a local animal rescue group, and began participating in protests against the fur industry and vivisection. I thought Janet was right on and I followed her lead. Janet and I became familiar to the small but dedicated LA animal rights movement, and, inevitably, I was approached to provide music at fundraising events. The organizers didn't care what I played, so I agreed.

I reached out to my pals Mark Goldenberg and Rusty Anderson, two of the best and most highly respected guitarists in the business and pitched my interpretation of the gig. "It'll just be us three on electric guitars, no bass or drums. I want you to play whatever comes into your head. Don't play real songs. Just make shit up and we'll see what happens when the three of us all get going." Mark and Rusty's faces lit up. Rusty laughed, "I can do that!" Mark chimed in, "I think we should call ourselves the Cruelty Free Noodlers." Sold.

We set up our gear on a balcony overlooking a small ballroom inside the Hollywood Roosevelt Hotel. Mark said, "Let's do this." Our no-rules guitar trio ventured to places we'd never gone before and never will again. We created music that was oddly beautiful, then hilarious, then like a spy theme, then Greek, back to beautiful, over to who knows where, and on and on. Certain passages caused us to piss ourselves laughing, but we played on, never knowing what was coming next. We'd take breaks, gather our wits, and then dive back in.

From the balcony, our view of the downstairs crowd was all hair and hats, so it was easy to spot the occasional upturned face of an attendee who'd noticed the sound of the Cruelty Free Noodlers. They'd look up, swivel their head, and try to locate the source of the weirdest damned music they'd ever heard. Mark laughed, "We've got one fan!"

The Noodlers gigs kept coming. Mark wasn't available for one, so Rusty suggested I call his friend Brian Ray, another excellent guitarist who'd played in Etta James's band when he was a teenager. Brian fit right in. As soon as he heard what Rusty and I were doing, he jumped in, laughing, and we were off. If there are any Paul McCartney fans reading this, I'm delighted you now realize Paul's band contains not one, but two members of the legendary Cruelty Free Noodlers. I'm waiting for Paul to make it three.

A WALK IN THE PARK

Janet and I hadn't lived together for the first eighteen months of our marriage. We stayed at one house or the other every night but enjoyed our separate homes as creative spaces during work hours. But, with both of us unemployed, we caved to cost-saving marital norms. We found a rental house atop another steep street adjacent to Elysian Park, home to Dodger Stadium, the Police Academy, and miles of walking trails.

Each day, I walked our coyote-like dog Algonquin into Elysian park and threw sticks for him to retrieve. That simple task, plus a couple miles of walking, nearly always resulted in a new song. Untethered from MCA, music poured out of me. I was free to write lyrics around my own truth, and, at that important point in my life, the truth was that Janet and I were becoming less financially stable by the day, yet even more in love.

We don't have a castle
That don't mean a thing
'Cause whenever I'm with you
I live like a king
("Live Like A King")

It's 2 a.m. my love's asleep
Somehow now it hits me deep
To watch her breathe, to know she lives
Is more than gold or silver gives
("Simple Things")

Last night I had the rent
Today I don't know where it went
I like Superman a lot
But I guess Clark Kent's all I got
It's okay, it's just one more day in the life
("One More Day In The Life")

I loved my new songs, and I loved loving Janet, but for the first time since I'd moved from New York five years earlier, I was unemployed in Los Angeles. I asked myself, should I swallow my pride and get a real job? (Did J.C. Penney have gas stations in LA?) I don't know if I'm selfish, driven, stupid, or stubborn, but I still clung to one dream—to be a successful artist on my own terms. I decided to keep my overhead low and trust that money would come from somewhere. I felt like my best move, as a broke thirty-seven-year-old, was to start a new band. I bet on myself once again.

P. HUX

The universe must've heard me. My old couch-provider and bass player Jen Condos introduced me to drummer Gordon Townsend, new in town from Philadelphia and looking for musical action. The handsome, twenty-four-year-old Mr. Townsend joined me in my rehearsal room with his champagne sparkle Yamaha drum kit, a slight Philly accent, and an appealing rat-a-tat laugh.

The first song we played together was one of my new ones, "One More Day In The Life." Gordon immediately latched onto the vibe I was going for and within a minute I knew he was the drummer I'd always wanted. Despite his youth—born in 1970, the year the Beatles broke up—Gordon reminded me of Ringo Starr and John Bonham: creative, rock-solid time, and plenty of power. I couldn't believe my luck.

After running through a half dozen new songs, Gordon mentioned he knew a bass player, a guy from Philly named Rob Miller whom he'd played with in Tommy Conwell and the Young Rumblers. I remembered *Rolling Stone* calling Conwell the Next Big Thing from the East Coast.

"Rob's good?" I asked.

"He's insane. He can do anything. We'd be very lucky to get him."

We got him.

Rob showed up in baggy blue jeans, black work boots, and a leather blazer over a thin T-shirt. He had clear blue eyes and long ringlets of blond hair framing his face. He was armed with a classic Fender Precision bass and a show-me-what-you-got attitude. I sensed that Rob appreciated Gordon's opinion of my songs but was holding out, wanting to judge for himself. Fair enough.

The three of us assembled beneath the skylights in my rehearsal room. I walked Rob through the chords of "One More Day In The Life," which he picked up easily. I counted the song off at the desired tempo, strummed my electric guitar, dug into the vocal, and listened to what Gordon and Rob cooked up.

I'd struck gold. Our sound matched the music I heard in my head on my walks with Algonquin. After two or three songs, I saw why Gordon was so high on Rob. I thought, "Fuck me. This guy has it." Rob's bass parts did the heavy lifting they were supposed to do—lock in with the drums, support the guitar and vocal arrangement, cover the low end—but the notes he chose and the phrases he fit them into gave our trio an extra quality. After one rehearsal, all three of us knew we had something special. We called our band P. Hux.

ALAIN

I had a new band, Janet a new script, and our house had a new occupant. We'd remained friends with Alain Romero's family from Janet's old neighborhood. Tragically, Milagro, mother of three boys, had died a terrible, prolonged death from AIDS. Janet and I had helped find her hospice care and assisted with the funeral arrangements. We offered to become legal guardians of seventeen-year-old Alain. He gratefully accepted and his younger brothers moved into a one-bedroom apartment with their stepdad. We had Alain for his senior year in high school. It went well for a while.

THE EASIEST ALBUM EVER MADE

After a few more rehearsals with Gordon and Rob, I got a call out of the blue from a guy named Matt Heimbold. He said, "You don't know me, but I just graduated from UCLA. *Sunny Nights* was my favorite album in college. I'm moving back up to Monterey where I'm starting a record label called Black Olive. I'd like you to be the first artist on my label, but only if you promise me you can make an album as good as *Sunny Nights*." Pretty good pitch on young Matt's part. I'd just rehearsed ten new songs with my incredible new band. I've never been more confident of a promise. I told Matt, "I can absolutely make an album as good as *Sunny Nights*." My first follow-up to *Sunny Nights* with Jeff Lord-Alge had failed badly. This time, things would be different. Truly, the world works in mysterious ways.

Young Mr. Heimbold and I worked out a budget and a plan. I proposed we record basic tracks to analog tape in Los Angeles, using an engineer I liked named Mike Bosley. We'd then transfer the masters to a new digital tape format called ADATs and do overdubs in Monterey. Bosley recorded us at Rick Parker's Sandbox and Doug Messenger's place out in the Valley, two comfy studios with great live sound. Doug Messenger's 3M tape machine was said to have captured Steely Dan's *Pretzel Logic*. Every LA studio has a story.

Bosley captured our sound perfectly as we ripped through eleven songs in no time. Rob's first takes sounded like keepers, but he'd say, "Naahhh, don't keep that. This next one'll be better." I'd look at Bosley, he'd wink back. He was keeping everything. Gordon and Rob's rhythm tracks were tight, punchy pieces of art, the perfect underpinning for my guitar and scratch vocals.

I drove the tapes five and a half hours to Monterey to begin overdubs at Black Olive Studios. During the drive, I listened again and again to a cassette of the basic tracks. California's landscape—soft golden hills, verdant valleys—added an element of romance as I filled four pages of a legal pad with overdub ideas. When I reached Monterey, studio owner Nick Olivo's first question was, "Do you have any thoughts on how you'd like to start?" I laughed. "Yes, I have some thoughts." We dove in.

Gordon and Rob soon joined me in Monterey, excited to pitch in on overdubs. It seemed like every idea worked just right. On "Here Comes The Savior," the three of us built a choir's worth of vocals that elevated the song immensely. Rob had one great idea after another for background vocal parts, adding spice to "It'll Be Alright" and "Every Minute." On a song called "California," I mused that a triangle would really sound good on the chorus. Rob said, "I know how to play triangle," and quickly put down an impressive track of a difficult-to-play percussion instrument I'd never used in my music.

As we continued to add killer overdubs day after day in Monterey, I'll never forget Rob saying, "This is the easiest album I'VE ever worked on." Noted.

"California" also had a bit of fun with some name dropping:

I shook hands with Brian Wilson
James Earl Jones, he loved my name
Played some pool with Edge from U2
But the best was Robin Lane

About that James Earl Jones reference. After a screening Janet and I attended in Hollywood, I spotted Mr. Jones in the lobby. Now, you're not supposed to bother stars in LA, but I couldn't resist. I approached him and said, "Sorry to bother you Mr. Jones, my name's Parthenon Huxley and I'm just a huge fan." He shook my hand and said, "Parthenon Huxley: that's a great name." My head nearly exploded. He didn't just say my name, he said my name with that voice. "I am your father, Parthenon." "I find your lack of faith disturbing, Huxley." "The force is strong on this one, P. Hux." I floated across the lobby back to Janet. "Darth Vadar just said my name!"

Matt Heimbold, promised an album as good as *Sunny Nights*, had deliberately stayed away from the sessions, wanting only to hear finished tracks. When he finally heard his label's first album, *P. Hux "Deluxe,"* his reactions were priceless.

One More Day In The Life. "Oh, I like that one!"

Simple Things. "Man, that one's good!"

Every Minute. "Oh, that's great! That might be my favorite so far."

Keep From Crying. "No, that one's my new favorite."

Matt had taken a chance. I'd made a promise. We'd both won.

Seven long years after the release of *Sunny Nights*, my album *P. Hux "Deluxe"* announced my return to the artistic driver's seat. The album immediately created a buzz not only in LA, but also on the nascent internet, where it was discovered by power pop aficionados around the world. Positive reviews came pouring in.

"Parthenon Huxley, a student of the masters...has become a master himself." – Magnet

"With each listen, I find a new favorite track which suggests they are all great." – Audities

"A smart, tough and consistently excellent release. Don't miss it." – Goldmine

"The perfect recipe for unforgettable pop gems. These guys deserve several hits." – Huh

"Worth the wait. Huxley sings...with gripping momentum." – Billboard

I licensed *Deluxe* to Pioneer Records in Japan, TWA Records in Australia, and Wagram Music in France. Rhino Records placed our single "Every Minute" on its *Poptopia: Power Pop Hits of the '90s* compilation. The Album Network featured both "Every Minute" and "It'll Be Alright" on their *Tune Up In-Store* CD collections. We opened for Chicago at the Greek Theater and did a Midwest/East Coast tour with Paul Collins' Non-Stop Pop Roadshow. Steve Vagnini, my stalwart supporter, brought us up to Monterey and Santa Cruz, repeatedly, for radio interviews and live dates. The positive response crescendoed when *Audities* magazine announced the results of its year-end poll of artists and writers: *P. Hux "Deluxe"* was voted 1995 Album of the Year. The editors added:

"Parthenon displays a rare talent, the ability to write lyrics with depth and substance (often with a dose of sarcasm or ironic insight) without compromising the visceral impact of the songs."

I felt like my return to music as my passion couldn't have gone better. I was the writer, singer, guitarist, and leader of a sensational band with an award-winning album. *"Deluxe"* was the record that cemented my reputation as an artist, and it had only taken me thirty-nine years to get my shit together.

All I had to do now was, once again, learn how to make money without a job.

DISHES

Janet and I felt good about our decision to become Alain's guardians. He had a room to himself for the first time, a job after school at the local ABC-TV affiliate, and a senior year in high school to enjoy. Sadly, the good vibes didn't last. Alain was still processing the loss of his mother and didn't have the bandwidth to accept us as the adults in his life. He began to resent us sticking our noses in his business. He became combative. He missed his brothers. We figured his behavior was typical of a teen, but Janet and I, untrained in parenting, still found it difficult to handle. The three of us entered counseling to lower the tension and get on the same page. It helped for a while.

We'd given Alain a single household task, washing the dishes, and he didn't like it. One night, Janet reminded him for the umpteenth time to keep the water in the sink and not make a giant mess. Regrettably, Alain's teen resentment boiled over and spilled onto Janet. "Fuck the dishes and fuck you, Janet."

It almost reads as laughable now, but after nine months of a difficult guardianship, it wasn't funny. We'd gone out of our way to do right by Alain, but we couldn't accept his resentment or verbal abuse. We asked Alain if he'd rather live with us or move in with his brothers. He said, "I would rather live with a million rats than live under your roof." It was a good line, and of course I put it into a song, but it hurt to hear it.

We began the process of legally reuniting Alain with his brothers and stepdad. Janet and I were disappointed, but also, truth be told, somewhat relieved. We loved Alain, but we couldn't have picked a more difficult time in his life to be his guardians.

PARTHENON HUXLEY'S OFF DAY

My dad, bless him and his Depression-era upbringing, worried about me and couldn't fathom how the music business worked. (We had that in common.) Unbeknownst to me, my conservative-leaning dad wrote a letter to the only person in Hollywood with values close to his own: Ben Stein. In an earnest letter to someone he admired, my dad mentioned my struggles in the music business and asked if Stein wouldn't mind giving me a call to offer advice and counsel from someone who'd made it in Hollywood. Ridiculous, right? Here's the kicker: Ben Stein called me. Here's the second kicker: I didn't know who he was. In fact, after he introduced himself on the phone, confidently saying, "Hi Parthenon, it's Ben Stein..." I said, "Hi, Ben. Do we know each other?" I could hear the air leaving the room on the other end of the line. Ben Stein had more than generously acted on my dad's earnest letter and only ended up embarrassed, thanks to my ignorance and the unfortunate truth that I'd never seen *Ferris Bueller's Day Off*. Stein said, "I'm sorry. I think there's been a mistake."

I called my dad and told him the story. Dad couldn't believe it. "He actually CALLED you? I'll be a son of a gun! He's a better man than I. I guess I should've let you know I'd written the letter...but I never thought he'd actually call."

I hope I get to apologize to Stein one day in person.

Chapter 13: The Easiest Album Ever Made

IT NEEDS MORE OBOE

A musician friend named Gus Black told me, "Parthenon, you should work with Kyle Vincent. His music is good but it's kind of wimpy. He needs your rock." I'd gotten pretty good at co-writing for MCA, so I decided to investigate.

Kyle Vincent may've been a skinny, dark-haired native of Berkeley, California, but his musical true north was 1970s LA pop: piano ballads, saccharine lyrics, treacly melodies, oboes, and strings. If "I'd Really Love To See You Tonight" by England Dan and John Ford Coley came on the radio, he'd turn it *up*, not off.

Like me, Kyle had been through the major label ringer. Mercury Records dropped his band Candy after one album. Kyle's MCA solo album never even got released. Was he willing to write new songs and take another shot at a major? Third time's the charm and all that?

Kyle lived in the flats of Burbank with a leopard-like cat and a roommate who was never there. We made each other laugh, and, in no time, we'd written a bushel of guitar-driven songs with big melodies. The ease of our collaboration got us both excited. Gus had made a good call. Ready or not, it felt like we had major-label material.

Kyle put together a four-piece band including me on guitar and background vocals. We showcased a short set of our best new songs at a rehearsal room in the Valley for a handful of reps from the majors. *Whatd'ya know*, Hollywood Records stepped up and signed my new songwriting pal. Our process had, shockingly, worked exactly as we'd hoped.

I co-produced the record with Kyle at *Lawnmower and Garden Supply* in Pasadena, a roomy, warehouse kind of studio that had belonged to the late, great Kevin Gilbert of Toy Matinee and the Tuesday Night Music Club. Gabe Veltri, a funny but low-key guy with too many credits to list on one page, co-produced and engineered. We used the P. Hux rhythm section of Gordon and Rob on our first single, "Wake Me Up (When The World's Worth Waking Up For)." "Wake" was a great example of Kyle's and my co-writing partnership. The lyrical theme and melody were all Kyle, and the guitar attack was heavily me. The two approaches blended perfectly.

Gabe mixed the thirteen-song *Kyle Vincent* album at LA's Ocean Way Studios. We knew our team had made a good record. All we could do was pray that Hollywood Records would invest in promotion and marketing.

They did. "Wake Me Up" ran up the charts and became a hit, especially in the Midwest. Before we knew it, Kyle and I were on the road for radio interviews and live gigs. We performed as an acoustic duo on bills with Bryan

Adams, Sister Hazel, Richard Marx, Kip Winger, and other '90s stalwarts. Even without a rhythm section, our songs were sturdy enough to entertain summer crowds of up to 20,000.

My favorite moment of the promotional tour reminded me of when I'd heard the Blazers on the radio at my old newspaper job. Kyle and I were being driven into Cincinnati by a regional Hollywood Records promoter when "Wake Me Up" came blasting out of the car radio. There's nothing like hearing your work on the air. We felt like stars as the deejay said, "That's 'Wake Me Up' by Kyle Vincent. He'll be onstage in Riverside Park tonight..."

CHAPTER 14
A FINAL TOUR

In 1995 our landlord reclaimed the house we rented from him near Elysian Park. Janet and I moved into a charmingly creaky 1915 wooden farmhouse in my old neighborhood at the corner of Baxter and Alvarado. We called it "Funky Farms." The walls were thin, the appliances out of date, but it stood facing west atop a hill in Echo Park with a million-dollar view of the entire LA basin. The vista made up for everything.

EVERYTHING'S WEIRD

One night, a few months after we'd moved in, I awoke in our attic bedroom at 3 a.m. to discover Janet absent from bed. Odd. I crept downstairs and found her in the living room, sitting on the couch in her robe, staring into space. I sat down next to her. Her lavish auburn curls spilled to her shoulders.

"What's going on, baby?" I asked.

"I can't get the taste of paint out of my mouth. It's strange. I've brushed my teeth three times and it hasn't gone away. I can't figure it out."

"That's weird. What do you think it might be?"

"I don't know," she said, looking at me, concerned. "I hope I don't have cancer."

"You don't have cancer," I said with a reassuring scoff. I wanted to sound confident, but neither of us could ignore that her older brother Joey had died of brain cancer. Not only that, her older sister Julie had died of Lupus back in the 1960s when it was a much less manageable disease. Janet, 37, was the oldest of five remaining siblings. Death was no stranger to the Heaney clan.

"Well, I hope no one in my family has died," she said, showing her typical concern for others.

"No one has died, baby. Come on back to bed. We'll figure it out in the morning."

She let out a breath. "Alright." We climbed back up the narrow, creaky stairs, got in bed and eventually went back to sleep. I didn't like this paint-taste thing, but if there was a living soul who might outlast us all, it was Janet. Janet was the kind of person who made the world go. She was all fire, all the time. Resolutely caring, she was the enemy of indifference, the backbone of her family, and a rock for friends to depend on. I couldn't imagine her being anything less.

At dawn, I suddenly awoke. The bed was shaking. Having lived in LA long enough to know, I thought, "Earthquake!" An instant later I discovered the world was moving for a different reason. Janet was in seizure.

"Oh, God! No!" My feet hit the floor.

As I hurried to Janet's side of the bed, I heard a voice say, "Your life is changing 180 degrees. Deal with it."

"No shit!" I said aloud.

I held Janet as she shook. Whether she could hear me or not, I pleaded to her, "Come back, baby! Please...I'm here!" I put my fingers in her mouth to prevent her from swallowing her tongue even as I doubted that was the prescribed thing to do. After fifteen or twenty terrifying seconds, she stopped shaking and gradually became still. The look on her face morphed from extreme agitation to one of calm, almost adolescent wonder. I thought to myself, "She looks like she's six years old." As I laid her head back on the bed, she stared out the window at the LA sky and said, "Everything's...weird." I couldn't have agreed more. I called 911.

Before I could ponder the insanity of hearing a disembodied voice giving me life advice or that I'd answered the voice aloud, I heard sirens howling up Echo Park canyon. Soon, a firetruck and an ambulance noisily purred outside in the driveway and a minute later our attic bedroom with its low, diagonally pitched ceilings was crowded with firemen and EMTs.

Janet sat on the edge of our bed in her nightshirt. An EMT examined her eyes. I heard him say, "Classic Grand Mal seizure."

"Yep, looks like," another agreed.

Janet said, "What're you guys doing here?" I smiled, happy to hear her speaking clearly. If I were Janet, I guess I'd be wondering that, too.

"We need to take you to the hospital, ma'am," an EMT explained. "You've had a seizure and we need to have a doctor look at you."

Janet looked at the EMT and scoffed. "A seizure? I don't think so." Janet the fighter was acting more like herself. My heart stopped breaking just a bit.

I knelt in front of her. "Baby, you have had a seizure. I called 911. These guys are here for a reason. We're going to take you to Glendale. It's the closest hospital. I'll follow the ambulance in the truck. We'll get you checked out and then I'll bring you back home. Okay?"

"If you say so, but I don't really think I need to go to the hospital." Her normal sense of independence and clear diction were almost comical under the circumstances.

I stood and said to one of the EMTs in a low voice, "Is this normal behavior?"

He kind of shrugged. "Can be. People can come out of seizures and not remember a thing about 'em. Has she had seizures before?"

"No."

"Make sure the doctors take a good long look."

"Okay."

180 DEGREES

A scan revealed a small smudge in Janet's brain. The doctors assumed it was encephalitis, a kind of "cold" that gets past the brain-blood barrier. We were told to get an MRI, nevertheless, which we did the next day. The brain specialist agreed he thought the smudge would clear up on its own, but being cautious, he booked a follow-up MRI for a month later.

Over the next few weeks, the taste of paint persisted in Janet's mouth. She began to lose her grip and dropped things like ketchup bottles. We were both uncomfortable with these developments, but we had the second MRI coming up and figured that would be soon enough to return to the doctor. When the day of her follow-up MRI arrived, Janet insisted on driving herself to the hospital to meet with the brain specialist.

I was in the yard at Funky Farms when Janet called from the doctor's office. She told me the second MRI revealed that in one month's time, the smudge had grown to the size of a tangerine. She had brain cancer. Dazed by the news, I remember doing two things. First, I began writing Janet's obituary in my head, being sure to use appropriately powerful language to describe what a sensational person she was. Second, I told myself to stop being a fucking idiot. She was alive. And as long as she was alive, I would never again let the thought of her dying enter my mind.

THE BATTLE

Janet and I met with a brain surgeon at Cedars-Sinai. After our consultation, I pulled him aside and said, "What are we looking at here, time-wise?"

He stared at the floor for a second, looked up and said, "We never like to project timelines in these situations."

I said, "I understand, but..."

The doctor told me, "When cancer's in the gut, it's easy to treat. The stomach opens up like a buffet." I blanched a bit. Doctor talk can be rough. He went on, "Brain cancer is hard to get to. We'll do our best, but it's much more difficult to treat."

I asked, "So, how long?"

He sighed and said, "Six months? Hard to tell. We just never know."

Janet underwent emergency brain surgery. The tumor was wrapped around an artery and couldn't be entirely redacted. In the recovery room, Janet bravely described her "sombrero of pain" but that didn't stop her from decorating her room with all the get-well cards she'd received.

The battle against the tumor was just beginning. After surgery, she consented to months of treatment with an experimental high-dose chemo regimen. We found her a hands-on healer, too. We did anything and everything over the next few months to fight the monster in her head. Slowly but surely, we made progress against the fastest growing glioblastoma multiforme our doctors at Cedar Sinai had ever seen. The tumor got smaller. I knew Janet could be the miracle girl. I just knew it.

Her pretty hair fell out and she wore ridiculous wigs, but otherwise she held up well during the chemo. One of my favorite images is of Janet laughing when her wig flew off during a highspeed ride with her cousin Carol and our friend Bianca on a go-kart track. That's my gal. Janet never complained about her pain, her baldness, her fate. We faced each day thinking she would get better, and we lived as normally as we could. Janet insisted I carry on with my music and not worry about leaving her at home when I needed to work. She'd never been anyone's burden and she didn't want to start now. Besides, her mom and her sister Jocelyn lived nearby and were available at a moment's notice.

ROCK 'N' ROLL TO THE RESCUE

I got a call from Len Fagan, a former drummer and big-hearted impresario who ran the Coconut Teaszer rock club in Hollywood. He'd heard about Janet's illness and offered to hold a fundraiser at his club to help us with medical expenses. I was floored by his kindness. Len and I put together a dream bill and started making calls. Every artist we contacted agreed to play. LA can feel like an impersonal, dog-eat-dog place at times, but on February 19, 1996, at the Coconut Teaszer it felt like the City of Angels. Len called the event Rock 'n' Roll to the Rescue and I'm still touched by the generosity and friendship shown by John Doe (X), Gilby Clarke (Guns N' Roses), Edna

Swap (with Rusty Anderson), Jason Falkner (Jellyfish) and E's new band, eels, for showing up when I was down.

SLOW DANCING

The good results from the experimental hi-dose chemo lasted only a few months. Janet's tumor began growing again and radiation became our last resort. I drove her to UCLA several times a week. Even in her compromised state, she insisted on shuffling unsteadily into the building by herself. She didn't want to feel helpless, and I tried to follow her lead. The treatments really took it out of her, but Janet put on a brave face. When her dad visited LA, Janet suggested we climb one of her favorite mountain trails in the Angeles National Forest. Cowboy Joe and I reluctantly acquiesced. The two of us walked on eggshells the whole way, checking in with Janet every twenty feet, asking if she was okay. "I'm fine, but you two worrywarts are gonna tire me out with your namby pamby inquiries." We smiled and shut up.

Janet and I took a drive up to Lake Arrowhead. We'd once fantasized about escaping LA and living in the mountains, but it was not to be. On this final trip, we parked on the side of a winding mountain road. The two of us wandered down into the quiet forest and found ourselves alone among the tall mountain pines. We locked eyes, I reached out, and we began slow dancing on a soft floor of pine needles.

P. HUX REDUX

Janet's illness had knocked the wind out of me, but I did my best to keep my head in the music game. I wrote a batch of new songs that felt like contenders for the follow-up to *Deluxe*. Gordon, Rob, and I convened in the West Hollywood garage studio of my friend Nic Pierone and effortlessly banged out a half dozen demos. Playing with Rob and Gordon was still a writer's dream. I could outline a song for them and have it fully recorded in less than an hour. After just one session at Nic's, a new album was taking shape.

We landed a photo session with the gifted rock photographer Henry Diltz. Henry's credits include the cover of Crosby, Stills, and Nash's debut album, *Morrison Hotel* by the Doors, Jimi Hendrix at Woodstock and so many more. Henry is one of the kindest, calmest people you'll ever meet, and it was a thrill to be a subject for his camera. He met our band at Funky Farms and positioned us in two or three locations with good natural light, Henry's preferred MO. Despite his easygoing, relaxed style of shooting, Henry captured us brilliantly. When we got the proofs, I circled several contenders for the cover of *P. Hux II*.

Unfortunately, P. Hux was about to run aground. We were musically successful and a favorite of critics, but we weren't generating any income. Rob had taken up computer programming and gotten so good at it that he landed a job at Geocities, an internet company that would eventually be bought by Yahoo. When Geocities relocated from LA to Aptos, California, up the coast near Santa Cruz, Rob decided to move north with the company. P. Hux had great demos and Henry Diltz photos, but we no longer had one of the best bass players I've ever worked with.

Before Rob left town, P. Hux gave a rousing final performance to a packed house at the House of Blues on Sunset Boulevard. The bill included Nic Pierone's band Head Popping Through, the Sunshine Club from San Francisco, and E's new band, eels. It was a great last gig for a fantastic trio that had given me so much musical joy.

A FINAL TOUR

A year after her diagnosis, Janet was determined to spend Christmas back East at Purgatory Falls Farm with her family. Her legs were unsteady, so she relented to being pushed in a wheelchair as we made our way through LAX. By this time, Janet had ditched her wig and instead wrapped her hairless head in an elaborate red kerchief, like a movie star from the 1930s. Her pretty face had become puffy and distorted from steroids and she spoke from one side of her mouth. Her spirit remained indomitable.

We landed in Boston, rented a car, and made the drive to Milford, New Hampshire, like we had so many times before. We were excited to see her dad, brothers and sisters, and closest cousin Carol. We pulled into the short driveway next to the centuries old original part of the house. It was a cold, dark December night. I told Janet to sit tight, I'd come around and help her out of the front passenger seat. She said, "No, don't bother. I want to make a good impression. I'll get out by myself."

Her family heard our arrival. Wooden doors opened, light spilled onto the dark frozen ground, and soon a gang of her loved ones were hurrying out to greet us and help with our suitcases. Janet pulled herself out of the rental car, stood and waved to everyone, and promptly collapsed in a heap. Good impression! All of us gasped and rushed to scoop her up. To my forever grateful ears, Janet was giggling about her fabulous stage entrance. Our hearts fell back into our chests.

Chapter 14: A Final Tour

Our week in New Hampshire was bittersweet. Janet's loved ones were happy to see her, but I could tell they were surprised and saddened by Janet's drug-altered appearance, her occasionally impaired speech, and her overall frailty. Janet put on a brave face, laughed at the usual Heaney clan jokes, and tried to put everyone at ease. Still, we all took note that once she was comfortably on a couch or soft chair, she didn't bother to move, and frequently nodded off to sleep. The rest of us would exchange glances and stoically bear what was obvious: this towering personality, this boldest of sisters, this dynamo of creativity was not the person she'd once been.

Still, Janet insisted we keep to our itinerary. After a week with her family, we visited her best friend Keke and Keke's husband Dave in Massachusetts. I think we tried not to frame our visit as a final tour, but it was hard to think otherwise. We then headed to New York City to see our friend Bianca Bob Miller. We stayed in the sleek West Village apartment of Robert Lamm. My sometime collaborator and Chicago keyboardist had, generously, let us have the place to ourselves for a few days.

At the end of our second day in New York, Janet was understandably wiped out from being in the city and gamely hanging out with Bianca. She'd used up her last bit of willpower to socialize. We were in the kitchen, me sitting, Janet standing with difficulty. Janet said, "I have to go to the bathroom, but I'm too tired to get there." The bathroom was fifteen feet away. I patted my lap and said, "Have a seat for a second, baby. Let your legs rest for a minute and when you're ready we'll get you over there." Janet sat on my lap. Huddled together in one small corner of the kitchen, I remember thinking we weren't exactly taking advantage of all the space in Robert's comfy apartment. We sat there, both of us still, Janet resting, neither of us talking. We looked at each other and smiled, and it was as if the whole saga of her illness took a few minutes off in recognition that, in the end, here we were, just the two of us, together no matter what, and more in love than ever.

Then she peed on my lap.

Janet's face caved a little, but she didn't move. "I'm so sorry, darling. I didn't mean for that to happen."

"I know you didn't, baby. That's alright." I had to smile. I said, "I wouldn't say it's my dream scenario...but I've never felt closer to you." We laughed. It was one of our last best moments.

P. HUX 2.0

We'd lost Rob to his computer future, but Gordon had an idea for his possible replacement in P. Hux. "Have you seen Tonic? The bass player is amazing. He's as good as Rob."

I scoffed, "I find that hard to believe."

Gordon was emphatic. "Trust me. He's great. They're playing Friday at Dragonfly. You'll love him. His name's Dan Rothchild."

Dan Rothchild?

I did some math. In 1985, I'd met a seventeen-year-old kid named Dan at Paul Rothchild's house up in Laurel Canyon. It was on my maiden trip to LA when I was writing a piece on *Star Search* for the *Spectator*. I remember I'd given him a demo tape. Could it be the same guy? Dan would be in his late twenties now. Hmmm.

Gordon and I scoped out Tonic. Really good band, including the guy on bass with lots of frizzy hair and an ignition key screwed into his Fender Precision. Afterward, Dan recognized Gordon and headed our way. Gordon introduced me to Dan, who shook my hand and immediately sang, "Psychic Waaaaitress..." Ha! I cracked up. Young Dan Rothchild had remembered my old demo tape, including the "joke" song that went over so poorly at Island Records. I instantly felt like we were friends even though we didn't know each other at all. Music will do that. Dan agreed to join P. Hux. We were lucky to get him.

AND IN THE END

After Janet and I returned to LA from our Christmas trip back East, my frail, suffering wife quickly went downhill. Janet had reached the critical juncture that our doctors had warned us about. She was unable to eat, and her pain meds no longer worked. With help from my neighbor (and engineer on *A Man Called E*) Jim Lang, we gathered up Janet's belongings, packed an overnight bag for me, and made poor Janet as comfortable as possible for the ride to Cedars-Sinai. Her doctors quickly determined that the brain tumor had returned bigger than before. Once a tumor impinges on the brain stem, I was told, there is nothing they can do. The doctors put her on a morphine drip, and Janet slipped into a coma. She didn't come out.

I was never alone at the hospital, and I'm forever grateful to my parents, Janet's family, and the many friends who stood vigil, holding Janet's hand, talking to her and keeping me company while we prayed for a miracle. I knew

Chapter 14: A Final Tour

we wouldn't get one. Janet died on January 9, 1997, thirteen months after her diagnosis.

I awoke alone at Funky Farms the next morning. My world had changed completely, 180 degrees as foretold by the mysterious voice I'd heard when Janet went into seizure in the same bedroom where I now slept. Outside, traffic streamed down the 2 Freeway toward Glendale Boulevard and downtown LA. Birds chirped. The sun shone. Life goes on, said Life. I thought, "Yeah? Go fuck yourself." I wanted the world to stop, to show Janet some respect. To acknowledge that she meant something, and that the world was a poorer place without her. It was appalling and unacceptable that she was gone while the world was still intact.

I drove to the Abbott and Hast Mortuary in Silver Lake to arrange for Janet's cremation. That's a task I never want to experience again. A week later, I hosted a wake at Funky Farms. I hung a huge print of one of my favorite pictures of Janet above the fireplace mantel. She looked radiant and beautiful, as we all knew her to be. My parents, my brothers, and their wives all attended. Janet's family and many of our friends from around the country flew out to California. I welcomed dozens of LA friends who'd been my bedrock during Janet's illness. Even young Mr. Alain Romero showed up and kindly apologized for how things had turned out when we were his guardians. I told him Janet loved him.

The following day, about thirty of us made a challenging two-hour hike to the top of Strawberry Peak, one of Janet's favorite mountains in the Angeles Forest. It was a beautiful, calm, sunny day. Odd gusts of wind took us by surprise as we climbed the mountain, and it felt like Janet was with us. I was comforted by the company of so many who loved Janet, and who loved me, too, I suppose. I was glad not to be alone. We ceremoniously spread half of her ashes at the base of a gnarled pine tree, saving the other half for Purgatory Falls Farm, her once and final home.

Two weeks later, I flew back east for a small service in an old New Hampshire church with Janet's family, cousins, and a few friends, including Robin Lane. Robin had moved to Massachusetts, but we'd remained close, and she insisted on driving up to be with me. The service included a recording of one of my many odes to Janet, "Offer You The World." Robin the writer said, "Wow, that's quite a song there, Parthenon." Robin's approval felt like a tip of the hat to Janet.

On that overcast winter day, we spread the rest of Janet's ashes in the lower pasture of Purgatory Falls Farm. As I walked up the incline toward the family farmhouse, where we'd had so many good times on visits from LA, I stopped to snap a series of photos from left to right that would form a panorama. When I got the photos back from the printer, one shot of the farmhouse had a striking crescent of golden light in the center of the picture. It could've been the result of a crimp in the negative, but I knew I'd seen something like that before. A few days later I realized it was from a scene in *The Sixth Sense* where a corkboard is covered with photos of dead people, all featuring a golden crescent. Wow. Classic move, JH! That photo would become the cover of my album in honor of Janet, *Purgatory Falls*.

LIVIN' ON THE EDGE

Widowerhood is an extreme state of being. It puts you on edge. Every move, every thought, every waking moment is connected to the part of your heart that is broken. You are required to move through the day, but you do it reluctantly, swamped by memories, good, bad, warm, painful. There's nothing you can do about it. You're trapped.

At the time Janet died, E (Mark Everett) was living in my old house just across the street on Baxter. He called me and said, "I don't know what your plans are, but there's a house on this side of the hill that's open. The entrance is right across the street from you." I knew the house. It didn't have the character of Funky Farms, but it was half the rent and would do fine. It would make for an easy move, too. I thanked E for letting me know.

I moved out of Funky Farms. On my last day there, the hundred-year-old wooden home was completely empty. Everything that represented my life with Janet was gone but for a single dry red rose I'd saved from her wake. I took in the desolate scene, and soon found myself lying in the fetal position on the barren floor of the living room, crying and sub-humanly howling like an injured wolf for about fifteen minutes.

Like I said, I was a bit on edge.

My favorite hippie massage therapist, a woman in the neighborhood named Julia, knew what I was going through. She was concerned that my grief was harming my body. She suggested I was a good candidate to undergo a unique process called Amané. I asked, "What's that?"

She said, "You'll see. I don't do it very often, but I think you should do it." I agreed to be treated.

I lay on Julia's padded table. Her treatment room always smelled great from the candles, and she piped in restful, drone-y music that helped calm my mind. Julia normally massaged my muscles, but this time she moved her hands above my torso in circular patterns. She said she was moving good energy in and bad energy out of my chakras. That's my understanding, anyway.

This gentle prologue soon became physically dramatic. She roughly pinched several spots on my torso and within seconds my arms and hands became paralyzed by muscle cramps. I couldn't move. I thought, "What the hell have I got myself into?" Had I not completely trusted Julia, I would've been terrified. She calmly led me through the process ("I'm redirecting energy") moving her hands over me and assuring me I was okay. I endured the shocking physical paralysis for what felt like forever but was probably twenty minutes. When the cramping finally began to ease, a torrent of grief suddenly overcame me. I began weeping uncontrollably and repeating "I love you so much, Janet…I love you so much."

When that part ran its course, my tears stopped, and I soon gave a little laugh. Julia smiled and asked what was going on. I told her I was laughing because…it seemed so cliched, but I saw images of Jesus and the Devil float by. I said, "I mean, how corny can you get?" She said, "You never know what's going to pass through. Just keep an open mind." A minute later, as I lay on my back, I had to gasp. My body felt incredibly good, and I clearly sensed, in the most realistic way possible, a huge, thick-stemmed rose lifting out of my chest. I mean, *it happened*. It was as clear as the voice I heard when Janet went into seizure. Trust me, I was as surprised as you would've been. When it was over, I walked home feeling completely drained and much less troubled. It was as if Julia had performed an emotional exorcism.

Widowerhood. It's weird.

STEER CLEAR

I went back to walking Algonquin in Elysian Park, as I'd done when writing *P. Hux "Deluxe."* We'd start at the same spot every day, a trailhead that led to a dramatic view of the San Gabriel Mountains. We could see the Angeles Forest and Strawberry Peak, where we'd spread half of Janet's ashes. Looking at the mountain's easily recognizable profile, I would say, "Hi, baby," and start a one-way conversation. Our talks inevitably ended with me breaking down and crying, my daily release. I'd wipe my face, pull myself together, and then Al and I would take our walk. These conversations went on for about six months before I finished one without tearing up. I noted my dry eyes and thought perhaps I was making progress. I also supposed that Janet wouldn't want me to be a babbling fool forever.

When I wasn't a mess, I did my best to function normally. I gradually grew less angry at life. I hung out with friends. I dated a bit, and even got into a relationship with a firebrand who filled my life with new adventures but also a lot of drama, confusion, and silly, but heated, arguments. I decided drama wasn't what I needed, so I stopped seeing people for a while. I wasn't ready yet. I was still damaged goods. I needed time to truly heal up. I couldn't be with someone else if I was still in love with Janet. I wrote a song on the subject called "Steer Clear":

If I were you, I wouldn't trust me
At least not now, not this year
I'm a ship without a pilot
If I were you, I'd steer clear
'Cause there's another woman in my head

HELLE

Gradually I began to feel like my old self. It had been more than fifteen months since Janet passed when, on a Friday night, March 21, 1998, I went to Club Largo with Gordon, my pal and drummer in P. Hux. Located in the Fairfax District of Los Angeles, Largo was our favorite hipster music venue. With booths along one wall and twenty small tables, Largo could squeeze in about 100 music fans. The stage was tiny, roughly 20 x 10. A small bar and kitchen anchored the back of the room. Perfectly intimate.

Gordon and I were there to see Jon Brion, known for his production work with Aimee Mann, Fiona Apple, and music scores for films like *Magnolia* and *Punch-Drunk Love* by Paul Thomas Anderson. Nice credits, but, for many of us in LA, Jon Brion was the guy who, by force of his transcendent musical talent, had transformed Friday nights at Largo into must-see entertainment. One of Jon's tricks was to ask musicians in the crowd to join him on stage for an improvised song or two. As it was LA, those musicians might be Elliot Smith, Rufus Wainwright, or Fiona Apple. One night, Jon called me up to play bass backing Robyn Hitchcock and Jon on the Beatles' "A Day In The Life." Wish I'd known the deceptively tricky bass part, but it was fun anyway.

On this night, Gordon and I had arrived too late to get a table, so we found standing room by the bar in back, ordered drinks, and settled in. Brion, dressed in a black thrift-store suit, disheveled white shirt, and loose tie, peered at the crowd from beneath a cloud of wavy black hair that loomed over his nearly kabuki white face. As he began his opening song on Largo's upright tack piano, I couldn't help but stare—not at the stage, but at a strikingly beautiful woman by the sound booth in the back corner. Trying not to be obvious, I'd pivot my attention back to the stage, but not for long. I couldn't help myself. Her eyes were electric green, her face expressive. A halo of blonde hair didn't hurt. Pretty girls are everywhere in Los Angeles, but I wasn't ogling. This was something else, something magnetic or deeper. You know it when you know it. Jon was on his fourth or fifth song when I said to Gordon, "I've gotta meet that girl in the corner."

Gordon looked over. "She's definitely cute. Go talk to her."

"I can't. She's surrounded by dudes."

Whoever she was, she was popular. A pack of men engulfed her. One was a young guy I'd met before, a drummer named Jaime O'Connell. There were three or four other hipsters I didn't recognize. Jesus. How many boyfriends did she have? I ordered another drink for me and Gordon. I'd just have to wait it out. After an entertaining but agonizing ninety minutes, Jon took a break and the bulwark of dudes around The Beautiful Woman momentarily broke apart. Fortified by two rounds of Dutch Courage I beelined to the corner. I had a solid opening line prepared.

"Hi," I said.

"Hi." She smiled.

This was going better than I'd hoped.

"Have you seen Jon before?"

"Yeah, lots of times. My brother plays drums with him occasionally. That's him over there."

I turned to look. "Oh! That's your brother? I've met him. Jaime, right?"

"Yeah."

And we were off.

Her name was Helle O'Connell. We talked easily. I decided to a get a third drink. Helle asked for water. Before long, I was on my fourth cocktail. I was plowed and she was stone-cold sober. Jon Brion started his second set and I sang along robustly with every song. Helle blanched, but I didn't catch it. Everything was going great as far as I could tell. So great, in fact, that Drunk Me asked Sober Helle if she liked backrubs. Helle's answer was classic:

"Eventually."

For the rest of the night, I did everything wrong, all the while thinking the night couldn't be going better. Thanks, vodka. Despite my litany of errors, Helle gave me her phone number on the back of a Largo appetizer menu. (We still have it.)

Unbeknownst to me, I wasn't the only guy interested in Helle O'Connell. A very talented record producer also asked Helle out that weekend. Sorting out her options, Helle called a musician/author friend to ask what he knew about me. His word came back positive. FYI, *of course* Helle's author friend had contributed to a book about the Beatles. Apparently, everything I do in life includes a Jungian tether to the Fabs. Okay by me.

Our first date the following Tuesday went just as well as the previous Friday. I called Helle at the appointed time from a restaurant by her house. She had dropped a bottle of nail polish in her bathroom. There was a lot of broken glass, and it would take a while to clean it up. She asked if I could I eat dinner by myself and pick her up after? Uh, sure. There I was on my first date with Helle O'Connell, dining alone. Probably deserved it after my somewhat sodden Largo performance.

The next week, I took Helle to a classic Spanish-style theater in West LA to see the world-famous comedic illusionists Penn and Teller. Surely a winner of a date. I laughed out loud at their tricks and banter and thoroughly enjoyed their act. At one point, fully expecting her to be equally amused, I turned to Helle, and…she was fast asleep! Wow. I was bummed, but also kind of amused and dumbfounded.

Date after date, we each blatantly ignored all the signs that this romance couldn't possibly work. I was forty-two years old, aka ancient. Helle was twenty-eight, aka stunning. I was self-employed (that's musician-speak for "unemployed"). Helle worked in the music department of New Line Cinema. I liked hiking through canyons and throwing sticks for the amusement of my dog, Algonquin. Helle didn't care for hiking trails and equated throwing sticks with "invoking chaos." Helle drove a groovy red Saab. I took her on dates in my dented white Ford Ranger pickup truck with a "Sexy Senior Citizen" bumper sticker on the tailgate. Finally, the coup de grace. Helle was single and I was already once divorced and once widowed. Damaged goods. We shouldn't have even been on the same playing field.

Music glued everything together.

One day, I sat leafing through Helle's CD collection in the small spare bedroom of her bungalow on Beachwood Drive in Hollywood. I found Grant Lee Buffalo, Elliot Smith, all the Clash except for Combat Rock, cool bands I'd never heard of like Liquour Giants, all the correct Elvis Costello albums, some Beatles, and much more. Helle had great taste. I kept flipping through the jewel cases and suddenly my world hit the brakes. I couldn't believe my eyes. Helle's CD collection included *Message From the Country* by the Move. This didn't make sense.

I shouted, "Helle!"

"What?" came the reply from her living room.

"You have the Move!"

"Of course, I have the Move."

"No! Not 'of course'! You're twenty-eight. You can't know about the Move!"

She laughed. "Well, apparently, I do. You're holding my CD."

How could I not love a girl of the '80s and '90s who owned a Move album from the '60s? We hadn't figured out how to go on dates together, but this revelation kind of fixed all that.

The other ultimate clincher was Helle's fearlessness. One of the greatest moments of my life was sitting on the edge of Helle's bed with a guitar, and telling her straight up, "I'm going to woo you with songs about my late wife." Did she gulp? Panic? Run away (like she probably should have)? No. Helle looked me in the eye and said, "Okay. Let's hear 'em." Maybe it really was possible to love again.

PURGATORY FALLS, THE ALBUM

The songs I played for Helle became an album called *Purgatory Falls*. After Janet had died, every time I played guitar or walked Algonquin in the park I'd written a song about her or what it was like to be alive without her.

I'm a ghost in my overcoat
A temporary number in the crowd
At war with this undertow
("Rubble")

Don't ask what's wrong
Please, I'd rather move along
'Cause I'll lie and tell you it's nothing
Yes, I'll hide behind my sweet nothing
I once had something
Now it's a scar
("My Sweet Nothing")

It doesn't take much
A book she never read
The last dress she wore
The first words we said
("Red Eyeliner")

The songs for *Purgatory Falls* were some of the most intense, personal things I'd ever written, and why wouldn't they be? I played a show at a popular coffee shop/performance venue called Highland Grounds. About forty of my and Janet's friends came to hear my musical eulogy, and pretty much all of them ended up bawling their eyes out. I'll never forget my friend Lissa Martinez, her eyes still red, saying to me after the show, "Parthenon, you can't do these songs forever. They're too much. I don't know how many times I could even bear to hear them." Lissa's heartfelt words reminded me that I needed to record my new songs sooner than later. It was important that I not lose my emotional connection to the music.

The only problem was, I had no record deal, no publishing deal, no job, and not much in the way of prospects. It'd been five years since MCA paid me monthly advances to live on. After I was widowed, every time I delivered my rent money, I called it the "monthly miracle." Somehow, a stray live gig, a surprise royalty, or a timely guitar session would save me. I knew I couldn't rely on that happening forever. It wasn't getting any easier to make a living doing music. I needed something to happen.

I agreed to do a writing session with Jesse Tobias and Angie Hart. They called themselves Splendid and were signed to Mammoth Records and Warner Chappell Publishing. Jesse had infamously joined the Red Hot Chili Peppers on guitar, only to be let go after just a month. He'd then met Angie while on tour with Alanis Morissette during the *Jagged Little Pill* phenomenon. They came to my house, next door to where I used to live on Baxter and just across the street from Funky Farms. While Jesse and I banged on guitars, Angie jotted down lyric ideas in her notebook. The phone rang. A guy on the line introduced himself as Eric Troyer from Electric Light Orchestra Part II.

Top: 2002. We may be the only band to get a useable photo at Glamour Shots. Middle: 2022. The Orchestra. L-R: Lou Clark Jr, Eric Troyer, Gordon Townsend, Mik Kaminski, PH, and Glen Burtnik. Cliff Hillis has since joined as our 7th member. Bottom: Glen does his job performing while Mik and Hux have a mid-show chat.

Top: 2013. My co-producer Mark Williams and I discuss a recording detail. We've worked together on my albums *Thank You Bethesda*, *This Is The One* and *As Good As Advertised*. Photo by Greg Dohler. Bottom: 2018. Ben Hoyt's world class violin chops make every gig we play an event to remember. Photo: Helle Huxley.

Top: 2018. L-R Gary Greene (Hootie), Duff McKagan (Guns N' Roses), PH, and Tommy Carlos (Boston) rock for the benefit of a homeless shelter in Rock Hill, South Carolina. Bottom: McKagan brothers Duff and Bruce. The McKagans are special men whose word is gold.

Top: 2000. Helle and I trade pick scrapes at our wedding. Bottom: Stephen Stills sang "In My Life" for us. Stephen and Helle's dad Terry became close friends in the early '70s.

Top: 2018. The late, great Jeffrey Foskett, who recommended me for the ELO Part II gig. How do you thank someone enough for changing your life? Jeff called me once and said, "Come down to Ocean Way Studio now. Trust me." Fifteen minutes later I joined Jeff on background vocals with Brian Wilson producing. "Those are some beautiful vocals, boys." Jeff insisted I pose with Brian and took the picture himself. Jeff passed away in December 2023 after a long battle with cancer. I miss him.

Top: 2014. Mik won Roger Daltrey's admiration for playing the fiddle part that ends "Baba O'Riley." Middle: 2018. The Orchestra in New Zealand. PH on the big screens. Photo: Kee Kee Buckley. Bottom: 2019. Besides writing the best cat song ever, Al Stewart is a very generous wine connoisseur. When Al's around, have your glass ready.

Top: 2023. We're called Parthenon Huxley and His Ridiculous Band for a reason. The talent around me is insane. L-R: PH in storytelling mode, Daniel Clarke, Ricky Wise, Dave Phenicie. Bottom: 2024. Imogen Huxley joins Dad and band at Jammin Java to sing "Don't Let Me Down." Both photos: Mike Landsman.

Top: 2017 The Huxley family all together at the Rewind Festival in Cheshire, England. L-R: Fiona, Imogen, Helle, PH. Bottom: Helle Huxley makes my life better every day.

PART THREE

IN WHICH WE FIGHT FOR OUR MUSICAL LIVES

CHAPTER 15

NO REWIND

After just one year, my grand new classic rock life was in jeopardy. Bev Bevan had announced his retirement. We were losing an original member of ELO, the founder of our band, and likely a bit of our cred. We had auditioned Gordon Townsend to be our new drummer and he'd blown us away as I knew he would. We were all set to keep touring. But there was a last second surprise. A big one. At Bev's farewell concert in Atlantic City on November 13, 1999, he'd announced that the show would not only be his last, it would be "the last show for ELO Part II." What? We'd heard him say it, but it didn't make sense. The rest of us in ELO Part II obviously had no plans to quit. How could he say ELO Part II no longer existed? Was he just talking about the name?

"ELO Part II" wasn't a cool band name, but it worked. It told fans we were a successor band to the original ELO, and, if you looked closely, you'd find musicians who'd played on most of the beloved ELO albums. Also, ELO Part II had invested ten years of touring and released two albums of original material to establish the ELO Part II brand.

Sagely, our manager John Regna told us to just do our jobs, to concern ourselves with performing and creating a new album. "You guys should just focus on being the great band you are and let me worry about everything else. We'll figure it out." So that's what we did. We had a new drummer, gigs to play, and an album to record.

HEAVENLY

Two months after Bev dropped his bomb on Atlantic City (and two weeks after the world didn't crash because of Y2K), Gordon Townsend debuted as our drummer at Selena Auditorium in Corpus Christi, Texas, on January 15, 2000. If the other guys had any worries about Gordon being able to handle Bev's duties, I didn't. I had no doubt Gordon would know his parts backwards and forwards.

He did. Even with the Corpus Christi Symphony Orchestra sawing away slightly behind the beat as string players do, Gordon's feel for the material was spot on. He nailed the set in his crisp and powerful style and the sold-out symphony crowd went completely bonkers for our band, rising in their suits and gowns to give us multiple standing ovations. I doubt anyone in the crowd was aware that we'd just played our first show without the services of ELO's legendary drummer. It was clear that Bev's departure was not going to be a musical disaster for our band. The opposite, in fact.

Our next stop without Bev was Maddies, a cozy rock venue/hotel in the rolling eastern Pennsylvania countryside. Gordon hails from Philly, so his sister and a gaggle of her friends made the short trek to our new drummer's second show. Once again, powered by Gordon's bashing precision, we sent the crowd into a crazy, joyous delirium (just stating facts). I was thrilled to have my old drummer in my new group, and I wasn't alone. After just two shows, even the Brits were content to have a third American in their once all-English band. Backstage at Maddies, Kelly and I clinked beer bottles. Kelly chuckled, shook his head and said, "Gordon's fucking great. It's like a completely different show for me now. Whatever I do, he's right there with me. It's heavenly."

IN THE YEAR 2000

Our tour included a night off in Las Vegas on January 19, 2000, so I was free to celebrate my first birthday of the new century. As a kid growing up in New Jersey in the 1960s, I'd more than once wondered what my life would be like *in the year 2000*. That centennial milestone had loomed like a mythical beacon in my unfathomable future. ("In the year 2000..." also became a pretty good recurring gag on Conan O'Brien.) I clearly remember my eight-year-old brain realizing with a shock that I'd be a *forty-four-year-old man*. Talk about unimaginable! I dreaded that I might end up riding a crowded commuter train, wearing a suit and holding a briefcase thanks to some boring job (no offense, Dad). I thought, "Is that going to be my life?"

Announcer voice: "*No, young Hux of the past, it's not*. When you turn forty-four, you'll carry a guitar case instead of a briefcase. You'll wear whatever clothes you want and travel by plane instead of commuter train. *Sound good?* To top it off, you'll celebrate your forty-fourth birthday in style...when you and Gordon Townsend head to the MGM Grand to see the one and only... Tom Jones!"

Thirty-five years after "Delilah," Jones's voice and stage command were stunningly intact. He was funny, engaging, a tad naughty, and totally captivating. Tom Jones, at fifty-nine years old, absolutely kicked ass. I doubt he saw that coming when he was a little kid in Wales stuck at home for a year recovering from tuberculosis. Gordon and I left the MGM Grand impressed and inspired.

Our next stop was the Surf Ballroom in Clear Lake, Iowa. If that venue rings a bell, it's because in 1959, Buddy Holly, Ritchie Valens, and the Big Bopper all perished in a plane crash after playing the Surf. Our band itinerary included a grimly playful note from tour manager, Greg Szabo: "January 22, 2000. Surf Ballroom. Finally! All 11 of us on the same flight!" Nice one, Greg.

Our New Drummer Tour carried on with sold-out shows in Michigan, Connecticut, and Florida. Gordon recalls it took him about ten shows to get excited about playing without being nervous. I could relate. I'd done the same just a year earlier. Playing the correct notes at the correct time is great, but truly owning the material is transformative. With Gordon locked in, we would not only survive Bev's departure, we'd reach new heights. We swung into spring 2000 with real momentum.

NO REWIND

In April, the band set up camp in Los Angeles to begin working on a new album. I couldn't wait to hear my songs recorded with rock's best violinist, an amazing orchestral arranger, terrific bassist, proven familiar drummer, encyclopedically knowledgeable keyboard player, three uniquely voiced singers, and one annoying egomaniacal guitarist. This was gonna be fun.

On my recommendation, the band chose Jim Jacobsen as our engineer and co-producer. I'd loved working with Jim ever since he'd introduced me to the creative process of digital recording. Jim and I'd done overdubs on my *P. Hux "Deluxe"* album, as well as recordings that would end up on *Purgatory Falls*. I'd introduced Jim to my collaborator, E, and, together, they'd won a Brit Award for "Susan's House" by eels. Based in LA, Jim was convenient for Gordon and me, the band's LA residents, and Eric and the Brits were more than happy to work in sunny Los Angeles. Once Mik'n'Lou located an English pub called The Fox and Hounds not far from Jim's studio, we were all set.

We began with "Over London Skies." It was an easy choice. We'd already road-tested it on our audience with great results. Lou had taken my meager ideas for string parts and created an arrangement that was stately and gorgeous. Bev's lyrics were still in there, of course, so our former drummer earned a co-write, but Gordon's drums would be heard on the record.

I had two other songs ready to record that I'd written during ELO Part II's 1999 UK Tour. "Jewel And Johnny" came to me on a beautiful spring day in London. I'd noticed young couples with mixed ethnic backgrounds holding hands and smiling, seemingly without a care in the world. I thought, "Wouldn't it be nice if this next generation didn't judge each other by surface appearances…" Conversely, I also wondered how the older, original generation of immigrants felt about their British-born kids living so freely in twenty-first-century London:

Jewel and Johnny walk to school each day
Holding hands and no one bats an eye
All their friends are pretty cool that way
No one knows why both their mothers cry

Two kids in love, that's all it ought to be
Still their parents grumble
This is how our cultures crumble
Love conquers all, except in families
All this bloodline squawking
Sounds exactly like the old world talking

I called my other new song "Can't Wait To See You," literally because I couldn't wait to propose to Helle at Abbey Road. Underneath that hopeful theme, however, was the idea that, on a certain level, I would likely always be damaged goods because of my widowerhood. In "Can't Wait To See You," I made sure to include a measure of self-doubt while still being excited about the future.

Your light always goes
To the places a sad man knows
Sometimes it gets a little close
And I run away
But I count the days
And I can't wait to see you

I wasn't the only writer in the band with new material. Eric's "No Rewind," "If Only," "I Could Write A Book," and "Say Goodbye" were all super melodic and lyrically riveting—full of lost love and painful regrets—really emotional stuff. Eric had also teamed up with Mik and written "Let Me Fly," a majestic piece with lyrics full of intriguing spiritual imagery. It had a beautiful repeating chord sequence over which Mik improvised a stunning solo on violin.

Kelly had demo'd a mournful song about a young Irish boy gunned down during the Troubles. It had a gripping melody that Kelly sang over a kind of pan-pipe track. The problem was it didn't really go anywhere. After some nudging, Kelly conceded to letting Eric and me turn it into a full, proper song. Eric and I noted that Kelly's lyrics were somewhat hymn-like, so we took his song in a gospel direction, added a chorus, bridge, and outro, and it all clicked. Eric's stirring vocal arrangements finished the job. Kelly's song became "Before We Go," a rousing plea for people to learn to live together. Kelly's son Chris said it was the best thing his dad had ever done. That added up to nine songs, almost enough for a full album.

A TWIST ON TWIST

We needed one more song. One day while Kelly recorded bass parts, Eric and I noodled on guitars as we sat overlooking the canyon that stretched below Jim Jacobsen's house in the Hollywood Hills. Eric said, "I have an idea for a cover."

"Let's hear it."

Eric slowly strummed his guitar and sang in a minor key, "Shake it up baby..." I almost didn't recognize the famous opening line from "Twist And Shout." Eric's minor key melody had changed the meaning of the words into a melancholy, mournful plea. It gave me chills. He played some more of his new arrangement and then stopped. "Not sure what it should do at that point..."

I wanted to jump out of my skin. "That's fucking great!" I said. "It's beautiful. Wow. I'm thinking that, somehow, it should make its way from this new sad place to the original rocking thing. It would just explode."

Eric said, "That's what I was thinking."

Arrangers, start your imaginations.

The trick of fleshing out the melancholy part and transitioning to the rocking bit ("WELL SHAKE IT UP BABY NOW!") was a fabulous challenge. We both knew in our guts it could work, but we had to figure out the journey. We couldn't just leap from melancholia to joy. We needed a gradual ramp-up to a moment when the song would suddenly *need* to blast off in its original major key. Eric and I ran through a dozen chord sequences and rejected anything that felt forced. I trusted Eric's deep knowledge of modes to help us navigate the terrain. Neither of us was willing to settle. We figured when we got it right it would click for us both.

We hacked away for hours and finally mapped out a seven-minute arrangement. It began with Eric's aching plea in moody B minor, dropped to E minor for several equally mournful passages, sneakily settled onto the we're-preparing-to-resolve-chord, A major, and finally exploded into the flat-out rock 'n' roll bit in joyous D major. For the outro, the band gradually faded away, allowing Mik's plaintive violin to dance around Eric's subdued vocal. The end part sounded like the audio equivalent of a cigarette after sex. We'd turned "Twist And Shout" into a thrilling mini concerto. My first collaboration with Eric may be my favorite cover, ever.

"Twist" soon became a highlight in our live set, alongside "Jewel And Johnny," "Can't Wait To See You," Eric's "No Rewind," and Kelly's "Before We Go." Our new songs fit beautifully with the hits from the '70s and '80s, bringing fresh energy to the show. We were becoming "a new sounding classic rock band" like I'd imagined, and less of a straight heritage act. I think we may've even played the new songs with a bit more juice, knowing the crowd would need some convincing when hearing unfamiliar material. We embraced the challenge.

APRIL IS THE CRUELEST MONTH

On April 26, 2000, thirty years after ELO began, the trademark for ELECTRIC LIGHT ORCHESTRA was registered in the UK for Jeff Lynne (file number UK00901628544). One can only speculate if that meant Lynne had *never* owned the trademark until 2000, at least in England.

Two days later, on April 28, 2000, we were in Robinson, Mississippi, for a casino gig. Just before going onstage, a stocky guy in a cowboy hat appeared at our dressing room door. He flashed a law enforcement ID and tossed a documents binder on a table. He said, "I'm just the messenger. Y'all have a nice day," and walked out.

The documents insisted we could not use the name "ELO Part II." We'd been told that already.

WORST NAME IN ROCK

Not long after Bev left the band in November, 1999, Regna had been informed by Jeff Lynne's management that "ELO Part II" no longer existed. Although that was news to us, it turned out to be correct. Back in 1990, in order for Bev to put together a new version of ELO, he and Jeff Lynne had agreed on four important points:

1. Bev could call his band "ELO Part II." He could never call it "ELO."
2. As long as "ELO Part II" was actively working, Jeff Lynne could not use the too-similar name "ELO."

3. If Bev left "ELO Part II," the name "ELO" would again be available to Lynne.
4. Also, if Bev left "ELO Part II," the remaining band members (in this case Mik, Lou, Kelly, Eric, me, Gordon) could not continue as "ELO Part II," as use of the name required Bev to be a member of the band.

Number 3 on that list worked out very well for Jeff Lynne. Bev "retired" and, just like that, the name "ELO" was Lynne's for the taking. A new version of "ELO" appeared less than two years later featuring Lynne, his girlfriend, and some studio musicians.

Number 4 on that list, losing the right to call ourselves "ELO Part II," worked out very poorly for us. Promoters all over the world enjoyed working with "ELO Part II." For us to reform under a new name would be close to committing commercial suicide. But we had to do it.

We needed a name that said our band featured former members of ELO and ELO Part II without using troublesome words like, you know, *Electric*, *Light*, *Orchestra*, *Part*, and *II*. Kelly and Mik had once formed a splinter group in the 1980s called Orkestra. We didn't like that name, but it led us to finally agree on a name we didn't loathe: "the Orchestra." It wasn't very catchy or memorable, but it spoke to our symphonic sound and it featured *one* of the words from Electric Light Orchestra Part II. Good enough, bro!

Regna then came up with the cumbersome but brilliant idea of adding a descriptive sub-name: "Featuring Former Members of ELO and ELO Part II." It made our name horribly long and difficult to fit on a poster. It was ugly to look at. "Former Members" likely cast doubt on our legitimacy. All that said, it was an accurate description of who we were. It was just unfortunate that it sounded more like a law firm than a rock band. Promoters would probably hate it, but if they wanted to work with us, they'd have to accept it and help us grow the name.

IDENTITY CRISIS

Most promoters went along with the new name, but some took liberties. We might contract with a promoter, say, in Chile, who would announce the show correctly as "The Orchestra Featuring Former Members of ELO and ELO Part II." She would then offer the band to regional promoters who, perhaps not knowing the fine distinction between "ELO Part II" and "Former Members of ELO Part II", might advertise us simply as "ELO Part II", or to make things even simpler, just "ELO." After all, they knew the music and it was originally made by "ELO", right?

When that happened, we might not see the incorrect promotional language until we'd traveled five thousand miles to South America, when it was too late to do much about it. We'd tear down incorrect posters in venue lobbies and off of telephone poles. (I thought back to working for the Cat's Cradle in Chapel Hill, putting up posters all over town. Now I was ripping down posters for my own band.) If our band name was incorrect on electronic signs, we'd ask that it be changed. If a local celebrity or national deejay planned to introduce us before a show, we'd write out "The Orchestra" and tell him or her, "Do not introduce us as 'ELO' or 'ELO Part II.'"

Unfortunately, our efforts were not always appreciated by concerned parties back home. If an ad calling us "ELO" appeared online, it made us look like we approved the ad. If fans posted videos and called us "ELO" or "ELO Part II", it looked like we hadn't done our due diligence to get our new name across. Our years-long struggle to play ELO music without being called "ELO" or "ELO Part II" was always nerve racking, occasionally ridiculous, and often costly.

All we wanted was to play ELO music and our original songs better than any band in the world. We had Mik Kaminski on violin, Kelly Groucutt on bass and vocals, Louis Clark on orchestral keyboards, and, when called upon, conducting orchestras. All three guys had been key components of ELO since the 1970s. Eric, Gordon and I weren't "original" members, but we were fans of the music and the kind of dedicated musicians who respected the catalogue and worked our asses off to get it across to live audiences.

No matter what problems arose because of the confusion around our name, the Orchestra's concert presentation was consistently incendiary. In Syracuse, we played a pair of gigs at the New York State Fair's main stage. We'd been playing a lot, and there's nothing better than performing when you're hot. Our shows were reviewed in the next day's *Syracuse Herald American*. After praising our band's performance and energy, the writer concluded, "It didn't even matter that Jeff Lynne, given the most credit for ELO's groundbreaking classical-rock-pop sound…was nowhere to be seen." That's a high compliment.

MEET THE NUPTIALS

Roughly a year after my awkward, but successful, marriage proposal at Abbey Road Studio Two, Helle and I tied the knot on May 13, 2000 in an ornate ballroom at the storied Willard Hotel in Washington, DC. Gordon and my LA pianist buddy Nic Pierone stood as my best men, each nicely cleaned up in dark suits and ties. I sported a wine-red sharkskin suit I'd bought on tour at William Hunt in London. I'm currently waiting for it to come back into style. My hair did its best Eric Carmen impression, puffed up on top of my head like a '60s suburban mom. I leaned on my long sideburns to reassure any doubters that I was the groom.

To no one's surprise, our wedding's theme leaned heavily on music. Helle and I thought "nuptials" sounded like a band name, so we created table decorations out of guitar picks and backstage laminates embossed with "The Nuptials". We modeled our wedding invitations on the Beatles' *White Album* with "The Nuptials" in light grey lettering in a field of white. Some obsessions can't be helped.

Helle looked stunning in her Badgley Mischka dress as her dad escorted her to my side to the tune of "All You Need Is Love." Our vows included a jokey "Xanadu" reference to Olivia Newton John, which our minister mangled to *Oliver* Newton John. It was funnier his way. At the end of our vows, which I believe mentioned the sanctity of Helle's CD collection, we happily kissed and then strutted out of the room to Free's "Alright Now." How're we doing so far?

Helle and I agonized over the choice of live music for our wedding. We agreed on one thing: we didn't want a typical wedding band. Helle eventually hit on the perfect, if ultimately obvious, idea. After the ceremony, the long cocktail hour, the sit-down dinner and the mostly heartfelt toasts (my dad felt obliged to say, "Parth, we hope this is your last wedding"), out came, for your entertainment pleasure...*the Beatles*. Well, okay, *the Fab Four*, a tribute band from Boston. They started with "I Saw Her Standing There" and the dance floor filled instantly. Did we know our crowd or what?

When the Fab Four took a break to change out of their Sgt. Pepper outfits and into their *Let It Be* period suits, I stood with Helle and her dad, Terry O'Connell, on the dance floor. Terry was a decorated Vietnam vet with the injuries to prove it, a presidential campaign manager, lobbyist, longtime Democratic operative and more. He said, "Oh, look, it's my buddy." We watched a man we knew well amble onto the stage with an acoustic guitar. Terry and his guitar-playing friend had had a fabulous time in the 1970s barnstorming from one political rally to another, wherever their services were welcomed.

Terry's pal was well known for writing some terrific songs himself, so Helle and I were surprised when he played "In My Life" by the Beatles. I doubt he knew it was one of my favorite "John" songs ever, and I'd even played "In My Life" at my brother Tom's wedding. When he finished to great applause and calls for more, he said, "I think I'm gonna quit while I'm ahead!" Before leaving the stage, he posed for a picture with the Fab Four. That was nice of you, Stephen Stills.

ADDITION BY SUBTRACTION

Before Bev Bevan left the band, the six members of ELO Part II were considered equals. Each of us was responsible for significant musical contributions, and we earned the same paycheck. There was, however, an undiscussed (of course) awareness that Bev was more successful than the rest of us. No one begrudged Bev living well. He'd earned it. As a founding member of ELO, he profited from sales of millions of ELO albums. Mik, Lou, and Kelly all joined the band after its formation, and never received a penny from album sales. In the '70s and '80s, when ELO toured to support each new album, they were paid tour wages and nothing more. And reportedly, "tour wages" were whatever amount their infamous manager, Don Arden, said they were. Take it or leave it.

With Bev gone, Gordon in, and our name changed to the Orchestra, an interesting leveling occurred. The English guys seemed to relax a bit and enjoy their status as former members of ELO without having to defer to Bev's seniority. Soft spoken Lou Clark and jokester Mik Kaminski felt freer to speak their minds and participate more earnestly in band decisions. Kelly Groucutt relished his role as band historian, authoritatively recalling how things had been done in the '70s on stage and in the studio, confirming every song's correct vocal parts, etc.

We bloody Americans stepped up as well. I took over Bev's job of creating the set lists and enjoyed my songwriting and production role on the new album. New Guy Gordon was still early in his tenure, but he was as obsessed as Kelly about playing parts precisely and finding spots to improve our sound. Senior American, Eric Troyer, assumed the role of band spokesman during interviews and press conferences.

Bev's friend, Phil Ackrill, who'd kindly driven me around Birmingham during my audition, resigned his position as band accountant soon after Bev's departure. (My one regret with Phil is that I never had the chance to ask him about his bizarre role in pop music's weirdest conspiracy theory. Remember when Paul McCartney was supposed to be dead? One theory claimed that Paul had been replaced by Phil Ackrill.) The band's accounting piece moved from Phil to our management company, World Entertainment Associates. Eric assumed the job of liaison between band and management. It was a great advantage to have even-tempered, raised-Mennonite Eric Troyer as band representative. Through Eric, we could relay our questions and concerns to Regna with full confidence that Eric would handle things reasonably and professionally. And Regna wouldn't have the rest of us pestering him.

With everyone on a more level playing field, a sense of band equality developed that hadn't been there before. We'd lost a de facto leader and become a more democratic organization—not that we ever discussed such a thing (*heavens!*) but, to me, the difference was palpable and pleasant. Good thing, too, because our new togetherness would be tested.

BEST NAME IN ROCK

Speaking of band names, after flying home from a string of dates back East, I exited baggage claim at LAX, relished LA's warm dry air, and was soon scooped up by a prearranged Town Car. My suitcase went in the trunk, but I kept my guitar with me in the back seat. My driver was a Black gentleman who looked a little older than me. He saw the gig bag and asked, "Guitar player, huh? Who you with?"

"Oh, I play with some guys who used to be in ELO..."

"Electric Light Orchestra? Really? No kidding!"

"You like ELO?" I asked. I was a bit surprised, simply because not everyone knows "ELO" until you sing 'em one of the hits, plus our live audiences were normally 99.9 percent White.

"Yeah! Oh, yeah. I love all that classic rock stuff. I grew up on it, you know, along with everything else back in the day."

"Alright, man," I said. "Back in the days of real musicians."

"That's right!" He laughed and met my eye in the rearview. "Back when you had to be GOOD!" We both laughed. I liked this guy.

I jumped in. "What classic rock bands do you like?"

"Oh, let's see...all kinds of stuff, you know...Led Zeppelin, Jimi Hendrix, the Cream..."

"Those are definitely some of my favorites." Two old guys on the same page. I loved it.

As we headed north on the 405 freeway, my driver threw me a curve. He asked, "Hey, uhhh, who was the one with the three names...?"

"Three names?"

"You know, it was like three last names..."

"Oh, ummm, Crosby, Stills and Nash?"

"No, they were good, but not them."

Hmmm. Three names. I doubted he was thinking of the Souther Hillman Furay Band. Who else was there? Outside the car, Los Angeles spread before me like a rock 'n' roll archaeological dig. I chipped away at the '60s and '70s hoping to discover a specimen with three names. Fortunately, my brain is chock full of useless rock 'n' roll knowledge. I took a stab.

"Was it West Bruce and Laing?"

"Nah. Who's that? I never heard of 'em."

"That was two guys from Mountain and one from Cream."

"Nope. That's not them."

There had to be others. I eliminated all the ones I could think of with two names. Not Zager and Evans. Not Seals & Crofts. Not Brewer and Shipley. Not Simon and Garfunkel. Not Chad and Jeremy. Not Sonny and Cher. Not the Mamas and Papas.

"You're not talking about Three Dog Night, are you?"

"No. It was *name* names."

"How about Bachman Turner Overdrive?"

"That's just two."

"True."

Suddenly, my new classic rock buddy said, "Oh, hey, I got it! It was, uh, how do you call it? *Jefferson...*"

"Jefferson Airplane? That's not..."

"Not Jefferson Airplane. The *other* one."

I laughed. "The *other* one? *What* other one?"

"You know, the one with three names. It was, uh, whatta you call it..."

I was stumped. I couldn't see where this was going.

And then suddenly my new pal got the name he was looking for. "I remember now!" He caught my eye in the rearview and victoriously proclaimed, *"Jefferson, Lake and Palmer!"*

I cracked up. Good for my guy to nail two-thirds of Emerson, Lake & Palmer, but the one wrong name made it funny as hell. Best airport ride ever.

FOLLOW THAT!

Two weeks after I married Helle, the Band That Was Not ELO Part II flew to Warsaw, Poland, for the Polish Telecommunications Music and Film Festival. We were greeted by the festival president outside Torwar Hall, a cavernous hockey and concert venue. He was accompanied by his staff and several supermodels in ankle-length gowns who presented us with bouquets of flowers. We expected nothing less.

Chapter 15: No Rewind

We entered the hall and found Art Garfunkel running through sound check with a Polish orchestra. We put our cases down and stood quietly out among the unoccupied seats, curious to hear one of the twentieth century's most recognizable voices. All seemed to be going well until Garfunkel suddenly grew agitated and shouted at the monitor engineer, "I told you to TURN DOWN THE OBOE!" It felt like everyone in the cavernous 6,000-seat hall stopped for a beat. Our band and crew exchanged uneasy glances. It's a given that the road can make one tired and cranky, but it's also a given that you don't scream and throw crew people under the bus. It's not good form. When it came time for our sound check, we went out of our way to make sure that the orchestra knew we appreciated them being there for us. Besides, it was true: Eastern European orchestral musicians are uniformly fabulous players.

Garfunkel headlined the festival, meaning he would play after us, a billing sequence our band interpreted as perhaps a bit of an insult and a challenge. I rarely consider music to be competitive—I think of it as magic, high art, a life-giving gift, a beautiful creative endeavor pursued by a giant community of talented dreamers. That said, there are times when my competitiveness, as a performer, gets aroused. This was one of them. My normally understated bandmate Mik Kaminski picked up on it, too. That night, our mix of rock 'n' roll, radio hits, exquisite string work, and balls-out harmony vocals had the 6,000-strong Warsaw crowd on its feet in a roaring euphoria. As we walked off stage, with the crowd noise battering our ears, Mik and I had the warrior gleam in our eyes. Instinctively thinking the same thing, we shouted at each other, "Follow *THAT*, Art!"

A half hour later, still adrenalized by our show, Mik and I stuck around to see how the headliner fared. Garfunkel's more sedate offerings sounded lovely—he is Art Garfunkel after all—but he didn't come close to matching our energy. After a few too many ballads, half his audience had headed for the doors. "That's enough of that, then," Mik said. "Time for a drink."

PULLING STRINGS

The Orchestra spent the end of August back in Los Angeles, recording *No Rewind* with Jim Jacobsen. To capitalize on all six band members being in one place, we doubled our recording options, engaging my new brother-in-law, Jaime O'Connell, at his home studio in Silverlake. While Mik did string overdubs at Jim's, the rest of us cut Kelly's song, "Before We Go," at Jaime's. We also managed to capture my sweet dog Algonquin's bark, which we put onto the end of *No Rewind*'s first pressing.

Eric created a short (:28) but stunning *a capella* piece for Kelly, Eric, and me to sing, which would precede the last song on the album, "Before We Go." Then Eric invited Jeffrey Foskett to sing with us, so I was in a vocal booth with guys who'd sung with the Beach Boys, John Lennon, Billy Joel, and ELO. Not a bad group. Once we'd arranged our parts, we began recording. I never wanted to stop. The sound of our four voices made my hair stand up. Harmony singing may be the purest, simplest, most holy experience available to humans. You don't need anything but your throat, and if you do it right, it's a beautiful way to connect.

We finished off *No Rewind* with string sessions in New York City. That may've been my favorite part of making the album. Lou Clark conducted twenty-two string players jammed together in a small live-recording room at Smythe & Co. Studios. Nothing compares to the sound of a room full of expertly bowed wooden instruments. A gaggle of violinists may read the same charts and play the same notes, but every musician brings something unique to a performance. Different hands create slightly different vibratos. A range of muscle strength varies the intensity of bow-hitting-string. The result is a glorious feast of harmonics and overtones that never vibrate through the air the same way twice. Chills! Once the orchestra had nailed a take, Lou had them double-track it by playing the exact same parts as closely to the original take as possible. This essentially doubled the size of the string section to forty-four players, making Lou's stunning arrangements sound massive.

My songs, "Jewel And Johnny," "Can't Wait To See You," "Over London Skies," and "Before We Go" all grew in stature once Lou's soaring string arrangements were in place. I'm thrilled to have had four songs arranged by my bandmate Louis Clark, one of the best in the business. Just ask the Royal Philharmonic Orchestra, Ozzy Osbourne, Air Supply, Roy Wood, America, and Kiki Dee…

CHAPTER 16

THE ORCHESTRA

We became a tighter sounding band when Gordon replaced Bev on drums. Don't get me wrong. It was an honor and a pleasure playing with Bev Bevan for the year that we were together. He was always loud as hell and I loved it when he unleashed drum fills that were quintessentially *him*, like his cascading tom-tom entrance to "Evil Woman." Bev had a sound all of his own, and he's a legend for a reason.

LET THERE BE DRUMMERS

When our bassist Kelly Groucutt exclaimed at Gordon's audition that he hadn't "locked into the fucking kick drum for thirty years" he was implying (perhaps a little unfairly, in Bev's defense) that when Bev's right foot stepped on the pedal that caused a little mallet to hit the kick drum, the mallet didn't always arrive precisely on time with the beat dictated by the tempo. This can be frustrating for a bass player, whose primary job is to pluck his bass exactly in time with the kick drum. During the audition at the Sands, Kelly fell in love with Gordon's accuracy immediately. That's what Gordon does better than any drummer I've ever known. He plays perfectly in time. I think the technical phrase is *accurate as shit*.

Gordon can also play with extra fire when he's in the mood. At a show in Louisiana, Gordon attacked his kit with such ferocity that a bearded, tattoo'd local dude attached himself to our drummer like a rescue puppy with a new owner. The fella had gotten so excited by the thunder coming from the stage, he stammered to Gordon, "Man, I swear to God, I just wanna...I don't know, you were so damned good on them drums, man, I just wanna...*take you home and cook you a steak!*" We all fell out. Gordon laughed and replied in his best Philly voice, "Taaaake it easy there, pal..." Dude ate steak alone that night.

My take on the latter part of Bev's career, if I can extrapolate just from my brief experience playing with him, is that ELO's popularity made Bev rich and famous, but ELO's music eventually cramped his flamboyant style. Prior to ELO, Bev's drumming with the Move blew people's minds. He played with swagger, innovation, and confidence—particularly on songs like the Move chestnut, "Hello Susie," where his drum fills are almost unfathomably cool. Bev's drums on Move recordings were as up front in the mix as the guitars and vocals and paired with some of the biggest bass tones ever put on vinyl. Bev's style screamed "Rock Drummer to Be Reckoned With."

By contrast, ELO songs are dense, multi-layered, ornate, decorated with flourishes of strings, multiple vocal parts, percolating synthesizers, and fuzzy guitars—a real kitchen-sink approach to sound. All that complexity and orchestral pizzazz were best served by a simplified drumming style, one that wouldn't rock the boat and knock heads with the other instruments. That style of playing, as far as I could tell, wasn't Bev's thing. The ultimate marginalization of Bev's skills in ELO can be heard on "Don't Bring Me Down." Bev's contribution was reduced to an endlessly repeating two-bar loop borrowed from his drum track on "On The Run." Innovative and successful concept? Yes. Precursor, even, to modern drum loops? Yes. Exciting drum performance by a legend? No.

DEN

In October 2000, The Orchestra Starring Former Members of Electric Light Orchestra and Electric Light Orchestra Part II arrived in Vejle, Denmark, for the first of four shows. Our UK-based front-of-house sound engineer Dennis York hadn't yet heard the band with Gordon manning the drums. Den could be parsimonious with his praise, so I was anxious to get his assessment. We ran through sound check at the gymnasium-esque Vejle-Centret Hall for an hour or so, with Den making his adjustments and, as usual, listening to the band from various spots in the hall to make sure the balance was good for as many paying customers as possible. When sound check concluded, I walked out to where Den stood at his mixing board.

"How does it sound?" is all I asked. I think he knew what I was waiting to hear.

Den is the quintessential even-tempered Englishman. He does not get excited easily. If Den and I were golfing in a lightning storm, I can imagine him saying, "Well, that's a par for me and a double bogey for you, Hux. Right, then, shall we attempt to find shelter?" As he prepared to answer my question, Den's expression grew serious. He intoned, "I've been mixing this band for I don't know how many years and in a multitude of settings, and I have to say," Den pointed at the stage, "*That* actually sounds...*alright*."

Huge praise!

Chapter 16: The Orchestra

He went on. "Look, we both know at times this band has sounded a shambles...the songs begin and end at the same time, but during the middle bits the wheels tend to come off...but this actually sounded *as it should*. I'm quite impressed." Dennis York saying the band sounded "alright" was like Vince Lombardi kissing his quarterback. Music to my ears. And Den's, too, apparently.

Just a few days later, I enjoyed yet another instance of cool, calm Dennis York getting "riled up." We were at a pub in the Danish city of Aarhus. Dennis and some of the crew guys were playing darts. After downing a pint or three of the local grog, I wandered over to watch. Beyond throwing a sharp-tipped birdy thing in the direction of a cork circle, I didn't know much about the sport. I asked Dennis to explain the rules of darts. He said something about going 'round the circle and hitting certain targets in order. I said, "I assume bullseyes are good, right?" Patiently, Dennis said, "Yes, bullseyes are always good, but the hardest place to hit is triple-twenty. It's where you get the most points, even more than the bullseye." He pointed to a small red crescent in the upper middle of the board. Not much of a target.

Kindly, Dennis asked, "Would you like to have a go?"

Sure.

Dennis handed me three darts and I settled myself behind a painted line on the bar floor, roughly eight feet from the target. Before I launched my first dart, I confirmed the plot. "So, I'm aiming for triple-twenty, right?"

"Yes. That's a good plan." Dennis was, undoubtedly, rolling his inner eyes.

My first dart landed in triple twenty. Dennis's face froze.

My beery thoughts told me, "Go on. No big deal. That's where you were aiming, wasn't it? Throw another one."

My second dart joined the first one. Triple-twenty again. I had 120 points after two darts. Dennis was respectfully keeping as quiet as he could while it was still my turn to throw. He took a long swig from his beer and his eyes stayed locked on the board. He may've stopped breathing.

The Danish beer continued to make my blood happy, and I prepared to throw the third dart. Suffice to say, *I was feeling it*. This was like going back to my days as a Little League pitcher. I blocked everything out but my target, aimed and threw.

Triple-twenty.

Finally, Dennis was free to react. He slammed his beer safely on a table and softly shouted, "Oh my God! Do you have ANY IDEA what you've just bloody done?"

I smiled, enjoying myself.

"Hux. *Listen*. I have been playing darts and watching darts for I don't know how many years, and I've never seen a beginner do that. It just doesn't happen."

The bartender noticed the hubbub and came over to verify that the darts were bunched together in triple-twenty. He asked, "It's a set-up, isn't it?" Dennis told him, "I know it looks like it is, but unfortunately, I have just witnessed it myself. He really did it."

I didn't have the same appreciation for my 180 points as Dennis. To me it was just beginner's luck, one of those weird moments where your brain and some beer enter a zone. But I enjoyed the hell out of doing it and I loved shaking Den's tree.

HEY, TROMMESLAGER!

In Copenhagen, we played the 1,100-capacity Vega Club, a general admission venue, all standing room, no seats. The fans were right in our face, fully inebriated (i.e., "being Danish") and demanding that we rock them into the ground. At least that's how I translated their Viking-esque fist pumping and screaming. The energy between band and crowd never let up, and we all did a bit more showing off than usual. Great show.

The lights came up, the crowd spilled onto the streets of Copenhagen, and we broke down our gear onstage. A terribly tipsy Danish lass loitered near the front of the stage and refused to leave the venue until Gordon acknowledged her. She even attempted a drunk version of lewd dancing and sweater lifting to catch his eye, but it wasn't working, poor thing. Gordon broke down his kit and avoided looking her way.

"HEY!" she shouted at Gordon. "TROMME...(burp)...SLAGER!" We figured that meant "drummer" and Gordon finally gave her a glance and waved with a forced smile, "Really nice to see you. Thanks for coming. Have a good night." What little light remained in her eyes went dark and she wobbled off as best she could. I love showbiz.

MACHINE GUNS AND BANANAS

Our final run of a dizzying year 2000 took us to Central America. I'll never forget deboarding in El Salvador to warm moist air that smelled like bananas. That's how life should be, isn't it? Our van took us into town on a hilly, winding road. With the windows open, bananas gave way to diesel fumes. Oh, well. We crested a hill and eased down into the capital city of San Salvador. The place was huge, spreading for miles before us, a tantalizing mix of festive, colorful buildings and dense green jungle. We learned that the verdant valley was called "The Hammock" because of how it swayed during frequent, violent earthquakes. Selling point?

As we entered the city, we were taken aback by the preponderance of security guards armed with little machine guns. They stood in front of nearly every business—hotels, restaurants, jewelry stores, nail places. This was my first time in Central America, and I'd never seen anything like it. Was armed robbery the national pastime?

Sort of. Local criminals preferred a robbery/kidnapping combo. Most were of the quickie variety, i.e., "We'll kidnap you at gunpoint and make your family get $2000 from an ATM. Once they deliver the money, we'll let you go. No harm done, other than the money and scaring the living shit out of you and your family."

During our visit, the promoter drove Eric and me—sightseeing buddies—to a popular roadside pupusa stand. We enjoyed the delicious cheese-filled pouches while taking in a nice view of the city. Our host spoke excellent English thanks to some years living in the States. After about ten minutes of chatting and answering our questions about San Salvador, he said, "We should go." Meaning, we should get back in the car and leave lest we hang out too long and get kidnapped.

Our hotel was surrounded by a tall fence and armed guards, but otherwise it was a lovely place with an easygoing tropical vibe. After registering at the front desk, we were frog-marched to a press conference. It was mid-afternoon and we hadn't had much to eat. No problem. The corporate sponsor of our show (including its mascot—some poor guy stuck in a hot parrot suit) had plenty of product to tide us over while a translator lobbed us questions. Unfortunately, the product wasn't food, but whiskey, or brandy, or scotch…I'm not sure, other than it was golden brown and delicious. We drank more and more as the press conference went on, and soon, we could barely put together a cogent answer without giggling or high fiving the parrot. We ended up answering most questions by saying, "We love zha Beatlezh!"

The next day we hauled our gear into a lush city park in search of our venue. The "International Fair Amphitheater" was a tiered rectangular concrete hole in the ground shaded by a flat tin roof with open sides—perfectly designed for anything but loud music. Kelly had come to the gig straight from a vacation in Cuba and was without his customary Esh bass. No problem: the backline company provided a bass that had three strings, which is, when you think about it, really close to the usual four. When we tried to power up the amps and P.A., nothing happened. We learned that the transformer hanging on a nearby pole had been blown up the week before by Starship ("We Killed This City"). Not to worry, we were told—they would fix it soon. We then learned that the sound company had not provided in-ear monitors as we'd requested, so hearing ourselves onstage was looking chancy. The gig was off to a rousing start. We had eight hours to fix everything before showtime.

Word got out about Kel's bass. A local musician ran home and brought us a fourth string. Alright! The bass was still a piece of shit, but at least it was a piece of shit with 25 percent more notes. After five hours of phone calls and repairs, the transformer sparked back to life, and we were able to power up for sound check. Next, a band booked for the following night arrived to inspect the venue. They were called Los Tigres Del Norte, from Mexico. We chatted with them for a bit. Nice guys. When they learned we had no in-ear monitors, they generously offered to loan us their system for the night. El Salvador taketh away, and El Salvador giveth back.

Laughing in the face of disaster, the show went miraculously well. Our soundman, John Shipp, wrangled a more-than-serviceable sound out of the gear he'd been dealt, and a delighted crowd packed the amphitheater and sang along with most of our set. It may've been the loudest, most reverb-y gig we've ever done, seeing as we were blasting our songs against tin and concrete, two materials not known for sound absorption. When I arrived home in LA late the next night and opened my guitar case, some reverb spilled out. No, seriously.

THE CENTER HOLDS

With our December El Salvador trip, an eventful Y2K was finally over. In a year of tumult, we'd held strong as friends and bandmates. We had a new name and we loved how the band sounded with Gordon on drums. Kelly said it was the best the band had *ever* sounded, including the original ELO. We'd written and recorded a new album, *No Rewind* (see Appendix C for *No Rewind* reviews), which would first appear on an Argentine record label, Art Music. We all looked forward to continuing our odyssey in 2001.

And, I'd gotten hitched for the last time.

WE'D BETTER GET ON IT

Helle moved in with me at my Baxter Street bachelor pad. She declared, "I will live here for a year. After that, we'll find a nicer place." I didn't doubt she was serious. Literally 365 days later, I found us a Spanish-style two-story duplex up to Helle's standards in Silverlake for twice the rent of Baxter. I'll admit it was twice as nice a place. I was learning.

My first two marriages had produced zero kids. Anistatia and I'd tried, but without luck. Janet and I were consumed by work, fun, career ambitions, and sometimes just plain survival. Kids hadn't fit neatly into the picture. As I grew older, whenever the subject of kids came up, I'd pretend to hold a baby in each arm, and say, "I can *feel* 'em, but I haven't figured out how I'm gonna *get* 'em."

My brilliant thirty-year-old wife got right to the heart of the matter. She asked me, "Okay, so how old will you be two years from now?"

"Forty-six."

Helle's face froze a bit. She was undoubtedly stunned anew by the fourteen-year chasm between us. She did the math, composed herself, and bravely declared, "Well, then, we'd better get on it." Now it was my face that froze. When your partner declares she will have your children...is there any greater declaration of love? My world tilted in the most profoundly beautiful way that day. Thank you, Helle.

Not long after our decision, I was in my little home office on the ground floor of our duplex when I heard Helle shout, "Parth! Come here!" I found Helle sitting on the stairs midway down from the second floor. Not a typical resting spot. She seemed a little shaken. She held up a pregnancy test and said, "There's a blue line." Holy wow. I was gonna be a dad. Helle a mom. Everything would be different. I couldn't wait.

WHO'S THE ORCHESTRA?

Now that we were called the Orchestra Starring Former Members of ELO and ELO Part II, it was, apparently, a hell of a lot harder for Regna to find us work. Some promoters were understandably concerned about selling tickets if they couldn't bill us more succinctly as "ELO Part II." Whatever the reason, the Orchestra began 2001 with a massive, disappointing thud: five months of inactivity. We didn't play a single gig until a life-saving run of eight shows in June. Regna assured us things would turn around, but the name change appeared to be killing us. My favorite quote of Bev's, "See you in Uruguay," seemed like a long, long time ago.

A CALAMITOUS MISCALCULATION

Speaking of name changes, in June 2001, Epic Records released an album called *Zoom*. Jeff Lynne performed most of the music, making it essentially a solo album, but it hit the market under the more commercially known name "ELO." Less than two years after regaining control of all variations of the name, Lynne and his new label put the ELO brand back to work. A massive US tour was booked to support the album. Below is a newspaper account of what happened.

Rock's Electric Light Orchestra Cancels U.S. Tour
By Dean Goodman

LOS ANGELES (Reuters) – Veteran English pop group Electric Light Orchestra, whose recent new album *Zoom* was greeted with a giant yawn, has canceled plans to mount its first North American tour in 15 years, the band's manager said Wednesday. The group, led by 53-year-old Jeff Lynne, had already scrapped the tour's Sept. 7 opening date in Albany, New York, while at least one show was shifted to a smaller venue. In a calamitous miscalculation, the group booked two-dozen shows in large arenas that seat up to 19,000 people, while the new album, *Zoom*, has sold just 52,000 units since its June 12 release in the United States. It spent two weeks in the top 200 pop album charts.

"That's like not even releasing a record when you're at that level," said Gary Bongiovanni, editor-in-chief of *Pollstar* magazine, a concert trade publication.

In a statement, Lynne's manager, Craig Fruin, blamed a combination of economic and logistic factors. "ELO wanted to put on the grand spectacle with a massive stage and light show that the group is known for," he said. "And that's just not logistically or economically possible in this marketplace at this time."

"Electric Light Orchestra" canceled the following tour dates, according to the band's publicist:

9/7 – Albany, NY @ Pepsi Arena
9/8 – Mansfield, MA @ Tweeter Center
9/11 – Toronto, ON @ Molson Amphitheatre
9/12 – Cleveland, OH @ Cleveland State University
9/14 – Uniondale, NY @ Nassau Coliseum
9/15 – Philadelphia, PA @ First Union Arena
9/18 – St. Paul, MN @ Xcel Energy Center
9/19 – Rosemont, IL @ Allstate Arena
9/21 – Columbus, OH @ Ohio State University
9/22 – Clarkston, MI @ DTE Energy Music Theatre

9/26 – Rochester, NY @ Blue Cross Arena
9/28 – East Rutherford, NJ @ Continental Airlines Arena
9/29 – State College, PA @ Bryce Jordan Arena
10/2 – Atlanta, GA @ Lakewood Amphitheater
10/3 – Nashville, TN @ Gaylord Amphitheater
10/5 – New Orleans, LA @ New Orleans Arena
10/6 – North Little Rock, AR @ Alltel Arena
10/9 – The Woodlands, TX @ C.W. Mitchell Pavilion
10/10 – Dallas, TX @ Smirnoff Music Centre
10/12 – Phoenix, AZ @ Arizona State Fair
10/13 – Inglewood, CA @ Forum
10/16 – Fresno, CA @ Selland Arena
10/17 – San Francisco, CA @ Shoreline Amphitheatre
10/19 – Chula Vista, CA @ Coors Amphitheater
10/20 – Las Vegas, NV @ MGM Grand

With the *Zoom* tour off the books, the new "ELO" filmed a couple TV appearances in front of studio audiences. One was a PBS special, which happened to air while the Orchestra was in New Jersey rehearsing for a tour of England. The six of us assembled in Eric's living room to watch Lynne play ELO songs with a band for the first time since the 1980s. Visually, Lynne's new group was strikingly different from the old ELO. Instead of being flanked by Kelly and Mik on bass and violin, Lynne stood next to his girlfriend Rosie Vela, a background vocalist. After three songs, Lynne said to the studio audience, "In case you didn't know, I'm Jeff Lynne and we are ELO!"

That hit home for the English members of the Orchestra. I wish I could accurately describe the collective sound created by Kelly and Mik 'n' Lou's reaction—well, okay, it was like an elephant, a buffalo, and a lion simultaneously groaning from acute stomach pain. Apparently they didn't equate a selection of talented LA studio musicians and Jeff's girlfriend with "ELO." We Americans enjoyed the spectacle of our English pals expressing their feelings.

We watched the broadcast for a couple songs before going back to work on our own show. If pressed, I think we all would've admitted that the band was fine and Jeff's voice sounded as good as ever.

9/11 AND 10/01

On September 11, Helle woke me at 6:30 a.m. and urged me to come downstairs to watch something on television. A jet had crashed into one of the World Trade Center buildings back east in New York City. Smoke streamed from the upper floors. At first, I thought, "This kind of thing happens occasionally in New York," but only with small planes. Big jets don't fly that low. Of course, a second jet hit the adjoining tower and 9/11 was in full disaster mode.

For my wife and me, 9/11 had an extra layer of concern. Helle was expecting our first child in just seventeen days. We could only think, "What kind of world are we bringing our baby girl into?" Unborn Fiona must've picked up the vibes. She decided to stay in her mother's womb past the due date. We scheduled a day to induce and instead of a panicky, water-breaking drive through LA traffic, we had a relaxed dinner of Mexican food before checking into the maternity ward. A day later, Helle brought Fiona into the world on 10/01/01. Cool zeros-and-ones birthdate.

The Orchestra hadn't worked much in 2001, but, naturally, we had a run of shows immediately after Fiona's birth that would take me away from home. This was all in keeping with the Touring Musicians Law: if you want to tour, schedule a super important family event for the same dates. When I expressed to my dad my concerns about leaving my daughter so soon after she was born, he assured me, "She won't remember you were gone. Helle might, but Fiona won't." Thanks, Dad.

TO BEV OR NOT TO BEV

The Orchestra Starring Former Members of ELO and ELO Part II treated sold-out crowds in six UK cities to spectacular shows accompanied by the Royal Philharmonic Concert Orchestra and a massive 100-person choir. On this high-watermark tour, I had the best seat in the house. As often as I could, I turned to watch the symphony and choir behind me, to drink in the sight and sound of more than 150 musicians and singers blending in with our band. I'd never been part of something so magnificent. For each show, I wore a black T-shirt onto which I'd ironed an image of my wee Fiona's scrunchy little pink face. Proud dad.

To the surprise of everyone in the band, Bev and his wife Val showed up backstage after our show in Nottingham. Bev was smiling broadly, standing on the outer edge of the crowd of well-wishers, looking pleased to be there and maybe even excited to see us. A rush of conflicting feelings hit me. I liked Bev and owed him a lot. I wouldn't have been in the band without his blessing.

We'd had many good times together. He was a boyhood idol. But when he took the name "ELO Part II" with him into retirement without warning us, it had caused a lot of expensive trouble. (Had we ever talked to Bev and expressed our disappointment and anger? Heavens no. Even we Americans knew that wasn't allowed in an English band.)

Despite our recent history, my instincts took over and I made my way over to our former drummer. We embraced, and soon enough we were chatting like old times. Nearly two years into his retirement, Bev said he was well and enjoying being a deejay with an oldies radio show. He marveled at our performance and commented that the band sounded fantastic. I wasn't about to disagree. I brought him up to date with Helle and shared my excitement about three-week-old Fiona. I was glad we talked.

We haven't seen each other since.

CHAPTER 17

LEAVING THE WEST BEHIND

When I joined ELO Part II in 1998, I fancifully mused it was as close as I'd get to joining the Beatles. In fall 2001, Paul McCartney hired my old *Sunny Nights* producer, David Kahne, to produce his next album. Kahne, as he always did when he needed a guitarist, hired my old bandmate, guitarist Rusty Anderson. After getting over the shock of working with a Beatle, Kahne and Rusty helped McCartney forge his first post-Linda LP, *Driving Rain*. When the recording finished, McCartney casually said to Rusty and the other studio musicians, "Well, I suppose we should take this on the road." And just like that, Rusty was in Paul's band. More than twenty years later, he still is. *That's as close as you can get to joining the Beatles!*

Thanks to Rusty, I have a few McCartney stories. Settle in.

On March 29, 2002, Rusty invited me to a McCartney rehearsal in Culver City (LA) at Sony Pictures Studios. I brought my baby Fiona with me in her stroller. I was among a small group of guests that included John Cusack, Rebecca De Mornay, Neve Campbell, and Cameron Crowe. You know, my usual crowd. Shortly after the last song of the set, "Hey Jude," reverberated around the vast indoor sound studio, I spotted Rusty and Paul leaving the stage area and walking toward me. "I'm about to meet Paul McCartney," I thought, brilliantly. When Paul reached the stroller in front of me, he turned to see the-cutest-baby-in-the-world Fiona looking up at him. "Ohhhh! Who's *this* then?" Paul said, smiling like a dad. He reached down and rubbed her smooth little cheek with his finger. I know it's absurd, but I thought to myself, "The finger that plucked the bass that changed the world just brushed my baby's cheek."

Rusty introduced us. I pulled myself together, shook Paul's hand and said, "Nice to meet you, Paul."

"Nice to meet you, Parthenon. We've got you in the show!" He was referring to the image of an ancient temple that popped up in their video graphics. It wasn't the Parthenon, but I wasn't about to correct him. Paul seemed friendly, open, and in good spirits. If I'd just rehearsed a show like his, I'd be in good spirits, too. When Paul walked off, I thanked Rusty for the introduction and said, "Looks like I won't be washing Fiona's face anytime soon."

Everyone was invited to have lunch, and we headed over to the buffet. I chatted with Cameron Crowe as the two of us assembled sandwiches. We both marveled how calm the rehearsal scene was, noting how a hundred-plus crew were going about their business without the slightest hint of tension or hubbub. We agreed it likely had something to do with the leader of the band. Crowe, himself, struck me as one of the least impressed-with-himself Hollywood guys I'd ever met. It's nice when that happens.

After lunch, Paul and a few members of the band sat in the empty audience space facing the stage to review the video graphics. I joined them, sitting next to Paul's new bassist/guitarist, Brian Ray, a friend whom I'd once hired to play guitar with me and Rusty on an animal-rights gig. The video featured random colorful images that changed at an ever-accelerating pace, creating a somewhat psychedelic visual experience. Accordingly, I mimicked toking on a joint and passed it to Brian. Brian smiled at my old chestnut of a joke, took my invisible joint, hit it and passed it to drummer Abe Laborial Jr. who laughed, hit it and passed it to Paul, who also laughed, nodded, and took a hit off the invisible joint. That's right. Paul McCartney smoked *my* imaginary joint. Boom.

GETTING BETTER

A month later, Rusty called me from London, where the McCartney band was in final rehearsals. "Paul's asking for suggestions for more songs to add to the show. Do you have any ideas?" Let's just hold on here for a second. *I was now being asked to help with Paul's set list.* Okay, we can continue now. I thought for a second and then said to Rusty, "Well, after 9/11 it'd be nice to hear something really positive, you know? What if you guys started the show with 'Getting Better' to kind of set the anti-terrorism tone? I don't think it's ever been performed live. It'd be a nice surprise. I think people would go nuts to hear it."

Cut to the Driving World Tour, Madison Square Garden, April 26, 2002. Eric Troyer, his friend Burt (who bought the tickets, thanks Burt!), Gordon, and I stood in the eighth row, center. McCartney, with Rusty to his right, had opened with three hits: "Hello Goodbye," "Jet," and "All My Loving." The band sounded huge and perfect. Paul's fifty-eight-year-old voice was fully intact, and I could barely get my head around the sight of my old guitarist

Chapter 17: Leaving the West Behind

hamming it up with Sir Paul McCartney. Life doesn't get much better, or more surreal.

A stagehand took Paul's Hofner bass and handed McCartney a Les Paul. Rusty's new boss said, "You know, there are times when you write a song, you record it, put it on an album, and then you forget about it..." *Well, maybe YOU forget about it, Paul, but yes, do go on.* "This next song is like that. It's from Sgt Pepper. I've never played it live before...and it goes something like this..." He started the staccato guitar riff of "Getting Better" and my head nearly exploded. Of course, I thought, "THIS WAS MY IDEA!" As if I'd written it. "Getting Better" had the exact effect I predicted. The crowd went mad. It felt so wonderfully powerful to hear it played live by Paul (and Rusty) in New York City itself, only a few miles from Ground Zero. I recall Eric and I both crying our faces off, failing to hold it together. It's a moment I'll always treasure.

ECHO, BANNED

Rusty hired me to co-produce his solo album. We finished work on three songs, and Rusty mused, "It'd be great if I could get the McCartney band to play on a track." I agreed that would be a treat. Rusty soon told me the great news that Paul, drummer Abe Laborial Jr., and Brian Ray had agreed to record a track for Rusty's album. The not-so-great news was that David Kahne would produce. Rusty said, "I just think things will go smoother if Kahne does it since he's already produced Paul, you know?" There went my chance to produce a Rusty Anderson song with McCartney on bass. I said to Rusty, "I understand your thinking on this, but I still want to be at the session." Rusty said, "Oh, for sure."

When I walked into Sunset Sound on the day of the session, Kahne saw me and said, "Lots of producers here today...!" I don't think he feared for his job.

The McCartney band ran through Rusty's song "Hurt Myself" a few times and then did a take or two. Kahne invited the band into the control room to have a listen. McCartney, standing next to me, said, "You know, it's kind of a pissed-off song and we're playing it too politely. We should play with a bit more anger." Heads nodded in agreement. Paul went on, "Sometimes it's good to have a kind of theme going into a project. I remember the Beatles did one album where we banned echo..."

"*Rubber Soul*," I said.

"Yeah, might've been," Paul answered.

I doubled down. "It was definitely *Rubber Soul*, Paul." I kind of laughed. That album was commonly recognized as a sea-change moment in the Beatles' recording career, with its more grown-up writing and in-your-face, *dry* sound. It dawned on me that we fans might be more familiar with some of the minute details of McCartney's work than Paul himself. And why wouldn't we? While Paul moved on to creating his next single or album or film, we kept on listening to the entire catalogue like our lives depended on it.

The band went back to work on "Hurt Myself," and I walked out of a McCartney session at Sunset Sound to keep an appointment across the street at S.I.R. rehearsal studios. I had promised to sing backing vocals at a label showcase with an artist whose name I've forgotten. There was no question in my mind that I needed to be there because I'd given my word that I would. The artist was late, the showcase ran long, and by the time I got back to Sunset Sound, Rusty and the McCartney band were packed up and leaving the studio. David Kahne came out of the control room saying, "Well, THAT was amazing," referring to the session I'd just missed. I still try like hell to convince myself I did the right thing by honoring my previous commitment. Damn.

GETTING WORSE

Our English tour at the end of 2001 with symphony and choir had been a great success, but, overall, our band's work calendar was grimly anemic. With 9/11 stirring up fears of flying, things would only get worse before they got better. There are a million reasons why gigs fall through, but I'm convinced that losing the use of "ELO Part II" rippled through promoter networks. We averaged about ten shows a year from 2001 to 2005, effectively shrinking our income by 75 percent. The band was barely more than a hobby, and no one was making a living. Our nadir came in 2003 with a paltry six gigs, fifty-three fewer than in 1999. Here's the ugly truth:

> 1999: 59 shows as ELO Part II, the year I joined the band.
> 2000: 43 shows during the transition from ELO Part II to the Orchestra.
> 2001: 15 shows as the Orchestra. USA (9) UK (6)
> 2002: 9 shows as the Orchestra. USA (8) Ireland (1)
> 2003: 6 shows as the Orchestra. USA (4) Chile (2)
> 2004: 9 shows as the Orchestra. USA (6) Spain (3)
> 2005: 16 shows as the Orchestra. USA (4) Chile (6) Dubai (1) Argentina (2) Spain (1) El Salvador (1) Guatemala (1)

FAB FIVE

Despite the struggle to find work, Regna doggedly refused to drop our price. He knew that if he devalued our worth, it would take forever to climb back to the income level and quality of venue we'd fought so hard to reach. We weren't playing many shows, but on the bright side, the ones we *did* play were memorable. Here are five of my favorites.

Noroeste Pop Rock Festival, Playa de Riazor, La Coruña, Spain

On July 30, 2004, The Orchestra headlined a pop festival in La Caruna, a port city in Gallicia, Spain's northwest corner. The festival site was Riazor Beach, a sandy crescent about a kilometer wide, right where the city met the Atlantic. We played to the largest crowd in band history, 70,000 people, a magnificent sight I'll never forget.

Vina Del Mar Festival, Vina Del Mar, Chile

Broadcast on live TV from Miami to Tierra Del Fuego, the Vina Del Mar Festival is a hugely popular over-the-top week-long celebration of Latin America's biggest musical stars. Each year, a single non-Latin act is invited to the festival as a special guest, and in February 2005 we were it. The audience, 17,000 fans packed into a huge outdoor amphitheater, is known as the Monster. If the Monster doesn't like you, they can boo you off the stage on live television before millions of viewers. Not good. Even more challenging, we began our set at 3 a.m. I'm happy to say that our thirty-five-minute hit parade was so well received that the Orchestra earned two gold statuettes, presented to us by dazzling celebrity hosts I didn't know from Adam. It was like being famous on another planet. Note to those familiar with my P. Hux albums: during our packed press conference the day we arrived in Vina, I assured the media we were not afraid of the audience, and in fact, we would "kiss the Monster."

Phillips Jazz Festival Dubai, UAE

Dubai is a place where the airport resembles Neiman Marcus, and a billboard on the way to our hotel declared, "Buy a condo, get a free Porsche."
The Phillips Jazz Festival took place outdoors on the beautifully landscaped corporate campus of Reuters, CNN, and Al Jazeera. The event was extremely well organized, and we were cared for by friendly festival workers. When our afternoon sound check was finished, I asked a group of stagehands if it was safe to leave gear on the stage. They reassured me, "No one will touch it." *Really?* "Yes. It is completely safe." Just to see what they'd say, I threw my wallet on

the stage. One of the stagehands laughed and said cheerfully, "It will be there when you return." Ha! I loved it. Great answer. I asked why it was so safe and one of the guys made a cutting gesture across his wrist. *Ohhhh. Thieves get their hands cut off.* Got it. I picked up my wallet anyway.

Pucon Gran Hotel, Pucon, Chile

Chile, a strip of land 3,100 miles long and facing the Pacific, boasts every climate and terrain. I've already told you about the desert moonscape of Antofagasta and the Mediterranean vibes of Santiago. In January of 2005, we ventured further south to a picturesque resort town called Pucon. Imagine Aspen on Lake Tahoe with a volcano towering nearby. For the first two days we were in town, the volcano, called Villarrica, stood solemnly, its peak cloaked by a puffy gray cloud that never moved. We were told the volcano was active, but we saw no evidence of it. Our hosts even drove us halfway up Villarrica's slope to a ski resort. Our guide pointed out a ravine that was the "usual route" of lava when the volcano erupted. I took in the view and asked, "If the volcano erupts, how much time do we have to get to, say, the lake?" "Seven minutes." *Right.* Still, no one seemed particularly nervous.

As usual, in Chile, our set didn't begin until midnight. When it was over, we had a few celebratory drinks and then retired upstairs to our rooms on the fifth floor of the hotel. It was a moonless night, and I opened my curtains to check out the view of the volcano. "HOLY SHIT," I yelled to myself. The volcano's cloud was gone. I had a crystal-clear view of Villarrica's ominous, bright-red, fiery smoking tip. I thought, "It's alive!" I ran down the hall and knocked on Eric's door. He opened it and before I could say anything, shouted, "DID YOU SEE THE VOLCANO?" We both stood at his window and looked up at the lava-filled monster in awe. There aren't many things more captivating or frightening on Earth. Man! No wonder they usually park a cloud on top.

Classic Superstars Live, Dover Downs, Dover, Delaware

For this all-day event, we shared a bill with CSN, Peter Frampton, Bo Diddley, Blood Sweat & Tears, and Creedence Clearwater Revisited (with the Cars' Eliot Easton on guitar). My father-in-law, Terry O'Connell, sat in the front row, delighted to see me share a stage with his best buddy Stephen Stills. In between sets, Terry suggested we visit Stephen in his bus behind the stage. Stephen welcomed us into his road abode. It was one of those deluxe jobs with soft lighting, nice carpeting, real wood features, a bedroom in the back, and sides that popped out to provide extra interior space. I'm sure it was bigger than my first New York apartment. Nice way to tour!

HERE COMES MY BABY

I hated my reduced income due to the Orchestra's decimated tour schedule, but I loved being a stay-at-home dad with Fiona. She was an easygoing, adorable baby. We went everywhere together. I'd prop Fiona on my Trader Joe's grocery cart and, without fail, a show would break out. LA is full of showbiz extroverts who'll never have kids, so babies are like magical aliens. Fi's big blue eyes would make strangers stop and they'd start to coo and ooh and ahh and comment and smile and laugh. I was only her handler, but I'd never felt more publicly popular.

Not long after Fiona was born, Helle and I bought a house in North Hollywood for half the price of an equivalent in Silverlake. Our migration from the LA basin to the other-side-of-the-hill Valley adhered to the classic plot line of coupledom in LA. You meet in Hollywood when you're young and renting, and you head to the Valley when you're older and ready to buy.

As soon as Fi was able to toddle, we enrolled her in a dance class called Tots and Tutus, an excuse to dress her up in tulle. Baby culture in LA is like secret daytime Hollywood. There was Eric McCormack from Will and Grace sitting in a "get to know you" circle with other parents, Eddie Murphy's nannie shuffling Eddie's tots into the dance room, and a singer from Three Dog Night sitting in the lobby waiting on a granddaughter.

HE'S SAM AND I'M OUT

Until Regna could restore our standing in the concert business, I needed to find work. Erin Scully, a friend of Helle's at New Line Cinema, invited me and some other musicians to an early screening of a movie called *I Am Sam*, starring Sean Penn. To my surprise, the soundtrack was loaded with Beatles songs—the original versions. I thought, "Can they *do* that?" The Beatles catalogue is the hardest to crack in the music industry. Original masters of their songs can't be associated with just any project. One of Helle's responsibilities when she worked at Sony Publishing was to caretake the Beatles catalogue, a duty we both equated with protecting the Holy Grail.

Erin spoke with me after the screening. "I'm sure you noticed the music."

I laughed. "I did. What's the deal?"

Erin said, "The creators of *I Am Sam* are convinced they'll be allowed to use the original masters."

"And you're not," I said.

"That's right. You and Helle, especially, know how hard it is to get permission." Erin then asked, "How would you like to record three Beatles songs for us? Do your own versions, but keep them pretty close to the originals?"

I finished Erin's thought, "And you'll temp them into the film, and the creators will see what it's like to have covers instead of originals."

"You got it," Erin said, smiling. Interesting gambit.

New Line gave me $3,000 to record "Lucy In The Sky With Diamonds," "I'm Looking Through You," and "Blackbird." I used my P. Hux bandmates Gordon Townsend and Dan Rothchild to knock out three close-enough-to-the-original covers and sent them over to Erin. Erin put my versions into the rough cut of *I Am Sam*, not knowing what reaction to expect from the filmmakers. Happily, they said, "Oh, that sounds great." Crisis averted. Good move, Erin.

If you've seen *I Am Sam*, maybe you're thinking, "So that was P. Hux I heard in the movie." Nope. In Hollywood, it's never so simple. New Line negotiated a soundtrack deal with Virgin (V2) Records. Virgin exclusively used Virgin artists to create the Beatles covers. Black Crowes, Sara McLachlan, Eddie Vedder, Nick Cave, Aimee Mann, Ben Harper, the Wallflowers, and Sheryl Crow were in. I was out.

HOUSE CONCERT

Jay Gilbert and Gail George worked at MCA (Universal) Records and loved power pop, including my album *P. Hux "Deluxe."* In 2001, Jay and Gail invited me to play an acoustic show in Jay's Simi Valley living room, my first "house concert," which was becoming a thing. Since joining ELO Part II, other than recording *Purgatory Falls*, I hadn't played my own stuff much at all. Performing twenty-one of my songs for an intimate audience was exciting but intimidating. Rusty Anderson agreed to join me, and, suddenly, the gig felt a lot more fun.

Rusty and I teamed up and laughed our way through songs from *Sunny Nights* including "Buddha, Buddha," "Double Our Numbers," "Shoebox," and even the little single that couldn't, "Chance To Be Loved." I dove into songs from *"Deluxe," A Man Called E*, and several as-yet-unreleased tunes about Janet that would end up on *Purgatory Falls*. Despite loads of nervous chatter and constant tuning of my guitars, the night was a big success and produced my *Live In Your Living Room* concert CD. I've performed dozens of house concerts since, in the UK, Finland, Maryland, Ohio, Virginia, California...

and they rank among my favorite shows ever. House concert audiences are attentive, the money is guaranteed, there are no opening acts, and there's normally a lot of food and drink. Compared to a run-of-the-mill club gig, house concerts are heavenly.

HOMEMADE SPACESHIP

My friend Kee Kee Buckley worked at Lakeshore Entertainment on the Paramount lot in Hollywood. In September 2004, I asked her to introduce me to Brian McNelis, head of Lakeshore's soundtrack division. I was hoping he might be interested in putting my songs into Lakeshore releases. Instead, he threw me a curve. Brian said, "Besides soundtracks, Lakeshore also does tribute albums. How would you like to do an acoustic ELO record?"

"Oh, geez. What would *that* sound like?"

"I don't know—you tell me," Brian said.

I asked, "Don't tribute albums usually have all different artists?"

"Yeah, but for this one, you could do the whole thing yourself. I figure you're the guy who could pull it off. What do you think?"

I thought it was an unworkable idea. *Acoustic* ELO? Without strings, electric guitars, bass, keyboards, drums, bells, whistles, and sound effects... what would be left? I said, "Hmmm. I don't know, Brian. I mean, it's an interesting idea. Let me think about it."

By interesting, I meant I wasn't interested. I was disappointed that Brian had skipped right over the idea of using my songs on Lakeshore soundtracks to pitch me his odd tribute idea. Yet another business meeting that left me shaking my head. And then, a funny thing happened. On my drive from Hollywood back to the Valley, I thought, "What if I played 'Sweet Talkin' Woman' really quietly, like I was in bed trying not to wake Helle?" When I got home, I grabbed my acoustic guitar and strummed the chords as softly as I could. Before long I had changed the key to support a softer vocal, altered the melody to fit the somber mood, and shifted from 4/4 to 3/4 waltz time. To my delight, the song became a completely different animal. The new arrangement worked *great*.

My opinion of Brian's idea did a one-eighty. I reasoned if "Sweet Talkin' Woman" could be re-imagined and still hold up as a recognizable song, why wouldn't others from the ELO catalog? I created a sotto voce version of "Ma-Ma-Ma Belle," which became the opposite of the howling original. It worked. Brian was right: I was the guy to do this. I called him the next day and said, "Okay, Brian, we're on." Before we discussed how I wanted to proceed, Brian told me Lakeshore's budget was $5,000, no negotiating. Ugh! Five thousand dollars used to be *demo* money, not a production budget. Just like that, I knew I wouldn't make a dime on this acoustic ELO album. Every cent would go to production. The back end wouldn't be any better, because all the songs were owned by Lynne's publishing. This was no way to make a living.

Despite the zero-sum financials, I took the deal. Why would I do such a thing? Why start a project that would take months to complete for literally no money? Because *I knew my concept would work*. That's it. I was driven to hear what I heard in my head. The classic artist's curse.

Luckily for me, my friend Michael Woodrum, a talented producer/engineer, was excited by the concept and just as financially insane as me. He agreed to record the album for $3,500, a ridiculously low fee. Michael never complained about the hours or brought up the money unless we joked about it, which we did. "You earned your $3.50 an hour today, Woodrum!"

During the last three months of 2004, I practically lived at Michael's studio adjacent to Burbank airport. Even with jets flying over the roof, his studio was quiet and comfortable. We worked on weekdays, and I had wee Fiona with me. We'd build a protective fortress of cushions on the floor, and she'd happily nap for hours.

The altered version of "Sweet Talkin' Woman" inspired me to reharmonize other ELO songs. For "Telephone Line," I reversed the melody—where the original vocal went up, I went down. For "Don't Bring Me Down," I created a Monty Python version, with spoken verses and a silly arrangement. I arranged "Do Ya" for my tiny, tinny-sounding Martin travel guitar.

My ideas for the project grew more complex, and I worried that I might be overdoing it. I called Brian at Lakeshore. Respecting his concept, I asked, "Hey, do you want *all* the songs to be acoustic?" Brian said, "No, man. Do whatever you want." He either trusted me or he didn't much care what I did. Either way worked for me.

For the non-acoustic songs, I brought in the Orchestra's Gordon Townsend, Kelly Groucutt (credited as Jelly Deal), and Mik Kaminski (Poppadom Screech). The highlight was Mik's first-ever vocal performance, a wooly Yorkshire recital of a verse on "Don't Bring Me Down." Rusty Anderson contributed goofy guitar parts. My neighbor and pal, Nic Pierone, laid down inspired piano when we weren't fighting over who was responsible for buying breakfast sandwiches. (I was.) Violinist Ludvig Girdland and background singer Angela Bartys turned "Evil Woman" into a menacing march.

Despite our demo deal budget, Michael and I created a record we both loved. I called it *Homemade Spaceship* in a nod to ELO's space pedigree and our humble funding. I sent the finished album to Lakeshore. Kee Kee told me she called Brian and said, "It's pretty fucking amazing, don't you think?" She said Brian was "blown away." I liked Kee Kee.

Not long after its release, *Homemade Spaceship* was nominated for Best Cover/Tribute Album by Just Plain Folks, an online community of more than 40,000 musicians. Helle and I were invited to attend the awards ceremony.

I mentioned to my old pal Matt Barrett that *Spaceship* was up for an award.

"Oh, congratulations," Matt said. "But don't you think that's somewhat ironic?"

"What do you mean?" I asked.

"Well, think about it. Here you are...the perfect guy to reinterpret ELO music, and you obviously did a great job of it because you're up for an award. And yet, the guy whose songs you're doing..."

Oh, right. *That* guy. I guess that is somewhat ironic.

Matt wondered, "Do you think Jeff Lynne's heard *Homemade Spaceship*?"

I had no idea. I'd like to think he'd heard it and enjoyed it. If I were he, I'd have gotten a huge kick out of it. I've had a few of my songs covered. I know how honorific it feels.

Ironic or not, Helle and I happily attended the Just Plain Folks awards ceremony at the Galaxy Theater in Santa Ana, California. We heard performances by rock bands, rap bands, spoken wordists, flautists, *a capella* groups, electric bagpipists, pianists...you name it. JPF has got to be the most inclusive, earnest, warmhearted music organization in the world. Even with all the trophies being handed out, the atmosphere tilted heavily toward inclusiveness, not competition.

A few hours into the ceremony, it was time for my category's winners to be announced. For Best Cover/Tribute Album, Just Plain Folks founder Brian Austin Whitney read off the sixth-, fifth-, fourth-, third-, and second-place finishers. I was the only nominee left. An excited realization passed between Helle and me: *Homemade Spaceship* had won! I walked quickly down the aisle and onto the stage to shake Brian's hand and accept my trophy. From then on, my little $5K album could rightfully be called the Award-Winning *Homemade Spaceship*.

Every few years, Michael Woodrum and I call each other and say the exact same thing: "I listened to *Spaceship* the other day...man oh man, I just can't believe how good it sounds." On one call, Michael mentioned an encounter with Charlie Bolois, an audio technician well-known in LA as the go-to guy for tuning control rooms and aligning tape machines in analog recording studios. Charlie said he used *Homemade Spaceship* as a reference CD. If *Spaceship* didn't sound good through a studio's monitors, there was something wrong with the *studio*. I can't think of a higher audio compliment.

WORKIN' FOR MCA, AGAIN

In 2004, the CD format was on the wane. Downloading was clearly the next platform for music retail (streaming was not yet a thing). Jay Gilbert, who'd first heard songs from *Purgatory Falls* when I played them at his house concert in 2001, helped convince his bosses at Universal (MCA) to form a new label in an all-digital format. Jay selected *Purgatory Falls* to be one of the first releases on Ume Digital. Just like that, I was working for MCA again.

Ume Digital's press release in Billboard made me laugh. It said the label's focus was on "acts that have a built-in fan base but don't play into a mass-market retail strategy." That was corporate-speak for "some people like these artists but not *that* many." They weren't wrong.

Universal managed to push my single, "I Loved Everything," to number one on *Rolling Stone*'s exclusive download chart. Yes, okay, I hadn't heard of that chart either, but my song was number one, end of story. I technically had my first number-one hit.

GO EAST, OLD MAN

By 2005, I'd toiled in LA for eighteen years and wondered if it was time for a change. I loved my friends, the food, the weather, the musical opportunities, and the sense of excitement, but I wondered, "If there's something I haven't done in LA after eighteen years, will I ever do it?"

One obvious thing I hadn't done was make it big. In LA, success is the only acceptable outcome. If you don't make it, the town has a way of reminding you. After writing with Robert Lamm at his exquisite Beverly Hills address, I drove home in the direction of ever-worsening zip codes to my humble Echo Park bungalow. Dave Wakeling and I wrote "I Want More" at my single apartment and then spent an evening playing pool where Dave was staying—Miles Copeland's Hollywood Hills mansion, once owned by Raymond (Perry Mason) Burr and rumored to contain numerous secret passages. I even spent an afternoon at Hugh Hefner's Playboy Mansion in west LA, but not as a high-profile guest. I was helping my neighbor deliver flower arrangements for that night's party. I'd never chased wealth, but I didn't *love* having my humbler status shoved in my face quite so often.

Chapter 17: Leaving the West Behind

Certain LA landmarks reminded me of Janet's last days. Cedars-Sinai Medical Center where Janet had passed; the Abbott and Hast Mortuary on Silverlake Boulevard where I tended to the gruesome business of arranging Janet's cremation; Strawberry Peak, visible on clear days, where we'd spread half of Janet's ashes.

I was married to Helle and raising Fiona now. A new setting might be good for all of us.

Helle's job in the Music Department at Warner Brothers Television required her to work late, often preventing her from seeing Fiona during the week. We knew that, in Washington, DC, the workday ended at 5 p.m. Helle's parents and extended family were there—a real support network. Helle's best friend, Ursula, had recently left LA and moved back to DC as well. As a member of the Orchestra, it didn't matter where I lived if I had access to a major airport.

All the above pushed me to suggest we move to Maryland. We thought there might be opportunities for Helle at Discovery Channel or National Geographic, two large media companies based in the DC area. Then, out of left field, a marketing position opened at a company called FedSources, a government consulting firm in Northern Virginia. Helle met with the heads of the company and won them over. Their response to meeting her was, "We were looking for a retired general with a large Rolodex, but we'd like to offer the job to you."

To get our North Hollywood house ready for sale, Helle emptied it of all our personal effects and made it look like a Scandinavian hotel. The housing market was hot, and we received twenty-nine offers on the first day. Through blind luck, we'd bought and sold at the exact right time.

Helle and Fiona flew to DC. I got in my first-ever new car and headed East with my best canine pal, the coyote-esque Algonquin. Al was perfect company for a long trip. He loved watching the Southwest roll by from his perch on the passenger seat. I snuck him into my motel rooms and gave him his own bed. He deserved it.

Departing LA was a big deal. Most musicians who dream of record deals and music careers head West, like I had, to seek fame and fortune. Now I was going against the migration pattern. When I'd told my dear pal bassist Jen Condos of my plans to quit town, she said, "You're *leaving*? How are you doing it? We wanna leave, too!" She's still there. It ain't easy.

I was leaving the land of opportunity, but I wasn't abandoning music. I would carry on with the Orchestra, create production music long distance with Jim Jacobsen, and, most importantly, finish my next album.

Our new neighborhood was called "Chevy Chase Section 3," an oddly impersonal name for a charming, leafy part of town. We rented a brick colonial house just a few blocks from Helle's parents. I learned that our neighborhood, and DC in general, was littered with ambitious do-gooders working in departments of government, dot-orgs, the military, scientific research, think tanks, and so on. Throw a stick, you'd hit a lawyer, researcher, or MBA grad. In LA, you'd probably hit a pizza delivery guy, also known as a drummer. *Badda boom*. I'm here all night.

We were warmly welcomed by our new next-door neighbors, the Murphys. Arantza was of Argentinian/Basque descent and her ex-Marine husband, Pat, worked as a lawyer for GE Health. They had four kids, including Lala who was just a year younger than Fiona, and all the Murphys seemed to enjoy a good laugh. We liked them immediately.

Not long after arriving in Maryland, Helle remarked that she felt freer to listen to music simply because she liked it, without needing to judge its placement potential for film and television. I had noticed the same thing. The perils of living in an entertainment-company town began to melt away. Music became *music* again, not "music supervision" or the "music business." I began to appreciate bands and songs without the weight of hipster relevancy or industry value dragging them down.

I reached out to my old songwriting/recording/touring pal, Kyle Vincent. "KV" had left his home state of California a few years earlier and settled in western Massachusetts. Kyle agreed to drive down to Maryland and spend a few days writing.

We cranked out a couple songs and excitedly got to work on a third. Writing back East away from Hollywood made us feel a bit freer to create. Late in the afternoon on day two of our writing session, I suggested we get out of the house, take a walk in my neighborhood, and see if we could finish the lyrics to a song we were calling "Emily Standing." We passed in front of the Murphy home next door with its wide front porch and wooden rocking chairs. My cheerful neighbor Pat called out to me. "Hey! P. Hux! Come and meet my friend, Killer!" We walked up to the porch holding our songwriting notebooks. I introduced my skinny, long-haired friend. "This is Kyle, he's down from Massachusetts to write songs. We made records together in LA."

Pat introduced us to his muscular friend with the jarhead haircut. "This is Killer. We were in the Marines together. I left. He stayed."

"Nice to meet you." I asked, "So, what do you do, Killer?"

Killer said, "I oversee a unit of seventy men that goes wherever we're told to go."

Pat laughed. "He's being modest, P. Hux. Killer goes on missions to hot spots all over the world where our best fighters are needed because no one else has the balls to go."

"Wow." Note to self: don't fuck with Killer.

Pat smiled and said, "What are you guys up to?"

"Yeah, we're on a pretty serious mission, too. We need a word that rhymes with Emily."

ELEMENTARY, MY DEAR HUXLEY

On a warm September day, a year after moving to Maryland, I stood outside Wyngate Elementary School holding Fiona's hand, preparing to walk her into her first day of kindergarten. I was fifty years old, living on the East Coast, and surrounded by younger, fitter, suburban parents and noisy whirlpools of children. I stared at the one-story brick school building. It looked strikingly like Hillview School in New Providence, New Jersey, where *I'd* gone to kindergarten. A thought struck me. "Oh, my God...*I'm back to where I started.*" It was as if my exotic childhood in Greece, my college and rock 'n' roll days in Chapel Hill, my dalliance with New York City, and my eighteen-year musical odyssey in Los Angeles had been nothing more than a fanciful dream from which I'd woken up in a throwback East Coast suburban neighborhood. Woah. I wasn't sure how I felt about that! Still, I was awestruck by life's ability to throw curveballs you don't see coming—until they hit you right between the eyes.

CANADIAN IDOL

Not long after my writing session with Kyle, I got a call from another West Coast friend and collaborator, Stevie Salas. I'd written lyrics for his *Colorcode* album on Island Records in 1990. Stevie hustled hard and always had something cooking. This time he was calling from Toronto. "P. Funk! I'm working with the winner of *Canadian Idol*, a talented kid named Kalan Porter. We've got a bunch of songs started for his first album, but we're kind of stuck for lyrics and I think you're the perfect guy to get us unstuck. What are you doing? Are you busy?" This East Coast thing was working out okay.

Electric Light Odyssey

Stevie and Kalan drove 470 miles in an ice-encrusted Volvo down to Maryland, arriving in a mega snowstorm. Kalan was a tall, skinny, polite young guy from Medicine Hat, Alberta. He had an interesting tone to his tenor voice and a fluid singing style not unlike Rufus Wainwright. On shows like *Idol*, you rise to the top singing cover songs. Winners are then expected to make an album of original music. Kalan had never written an album before, and the pressure was on to decide what his sound was going to be. Stevie was steering him in a semi-hard rock direction, but Kalan wasn't fully convinced. This was a problem. If an artist is unsure of his targeted sound, it leaves co-creators shooting arrows in the dark.

Kalan's situation reminded me of an encounter I had with Don Dixon and T-Bone Burnett when they were producing an album for Tommy Keene. I'd stopped by Reflection Studios in Charlotte, North Carolina, to say hi to Dixon. I was heading toward the building when he and T-Bone bolted out the door. Dixon saw me and said, "Hey P. Hux! What are you doin' here? C'mon and take a walk. We've got to get the hell out of the studio." The two producers seemed stressed. Turns out Dixon and T-Bone had spent all night mixing a track. They felt they'd nailed it. When they played it for Tommy the next day, he said, "I don't like it." Dixon and T-Bone swallowed their disappointment and asked, "How would you like it to sound? What would you do differently?" Tommy's answer was "I don't know." Thus, the angry walk around the neighborhood. Dixon and T-Bone were lamenting their untenable situation. If an artist doesn't have a vision, how can a producer help bring it to life?

I took Stevie and Kalan to Suckerpunch Studio in Bethesda, owned and run by my engineer of choice, Mark Williams. We demo'd a half dozen of Stevie's song ideas and I did my best to find lyrics Kalan could comfortably sing. The young *Canadian Idol* winner couldn't decide what he liked until I played a song of mine called "Out Of My Head." It was an introspective ballad, and Kalan responded to it right away. Kalan and Stevie accompanied me to a show I was playing at a local live music venue in northern Virginia, Jammin Java, and Kalan guest-sang "Out Of My Head" live. The audience loved it, and that may've been what Kalan needed: a response. "Out Of My Head" was the only song from our writing sessions that, ultimately, made it onto Kalan's debut album, *Wake Up Living*. We'd worked hard as a team, so I granted Stevie and Kalan each 17.50 percent of "Out Of My Head," a song I'd written pretty much entirely on my own.

The young Mr. Porter ultimately parted with Stevie and went with a different producer. His album *Wake Up Living* mostly put people to sleep.

Stevie was deservedly frustrated. He'd busted his ass to get Kalan excited about making a rock album and come up empty. Happily, the Kalan story had an epilogue.

One of the last songs we'd worked on with Kalan was "Mister Black Sky," a tune I'd begun with a Nashville writer named Bill DeMain. Stevie loved "Mister Black Sky" and never forgot it. A few years after the Kalan fail, Stevie played it for a Costa Rican band he was producing called Gandhi. They flipped. The only problem was that they sang in Spanish. Stevie suggested they write their own words. Gandhi transformed "Mister Black Sky" into a Spanish-language song called "Simple." That gave them fifty percent ownership. "Simple" became a huge hit in Costa Rica. Stevie called me up one day and said, "P. Funk! Congratulations! You and I are Rock Composers of the Year in Costa Rica!" Stevie presented me with my trophy the next time he visited DC.

"Mister Black Sky" wasn't done. Years later, Stevie played it for a Japanese hard rock legend named Koshi Inaba. He loved it as well, and wrote all new lyrics, resulting in "Mister Black Sky" becoming the Japanese-language song "Blink." It appeared on the album *Chubby Groove*, which debuted at #2 on the Japanese album charts. I got a nice check in the mail. Stevie toured Japan with Koshi.

I have, at last, recorded my own version of "Mister Black Sky." It's on my 2023 album *As Good As Advertised*. It's the first version recorded in English and the first to keep the original title. Third time's the charm, right?

SMART FI

This isn't a music story, but I have to share it. One day, I was driving through Bethesda with five-year-old Fiona in her car seat in the back. I complained about a slowpoke driver in front of me. "What's wrong, Dad?" Fiona asked. I said, "Well, I'd like to pass this slow driver, but I can't." She asked, "Why not?" I launched into one of those *I'll be a good Dad and educate my daughter* speeches. "Well," I explained, "see the two lines of yellow paint?" Fiona peered over the front of the car and said she did. "Well, those two lines of paint are telling me I can't pass another car right now. And the white paint on the right side of the road tells me to stay on this side of that line. And the big white arrow of paint tells me I can turn left. You know what I mean?"

Fiona thought for a second and said, "Smart paint."

I laughed out loud. Smart daughter.

THE KING

In 2006, after five years of barely touring, the Orchestra Starring ELO Former Members finally emerged from the pall cast by Bev's departure and our loss of the name "ELO Part II." Our workload rebounded spectacularly to the tune of fifty gigs, an impressive number for a band with the worst name in rock. We could barely believe the good news. Had we finally turned a corner?

The year began with a short run in Spain. We were with our Spanish promoter, Robert, at a hotel bar in Madrid, on the last night of our four-date tour. Robert, with his thinning dark hair pulled back into a long ponytail, was a veteran promoter who enjoyed talking shop. After a few drinks, he asked, "Hey, do you know Ian McDonald?"

I said, "The guy from King Crimson? Woodwind player?"

He said, "Yeah. He's a friend of mine. Do you know he's in his sixties…and he just married a girl in her twenties! Can you imagine that? What a man he is!" Or something to that effect. I wondered what interests Ian and his young bride might share, but I said, "Yeah, good for him." Go along to get along.

I suspected that in Spain, a country where machismo still held some sway, marrying younger could be seen as an accomplishment, a confirmation of one's manliness. I didn't see it that way. The musicians I know who have younger wives or girlfriends are some of the least macho people I've ever met. I think it's actually *music*, not manliness, that blurs reality and, in many cases, makes older musicians seem younger. Of course, good old immaturity helps, too, speaking for myself.

I sipped my drink and glanced around the bar at my Orchestra bandmates. A thought occurred to me.

I shouted to our 60-year-old bass player, "Hey Kelly, how many years older than Anna are you?" Kelly replied, "Twenty-two."

"Lou, how much older are you than Gloria?" Lou, 58, burped and said, "Twenty years."

"ET, how about you?" Eric came back with, "Eighteen years." Eric was 56.

I was 50. I added, "I'm fourteen years older than Helle. Mik, how about you?"

Mik, a spry 54, said, "Twelve years older than Jackie."

Gordon, the youngest guy in our band at thirty-five, wasn't seeing anyone at the time, but a future partner was probably just finishing up high school or college. Marrying younger is not a competition, but I couldn't help saying to our promoter, "How about that, Robert? We're all double-figures older!"

Robert, not giving in, said, "Ian's still got you beat." Fine. Congrats to the Crimson King.

One more thought. Now that women dominate rock, in a few years will we see strapping young men (or women) on the arms of aging female rock stars?

LEAVING THE WEST BEHIND
Note: this story takes place eighteen years before Russia's brutal invasion of Ukraine. It remains as originally written.

Next up in our resurgent touring year was Russia. I'd always wanted to go, if only to put my eyes on a place few Americans visit, but which looms so large in our psyche. Growing up during the Cold War, my flipbook impressions of Commie Russia were missile parades in Red Square, cosmonauts, food lines, Khrushchev banging his shoe, twenty million dead in WWII, the Cuban Missile Crisis, tanks rolling into Czechoslovakia, furry hats with earmuffs, vodka, Siberia, the gulag, and funny looking cars. Not exactly images from a vacation brochure. Even communism's hammer-and-sickle logo felt like a stick in Uncle Sam's eye. Things changed, of course, when Gorbachev helped bring down the USSR in the early 1990s, and our two countries even began to share a space station. Still, I figured Russia's Russia. I expected her to be different.

On April 27, 2006, the Orchestra landed at St. Petersburg's Pulkovo Airport. A thin-haired sunken-cheeked fellow named Igor greeted us at baggage claim. Our Russian promoter's name being *Igor* didn't strike any of us as clichéd or kinda funny, I can assure you. Igor's clothes looked a little rough and worse for wear, like he'd already traveled a long way to meet up with us. Maybe he had. His limited English and our non-existent Russian hampered our ability to communicate, but we knew the drill. We stuffed our bags, guitars, and road cases into a large van, and Igor drove us into the city as night fell.

The three-lane highway was like a typical western road, except it had no exits. Hmmm. When we reached the city, the highway finally curved and became an elevated off ramp. As we decelerated, Gordon and I noticed that we were circling dozens of small earthen huts jammed close together like a muddy hobbit village. "What the fuck are those?" Gordon asked. The huts had tiny wooden doors, and smoke rose from primitive metal smokestacks. Were they curing meat? Boiling bones? Dunno. Weird first impression of a major city.

Peter the Great founded his namesake town in 1703, intending it to be the Venice of the North. Modern St. Petersburg featured urban waterways and long blocks of handsome eighteenth-century buildings painted in a variety of striking colors. We were told the buildings were difficult to upgrade to twenty-first-century standards because the walls were too thick to install new water and electrical pipes. Infrastructure would be a recurring theme during our stay in Russia.

Igor got us to the Novatel hotel, a modern, comfortable hi-rise. After a full day's trip slogging through multiple airports, I looked forward to a nice hot bath. I thought better of it when the water pouring out of the gleaming faucet turned muddy brown. Did I mention infrastructure?

Our first Russian venue was a professional ice-hockey rink with lively acoustics. The stage crew weren't ready for us to sound check and even seemed a bit surprised that we'd arrived on time. Silly us. Igor, dressed in the same clothes as the day before, reassured us that the delay was "not problem," the first of ten thousand times we'd hear Russia's most beloved phrase.

That night, we played to a well-dressed crowd of three thousand general admission fans. From the first song, they were ready to go, all smiles and dancing in place. We were joined by a thirty-piece string section for the last third of the set. We've found Eastern European musicians to always be top notch, and the show went down a storm. All in all, a nice start to our first Russian tour. The gig began at 7:00 pm, early for us, but apparently the norm over there. After the show, we checked out of the Novatel and hurried to catch an overnight train to Moscow.

Igor's partner, Herman, met us the next morning at the Moscow train station. Our promoters checked us into our hotel and then took us straight to the Applesin (oddly, it means "Orange") Club, a slick, multi-storied operation with a large stage, huge bar, comfortable dressing rooms, a bowling alley, and restaurant. After sound check, we assumed we'd go back to our hotel to rest up. Instead, we were frog-marched into a van and taken on an hour-long slog through rush hour traffic to an unannounced location. Our driver swore under his breath at every red light. A grim-faced handler we hadn't seen before stared anxiously through the windshield. Who was this guy, where were we going, and what the hell was the rush? We had no idea. We just hoped it was *not problem*.

RUSSIAN IDOL

We pulled into the gated parking lot of a large, unmarked building and were greeted by a dozen nicely dressed and very excited men and women. Smiling

Chapter 17: Leaving the West Behind

and gesturing, they led us into a reception area, speaking excitedly into their walkie talkies. We were shown into small makeup rooms and given the face powder treatment. I thought, "Oh! We're going on television. *Nice to know.* Glad I wore my best sound check outfit." Have Russian promoters ever heard of an itinerary?

Our handlers beckoned us to a brightly lit TV studio divided into makeshift rooms by large sheets of thick, opaque plastic suspended from the ceiling. We were seated in what looked like a groovy, space-age lounge. Across from us, sat nine very young men and women, all fashionably dressed and impressively telegenic. Mik quipped, "They must be thinking 'who are these horrible old geezers?'"

A guy with shoulder-length blond hair, jeans, and a hoodie sat between the contrasting groups. He spoke excellent English and appeared to be the director. He explained that the kids were contestants on *Star Factory*, the Russian version of *American Idol*. Holy shit.

Star Factory took the Idol concept one step further by isolating the kids in this Big Brother-like TV studio—where we now sat—for the duration of the show. It dawned on us that we were that week's international superstar guests—mentors brought in to offer professional advice. Might someone have told us we were going to appear on Russia's most popular show?

None of the contestants spoke English, but *not problem*, the director translated. One asked us what it was like to be so popular. Mik took the lead and said, "How would we know?"

Another asked for words of advice. Mik's advice was, "You don't want to end up looking like us, do you? Don't go into the music business!" In between laughs, I'm sure we offered some sage thoughts to these young contestants that undoubtedly changed their lives forever. Or not.

A tall, skinny contestant named Alexei had been selected to sing an ELO song with us. From all the songs in ELO's catalog they'd naturally chosen "Ticket To The Moon" and...wait, what? *You don't know "Ticket To The Moon"?* Trust me, before I joined the band, I'd never heard of the song either, much less performed it. "Ticket" is an overtly dramatic ballad from ELO's *Time* album, written in the saddest of all keys, D minor. It's perfect for Russia, where it's a huge hit.

On a small stage, the show had assembled drums, bass, keyboard, and guitar. Alexei and one of the female contestants sat at the piano and gave a performance of "Ticket." Their Russian accents suited the song, and we all applauded generously. Then it was our turn. Eric, Kelly, and I performed an abbreviated version of "Telephone Line," which seemed to go over well, especially with the director and older production staff.

Our mission completed, the producers and our mystery handler then frog-marched us back to the van for another rush-hour drive to a massive, fenced compound. Multiple buildings sat surrounded by large green lawns and dwarfed by the enormous Ostankino television tower, 1,772 feet tall, and one of the tallest buildings in the world. We'd arrived at the headquarters and studios of Channel One, Russia's leading TV station. We were led inside and marched down a wide hallway with high ceilings and crumbling marble tiles under our feet to a warren of makeup rooms. This time, my shiny forehead was powdered by none other than Gorbachev's granddaughter, Ksenia Virganskaya-Gorbacheva.

Fuck yeah, Glasnost.

Faces powdered, we passed through large gray doors to the glittering *Star Factory* stage set. A director with headphones and an authoritative attitude pointed out our marks. While we prepared for our segment, Eric repeatedly told the show producers we were "the Orchestra" and could not be called "ELO" or "ELO Part II." Of course, the response was, "Yes, yes, not problem," but we were hardly reassured. Fortunately, we had a box of T-shirts, all with "THE ORCHESTRA" on the back. We put shirts on Alexei and his co-contestants with "THE ORCHESTRA" facing forward. The show runners frowned and shook their heads at the look, but Regna would've been proud.

We ran through "Ticket To The Moon" three times with Alexei taking the lead vocal. Our performance was filmed without an audience, but we did our best to make it authentic. The producers seemed well pleased, and our nameless, dour handler wore a look of relief. He'd successfully herded the cats. We heard later he'd also successfully picked up a check for our performance and kept it for himself. *Problem!*

CLANG, CLANG

Our gig at Applesin Club didn't begin until 11:00 pm We'd never played Moscow before, so we were excited to see the room jam-packed, standing room only, with fans pressed up against the stage, our favorite setting for a show. We opened with "Evil Woman" and the Muscovites exploded. Inspired by their energy, we gave it right back. Nothing like a sea of deliriously happy faces to make us sing harder and show off a bit more than usual. The applause didn't subside until ten minutes after we'd left the stage.

Chapter 17: Leaving the West Behind

Quite a day. We'd traveled by train from St. Petersburg to Moscow, filmed two TV segments that would be watched by forty million people, and knocked out a sold-out gig at Moscow's coolest club.

Our Russian schedule was just getting warmed up.

The next morning, band and crew assembled with luggage in our Moscow hotel lobby promptly at 5:45 am for our ride to the airport. We patiently waited for Herman and Igor to join us. They had the plane tickets, so we wouldn't be going anywhere without them. We thought they might already be up and getting the vans for us. When they still hadn't shown up twenty minutes later, Eric had the front desk ring their room. We woke them up. "Oh, my God, those numbskulls...", Eric muttered. Waiting on slackers at the crack of dawn with no coffee and not much sleep was not our favorite scenario. We were pissed.

An agonizing ten minutes later, we heard noises from a stairwell mixed with laughter: "CLANG, clang, HA HA HA, CLANG, clang..." Herman and Igor burst into the lobby laughing their heads off. Igor was struggling to carry a huge, black plastic garbage bag filled with bottles of beer and wine they'd taken from our backstage hospitality in St. Pete and Moscow. They clearly thought it was hilarious, but Herman saw our faces and sobered up quickly. He ran to fetch the vans. We had an early evening gig that night in Yekaterinburg, seven hundred miles east of Moscow on the other side of the Ural Mountains. We could not afford to miss our flight.

The bag of bottles was all Herman and Igor carried. Neither one of them had luggage, and each wore the same clothes as the day before. *Wow.* That is a commitment to traveling light...or maybe just not giving a shit. Thus began the Herman and Igor Show. It would become legend in band history.

Moscow has four airports. We were headed to the not-yet-modernized domestic flights terminal. Tensions ran high during the forty-five-minute ride from the hotel. If there's one thing that goes down poorly in the Orchestra, it's running late for a flight or show. Herman and Igor were in our crosshairs.

We parked in front of the snow-covered terminal and hurriedly unloaded our mountain of bags and gear, while Herman and Igor ran inside and began yelling at everyone at the check-in counter. We couldn't quickly enter the building with all our stuff because the entrance was blocked by an x-ray luggage conveyor. We had to prop open the doors to the freezing-cold air and heave all our gear onto the slow-moving conveyor. There was no airport security staff checking to see if our bags contained weapons. Our stuff just plopped onto the floor on the other side. Completely pointless.

Herman and Igor pushed other customers out of line at the ticket counter and insisted the airline check in all our luggage first. It was cringeworthy, but impressive. Our promoters knew they'd crossed a line with us and were hell-bent on making things right. *Sorry*, bystanders.

Miraculously, we made it to the gate on time. Herman and Igor were beaming, proud of their successful maneuvers at check-in. The rest of us were relieved, but mostly frazzled and shaking our heads. The Keystone Cops routine could've been avoided if our promoters had merely gotten out of bed on time. Putting a cherry on top of the morning, the plane we were about to board was an elderly prop jet, with wings above the windows and a rear entrance. We entered the plane walking up a cargo ramp beneath the tailpiece. That was a first for me.

Igor's carry-on bag went clankety-clank. No one stopped him.

The prop jet flew so slowly and smoothly I could, practically, count trees on the ground. We arrived safely in the sprawling, modern city of Yekaterinburg, where we would crash for a few hours at the brand-new Voznesenski Hotel. It turned out we were the hotel's very first guests and the staff took photos, including a shot of me and Mik'n'Lou in the lobby. More on that photo later.

Yekaterinburg is best known as the remote location where Bolsheviks murdered the Imperial Romanov family, effectively ending Tsarist rule. A cathedral now stands on the spot where the family was imprisoned before their demise. On a cheerier note, our 7:00 pm show at a large venue called KKT Kosmos got off to a pretty exciting start. A few songs into the set, Kelly, our fearless ringleader, pointed out an open area between the first row of seats and the stage. He generously invited everyone sitting in back to come down and stand at the front. They did, about a hundred of 'em, in a delighted mass stampede. The folks in the first few rows weren't happy to have their view obstructed. One lady in the second row leaned forward and swung her large purse, hitting one of the happy newcomers upside the head. He flinched but didn't retaliate, thankfully, and we carried on without further disturbances.

Done with our show by 8:30 pm, we scurried back to the hotel to watch *Star Factory*. Our segment had been skillfully edited to make it look like we were performing for a cheering audience. To our relief, the Orchestra T-shirts were plainly visible. No one could claim we were trying to call ourselves "ELO" or "ELO Part II."

We had a show to play the next night and less than twenty-four hours to get there. Off we went to Yekaterinburg-Passazhirsky, the city's main train terminal. We were scheduled to leave at 10:00 pm local time, so when we arrived at 9:45 pm the large clock in the center of the station naturally read...7:45 pm?

I pointed this out to Herman. He nodded and said, "Moscow time." That was the time in Moscow, 700 miles away. Okay, but why did the clock say 7:45 pm...*here*? Herman said, "Moscow time...everywhere." What the what? It turned out that every train schedule across Russia's eleven time zones ran on Moscow time. Why? I loved this official explanation: *to avoid confusion*.

GETCHYA UFA TWO-FA

Our next gig was in Ufa, capital city of the Russian Republic of Bashkortostan. Flights to Ufa took four hours, so I'm not sure why Herman and Igor had us travel by train. In retrospect, I'm glad they did. Our slow crawl across central Russia is etched in my mind as a unique, I'll-never-do-this-again experience.

Our train was an early-twentieth-century iron horse from an age before the existence of modern, lighter materials. The sliding doors and windows were framed in heavy steel and took some effort to open. Each car featured a giant silver tea dispenser, or samovar. Uniformed attendants patrolled the corridors.

Gordon and I shared a cabin. We inspected the bedding for cleanliness. "Wonder who slept on these sheets last night?" Gordon asked. "Let's pretend no one," I offered. We cooled off our post-gig adrenalin with several excellent Russian beers and laughed ourselves silly with a dumb scenario we concocted about a Russian T-shirt guy pimping bootleg Orchestra shirts outside our Ufa gig. "TWO for the price of one! Get your UFA TWO-FA right here!" Yeah, you had to be there, which we were. We drifted off to sleep, lulled by the chugga chugga chugga sound of our train and the pitch-black Russian night. Ufa here we come.

The next morning, a pale dawn light spread over a vast forest of aspen and birch, white tree trunks contrasting with dark brown earth. We passed by villages of simple wooden houses huddled on mud streets. Straight out of Dr. Zhivago.

Eric, Gordon, and I sought an early breakfast in the cozy cantina car. We were served by a genial hermaphrodite who prepared our eggs on a massive coal-burning stove that must've weighed two tons. As we sipped coffee, a tall, disheveled Russian youth barged into the dining car, teetering next to our table. It was clear he hadn't finished drinking, despite the early morning hour. He loudly banged two huge beers on our table, shaking our coffee cups. He smiled and raised his eyebrows, semaphore for "You guys wanna party?" Our stoic looks rebuffed his charming offer. Crestfallen, he stared at us through drooping eyelids for a minute, searching for any signal that we were warming up to him. None was given. Eventually, he slurred something in Russian, took his bottles and left.

Mile after mile of forest passed slowly by the windows, a picturesque monotony. We strolled up and down the corridors, killing time. We got back in our bunks and read books. We looked out the windows again. Anybody see a city? Ufa, you out there?

Chugga-chugga-chugga-chugga.

The train started to brake. Yes! Are we there? We ran to the windows. Dang. We were still in the middle of nowhere, but the endless forest had given way to a remote town. We stopped next to a concrete platform that featured a bare-bones, impromptu flea market. Roughly dressed vendors had spread blankets on the ground and set out their wares. I stepped off the train to investigate—nervously, lest I get left behind in the Urals—and ended up bartering for some oddball souvenirs. I picked up a folksy coffee cup decorated with a picture of a smiling Russian citizen. When the cup filled with hot liquid her bikini magically disappeared. *Quaint.* I bought two. Nervous of getting left behind, I ran back to the train. The brakes released and off we went.

Chugga, chugga, chugga, chugga. Our show was scheduled to start at 7:00 pm Surely, we were closing in on Ufa. We rolled along the top edge of a curving canyon wall a thousand feet above a muddy river. On the opposite shore stood the rusted steel skeleton of an abandoned industrial plant. It would've made a fantastic post-apocalyptic movie set. After seventeen hours and four billion birch trees, our brakes, at last, engaged and we rolled cautiously into Ufa, population one million.

A small convoy of cars and trucks rushed us to the gig with just enough time to set up gear, grab a quick bite, and jump into our stage clothes. Sound check? Not so much. Oh, well. At least we were off the train. I recalled a catchy Russian phrase I'd seen in my cultural guide: "We'd hoped things would be better, but as usual they turned out normal." I was beginning to understand what that meant.

The Ogni Ufi Center in Ufa featured dicey electricity (everything hummed), but the dressing rooms were big, and the young staff treated us nicely. The place was a rock joint, but, for our show, folding chairs had been set up to make it feel more like a concert.

We banged into our show, fully expecting the kind of raucous reaction we'd received in St. Pete, Moscow, and Yekaterinburg. We sounded good, we rocked hard, we sang well, we did all our show-off bits. We could see people smiling and dancing in the back, but the seats closest to the stage were filled exclusively by quiet, unsmiling men. They were as fun as a fucking oil painting. I looked over to Kelly and shrugged my shoulders to say, "What more can we do?"

After the show, we were approached by some friendly Canadians. I mentioned our frustration with the first few rows. They laughed and explained that the men in the expensive seats were from government and business—important guys in Ufa society. They weren't about to make fools of themselves by acting silly at a rock show. The Canadians assured us that everyone else had a fantastic time despite the fat cats hogging the best seats.

That made sense. Kinda like the Grammys.

SAFE AT LAST

Early the next morning, we flew back to Moscow. Our next gig was four days hence in Denmark, so Herman and Igor (clink, clink went the bottles) drove us to Zavidovo, a resort on the famous Volga River, where we would chill for a couple days. Herman assured us it was the best quality, mentioning several times that "Putin was stayed here!" Zavidovo (nowadays covered in high rises) was less a resort and more a huddle of wooden cabins—think northern Michigan.

Since arriving in Russia, we'd traveled 2,500 miles, played four concerts in four cities in four days, and taped a national TV show. Our reward was a cabin in the woods with bugs. We were all bored to tears by mid-afternoon. Fortunately, the youngest, least experienced, and most expendable member of our crew decided that Zavidovo was the perfect place to air his grievances about our band, his job, and his life. Thank God! Something to do! We listened stoically as he told us how we'd broken promises, roped him into doing horrible tasks, sabotaged his songwriting career, and so on. It was entertaining up to a point, but once we'd heard enough, we patiently took turns explaining to him that he was quite full of shit, a bit whiny, perhaps delusional, frequently drunk, often obnoxious, and not very good at his fucking job in the first place.

And, he was fired.

To his credit, the young man owned up to most of his bullshit. He simply wasn't happy—and he came to recognize that he'd blamed his unhappiness entirely on us. We were, in fact, some of his staunchest allies, and still are. He just wasn't meant to be a roadie. He was a songwriter. Fucking musicians!

Before we left for Denmark, all that remained on our itinerary was to have one final kerfuffle with Herman and Igor, and they came through. The bottle brothers decided it was our responsibility to pay for our stay at Zavidovo. Eric thoughtfully told them that was ridiculous. They were the promoters and hosts, and we would not pay. Igor nearly had a meltdown. For all we know, he tried to pay the bill with bottles of beer.

When our Delta flight (USA!) went wheels up and Russia receded below, I let out a sigh and thought, "Ahhhh, safe at last." I've thought about that moment many times because I can't say, and will never know, if we were ever in danger. I think not. We'd actually had a truly memorable time in Russia and would again in the near future.

But still, we'd never been granted access to operational details. I never saw an itinerary. We never got explanations in response to normal inquiries. Russia is the *only* country where that has ever happened. Plus, we didn't speak Russian and we didn't know the identity or role of at least one of our handlers. We felt a little too vulnerable, exposed, and not in control. That's not good when you're far from home and not protected by any legal authority other than a passport.

As uneasy as we sometimes felt, I'll admit my assessment of Russia is unfair to the people, Herman and Igor included, who worked hard to show us a good time, got us to our gigs, took us to excellent restaurants, and so on. We were treated, mostly, extremely well, and our audiences were fantastic, other than the stiff bigwigs who took the first couple of rows in Ufa.

SWINGIN' '70S

In Denmark, it was a relief to discuss business in perfect English and operate on a precise schedule. Everything happened as planned, and a highly organized time was had by all. Truth be told, it was kind of boring. Was I pining for Herman and Igor? I wouldn't go that far.

The Esbjerg '60s Festival starred the Swinging Blue Jeans, Marty Wilde, the Searchers, the Merseybeats, and…us. We felt like interlopers from the '70s. The "festival" was pretty much just a large beer hall with a stage, all tucked under an enormous tent. Once again, the lovely audience of happy Danes fulfilled their reputational obligation by getting absolutely drop-dead pissed drunk by mid-afternoon. *Represent.*

We arrived in time to catch the Swinging Blue Jeans ("Hippy Hippy Shake"). Defying their age, they sounded in fine form, playing simple, catchy rock 'n' roll. They also pulled off an amazing trick as only a veteran band could. After listening to two or three songs, I noticed that the Blue Jeans' drummer had the unfortunate habit of rushing fills, meaning, whenever he pounded out a didda-lidda/didda-lidda/bumm, he would finish slightly ahead of the downbeat. The band's trick, and it took me a while to figure it out, was to rush along with the drummer. Everybody landed ahead of the beat! They'd made it a part of their sound. That's togetherness.

After our show, Marty Wilde (UK pop legend and father of Kim) mistakenly boarded our bus. He saw our mugs, looked confused, and then Mik helped him out, shouting, "Wrong bus, Marty ol' chap. This one's the '70s."

CHAPTER 18

DAD

After Denmark, we were excited to return to the UK for a proper long tour. It was the band's first extensive run in the UK since 1999 and the memorable climactic show at Royal Albert Hall. Tony Denton, an established promoter, put together an exciting twenty-five-city itinerary, including stops in Liverpool, Manchester, Oxford, Birmingham, Newcastle, Edinburgh, Cardiff, and more. If there was one particular show circled on the tour calendar it was May 23 at Shepherds Bush Empire in London. That was a high-profile gig, and it was positioned perfectly: gig number nine. By that point in the tour, every lick, lyric, and vocal harmony would be locked down tight. We'd be free to simply perform, which is the dream. It's also called kicking ass.

Shepherds Bush Empire is a beautiful rock venue, modeled like an old opera house with stacked balconies and a capacity of 3,000. There are no seats on the main floor, just general admission, so band and crowd are eyeball to eyeball. Our show was sold out and packed to the gills. We opened with "Evil Woman," and when we reached the first chorus, the audience sang it louder than we did. We were all blown back on our heels. Fantastic! The crowd was fully with us, and from that moment on, my band entered a state of pure bliss. We played *fucking great*. Song after song after song, we were riding the tiger and the audience was right alongside us for ELO classics and our selections from *No Rewind*.

OK IN THE UK

A show like Shepherds Bush is as high as a performer can get. I'd glance at Eric or Kelly, and they'd give back a quick nod or a fleeting smile—but no more. You mustn't interrupt the ride when you're at one with an audience. I wish words could better convey the joy I experienced during that performance and the love I felt for my bandmates, for music, for life itself. It was that powerful. What an incredible night.

In 2006, we worked with a veteran tour manager, Brian Coles. Brian told us about his time on the road with Peter Frampton. He was there before, during, and after *Frampton Comes Alive*, the album that helped push the former Humble Pie guitarist to superstar status in the '70s. "I saw the whole rise and fall," Brian said. "In three years, we went from clubs to theaters to arenas to stadiums, and then back to arenas and theaters. The band and the songs weren't much different the entire time! It was just an instance of ridiculous fame singling out a guy who was good at what he did."

We accidentally bestowed Brian an Orchestra story when we drove off and left him at a motorway service area. We'd been rolling down the road for at least ten minutes before I happened to notice his absence. I shouted, "Brian, if you're on the bus, please speak up." When no one answered, Dave the driver said, "Oh, bollocks!" Back we went. Brian was nonchalant about it as he boarded the bus. "I thought you might miss me a *little* sooner..."

We wrapped up the first leg of the tour, thirteen gigs, at the end of May. We went home to our families for two weeks and then returned to the UK for twelve more shows. At a venue called the Anvil in Basingstoke, I cashed in one of the benefits of being in a touring rock band. I left tickets at Will Call for a London taxi driver named Dave Bromiley, who would attend with his daughter. I'd last seen Dave when he was a skinny, long-haired hippy living in a Volkswagen van behind the American Youth Center in Athens, Greece. His van mates, Derek and Trevor, were the guys who'd teamed with American kids in a band called Monty Python's Flying Circus. Thirty-five years later, here we were, talking about our time in Greece like it was yesterday and laughing our heads off.

DAD

Halfway through the second leg of our UK tour, I was asleep in a hotel after our gig in Newcastle Upon Tyne, a river city in Eastern England and home of the Animals. At 3:00 am my room phone rang. Groggily, I thought, "This can't be good." It wasn't. Eric was on the line. "Hux, sorry to wake you.... I just got a call from Helle on my cell phone. Your dad passed away."

"Oh, crap." Breath left my lungs. My comfy hotel room suddenly looked forlorn. And far from home.

Eric said, "Sorry, man."

"Yeah. Thanks. Sorry you're the only one whose phone works over here."

"That's alright. I guess we'll talk in the morning and figure out what to do about the rest of the tour."

"Okay."

Oh, hell. Right. We still had six shows to do. In a few hours, we'd be leaving for Edinburgh, Scotland. We had a gig at The Playhouse. The next

Chapter 18: Dad

night we were booked at DeMontfort Hall in Leicester. There was no way I could go home just yet.

I called Helle from my hotel phone. The first thing she said was, "I'm so sorry about your dad, baby. Will you be coming home tomorrow?"

I said, "I can't. If I leave right away, we'll have to cancel a bunch of shows. I'm not gonna leave the band in a bind."

"Baby, you need to come home," Helle said.

"I know."

I couldn't sleep. I thought about Dad. The quintessential great guy. All my friends, male and female, from high school into adulthood—everybody loved my dad. He always had a smile, a joke, an anecdote to lighten the mood or make a stranger feel like a friend. He was kind and thoughtful, responsible and caring, strong but easy-going. Smart as hell, too. A terrific guy.

His lungs had failed him. Chronic emphysema. A chlorine explosion at the Baton Rouge refinery where he worked in his twenties probably hadn't helped, and he'd smoked cigarettes until he quit cold turkey at age forty in Greece. His last year had been tough. His body couldn't get him enough oxygen, and he hated dragging his portable oxygen tank around the house. He'd told me with a bitter chuckle, "This is no way to live."

I'd miss him terribly, but I wasn't mad that he'd passed. I thought, "You can breathe now." I was relieved for him. He'd lived eighty-one years, twenty-five years longer than *his* Dad. He died at home. No hospitals. No paperwork. No bullshit. Sense and senses fully intact to the end. His finances were all in order so my mom could go on with her life. You can't leave on much better terms than that.

I got a new guardian angel, too.

I needed to go to South Carolina, but not yet. I had enough time to play the next two shows, Edinburgh on Saturday and Leicester on Sunday. After that, things would get complicated.

I called my mom. She didn't want to delay the funeral. It was scheduled for the following Wednesday. The Orchestra had gigs on Tuesday and Wednesday in Truro and Cardiff. If I was going to attend my dad's funeral, I would have to miss those two shows. That meant we had one day to find a sub, which was insane. Who could possibly take my place on such short notice? There was only one guy who could do it...one guy who knew our show, knew the arrangements, and could pull it off without tons of rehearsal. That was Phil Bates, the singer/guitarist I'd replaced eight years earlier. Of course, we had no idea where Phil was, no idea if he was available, or if he'd even be willing to do the gigs. I thought, "Hey, Dad. We could use some divine intervention right about now."

You'll never guess what happened.

REVOLVER

Kelly knew Phil the best, so he started making calls. Lo and behold, he located Mr. Bates out in the Black Country, northwest of Birmingham, not far from where Kelly lived. The problem was, Phil wouldn't be in England long. He needed to get back to Berlin. He was willing to cover for me, but the only days he had available were Tuesday and Wednesday.

Tuesday and Wednesday. Those were our gig days. Phil could do it!

Thanks, Dad.

Judy LaMarca, the band's longtime travel agent, found no available flights to Charleston, but she was able to get me to Savannah, Georgia, a hundred miles south. Close enough. Helle and five-year-old Fiona drove from Charleston to Savannah through a scary, pummeling downpour to meet me at the airport. My poor wife was frazzled, and Fiona seemed distracted rather than excited to see me.

When we had a moment, I whispered to Helle, "What's the matter with Fi?"

"She's mad that I wouldn't let her see your dad at the funeral home viewing."

Surprised, I said, "She wanted to see him in the casket?"

"Oh, yeah. She yelled at me, 'Mom, you *never let me see dead people!*'"

I laughed hard. Fi's gripe became legendary in our family.

Contrary to all his success as a businessman and a volunteer leader at Habitat for Humanity and other charitable causes, at heart, my dad was a wise-ass kid from Northern Michigan who loved to laugh, and my brothers and I inherited that gene. Still, you never wanted to cross him or do something he felt was wrong. He'd call you on it.

In my eulogy at the church service, I told a story about traveling with Dad from Greece to New York City. "Dad and I stayed a few nights at the Essex hotel and when we packed up to leave, I stuck a towel in my suitcase. Dad looked at me and said, 'What're you doing?' Whenever Dad's voice got serious, I knew I'd done something wrong. I mumbled, 'I'm just taking a souvenir.' He said, 'No. That's not a souvenir. That's stealing.' I took the towel out of my suitcase. He didn't say anything more. I learned a valuable lesson that day. Dad set me straight about stealing stuff, and I think about him every time I take a towel from a hotel." The congregation laughed (the priest didn't), and I felt like my joke had done my dad proud.

Chapter 18: Dad

After more tears and laughter with my family and friends, I returned to the UK in time for Friday night's gig. Jet-lagged and emotionally drained, I lay down in the back of the cab for the sixty-mile trip from Heathrow Airport to Dartford. After an hour, I felt the car slow down and I rose to see where we were. Directly out my window was a building with a sign that read *Mick Jagger Centre*. Back in England, indeed.

The cab dropped me off at the Orchard Theatre, and, just like that, I was back on tour. What an odd life I led. Phil had subbed for me in Truro and Cardiff, two of my favorite spots in the UK. Truro was home to the cathedral where, in 1999, I'd had my deep communion with Janet. That same year, in Cardiff, I'd assembled the Beatles boxes for my marriage proposal to Helle.

I ran into Mik backstage. He said, "Mr. Huxley! You've returned."

I nodded. "I have. How'd Phil do?"

Mik said, "Huh? Oh, right. You weren't there for that, were you?"

"No."

"It would've been quite odd had both of you been there, I suppose." Mik laughed.

"Yes. Phil and I aren't allowed to be in the same space at once. It would upset the universe."

Mik said, "Yeah, he did okay. About as good as possible I suppose. He had cheat sheets all over the floor in front of him, but he did well, yeah. People were a bit surprised to see him, but we explained your dad had passed, so…"

That's about all I got. Funny how nonchalant we were about our miracle. Oh, sure, Phil Bates dropped out of the sky to rescue the band in its hour of need. Ho-hum. Put on the kettle.

CHAPTER 19

BACK IN THE (FORMER) USSR

The Orchestra returned to glorious Russia in September 2006. We didn't use Herman and Igor again, despite their memorable performance. Instead, we were paired with a once-in-a-lifetime character named Ulyana Turnes, an ambitious promoter and businesswoman from Yekaterinburg. Still in her twenties, Ulyana appeared to be quite taken with her five-foot self, strutting on loud chunky heels and donning knee-length fur coats as if she were incredibly beautiful and fun to be with. With her long wavy hair, big red lips, and gap-toothed smile, Ulyana brought a dramatic flair to the simplest transactions.

Eric, speaking like a normal human: "Ulyana, have you confirmed a sound check time for tomorrow's gig?"

Ulyana, moaning like a jilted lover: "Oh, Err-reek, *Err-reek*...please don't worry about such things, it is all taken care of."

We never rolled our eyes so much.

Despite, or perhaps thanks to, her over-the-top persona, Ulyana had put together an ambitious itinerary. We traveled more than six thousand miles and performed in ten cities, mostly places I'd never heard of, perhaps not surprisingly. During the Cold War, major cities in Russia's interior, mysteriously, didn't exist. Important manufacturing centers, sensitive military installations, and research centers were purposefully removed from official maps to confuse us capitalist dogs and our intercontinental ballistic missiles. Imagine Houston not appearing on a US map. Nothing to see here, comrade.

We played to packed houses all over the Russian hinterland. Audiences welcomed us like old friends, despite our origins on the other side of the world. How far from home were we? When we rocked Volgograd, formerly Stalingrad (where Nazi invaders ran out of gas), we were as easterly as Baghdad. Our gig in Samara pushed us further toward Asia, on a line with Tehran; and, if we'd asked our bus driver to head south from our gig in Tyumen, we'd have eventually reached Pakistan by way of Kazakhstan, Uzbekistan, and Afghanistan.

Our old pal infrastructure roared back on this trip. During the spring tour, we hadn't been thrilled with the agonizing seventeen-hour train ride to Ufa, so we decided to skip trains this time and hire a bus for the shorter distances when we didn't need to fly. The idea was to have more control over our itinerary, fewer 4:00 am wake up calls, etc. What could go wrong?

We got off to a memorable start in Sochi, back then still a sleepy seaside resort on the eastern shore of the Black Sea, just up the coast from the country of Georgia. It's not so sleepy now, after the Russian government invested $50 billion there for the 2014 winter Olympics. There were so few hotels in 2006 that we debunked to a house high in the hills near town, like an Airbnb, run by a married couple who shared meals with us in their kitchen. Cozy.

To our great disappointment, Kelly and Mik, traveling from the UK, missed connecting flights in both Milan and Moscow and were unable to reach Sochi in time for our opening show. Our Russian soundman, Misha, also got held up in Yekaterinburg and couldn't make it on time. We would have to cancel Sochi. Ulyana hatched a plan. She would accompany Eric, Lou, and me to the site of our gig in Sochi's city park. We sat in plastic chairs on the empty stage, and, with Ulyana translating, told the early arrivers about the flight problems and that there would be no show. Ulyana then reassured the growing crowd that we would come back and play the following night. After an hour or so of repeating the story, the word got out, people left the park, and we went back to our house.

The only problem with Ulyana's plan is that it wasn't true. We would be playing up the road in Krasnodar the next night. She insisted that telling a lie was the best way to handle the situation, and that the people who bought tickets for Sochi would get their money back. "If we told them the truth now, we would never get out of here tonight. Everyone would want us to buy back their tickets. Don't worry, it's okay. I will take care of it." We were on Ulyana's turf, and we deferred to her way of handling it. Under any other circumstances, I don't think we would have even considered pulling a stunt like that. I still feel shitty about it, and I hope our disappointed fans got their money back.

Mik, Kelly, and Misha finally joined us in Krasnodar, and we were able to properly start our tour. Other than "Krasnodar" sounding like a Star Wars trading outpost, its main charm was our hotel, a nineteenth-century resort with walls covered in headshots and album covers of Russian pop stars. I didn't recognize a single one, and I felt like I'd been dropped into an alternate entertainment universe. Which I had.

From Krasnodar, we flew 2,500 kilometers northeast to the city of Perm (population one million, closed during the Cold War). We played a sold-out show for 1,500 geographically isolated, but ecstatic, classic rock fans experiencing their favorite ELO songs live in person for the first time. They even shouted in English, "We love you!" Their applause stayed at a crescendo longer than we were accustomed to, and their rhythmic shouting and clapping felt like a release of pent-up emotion. Western rock music was banned during the Soviet period, forcing these (then young) rock fans to circulate well-worn bootlegs in secret. Imagine how precious a tape of ELO must've been? As a performer, you can tell when there's something extra in the air, and I had no doubt the people of Perm had waited years for this night to happen. It was an honor to get a reaction like that so far from home.

We'd begun rocking Perm at Russian showtime, 7:00 pm, so it wasn't even 10 o'clock when we boarded a large private coach, ready to take the Orchestra on its inaugural Russian road trip. No more trains for us. Ulyana relayed that our driver and local promoters had insisted we leave Perm immediately after the show. They were nervous about making good time to Yekaterinburg. The band consensus was, okay, you know best—it must be a long drive. How far is it?

"Three-hundred kilometers."

That's less than 200 miles. I thought, "We have to drive overnight? To make 200 miles?" That seems overly cautious, doesn't it?

Our coach pulled away from the venue and eased onto one of Perm's wide city avenues. As we reached the edge of town, streetlights gradually petered out and our surroundings grew dark and rural. I settled into my seat, expecting to spot the highway to Yekaterinburg any minute. The road out of Perm narrowed and turned to dirt. The ride grew bumpy and soon progressed to jarring. Bam! Bam! Bam! Stuff bounced out of the overhead storage spaces as our driver downshifted dramatically. The dirt road was ribbed and rock hard. Had we made a wrong turn? What was going on? The whole bus shook and shuttered. Holy shit. I hung on to the seat in front of me as the ride remained unbelievably rough for another fifteen solid minutes. I gritted my teeth and thought, "Wow, Perm. Nice road!" How much farther was the highway? At last, we hit a stretch of paved road. The bouncing stopped and the driver eased into a higher gear. Ahhhhhhhh. Jesus. That was horrible. I wonder why the road was so...

Bam! Bam! Bam! Bam! The bus shook again like it was under attack. The paved road might've lasted a quarter mile. I leaned into the aisle to get a look through the windshield. Our headlights confirmed we were back in road hell. The driver downshifted again to minimize the shaking, while maneuvering his poor bus around massive potholes.

And then it hit me. We weren't heading for a highway...this gut-shaking cow trail *was* the highway! Oh-my-f-God. It was worse than a shepherd's path on a Greek island or a logging trail in the Upper Peninsula of Michigan. I swear I'm not being a dick-ish American. With apologies to Han Solo, I've been from one side of this world to the other...I've seen a lot of strange stuff... but I've never seen a road that bad.

By the way, we weren't on some secret back route. We were on *the* major artery from Perm to the east of Russia. Everyone and everything, people and products, had to traverse this trail of torture. I thought, "How do they conduct business in this country? How do they supply cities with basic goods? Can't the government afford to build decent roads? Don't they want their people to be able to move around freely?" Hmmm.

At a later point on our trailblazing bus tour, we asked a hotel concierge how long it would take to travel by bus from Kazan to Samara. Simple question, right? He came back with, "*Why would you go?*"

Back on the highway to hell, it was no wonder our driver wanted to leave Perm early. It took all night to go 200 miles. Had we gone any faster, I swear our poor driver's bus would've shaken to pieces. At one point, the smokers onboard requested a cigarette break and our bus driver pulled over. We were the only vehicle on the road, in the middle of absolute nowhere. I got out, too, and was glad I did. The black sky was flooded with stars. Wow! As a city dweller, I tended to forget about skies like that. Surrounded by endless forest, Misha, John Shipp, Kelly Groucutt, and I stood in the black silence, raised our eyes to the heavens, and marveled at the vast ocean of heavenly bodies above us. The stillness was stunning, the only audible sound our shoes on gravel. After a minute, I thought, "No matter how weird it sometimes gets, I love traveling with these guys and, oh my God, look where we are." Almost as much as the shows themselves, moments like that are what make touring unforgettable.

About that forest. As vast and beautiful as it was, it had a spooky quality: no discernable animals. We literally drove for hours and saw nothing alive. No reflective eyeballs in the woods. No birds. We didn't even see roadkill. We couldn't fathom it. Had the Russians eaten everything that moved? Was the forest empty because of Chernobyl? We didn't know what to think.

Misha said he read a story in *National Geographic* about the Ural Mountains (where we were) and Canadian Appalachia. The story said these two ancient mountain ranges had the highest levels of natural radiation on earth, with one key difference: no one lives in Canadian Appalachia, but six million people live in the Urals. Maybe Canadians and animals know something Russians don't.

WE ARE TRAVEL

Misha was the secret Russian sauce that made our bus tour tilt toward pleasure and away from chore. At the time, he was thirty-three, a father of two with another on the way, and he knew WTF he was doing. He expertly ran monitors for us and pressured the backline companies to do their job well. During that bone-shaking overnight drive from Perm to Yekaterinburg, Misha gave me a much-appreciated dose of perspective. He wasn't mad at the crappy road or wishing he were asleep in a hotel. He was in *heaven*.

Conjuring his limited English, Misha told me, "It's like dream to me... ever since I'm boy...to go on bus tour with beeg band."

I smiled back at him. "Yeah?"

"Oh, yes," Misha nodded and spoke earnestly. "At first, I learn guitar. Then I learn you need cord, then amp. Then I learn there is monitors and microphones and many more interesting things than just guitar. So, I quit guitar and learn all this more interesting things. And now here I am! Fantastic. It's like dream. I thank you for this." Misha raised his arms in victory and shouted, "We are travel! With beeg band!"

I was delighted to know we were a beeg band. I decided to gauge how big we were.

"So, Misha, is this better than being out with, say, Procol Harum?"

"Oh, yes. Is better."

"Deep Purple?"

"Better."

"*Alright!* Better than Deep Purple!" Think what you will, but that resonated with me. When I was a kid living in Greece, Deep Purple was always the biggest hard rock band in the world outside the States. Misha ranking us higher was a delicious victory for me.

Feeling good, I went for broke. "Okay, Misha, is it better than being on the road with Pink Floyd?"

"Mmmm...*no*. Not better than Pink Floyd."

We laughed. I figured there was a classic rock ceiling we wouldn't crack.

Misha gave me a sense of how progressive it was for us to be visiting so many cities deep in the Russian interior that not long ago were off limits to foreigners. "The new direction of Russia is freedom," Misha said emphatically. "We can't go back. Everything is change. Ten years before, even five years, this tour *not happen*. You cannot go to all these cities. It is *amazing*. Believe me."

I thought, "Wow. Sounds like we're doing something kinda special. Bringing the rock to the far reaches of Russia." Trust me, I don't confuse entertainment with the work of doctors, teachers, etc. But our small part in Misha's happiness, and his confidence in a freer future really made me feel good.

SAME, SAME

In Yekaterinburg, we returned to the hotel we'd christened at the end of April. It still looked brand new, but now the walls were decorated with photos of celebrity guests. After lunch with Mik'n'Lou, I spotted our picture among the celebs. "Hey, there's us, boys. We're famous in Yekaterinburg!" We had a chuckle, and then I noticed something. I looked back and forth from us to the picture. I couldn't believe it. Well, honestly, I could. The photo taken in April revealed that five months later, all three of us were dressed in the *exact* same clothes. I mean, shirts, jackets, pants. All the same. We laughed our asses off. Men are such simple creatures. I asked one of the staff to take another picture of us in front of our picture, kinda like Pink Floyd's *Ummagumma* album cover.

GOOD PIPE

Although the roads were horrible, traveling by bus afforded us a closeup look at the real Russia. We got a perverse kick out of the blocky, Soviet-era apartment buildings. They were uniquely ugly, unimaginatively designed, and poorly built. Most sported rusty AC units in the windows, hand-jiggered electrical wires, and crumbling concrete foundations. Workers' paradise!

We marveled at the countryside's bedraggled villages, typically built on denuded land—no trees, no bushes, no grass. Most featured mud lanes and humble wooden houses that tilted at odd angles. I tried to imagine Russian foot soldiers at the end of World War II chasing the Nazis all the way back to Germany. They must have been stunned to see the picturesque, idyllic villages of their savage enemy.

Our favorite inanimate thing in Russia, by a landslide, was above-ground utility pipe. Unlike in the West, where gas and water travel underground, Russia has miles and miles of large-diameter pipe running above ground

Chapter 19: Back in the (Former) USSR

alongside its roadways. Resting on metal supports and wrapped in often-tattered silver insulation, this eye-grabbing tubular infrastructure snakes up and over gates, folds around trees and street signs, angles off to apartment buildings, and so on. It looks bonkers and we couldn't get enough of it. Our soundman John Shipp would shout from his side of the bus, "Got some good pipe over here!" Whatever was in there, moving it above ground undoubtedly made repairs easier, so there was a certain logic at play. I've read it's mostly a cost issue. The government won't invest in burying pipe. Fine with us. We loved looking at it.

The city of Tyumen represented the farthest east we would travel. It's straight north from Pakistan, yet still only a third of the way across Russia. Our roadside hotel was barely adequate, the weather cold, the gig unmemorable. On most tours of any length, there's a point where the adventure aspect gets old, the adrenalin decreases, your dirty clothes outnumber your clean, you're tired of lugging your bags to yet another hotel room, you arrive somewhere too late to eat, you miss your family, you hate the bus, and you wanna go home. In an odd way, it's good to reach the nadir. It usually only lasts a day or so, and once you get past it, you can appreciate what you've accomplished and look forward to finishing things off in good spirits. We bussed to Chelyabinsk, another Cold War secret city, and the road wasn't so horrible. A gift to the weary.

COWBOYS

Before heading to sound check, I ate lunch alone in our Chelyabinsk hotel restaurant. I gave my order to the waiter and then settled in with a Michael Connelly book, enjoying my solace. A couple of chapters later, I looked up from my book to reset my bearings in real life. The place was packed with Russians, naturally, and then I spotted a Black guy sitting by himself across the restaurant. I had a hunch he was American, judging by his clothes. I caught his eye and said just loud enough for him to hear, "Wanna join me?" He gave a slight nod and came over.

We introduced ourselves. I told him about the Orchestra and our tour and then asked, "So what are you doing all the way out here?"

He said, "I'm part of a team that's working about a half hour outside of town. Today we've got R&R, so a bunch of us drove in."

"What kind of work are you doing, if you don't mind me asking?"

"I don't mind. I'm installing computers in a facility we're building that will be used to destroy Russia's old nuclear stockpile."

Holy crap. "Well, on behalf of me and the rest of the world, thank you."

"You're welcome." He smiled.

I asked, "So...why are a bunch of Americans over here building a facility that the Russians probably ought to be building themselves?"

He nodded. "It makes you wonder, right? Yeah, well, it's logistically complicated and a very expensive project and the Russians don't consider it a priority, so they're not interested in doing the work. Americans *do* think it's a priority, we can afford it, and we're more than willing to do the work, so here we are."

He disarms nukes, I sing to hinterland ELO fans. Just a couple cowboys ridin' the Russian prairie tryin' to make the world a better place...right?

Our show in Chelyabinsk went down a storm, another high-energy exchange between the Orchestra and rock-starved Russian fans. We couldn't have asked for more excited crowds.

The next day, Kelly Groucutt flew back to England to attend his dear mom's funeral. Fortunately, our next show wasn't until three days later in Kazan. He would make it back on time. Kazan was a handsome 1,000-year-old city known for its kremlin, a heavily fortified hilltop citadel rising above the confluence of two rivers. The kremlin dominates the city skyline with its domed cathedral, ornate mosque, and highly decorated towers. We walked around Kazan, which was uniquely well maintained and landscaped. We played at a massive glass entertainment complex called The Pyramid, built in the shape of a...yup.

During breakfast at our hotel, I struck up a conversation with three dudes at a nearby table sporting mussy hair, American clothes, and jet lag: clearly musicians. They were the backing band for a well-known Russian act called t.A.T.u. that had sold millions of albums worldwide. I asked where their tour would take them. "Oh, we're not on tour. We're just doing a one-off." Really? They'd flown all the way from Los Angeles to Kazan...to play one show? "Yeah. Crazy, right?"

Yeah. Crazy.

WHY WOULD YOU GO?

But maybe not as crazy as the next leg on our bus tour, the 220-mile endurance test from Kazan to Samara, also known as the "why would you go?" trip, during which our bus averaged less than 30 mph. The highlight of our trip came when our driver, dismayed by the poor condition of the highway, decided to try a shortcut. We figured he knew what he was doing and, what the hell, how much worse can it be?"

We found out soon enough, on a country road that took us past typically distressed Russian villages with mud streets, loose chickens, and tilting houses. The road was practically destroyed. It looked like it'd been bombed in World War II and never repaired. Our driver smoothly navigated around broken pavement until we saw *it*, the mother of all potholes, stretched across the entire road. There was no way around. The driver stopped. He spoke with Misha, who told us, "The driver say he not sure if bus make it. Maybe hole too deep to get out." We stared through the windshield. We couldn't argue. It was hard to tell how deep the hole was without someone walking through it.

"Mik? Wanna put on your cossie (English for bathing costume) and show us how deep these potholes are?"

We sat for a minute, not knowing what to do, weighing our options, which were none, really. The driver must've thought the Russian equivalent of "fuck it," because he suddenly put his bus in gear and slowly eased us into the pond-hole on the right. Our fate decided, we all crowded into the aisle to watch through the windshield, shouting, "Holy shiiiiiiitttt, c'mon bus, you can do it!" As the right front wheel entered, we tilted at a very concerning angle, causing us to hold onto headrests. We didn't roll over or disappear underwater. So far so good. Then the back wheels thumped awkwardly, and the bus tilted heavily to the right. We took turns yelling "Woah!" and "Hang on!" Our bus caused brown waves to lap against the edge of the hole. Now the moment of truth. We were fully in the hole. Could we get out? The driver downshifted one gear and headed for the far edge. We tilted again as the nose of the bus raised up, but our driver steadily moved forward and soon we found ourselves safely on the other side of Lake Holyshitski. Whoops of victory broke out and our driver even managed a relieved smile. Good times. It took us eight hours to travel the roughly 220 miles to Samara.

FROM SALT LAKE TO SAMARA

If Antonio Gaudi had designed a concert venue, it would've looked like Samara's Philharmonic Hall. Curvy banisters, paramecium-shaped ceiling panels, seashell balconies...the place was too cool for words, a real art nouveau treasure in another city once left off Cold War maps. After yet another rousing show well appreciated by Russian fans, we were boarding our bus when a small pack of college-aged kids approached us in a run. They looked kind of familiar in their dark pants, white shirts, and backpacks. To our surprise, they shouted in American accents, "Hey, Orchestra! We loved the show!"

I said to the group of freshly scrubbed faces, "Glad you guys enjoyed it. You're a long way from home, huh? What are you doing in Samara?"

"We're Mormon missionaries!" Bingo. I knew I knew that look. Guileless and happy.

"How's that going?"

"Pretty good, yeah, it's going well. We're having a good time!"

Lots of cowboys out here on the Russian prairie…!

DEEP TOUR

Moscow is staggeringly huge, ringed by a four-lane highway and served by four airports. New cars clog the streets. Construction cranes puncture the skyline as modern apartment buildings and offices rise in every section of the city. A gazillion billboards trumpet the latest fashions and gadgets. Small sidewalk casinos flash their gaudy signs on every other block, and the streets teem with smartly dressed urbanites hurrying to and fro. I'd wanted to see Red Square when in Moscow, but the city was so huge I still hadn't been near it.

We were in the capital for a return engagement at Applesin, the large, posh club we'd played in the spring after our Star Factory appearance. I struck up a conversation with one of the club's owners. He spoke excellent English and his sophistication was typical of the Muscovites we met. He asked me how things were going.

I said, "Great. We've had a very interesting trip."

"Where else have you gone on this tour?" he asked.

"Well, let's see…Tyumen, Yekaterinburg, Samara, Krasnodar, Kazan, Chelyabinsk, Perm…"

I couldn't help but notice his widened eyes. He replied, "Really? All these places? That is very unusual. Most bands only go to St. Petersburg and Moscow and then return to the West. That is very impressive."

My touring ego puffed up a bit. "We've enjoyed it. The crowds have been great," I said. I was feeling smug. Take that, wimpy western bands! I don't see *Krasnodar* on your world tour T-shirt.

My new acquaintance went on. "Yes, ten cities. That's very good. I can think of only one band that has done more…"

I came up short. "Huh?"

"Yes, and even more impressive, they started their tour all the way in the east, at Vladivostok, and traveled west, playing city after city…maybe twenty or twenty-five places."

I tried to hide my deflated feeling. "Wow. That's amazing…"

"Yes. Amazing. Do you know...*Deep Purple*?"

BOSS OF BANNER

We were ecstatic to be touring again in 2006, but it didn't mean we could let our guard down regarding misuse of the old name. At our second Moscow gig, a banner with incorrect billing hung over the street in front of the club. As soon as we saw it, we pleaded with the venue to take it down. They said they would, but they didn't. We asked again and again. Always, they said, "Yes, yes, not problem" without solving the problem. As show time approached, we seriously weighed the risks of not playing the gig because of the banner. If we played as incorrectly advertised, we would look complicit. If we didn't play... we'd be at odds with a Russian nightclub whose security staff were, how shall I put it, *serious-looking guys*—the kind with crewcuts, thick necks, and leather blazers. I couldn't exactly picture Mik fending them off with his bow should we come to a major disagreement.

To our great relief, the club relented and removed the banner. We stood in our dressing room and did a show of hands whether to play or not. We all elected to play. Still, I felt compelled to add some insurance. I found a poster for a Russian band, turned it over and wrote with a Sharpie: "Tonight's band is called the Orchestra and is not 'ELO Part II.' If you don't want to see the Orchestra, please ask for your money back." I pinned it up at the club entrance and took a picture. I thought, "I can't believe I'm doing this shit instead of warming up my voice."

ONE FOR THE MONEY

As great as it was to play fifty shows in 2006, there was a downside. I was apart from my family for 108 days. My absence forced Helle into the role of single mom on top of working her full-time job. Not what she signed up for. Every touring musician with a family at home butts up against this untenable scenario. It's a shame that a great year for the band had to have a negative impact at home.

As if on cue, our 2007 schedule cratered to eleven gigs. I'd be home more often but my income would shrivel. I understood it was too early to return to Russia, Spain, and the UK, but God knows why the drop in work was so precipitous. The news that we'd been taken to court couldn't have helped settle any promoter nerves, even though we'd won the case.

Nine of our eleven dates in 2007 were one-offs, or as we call them now, fly-outs. I'm not one to bitch about gigs (*much*), but one-offs can be maddening. You pack your bags and gear, fly thousands of miles, meet your promoters, drive to the hotel, unpack, sleep off jet lag, do your sound check…all the things you do to start a tour…and then you play one show, sleep it off, get back in the van, go to the airport, and fly all the way home with one day's pay. It *is* "hard work" as Mik would say. It made me crazy to think, "We've flown all the way to Chile (or Mexico, or France, or Argentina) and there's not a second gig to be had anywhere in the whole country? How can that be?" One-offs take the best part of touring (exotic travel) and turn it into the worst part of touring (we flew 7,000 miles, now let's go home).

Whenever I got frustrated with our workload, or lack thereof, I'd feel the urge to call Eric or John and ask, "What's going on? Why can't we play at least two shows when we're already flying thousands of miles to a foreign country? What happened to the Australia tour? And India? Weren't we supposed to team up with another classic rock band in the States and do sheds?" Each time I made these reasonable—I thought—inquiries, Eric would exhale and say, "Do you really want to know the reasons those gigs went away?" Sure. Eric would calmly lead me on a tour of the booking agent sausage factory, where gigs do occasionally come together, but, more often, end up on the killing floor. "We were told that the Indian promoter had a terrible car accident on his way to the bank to send the deposit." "We found out at the last minute, luckily for us, that the Australian promoter's offer was in *Australian* dollars, which would have cut our fee in half." "We were ready to tour with such-and-such band, but it turned out none of our promoters wanted to work with that band's management." And so on. There are more reasons gigs don't happen than actual gigs themselves. I appreciated Eric's patient willingness to share, and his deflating stories usually kept me from asking about the sausage factory for a couple of years!

TWO FOR THE SHOW

I hated one-offs, but sometimes the gigs were so much fun it didn't matter.

A British realtors association held their annual corporate bash under a tent on the beach at Cannes, France. Their chosen entertainment? The Orchestra, with a guest solo set from Rick Wakeman. The beyond-legendary English pianist and member of Yes joined us for a boisterous pre-show dinner at a crowded café in Cannes before the show. I was delighted to discover that Wakeman was funny as hell, loved to laugh, and bore no pretensions about his musical importance. Just a big (6'4"?) lovely guy…who happened to have played piano on Bowie's "Life On Mars," created indelible keyboard hooks on tracks like "Roundabout," and so on. In fact, Yes was my first concert, when I was seventeen. I think I kept that to myself.

Wakeman borrowed Eric's keyboard and did a twenty-minute solo set during our intermission. He turned the keys into a comedic foil, playing dazzling runs that would suddenly veer off drunkenly into notes that screamed comedy. All the while, he kept up a monologue with the audience that was just as funny as the musical gags pouring forth from his dancing fingers. I could've watched him all night. When he finished, the Orchestra gathered around Rick to say how much we enjoyed his show. Mik looked at Eric and quipped, "It's funny, Eric, when *you* play the very same keyboard, it doesn't seem to have nearly as many notes."

Wakeman kindly mentioned us soon after in his newsletter: "The opening months of the year included a trip to France to play with the former members of ELO, now called the Orchestra. What a great bunch of guys and a good band, too. They're going to be touring next year, and they're well worth going to see."

Our next one-off took us to Zacatecas, Mexico, an historic hilltop town hosting our open-air concert as part of the Festival Cultural La Jornada. A large stage took up one side of the main city square, which was dominated by the Cathedral Basilica of Zacatecas. It felt like we were in Spain.

I'd invited a high school musician pal from Greece, Paul Voudouris, to the show, and he generously made the 224-mile drive from his home in San Miguel Allende to meet up with me. We hadn't seen each other in years, but we picked up wherever we'd left off and spent most of our time together laughing. After high school, Paul had been half of *Spheeris and Voudouris*, a new age musical act that recorded for Columbia around the same time I did in the late '80s. Two acts on Columbia Records is pretty good for a graduating class of 140 kids at the American Academy in Athens, Greece.

Our show in Zacatecas was part of a week-long festival, clearly the event of the year. We went down a storm, with "Last Train To London" bringing the crowd to a happy frenzy like it always did in Latin parts of the world. The next morning, Paul and I headed to breakfast at the Acropolis Restaurant (the Greek diaspora at our service). Unfortunately, I was recognized as the guitarist from the night before, and soon swarmed by Zacatecans asking for autographs and pictures. It was cute, but it literally took us a half hour to walk two blocks. Once we were seated in the restaurant, the autograph and photo requests continued during our eggs and coffee. Paul and I did our best to laugh about it, even after it grew tiresome. I've never felt so much like a celebrity and, I have to say, it's not for me. Five or ten minutes was fine. After that, ugh. I thank God I'm not famous.

A RAY OF SUNSHINE

Whenever the Orchestra traveled to Russia, each band member had to secure a visa at the nearest Russian consulate or embassy. For me, it meant driving five miles down Wisconsin Avenue in DC to the Russian Embassy, which overlooks Georgetown. A small, separate travel office is accessible at the rear of the large complex, negating the need to enter the Embassy grounds. When the band required visas in a hurry, we paid extra for expedited service. I'd hand over my paperwork with a check in the morning and pick up my passport in the afternoon with its shiny new visa glued to a page.

I'd become a frequent visitor to the little office, and I began to recognize some of the Russian employees on the other side of the thick glass. One morning, I decided to include a CD of the Orchestra album *No Rewind* with my paperwork. I slid it under the glass barrier, pantomimed playing a guitar, and said, "my band." The official on the other side blushed a bit and nodded thank you.

That afternoon I returned to pick up my visa. When I approached the thick glass wall, the employee who took the CD signaled me to wait and disappeared through a door. I thought, "Oh, shit. Did I go against protocol or something?" She came back with her boss, a guy in his early thirties, who said, full Russian accent intact while showing me the CD, "Thank you so much for this gift of generosity. It was too much kindness of you. You have brought a ray of sunshine into our otherwise miserable existence." I tried to keep my face straight and said, "You are very welcome."

As I left the little office with the new visa in my passport, I thought, "*a ray of sunshine into our otherwise miserable existence*? That's a bit over the top for a *CD*, isn't it?" They could surely buy CDs, couldn't they? Also, they lived in America, not Siberia. I wondered if they were allowed to leave the embassy. Russia never stops surprising.

78.5 HOURS

Not all fly-outs included Rick Wakeman in Cannes or old pals from high school in Mexico.

The Russian province of Kaliningrad is not connected to Russia itself. It's a separate enclave on the Baltic Sea, surrounded by Lithuania and Poland.

Once known as the German city of Konigsberg, Russia took it in 1945 so they could have a port on the Baltic that didn't freeze in winter.

We flew to Germany and Poland, and, from there, our Russian handlers drove us to Kaliningrad. Gordon and I were in a Nissan sedan behind a Toyota van carrying the rest of the band. Our lead-footed driver accelerated to 70 mph and locked onto the ass of the Toyota. Gordon and I requested, through hand signals and pleading voices, that the driver kindly slow the hell down. He didn't. The police pulled our driver over for speeding *twice* on a one-hour drive.

I'd been up for twenty-four hours, and my nerves were getting travel crispy. I tried to doze, but a Russian rap act doing *Straight Outta Krasnodar* blared from the car speakers. I killed time by eating a scrumptious dinner of cheese puffs and Powerade.

We finally took our place in line at the Russian border, plumes of exhaust rising slowly in the freezing air from every idling car. After an hour-long crawl, we got out of the car and trudged over frozen mud to present our passports to an official in a small, mud-splattered hut. Through a dirty window, I watched the border officer flip slowly through every page of my passport. He checked the visa. He looked through my pages a second time. He cross-checked it with a computer. He looked at my face and gave a long frowning look at my hat, as if it insulted him. I didn't think my hat was that bad. He moseyed through the pages one more time, found a spot to stamp, and handed my passport to me with the most bored expression a cog in the machine could possibly manifest. Have a nice day, Comrade.

We got back in the car, thinking we were done. Instead, we drove fifty feet and stopped. Soldiers signaled us to roll down the windows. We were handed entrance forms to fill out, twice. This took another twenty minutes. A guy in a trailer peeked at us through vertical blinds. The soldiers gave us suspicious looks and strutted like bantams around the car. They opened the trunk. No bodies or booze. At last, we were permitted to drive away.

Not so fast. We stopped after another twenty feet, where an automated boom barrier lowered to block our path. Several tractor trailer trucks in an adjacent lane were allowed to rumble into Russia before us. When they were done, we got the okay to proceed, and we drove past a sign that said, "Welcome to Russia." I couldn't have said it better myself.

At 2 a.m. we arrived at the hotel, where our memorably oddball promoter, the theatrical Ulyana, welcomed us back to Russia. It was strangely nice to see her, despite her eccentricities. At the very least, she was a familiar face in a foreign land. The hotel architect had forgotten about elevators, so I hauled my bags to the third floor, every muscle straining. The cheese puffs hadn't quite done the job for dinner, so I called Ulyana's room and asked if she might have the kitchen prepare me some eggs with bread, the easiest, most universal meal I could think of. Before the food arrived, I fell fast asleep. An hour later Ulyana persistently rapped on my door with a to-go container of peas in mayonnaise. *Perfect.* I stuffed 'em in the mini fridge and crashed hard.

The next morning, I felt a hundred times better, which brought me up to 50 percent of how I normally feel. I found an entertainment magazine in the room with a familiar picture of us on the cover. I can't imagine another band getting as much mileage from a group photo taken at Glamour Shots in a Florida mall.

After breakfast, we headed to sound check. There were plenty of modern buildings and up-to-date cars in K-grad, alongside the old Soviet ice-cube-tray apartment buildings. In addition to neighbors Poland and Lithuania, Sweden and Denmark were just across the water. I wondered if it was frustrating to be an educated, ambitious Russian citizen living in K-grad surrounded by democracies. The West is far from perfect, and democracy is messy, but as my dad used to say, "it's way ahead of whatever's in second place."

The venue was a narrow multipurpose hall, longer than it was wide, with the stage at the far end. A bank of stage lights that should've been high overhead was stuck five feet above the stage because the lifting mechanism was broken. Our sound check felt a bit dicey with a thousand pounds of metal dangling right above Gordon's head. Impressively, three guys eventually arrived carrying a brand-new light lifter. They installed it in no time, and it worked.

At dinner, my order of salmon arrived as white fish in mushroom sauce. Close enough, and quite tasty. The deliciousness of its food may be Russia's biggest secret. At 6:30 pm the crowd poured into the venue, and, by 7:10, the natives were restless—hooting, whistling, and chanting Or-ches-TRA! Or-ches-TRA! Our contract called for a short, sixty-minute show, which made no sense, but delighted Mik'n'Lou. Our string section's affection for shorter sets was a long running band trope. I thought, we'd come all this way, why not play all night? As we're about to walk onstage, Ulyana tells us we can just do fifty-five minutes. *What?* Why are we trying to shorten the only good part of this trip?

The crowd was standing room only, packed in tight, smiling and yelling, pumped and ready to rock. We slammed into our set and the audience's joy went up another level. It was loud onstage, but I still decided to loosen my in-ear monitors so I could connect to the energy in the room. Band and fans stayed in lockstep for the entire show, and we gave them a couple extra songs at the end. I could've played another hour. I managed to shoot some video during "Don't Bring Me Down." When it was the crowd's turn to sing, they nailed the "woc-hoos," but hilariously fell apart during the chorus, mangling the pesky English words. Endearing. Our communion complete, we waved goodbye, and the sated crowd retrieved their heavy coats from the cloak room and went out into the not-yet-dark night.

Afterwards, we drank some wine in the dressing room and discussed our plan to exit Russia. Unfortunately, we wouldn't return to the hotel for a good night's sleep and a reasonable morning departure. Instead, we would pack our bags and meet in the hotel lobby at 11:00 pm Why anyone thought this was a good idea, I don't know. I suspect we were trying to save money or attempting to cross into Poland when the lines weren't long, or both. In any case, my gig adrenaline was gone. Jet lag kicked in.

This time, the kamikaze driver was joined by one of our promoters, Vadim, who spoke good English. On our approach to the border from the Russian side, hundreds of tractor trailers were lined up on both sides of the road, idling in the snow, stalled by Russian and Polish red tape. I asked, "Is it always congested like this?" "Yes," Vadim said, with a solemn nod, "sometimes much worse."

I noticed a separate line of cars, about a quarter-mile long. Vadim told us those cars belonged to guys who made their living transporting vodka, cigarettes, and a tank full of gas to Poland, where they could sell everything for twice what they paid for it in Russia. Some of these guys, Vadim said, got out and pushed their cars through the checkpoints to save precious gas. They were allowed to take only so much vodka and so many cigarettes, so they stuffed their wheel wells, doors, and trunks with extra contraband. They made the crossing around ten times a month and hauled in about a hundred dollars per trip. I said, "That's a shitload of work for a hundred bucks." Gordon added, "Minimum wage never looked so good."

This time, it only took us forty minutes to engage our jolly friends at passport control and get through the checkpoints. Vadim, pleased, called it "an excellent result." Once through the border, we headed to Gdansk, where we checked into a hotel at 3:30 am We would sleep for two hours. Our alarms rang at 5:30, and Gordon said he'd rather stay in his Polish bed than fly home. Same here. This was no way to live.

Four hours later, we managed to board our first flight of the day. A talkative gaggle of sturdy-looking men settled into nearby seats. One of them announced, "Looks like I'm seated across from Led Zeppelin." I thought that was funny, but did he think Led Zeppelin didn't speak English? I set them straight and discovered they were a bunch of ship pilots from Vancouver. They'd been learning how to maneuver large container ships on a lake south of Gdansk at the Ship Handling Research and Training Centre. Apparently, the facility is one of the best in the world. I Googled it and found videos of burly men learning to park *miniature* container boats. It looked silly as hell, but, apparently, the training works. Now you know.

After two more flights and sixteen hours of travel through eight time zones, I landed back in DC. My hallucinatory one-off to Russia had taken over seventy-nine-and-a-half hours. That's one hour on stage and seventy-eight-and-a-half hours of no-thank-you. All for a single check. I resented just about every minute of the trip, except the show itself, which was like a ray of sunshine in my otherwise miserable existence.

SPLIT DECISION

With our touring schedule, again, reduced to a handful of dates, I wasn't making much money with the Orchestra, while Helle, stuck at home without her husband, wasn't having much fun. She knew, going into our marriage, that I was committed to the musician's life with all its attendant risks and rewards, good years and bad. It's who I was. But even if we understood each other, the nature of my job and my time away had become a wedge between us. It didn't make it any easier for her to work full-time in government consulting and care for Fiona, while I went on adventures with my band buddies.

Fiona was already six years old and still an only child. Helle and I grew up with five brothers between the two of us. We desperately wanted Fiona to have a sibling. My erratic schedule wasn't helping our chances.

I felt like forces were closing in on me, and if I didn't make some kind of move, I'd slowly get crushed. The Orchestra guys were some of the best people I knew, and I loved playing with them. I didn't want to leave the band, but to make things better at home I felt maybe I ought to. I struggled to make a decision and when I finally did, I had no idea if it was the right one. Maybe things would've turned out differently if I hadn't resented the Kaliningrad gig so much. More than anything else, the ever-widening disconnect with my wife and daughter sealed the deal. If I lost them, I would lose everything.

I decided to quit the Orchestra. It made me sick to my stomach.

I was at Eric's studio in New Jersey, recording guitar parts for an Orchestra project. I had about three hours of work to do and, the entire time, I was dreading the moment when I'd tell my pal, the guy who'd changed my life when he contacted me about joining ELO Part II, that I was leaving. When the time came, I felt like a scared kid guiltily confessing to a parent. I got emotional and could barely get my words out. I don't remember calmly explaining my reasons. Maybe I did, I don't know. I do remember packing up my gear and practically running out of his house. I felt so shitty about it. The sense of loss was beyond what I'd expected. My four-hour drive to Maryland was pure misery.

LOVE AND MARRIAGE
I'm still glad I did it.

My marriage to Helle means everything to me. This book may be about my love for music, but the secret sauce is Helle Huxley. She's a fearless genius and an amazing wife. Her understanding of emotional intelligence is profound. Through her patient and, sometimes painful, guidance we got to the other side of our issues. We found a place where we saw eye to eye and agreed on what mattered most to each of us. Our marriage is stronger because of the work we did after I left the band. And, to our incredible joy, Fiona got her sibling when Imogen arrived in August of 2008. Her middle name is George, honoring my dad.

TITS FOR TATTS
The Orchestra brought Phil Bates back through the revolving door. In 1998, when I joined the band, it was the other way round. When my dad died in 2006, back came Phil for two shows. When I quit in 2007, Phil came back again. Truth be told, the guitarist gig belonged to me or Phil because the band dreaded the thought of rehearsing someone new.

Before Phil could take over, I played *Rockin' the Rivers*, a festival in Montana. We stayed at the Sacajawea Hotel in the town of Three Forks. Real Wild West stuff. The festival site was out in the country. A panoramic grass hillside gently sloped down to a massive festival stage. We arrived late-morning for sound check, got our levels organized, and returned to the hotel until showtime.

As the headliner, we took the stage last and slammed into "Evil Woman," beginning my final gig with the band. Mik's violin screamed in my in-ear-monitors. I couldn't hear my guitar or my vocal. This was not good. I looked at the other guys, and *everyone* was pointing to their ears in a panic. Somehow all our settings from the morning sound check were gone. There was no way we could do a show without being able to hear what we were playing or singing. We stopped in the middle of the first verse and spent ten minutes re-setting all our in-ear monitor levels.

This had never happened to the Orchestra in my nine years with the band. I was so disappointed. We took immense pride in our professionalism and consistently good performances. Although it wasn't really our fault, I was bummed to look so amateurish. Adding to my displeasure, I'd noticed that Art Alexakis and the members of Everclear had stuck around after their set to hear us play. It was painful to see them standing at the rear of the stage watching our shitshow. Ugh. I always want to kick extra ass when other bands are watching.

The audience was perfectly patient and understanding while we sorted out the mess. It's not like they were going anywhere. Soon enough, we restarted the show, but I felt like we were fighting uphill the whole time. Our mojo had been severely compromised by a technical fuckup…at my last show.

Afterwards, we were changing our clothes and having a drink in our band's assigned tent backstage. We never saw her coming, but a fan was suddenly in the tent with us, talking loudly and inserting herself into our conversations. She was in her fifties at least, skinny, drunk, a few teeth missing, and dressed in dirty shorts and a T-shirt with no bra. She lifted her shirt, giving us an unwelcome look at her fake breasts, which were covered with black Sharpie autographs. "Sign 'em! You guys gotta sign 'em! I already got all the other bands." Fucking hell. What's it like where *you* work?

The next day, I had lunch with Mik and Kelly. We talked about my plans, such as they were, and wished each other good luck. The English are normally not touchy-feely, but I have some cherished photographs of me with my arms around both the guys. I would miss their companionship. Back at the hotel, Eric, Gordon, and I sat in rocking chairs on the front porch of the Sacajawea Hotel, waiting for our ride to the airport.

I said, "This is where we're all gonna end up, boys. Sittin' in rocking chairs on the porch."

Gordon laughed, "Yelling at neighborhood kids."

Eric shouted, "Get off my lawn!"

CHAPTER 20
THANK YOU BETHESDA

It felt odd to not be a member of the Orchestra. Although it had never been my dream to join a classic rock band, for nearly a decade, I'd hung my hat on being part of the ELO universe. I'd had a good answer to the Airport Question and had routinely flown to exotic locales as a part of my job. In busy years, the money was pretty good, too. When I told friends that I'd quit the band, most were shocked and said things along the lines of, "It seemed like such a perfect gig." I knew how they felt.

After I quit, I peeked at the band calendar and saw they'd gone Deep Purple on me and traveled all the way to Vladivostok, Russia, just across from Japan. What an adventure that must've been. I couldn't help feeling a little jealous, but I was glad Phil Bates had agreed to come back and replace his replacement. I hadn't wanted to cause the band any disruption. Phil's nine years away had apparently done him some good, and I'd heard he was glad to be back.

DREAM NUMBER ONE

With ELO music no longer occupying my mind, my focus returned to obsession number one, making records. I'd begun my latest album in LA before moving to Maryland. The working title was *Everything's Different Now*, inspired by the birth of Fiona. When I saw that Til Tuesday had an album with that name, I went with *Kiss the Monster*, which originally referred to the notorious Vina Del Mar Festival audience but carried new meaning in 2007. I was facing a major unknown, a future without my Orchestra crutch. If the unknown is a monster, then kissing it, and embracing it, felt like a sound plan.

Helle inspired no fewer than four songs on the album: "Wear My Ring," "Yet To Say," "Better Than Good," and "Bones," a ballad that cuts to the heart of our early relationship:

Things are much better now
And I've got you to thank
'Cause I came pretty close

To goin' in the tank
I was goin' down
How did you know we would make it?
How did you know you could take it
When you took me on?

Kiss the Monster also included "Everything's Different Now," a song I wrote for Fiona with some lyrics I'm particularly fond of:

Everything's in its place my beautiful little Fi
One day you'll get me back for making you look like me

After *"Deluxe"* (life with Janet) and *Purgatory Falls* (life without Janet), I felt like *Kiss the Monster* (life with Helle and Fiona) completed a trilogy of sorts. My manager, David Bean, and I secured a deal for KTM on Voiceprint, an English label. I think it's one of my strongest albums.

HOW THE MIGHTY HAVE FALLEN

My studio albums are my best work and proudest achievements, but they're rarely lucrative. Without my Orchestra income, I sought out music-related work. I played house concerts, wrote production music for Killer Tracks, and landed an adjunct lecturer position at The Omega School of Recorded Arts in Rockville. The universe then steered me to an income stream I hadn't seen coming. One morning, I stood with Fiona at her school bus stop when a neighbor asked if I gave guitar lessons. I didn't, and was about to say so, but suddenly thought better of it and decided that, yes, in fact, I did teach guitar. I took myself by surprise.

I created a lesson plan on the fly and started out with a student or two from the neighborhood. I called Eric Troyer and asked him for advice. Eric said, "If they've never touched a guitar before, teach 'em 'Twinkle, Twinkle, Little Star' and go from there." Eric knew what he was talking about. Within a year, I was up to twenty students per week, ranging in age from eight to sixty-eight years old. As expected, my adult students were interested in learning classic rock hits from their youth. The biggest surprise was when I asked teenagers what bands they liked, they often said, "AC/DC, Deep Purple, Led Zeppelin..." Cracked me up! My go-to joke became "Dude, did we go to high school together?"

Laptop software allowed me to slow down any song my students wanted to learn without changing pitch. Note by note, I studied all my favorite guitar-

Chapter 20: Thank You Bethesda

ists like Jimmy Page, Jimi Hendrix, Ritchie Blackmore, Jeff Beck, Dave Davies, Mick Ronson, Wally Bryson, Keith Richards, George Harrison, Joe Walsh, Bill Pitcock IV (guitarist for Dwight Twilley), Mark Knopfler, Angus Young, Stephen Stills, Paul Kossoff, Tony Iommi, Alvin Lee, Eric Clapton, and so on. As fun as it was for my students to learn how to play guitar correctly, *my* skills improved enormously. There's nothing like having a guitar in your hands six days a week.

I created a poster advertising my lessons with my phone number, a picture of me and "Guitarist for ELO Part II." I thumbtacked a few at local grocery stores. After a few days, I noticed on one poster someone had bothered to scribble, "*How the mighty have fallen.*" Damn! A real-world troll!

A kid named Ben Hoyt sought me out for guitar lessons. I thought I recognized him from the local high school orchestra. I asked, "Aren't you a violinist? I'm happy to teach you guitar, but can you bring your violin next time, too?" Thus began one of my favorite collaborations. Ben is the rare classically trained musician who can also improvise, meaning he can literally do anything on the violin (he's pretty good on piano and guitar, too.) Over the years, he's played on my albums, joined me for house concerts, and even traveled to gigs in LA and Carmel. Despite our 40-year age difference, Ben and I are locked in musically and comedically. He never fails to elevate a proceeding.

Ben has also played lifesaver for the Orchestra, subbing for ELO legend Mik Kaminski when Mik was unable to leave England due to Covid, visa problems, or an erupting volcano in Iceland spewing soot into flight paths. His first show with us came at Nemacolin Resort in Pennsylvania. With cheat sheets spread across the stage floor, Ben nailed the Lou Clark-composed string parts with pizazz. He doesn't need cheat sheets anymore.

SERIOUSLY, MUZAK?

Before I left the Orchestra, I'd attended a music conference in DC, my attempt at networking. I befriended a fellow named Bruce McKagan, who worked at, of all places, Muzak. He disarmed me a bit and said, "I know, I know. Elevator music, right? Well, that's not what we do any more. We have one of the biggest music libraries in the world. What do *you* do, Hux?"

"I play with some guys from ELO."

"Oh, really? My brother's band just cut an ELO song on their latest album."

"Oh, yeah?" I assumed his brother's band was unknown. "What's the name of the band?"

Bruce said, "Velvet Revolver. Have you heard of 'em?"

Uh, *yeah*-eah. "Who's your brother?"

"He's the bassist. His name's Duff."

Duff McKagan. Of course. Bruce's little bro was Duff from Guns 'n' Roses. Bruce was justifiably proud. I remembered the track he was talking about. I said, "I think they did 'Can't Get It Out Of My Head.' I'll have to check it out again." (I did check it out. Velvet Revolver's version is thick with cool fuzzy guitars and big bass, but, oddly, Scott Weiland either changed or didn't know some of the lyrics.)

Bruce handed me his card and I reciprocated. He said, "Let's figure out how to do something together." I liked Bruce and wholeheartedly agreed. That said, conference networking rarely pays off. It's easy to get chummy for a minute and promise to stay in touch, but it rarely happens. Surprise, surprise, a few weeks later, Bruce called me. "Hey, P. I'm giving a boring speech to some of our regional salespeople at a casino in Mississippi next month. How would you like to join me and play a few songs after my talk to make me look good?"

I liked this Bruce guy.

He said, "I'll cover flights, and you'll have your own room, of course. So, what's a reasonable fee? Would $1,000 work?"

For two or three songs? Yeah, that'll work.

Over the next couple of years, Bruce and I collaborated on special projects. I produced recordings of original songs by his employees and played live at Muzak's summer bash. I wrote a Christmas song for a special Muzak holiday CD and performed it at the company's space-age headquarters south of Charlotte, North Carolina. I was flattered that he kept coming back to me and I was always happy for the work now that I was without my Orchestra gig. Bruce changed my perception of Muzak—long a meme for schmaltz—from a joke to a much hipper place than anyone had the right to imagine.

In 2009, two years after I had quit the Orchestra, Helle said, "You like Bruce and Muzak, right? Well, they've got a job opening here in DC. You might wanna check it out."

I liked Bruce and Muzak and their cool headquarters. But. Hold on. A *Jay-Oh-Bee*? I hadn't had one of those since 1986 at MacMillan in New York. Not really my thing. (Did they pay by the Rick Hour?) The position was accounts manager or client representative or something. I wasn't sure what that meant, but oddly enough, I was kind of intrigued. I was fifty-three. I liked people. Maybe I could pull it off. My buddy Bruce was taken aback when I brought it up. His voice dropped to a serious tone, and he said, "That's… that's a hard job, P. It's not anything like the stuff you and I do together. But, if you're really interested, I'll be more than happy to talk to the people doing the hiring." I decided to go for it.

What had gotten into me? Was this a rock 'n' roll backwards mid-life crisis? Was I suddenly going straight? Was there a minivan in my future?

In a new suit(!), I made the half-hour drive to Springfield, Virginia and walked into Muzak's boring un-space-age DC offices. I was a fish out of water, but the strangeness of the experience kind of appealed to me, as if work had become an exotic adventure. If I got the job, I'd be joining a company I already liked, but in the trenches. My interviewers asked me what I'd done previously, though I'm pretty sure they already knew thanks to Bruce.

"I toured the world playing guitar with some guys from ELO."

They shook their heads. "That's the job *we* want! Why the hell would you want *this* job?"

"Touring took me away from my family. I left the band so I could stay home. I've done special projects with Bruce McKagan and I've been to your headquarters a bunch of times. I like the company."

They still didn't believe me, I don't think, but the interview went fine. I got the job, most likely because Bruce advised them to hire me. The pay wasn't great, but I felt up for a challenge. I also felt like, if it didn't work out, I would forever have the right to say, "Yeah, I *tried* doing a real job once…"

I underwent some training at headquarters near Charlotte. I had a huge learning curve regarding Muzak's services, packages, technology, reporting methods, terminology, and so on but, mainly, my job was simple. It required me to interface with Muzak clients all over the DC area and service them in one of three ways. If they already had Muzak, keep them happy. If they were threatening to leave Muzak, convince them to stay. If they'd already left Muzak, try to get them back.

It was a long way from Albert Hall.

I spent the next year introducing myself to owners of gas stations, restaurants, retail stores, shopping malls—any place of business using Muzak's dizzying array of music players and speakers. Some systems were brand new, and others had been stuck in closets for forty years. Bruce was right. It was a hard job. Most clients never thought about their music service unless it was malfunctioning or costing too much, so they weren't all that jacked up to talk to a rookie Muzak rep they'd never seen before. It was mostly thankless work, but some clients were genuinely grateful for upgrades, good deals, good service, and a sense of humor, all of which I tried to provide. The owner of a grocery store in Baltimore loved me for the new system we installed. When

I'd pay him a visit, he'd shout out, "Hux! There's my man!" I had a few clients like that, but not many. Most were business owners just trying to survive on narrow profit margins, and when business was slow, Muzak looked a lot more superfluous—an unnecessary expense. I tried to lower clients' costs whenever I could.

Helle had told me before I started the job "You will actually appreciate one thing about corporate culture. When you do something well, you'll get acknowledged right away. As you know, in music, there's rarely anyone around to pat you on the back for that great lyric or bridge you came up with. Musicians don't get any recognition until a record finally comes out or you play for an audience." She was right. I won employee of the month three times at Muzak and, although it was an acknowledgement of work that I wasn't particularly geeked up about, it did feel good to be recognized.

It turned out that us guys in the field were in a completely different world from fancy-pants Muzak headquarters. Down there, teams of young music curators sorted through Muzak's gigantic library to create cool new programs. They were like deejays making playlists. Pretty fun. As an account executive, I was more likely to be in the basement of an ancient Baltimore law firm digging around stacks of old files looking for disconnected speaker wire. Some businesses couldn't even remember where they'd stuffed their Muzak hardware. I got to see some weird spaces. One of my favorites was the Baltimore Mint. Even though I had an appointment, the security checks were endless, since I was entering a building literally stuffed with money. I saw pallets piled high with hundred-dollar bills. The Mint went with *soft rock*.

Muzak gave me a taste of corporate culture, good and bad. I was amazed that anything ever got accomplished. Headquarters kept coming up with new schemes and themes and price tiers and terminology, when all we really needed in the field was a few good products that were easy for customers to use, didn't break, and didn't cost an arm and a leg. But what did I know?

One day, on a lark, I called up my old VP from MCA Publishing, Betsy Anthony. I told her what I was doing and how I now appreciated what she'd faced in the corporate world. Full of insider pride, I said, "It only took me one conference call to learn that you should never, *ever* voluntarily speak up on a conference call." Betsy laughed and said, "Oh, my God. P-man! I can't believe I'm hearing this from you." I know how she felt.

A year into my job, I drove south around the DC beltway to Springfield to meet with a supervisor. We sat in the conference room, and I took out my computer as usual. She said, "Don't bother opening that up." I was taken aback. We had a good rapport, and she was normally much friendlier. "I'm sorry to tell you that you've been let go. Muzak just got bought by a finance company and they're downsizing. Since you're new, you're at the top of the list to go. If it makes you feel any better, some people who've worked here for many years will also be leaving." She wasn't mad at me, she was sad.

I was speechless. Such a thing had never happened to me, since, to *lose* a job, one must *have* a job. At first, I felt kind of insulted (Employee of the Month!) and strangely unprotected (couldn't Bruce have stepped in?), but then she said, "Be sure to apply for unemployment right away. We'll send the state all the information they need from us. It won't be complicated. I'm gonna miss working with you." And that was pretty much it. No use hanging around the office. I drove home. I had no real job anymore. Familiar terrain.

I had never known the wonders of unemployment benefits. It turned out that doing nothing (by which I mean searching daily for a new job) earned me almost as much as installing a Muzak system at Patel's Exxon down by the Bay Bridge. Fuckin' A! And even better, it was 2010, and the President extended unemployment benefits beyond the normal eligibility. Thanks, Obama! I think I legally got two years of checks for one year of work. USA! USA!

UNION JACK'S

Helle's brother Jaime left LA and returned to Maryland a few years after we did. Jaime took over a Sunday night open mic in Bethesda at a place called Union Jack's English pub. Any musician or singer could sign up and play two or three songs with the house band, which was Jaime on guitar and a rhythm section of drummer Ricky Wise and bassist Dave Phenicie. All three were amazing players and singers. I spent a year going to Union Jack's as often as I could so I could sit in with the house band. With *two* guitars, bass, and drums and all that vocal power we could cover pretty much anything, and our loose repertoire grew to more than a hundred songs. The four of us had a shitload of fun playing classics like "Funk #49," "The Weight," "Woodstock," "A Little Help from My Friends," "What Is and What Should Never Be," "Day Tripper," "Immigrant Song"—all great tunes that I either knew or could fake my way through with enough Sunday Night swagger.

That year at Union Jack's turned out to be the perfect way for a band to gel. Without rehearsing or even trying very hard, we'd established a raucous sound and a discernably fun stage presence. My friend from *Spectator*, Jonathan Mudd, caught our act in Bethesda and said, "Dude, this is the best band you've ever had!"

It was a no-brainer to have the guys learn a set of my songs, and voila, I had a kick-ass original band. I began booking us at Jammin Java in nearby Vienna, Virginia, one of my favorite places to play. The club is owned and run by musicians, and artists get treated well. Backed by my ridiculous band, an audience found me, and they've been coming to see my band at Jammin Java ever since.

TOO TALL INDEED

In February 2009, Eric Troyer called me with the awful news that Kelly Groucutt had died. The heart and soul of the Orchestra had experienced terrible bouts of chest pain that would knock him down and then mysteriously go away. He'd been checked out by a doctor and given the okay, but his wife, Anna, begged him to see a specialist. Kelly didn't, true to his stubborn core. As he was getting ready to leave England for an Orchestra gig in Berlin, he wasn't feeling well, and Anna pleaded with him not to go. Kelly said, "We need the bread. I'll be fine." In Germany, he continued to have painful episodes. The rest of the guys were alarmed and urged him to revisit the doctor. When Kelly returned to England, he went to see Anna at her work and suffered another attack. He was rushed to Worcestershire Royal Hospital where he died the next day. Hard to believe such a lively, lovely guy was gone.

I flew to England to attend the funeral on March 9, 2009. Not the way I'd envisioned reuniting with the band. Inside a grand church in the village of Coseley, Kelly's friends and family members gave tear-jerking tributes to a man loved by so many. Kelly's son, Chris, acknowledged his dad's enthusiasm for new gadgets with a great line: "Dad was, of course, the first in the county to have a Wii." Everyone laughed.

When I'd first joined ELO Part II in 1998, Kelly picked up on my Move-influenced musical taste and was thoughtful enough to invite Roy Wood to join us for dinner in Birmingham. I'd been super-excited to meet him, Roy being a musical hero and one of the reasons I was so pleased to have a small stake in the ELO/Move legacy. Unfortunately, Roy was late to rendezvous with us at our rehearsal room and I missed meeting him. I didn't get another chance until, sigh, Kelly's wake, eleven years later. Roy and I chatted for a few minutes, but it was just too strange and sober a day, and I couldn't muster up much of a conversation. It felt like Kelly had finally gotten me to meet Roy, but the musical hero I desperately wanted to talk to in 2009...was Kelly Groucutt. When I got home, I posted this eulogy:

Chapter 20: Thank You Bethesda

In late 1998, I walked into a large, well-worn rehearsal room in Birmingham, England, for my audition with ELO Part II. I wasn't sure who everyone was, but immediately Kelly Groucutt positioned himself directly in front of me, tilted his head upwards and said, "You're TOO TALL!" We laughed. Leave it to Kelly to be the icebreaker.

Of course, Kelly needn't have worried about my height. He was the real giant.

He's rarely mentioned when rock media list Greatest Bass Players or Greatest Front Men, but he was among the best I've ever seen, much less had the privilege to work with. Kelly's voice was always front and center in our sound (he was louder than everyone else!) and the bass parts he commandeered while singing on every song were astounding. Try singing "Hey there Mister Blue/We're so pleased to be with you" whilst nailing the bass part of "Mr. Blue Sky" and you'll get an idea.

Kelly never had an off night. Sure, he'd throw a clam on the pile—we were all guilty of that—but he never phoned in a performance. No matter how sick, tired, or jet-lagged, he always gave everything he had. "Never punish the ones who show up" was his mantra. He loved the fans and respected them. It didn't matter who they were or how many of them were in the seats.

Fans of ELO Part II, and now the Orchestra, will attest that Kelly was always available after a gig for an autograph, a photo, a cigarette, a drink, whatever was happening at that moment. Hours after a performance, the last thing fans heard in the parking lot was usually a tour manager shouting, "Kelly! The bus is leaving!" He gave the fans every spare minute he had.

Kelly was a tinkerer, a gadgets freak, a student of puns, an expert Country & Western singer, a walking encyclopedia of music history (song title, artist, year released), a loving Dad, a smoker, a drinker, a traveler (China, Cuba, Chile... hmmm...never noticed how much he liked "C" countries), a joke teller, a tireless chatter bug, a generous friend, a lyrics freak, a willing accomplice.

I was with Kelly in planes, trains, and automobiles, but my cherished memories will always be our time on stage. I don't know how many shows we did together, but it's many hundreds. Over the years, Kelly and I developed several moments in the set that were "ours"—just dumb little things that we acknowledged with a covert grin or an overt laugh. When I'd join him on his mic for the "George and Paul" vocals in the chorus of "Twist And Shout," he'd move his bass neck out of my way in an exaggerated "showbiz" sweep; in "Xanadu," we'd mouth the words "people are wanking" during the four beats between the title repeat in the chorus; in "Shine A Little Love" I knew he'd be looking over at me during the third verse, the lyrics of which I was prone to botch. Kelly would jump in singing if I missed one syllable...

It seems absurd that Kelly's gone. His spirit is that of a giant's. I wouldn't be surprised if, at Heaven's Gate, he has to duck to get in. Too tall, indeed.

Over the next few years, Kelly's family and friends led a fundraising drive to secure a Blue English Heritage Commemorative Plaque to be placed on the house where Kelly had lived from 1945 to 1971. Their campaign succeeded. The Blue Plaque reads:

Kelly Groucutt
Musician and Songwriter
1945–2009

Bass player with the
Electric Light Orchestra
1974–1983

Lived here
1945–1971

Dudley Metropolitan Borough Council

THANK YOU BETHESDA

In 2009, I began work on what would become my eleventh studio album, *Thank You Bethesda*. Weirdly, I'd written the title song years before setting foot in Bethesda, Maryland. The lyrics refer to a Thanksgiving break I spent with a nursing student in Chapel Hill, who had procured forbidden pharmaceuticals from Bethesda Naval Hospital. We shared a wonderful day together.

> *My, don't all the leaves look extra shiny out behind the house today*
> *Maybe it's just me but possibly the world could always look this way*

I was excited to work again with producer/engineer Mark Williams at his Suckerpunch Studio. Mark has recorded all my output since I moved to Maryland in 2005, and we make an excellent team. He has helped me do some of my very best work, including the albums *Thank You Bethesda*, *This Is the One* and *As Good As Advertised*.

I was long past my last record deal, so after going out of pocket to cut tracks with Gordon on drums, Dan Rothchild on bass, and Daniel Clarke on keys, I decided to look at Kickstarter. I'd shied away from funding sites, mistaking them for platforms where musicians begged for money. A Kickstarter video by an artist named Bleu changed my thinking. His pitch in support of his album *Four* was hilarious, well written, and honest. He made the point that recording music without funding from a label was prohibitively expensive and time consuming. Why NOT appeal to fans who'd want to hear the album anyway?

I set my goal at $8,500, stitched together a video, and created twelve reward levels ranging from $10 to $1,500. It took about three months to get all that together. At 12:01 am on my daughter, Fiona's, birthday, I launched my thirty-day campaign and crossed my fingers that someone from my 1,500-person mailing list might respond with a pledge.

The next morning, I had $400 in pledges before 8:00 am I could've wept with relief. In just two weeks, I raced past my target of $8,500. After thirty days, my pledges from 178 backers amounted to $15,390. That money allowed me to finish recording, pay for mastering, and manufacture 1,000 CDs with a massive twenty-four-page booklet. Kickstarter was a game changer, and it didn't feel like begging. The secret sauce of Kickstarter is that *people enjoy supporting each other*. I've pledged money to five Kickstarter projects, happily.

HEY, THESE GUYS ARE GOOD

On April 17, 2010, the Orchestra was booked into the Resorts Superstar Theatre in Atlantic City. I made the three-hour drive from Maryland with eight-year-old Fiona as my sidekick. Fiona and I met up with the band backstage before the show. Everybody fussed over Fi, I gave a big American hug to Mik, and happily shot the shit with my old bandmates. It'd been three years, but the pre-show vibe was all too familiar. Mik'n'Lou nursed glasses of wine, Eric did vocal warmups in the bathroom, and Gordon knocked out paradiddles on a table with his sticks.

I'd replaced Phil Bates in 1998 and heard stories about him, but since we were two men for one job, we'd never met. We finally occupied the same room backstage in Atlantic City. We shook hands and had a laugh about our combined presence disturbing the universe. Someone in the room was showing unflattering phone photos and Phil said, "I saw myself in the mirror the other day and thought, 'Who's the fat hippie?'" I liked him.

I also liked the band's new southpaw bassist/singer, Glen Burtnik. Kelly Groucutt might've been a little guy, but he'd left big shoes to fill. Glen was engaging, funny, and other than being American (oops) a perfect fit for the Orchestra. A New Jersey native, Glen had played Paul in Beatlemania, released a couple of major label albums, written a hit with Patty Smyth and Don Henley ("Sometimes Love Ain't Enough"), and spent ten years with Styx, among other things. He'd even subbed for Kelly a time or two back in the day before I joined ELO Part II.

Fiona and I watched the show from the front row. I'd been gone from the band long enough for the songs I'd spent so much time memorizing to finally vacate my head. I was able to experience the Orchestra with fresh eyes and ears, and, for the first time ever, from a fan's perspective. What a revelation it was. I finally understood why audiences loved the Orchestra so much, why some of our fans had seen us more than two hundred times: *the show is relentless*. It grabs you and never lets you go. There are no jams, no joke songs, no bass solos, no blues exercises, no boring bits. All the songs are hits, with clever arrangements that never sit still, one after the other, presented by a personable, likable bunch of guys who sing like angels and happen to all be fantastic, first-rate musicians. What's not to love?

At the end of the set, the band brought me up to play on the perennial encore, "Don't Bring Me Down." As I crossed the stage to grab a guitar, Phil said into the mic, "Hux will probably replace me again when I drop dead in a few years." Phil and I laughed. Life is funny sometimes. That was the only time Phil and I were ever on stage together.

COKE AND RED WINE

Four months later, Phil didn't drop dead, but he did inform the Orchestra that he would not be available for an August 27 gig in Bilbao, Spain. Apparently, Phil wasn't 100 percent onboard with the Orchestra's direction and had started booking gigs with a band of his own in Germany. The Orchestra's "please don't make us rehearse someone new" rule still applied, so you'll never guess who they called to fill in.

I told Helle about the gig. We were in a much better place as a couple, almost like we were different people with a deeper understanding of each other. She said something as breezy as, "Oh, that sounds like fun." I couldn't have agreed more. Three years after severing ties, I was incredibly excited to play with the guys again. It felt like I was returning from exile. I didn't mind that it was just one show. My aversion to one-offs had eased up considerably during my time away.

Eric sent me the band's set list so I could prepare. The first thing I noticed was that all twenty-one songs were old ELO hits. I hadn't expected to see "Jewel And Johnny" in the set without me around to sing it, but I was surprised there weren't any original songs of Eric's or Phil's or even our version of "Twist And Shout." I got to work refamiliarizing myself with material I'd played a thousand times. It didn't take long to get my chops back. Vocally, the band was doing some different things with Kelly gone and Glen in, but we didn't have a lot of time to work out parts, so it was agreed that I would stick with what I'd sung three years before.

Our gig was part of a weeklong city festival in Bilbao. The streets overflowed with revelers day and night, and our hotel was right in the middle of the action. A long-time Orchestra fan from Spain named Victor joined Eric and me, showing us around the old part of the city. I noticed young people carrying huge, clear plastic bottles filled with red wine. Victor explained it was actually red wine mixed with Coca-Cola. Eric and I both blanched. "It's not as bad as you might think," Victor insisted. He ducked into a small shop and came out with the ingredients, which we poured in equal amounts into three cups. I was prepared to barf, but instead, I was shocked by how tasty it was. "Oh, damn. That's delicious." Victor exalted in his victory. "You are now a little bit Spanish, Hux, or maybe even Basque!"

Our stage was set up on a massive asphalt plaza across the river from downtown Bilbao. Muscle memory had brought the songs back into my hands with only a few hiccups, so performing in front of thousands of people wasn't a problem. My challenge was fending off emotions and a bizarre sense of time collapse. I felt a huge sentimental attachment to my place on stage with my old friend Gordon behind me pounding away; Eric to my right on his riser, ready to catch my smug smile or an exaggerated look of mild panic depending on how the show was going; Mik meeting me at center stage for competing solos in "Rock 'n' Roll Is King." I was right at home, as if three years had been nothing. It was my first show with Glen, and I felt perfectly at ease with him. I imagine he may've found it odd to have a stranger up there who knew all the parts.

The gig in Bilbao reignited my joy and appreciation of playing in the Orchestra. Great bandmates, big stage, huge crowd, nice hotel, exotic location, good paycheck...nice work if you can get it. Even nicer if you can get it back.

BIG LEAGUES

I don't know if my availability for the Bilbao gig encouraged Phil Bates to book more shows of his own, but that's what happened. In March 2011, the Orchestra brought me to Mexico City's prestigious National Auditorium on a bill with Alan Parsons. Parsons's achievements include his Alan Parsons Project albums, his engineering work on *Abbey Road*, producing Al Stewart's *Year of the Cat*, Pink Floyd's *Dark Side of the Moon*, and more. He helped put together the Beatles' rooftop concert at Apple headquarters when he was seventeen. Nice career.

The Mexico City gig reconnected me with P.J. Olsson, a songwriting friend from my LA days who'd become the lead singer for Parsons's band. P.J. is from the Upper Peninsula of Michigan, which makes him one of the few people on Earth familiar with my dad's hometown of Ishpeming. Big points. When we spotted each other backstage in Mexico City, we shouted, "Look who it is!" and immediately became goofier versions of ourselves. P.J. has a memorable machine-gun laugh, and it was like we'd never stopped hanging out. During the Parsons band sound check, I went out in the seats of the hall and listened to P.J. sing "Time," a lovely ballad from the Alan Parsons Project album *The Turn of a Friendly Card*. P.J. owned it.

Playing guitar again with the Orchestra and watching P.J. sing with Alan Parsons, I marveled at how many friends of mine had been promoted to the big leagues of Classic Rock. VeG drummer Winston Watson toured for five years with Bob Dylan. P. Hux bassist Dan Rothchild joined Heart. My old drummer Rob Ladd backed up Roger Daltrey. Glen Burtnik spent ten years in Styx. Jen Condos played bass with Don Henley and Stevie Nicks. Kevin McCormick, the bass player who led me to the show where I met Janet, toured with Crosby Stills and Nash. Jeff Foskett became Brian Wilson's musical director and toured as a member of the Beach Boys. My co-writer, Stevie Salas, played guitar for Rod Stewart and Mick Jagger. Topping us all, my old pal and bandmate, Rusty Anderson, has been Paul McCartney's guitarist for more than twenty years. I think all of us would publicly admit it's a thrill and an honor to play with the artists who made our favorite records. What we'd only admit to each other, is that we felt we were talented enough to work with the best in the business.

KISSING ASS

After the Mexico City show in March 2011, I subbed for Phil Bates again in June, July, August, and September. A pattern was developing, and I wasn't complaining. The highlight had to be the Salmon Festival in Grand Falls—

Windsor, Newfoundland—and not because I'm a pescatarian. The bill featured the Orchestra, Smashmouth...and KISS. I have never been a fan of KISS's dumbed-down rock, but there's no disputing the band's astounding commercial success and cultural presence. To be fair, in my more tolerant musical dotage I have softened on certain KISS songs and will admit that "Rock And Roll All Nite" is exquisitely fun and stupid. That's praise, right?

Gordon *loved* KISS. His first-ever concert had been KISS live in Philadelphia when he was seven years old, and he never stopped being a fan. I respected that completely.

At the time of our rendezvous with KISS, Gene Simmons was not only a fire-breathing demon bassist, he was also a reality TV star on the A&E network's *Gene Simmons Family Jewels* (no surprise Simmons would star on a show named after his balls). At Gordon's urging, I had caught a few episodes and learned that Gene's mom had been a Holocaust survivor, and the "SS" in "KISS" represented Gene's revenge on the Nazi SS. That put some perspective on his impressive drive to succeed. I also knew that the season-ending episode left viewers wondering if Gene would finally propose to his partner Shannon Tweed after a twenty-year relationship and two kids. Gordon could barely contain himself. "He's GOT to ask her!" I loved Gordon's devotion.

If that wasn't enough, there was Eric Troyer's history with Gene Simmons and Paul Stanley. In the early '70s, Eric hung out with both guys before they formed KISS. Gene had even queried Eric about forming a new band. Eric declined, confident his musical destiny lay elsewhere. It's fun to imagine Eric's makeup had he joined KISS. Alongside Starchild, Catman, the Demon, and Spaceman, maybe Eric could've been "Helpful Menonite Man" with a hammer on his forehead and a nail through his lip? Just spitballing here, folks.

As fired up as we were to play with KISS, we almost didn't make it. We ended up stranded in St. John's, New Brunswick, with no way to get to Newfoundland. Eric resignedly called the promoter and told him we weren't going to arrive in time. The promoter's response was, "Hold on! I'll call you back in ten minutes." Just like that, the promoter managed to book a tiny, six-seat plane for us, our bags, and gear. We were relieved and scared to death. Rock bands and small planes: not our favorite combo.

Gordon, Glen, Eric, and I sat behind the two pilots. We watched our takeoff through the front windshield. When the little plane wasn't jolting side to side in the wind (terrifying), it was a cool trip. We flew slower than 200 mph, and not very high, so we had a clear view of the coastal scenery beneath us.

Our terror of small planes receded a bit, and we got back to the subject of KISS. At one point in our conversation, Eric suddenly let out a groan. Gordon, his interest piqued, asked, "*What?*"

With a sad chuckle, Eric responded, "I just remembered, I still haven't completely paid Gene back some money he loaned me back in the '70s."

Gordon, Glen, and I convulsed with laughter, delighted by this new plot point.

Gordon said, "He's not gonna ask you for it, is he?"

Eric said, "He will *absolutely* ask me about it. I bet you a thousand bucks he brings it up." I guess Gene didn't get rich by losing track of his debtors. We had to ask Eric, "How much do you still owe him?" Eric said, "It's not even that much. It's like sixteen-hundred bucks…but he never forgets stuff like that."

We landed not at an airport, but on a bumpy strip of asphalt surrounded by thick brush. We were met by a van. Our driver told us the festival was going well…at least I think that's what he said. His Newfie accent was spectacular, a kind of Irish/English old-world mishmash. We drove through windblown, scrub-covered countryside until we were suddenly among a sea of fans, all headed on foot toward the huge festival stage. Our van reached the backstage area and Gordon yelled, "Oh, my God! Look!" Four black KISS costumes were hanging limply in a tall, open road case. Gordon said, "That's amazing…" This was gonna be fun.

We decided to check out Operation Kiss. Behind the stage we found a dozen 4 x 4 speaker cabinets. Instead of "Marshall" or "Hiwatt" they had "KISS" logos on the front, and all the cabinets were empty. They were just stage props, to be stacked behind KISS to form an illusory wall of amps. I totally got it. Every drawing of a band in my ninth-grade notebooks included enormous stacks of speaker cabinets. Of course, in the old days before adequate PA systems, bands like the Who, Cream, Blue Cheer, and Black Sabbath would play through *real* stacks of amps and speakers to get their sound across. (Tinnitus, anyone?) Nowadays, any size amp will do. You just stick a mic on it and crank it through the PA system.

Gordon and I found Eric sitting with Gene Simmons at a picnic table outside Gene's trailer. Gene sported a purple paisley button-down shirt and dyed-black hair spilling from beneath a "FT Hood TX Armor" baseball hat. Eric introduced us to Gene. "This is our guitarist, Hux." Gene shook my hand and said, "Pleased to meet me." Badda boom. Henny Youngman lives.

Chapter 20: Thank You Bethesda

Gene was perfectly as ease shooting the shit with us, but, at one point, he went on a heated anti-Michael Jackson rant, railing about Jackson's bizarre and well-documented relations with underage children. This was not exactly news, and more to the point, Michael Jackson had been dead for two years, passing away under controversial circumstances. That didn't matter to Gene, who was all fired up and acting as if he were preparing to grill Jackson in court. Not sure why that was the topic of the day.

Finally, the subject drifted back to those present, and right on cue, Gene said to Eric, "Hey, you gonna pay me that money you owe me?" Gordon and I tried not to guffaw, but Eric wasn't surprised and took it calmly. I learned later that Eric, on Gene's suggestion, sent a check for $1,600 to the Wounded Warriors charity, a thoughtful resolution on Gene's part.

Soon after arriving, we were dressed and onstage for a line-check. Unlike a sound check, a line-check merely confirms that all the equipment is *plugged-in and working*. It's not a confirmation that the gear *sounds good*. Such is the case at most festivals. We were dead tired from travel and nervous about getting rained on, but we confidently knocked out a performance that won over a crowd looking to bang heads with KISS. Paul Stanley watched our whole show from the side of the stage with a big grin on his face. It looked like he was genuinely thrilled to watch his old pal Eric sounding so good. When we finished our set and walked off, Paul and Eric bearhugged and Paul couldn't say enough nice things about how great the band sounded. What a cool guy. I was starting to get a picture of the yin and yang personalities driving KISS.

I came away impressed by the KISS operation. The crew were all in great spirits and worked easily together, an indication they were treated well by their bosses. Gene and Paul hung out in bathrobes with towels over their shoulders. They still applied their own makeup after all these years. They hobnobbed with fans who'd purchased backstage access and, once in full costume, posed in a photographer's tent with hundreds of fans for at least an hour. KISS put in a full day's work before they even hit the stage. Admirable.

Gordon and I chatted with KISS manager Doc McGhee, an industry heavyweight whose other clients included Bon Jovi, Motley Crue, and Hootie. We were a little surprised that Doc had ventured out to a gig in Newfoundland, but he seemed right in his element. Doc asked if we were sticking around for the show. We said, "Wouldn't miss it." It suddenly began to pour, and Doc was kind enough to have one of his guys escort me and Gordon to the tent that covered the front-of-house mix engineer. A nice gesture, and Gordon and I had the best view in the house.

Just before showtime, a dozen VIPs ducked into our tent, including a six-foot tall, drop-dead gorgeous woman who stood right next to me. "Hi," she said. "I'm Shannon. Want some gum?" Yeah, so, Gordon and I, of course, watched the KISS show with Shannon Tweed, the star of *Family Jewels*. She was disarmingly friendly, without a whiff of entitled star on her at all, which figures: she's Canadian. Shannon was funny, too. At one point, she said, "Oh, the band hates this song, but they have to play it." Gordon and I stayed cool for most of the night, chatting easily with Ms. Tweed and enjoying the wiz-bang theatrics and pyrotechnics lighting up the stage. Toward the end of the night, fanboy Gordon couldn't contain himself any longer. He leaned across me and asked, "So, Shannon…is Gene gonna propose or not?!"

Shannon was not about to give away a reality show plotline. "Oh, you'll have to wait and see…" Total pro.

WHAT GOES AROUND

I subbed for Phil again in August, September, and October. I began to feel like I was back in the band. I got along especially well with the newest new guy, bassist and singer Glen Burtnik. Glen and I are roughly the same age, and he grew up in New Jersey, like I had before I moved to Greece. I mused, if I'd stayed in Jersey, would I have ended up like Glen? I guess it doesn't matter since I ended up like him, anyway. Our musical tastes aligned almost perfectly, and we had a knack for referencing all the same rock 'n' roll historical info. If I had trouble coming up with an obscure band name, Glen usually could, and vice versa.

In October 2011, the Orchestra calendar included dates in Punta Del Este, Santiago, and Buenos Aries. The itinerary was nearly identical to my maiden voyage with ELO Part II in 1999. I didn't want to get greedy, but I would've loved playing Uruguay, Chile, and Argentina again.

Alas, Phil did the gigs, but the consequences of his trip to South America were far more serious than me missing out on a bit of nostalgia. On their final night in Punta Del Este, a van waited to take the Orchestra from their hotel to the show. Instead of taking an elevator, Phil chose to exit the hotel by hopping down several flights of poorly lit stairs. He misjudged a step, landed awkwardly, and shattered his ankle. Our sound engineer Scott Harrison found him in the stairwell, barely able to walk. The van took Phil to a clinic, and Eric called the promoter to cancel the show.

Fortunately, the promoter wasn't upset. He simply announced to the audience that the gig would happen the next night. The easygoing beach crowd at Punta was fine with that. The bad news was that Phil's ankle was diagnosed with multiple fractures and some internal bleeding. Phil declined to have surgery, preferring to get it done in England. The internal bleeding would make flying risky, but Phil insisted. The clinic ended up just wrapping Phil's ankle as tightly as possible. The next night, with his foot up on a chair, Phil gamely played the rescheduled gig and flew home the following day.

Shortly after returning to England, Phil decided his broken ankle and inability to fly equated to his break from the band, and for a second time, he quit.

YOU'LL NEVER GUESS WHO...

The Orchestra was gearing up for a month-long tour of Eastern Europe beginning November 6, 2011. With Phil Bates out of the picture, they were in a tough spot. I'd happily subbed for Phil roughly once a month over the previous year, but his official departure changed things drastically. Eric called and asked if I would be interested in coming back full-time and starting things off with a month away from home? The tour would take the band to Poland, Lithuania, Belarus, Ukraine, and Russia. I was excited, but also hesitant to commit. A lot had changed for the better in the Huxley household during the four years I'd been away, and I didn't want to jeopardize our gains. That said, Helle didn't hesitate to support my return to the band. She knew that performing and spending time with the guys made me happy, and we both understood that a part of my identity was wrapped up in the legacy of ELO Part II and the Orchestra. The paycheck wasn't bad, either, especially for a job that wasn't a *real* job. Finally, what was the band gonna do if I said "No"? *Rehearse somebody new*? God forbid. Four years after painfully leaving a band I loved, I was officially back in the Orchestra—my home away from home.

EPILOGUE
BACK IN THE FOLD

Since my official return to the Orchestra for the 2011 East European Tour, I've performed with the band 239 times in 28 countries. We've played some stunning locales, including Norway, Chile, Ecuador, Italy...but at the top of the list are three festival shows in New Zealand on a bill with Alanis Morrisette and Colin Hay from Men at Work. We played to more than ten-thousand fans at each stunning outdoor setting. I'd wanted to put my eyes on New Zealand since I was a kid, and "Scotland in the South Pacific" did not disappoint. I recommend you visit, but only if you like snowcapped mountains, endless waterfalls, pristine rivers, and friendly people.

On March 23, 2024, I played my 500th show with ELO Part II/the Orchestra. More ambitious touring bands can bang out 500 shows in just a couple years, but not us. We average about twenty-five gigs per year. Instead of the usual theater-and-club circuit in the States, we'll travel to places like El Salvador, the Canary Islands, Dubai, Israel, Chile, Ecuador, Slovakia, etc. Fewer shows, but more adventures. With all the off time, I'm able to be with my family and work on my own records, too. Would I like to play more shows with the Orchestra? Sure. Do I want to stick my nose into the booking agency business? *No*.

ELO: WITH OR WITHOUT YOU

There's an ELO culture war that sometimes flares up on the internet. I try not to pay it much attention, but here's the gist. On one side, staunch fans of Jeff Lynne consider him to have been 100 percent responsible for ELO, as if the band had been a sixteen-year-long solo project. After all, the argument goes, he wrote the songs, produced the records, and sang lead vocals. Without Jeff, there is no ELO.

It's not a terrible argument.

Other fans of ELO acknowledge Lynne's primary contribution, but also appreciate Bev Bevan's thunderous drumming, Mik Kaminski's peerless violin playing, Lou Clark's beyond-gorgeous string arrangements, Hugh McDowell's skills as a cellist and stage performer, Richard Tandy's creative keyboard contributions, Kelly Groucutt's superb bass playing and deft vocal harmonies, and other contributions from the many musicians who spent time in ELO. Fans on this side believe ELO wouldn't have sounded like ELO without the other band members. It's also not a terrible argument.

Whether you prefer the band vibe or the single-genius theory, I think we all can agree that Lynne is one of the most important creators of twentieth-century rock music. I have played "Evil Woman," "Do Ya," "Mr. Blue Sky," "Can't Get It Out Of My Head," "Showdown," and so on hundreds and hundreds of times and I have yet to grow tired of his music. That is one of the highest compliments I can give any writer.

APOSTROPHE OR POSSESSIVE?

In September 2014, after being goaded on-air by London deejay Chris Evans to play live, Jeff Lynne performed in front of 50,000 fans as part of the Festival in a Day concert in Hyde Park, London. Accompanied by one former member of ELO, pianist Richard Tandy, members of Brit pop group Take That, the BBC Concert Orchestra, as well as some pre-recorded strings, Lynne's return went over big time. It must've been a fun gig for Lynne, because fifteen years after acquiring the rights to "ELO" he suddenly got the tour bug again and hit the road as "Jeff Lynne's ELO." It's unclear if the apostrophe after his name is intended to be a contraction for "is" or act as a simple possessive, but Lynne's attachment of *his* name to *the* name did all of us a favor. It's very clear that "Jeff Lynne's ELO" and "the Orchestra" are two different bands.

Unlike the ill-fated *Zoom* tour, Lynne's second attempt at an ELO comeback was timed perfectly. Tickets quickly sold out at huge arenas in the U.S. and Europe. Lynne's set list is, unsurprisingly, nearly identical to ours, but Jeff Lynne's ELO and the Orchestra present two very different concert experiences. I haven't seen Lynne's live show, but Richard Stoeger, a music writer for New York's *ROCK NYC*, saw both bands and offered his thoughts.

Stoeger pointed out that Lynne's show is built for arenas, with giant video screens, hundreds of lights, and a massive sound system. He saw Jeff Lynne's ELO from the nosebleed seats at Madison Square Garden and, while appreciating the spectacle, didn't feel connected to the artist. He pointed out that the Orchestra's show is scaled to theaters (we sell fewer tickets) with the audience closer to the performers. I think Stoeger appreciated that we sound like a band that has played together for years and sport a range of engaging personalities on stage. Stoeger's August 23, 2018, headline read:

Epilogue: Back in the Fold

Jeff Lynne's ELO At MSG: The Orchestra Next Time
The next time I want to drench myself in ELO's amazing discography, I will go and find really great seats for the Orchestra. Musically, they are more ELO-like than Jeff Lynne's latest performance at the Garden. If you don't give a rat's ass about the light show, then find yourself great seats for the Orchestra.

As much as I appreciate Mr. Stoeger's take, and I do, I would note that an advantage of seeing Jeff Lynne's ELO is that you get to witness the writer, producer, and singer of this amazing music. I'm sure that's a bucket-list item for most ELO lovers. In July, 2025, fans will have a chance to catch Jeff Lynne's ELO in England on the Over and Out tour.

The Orchestra's 2025 calendar includes the Rock and Romance Cruise, plus dates in Florida, Pennsylvania, and Chile.

…COMES AROUND

In spring of 2024, Jeff Lynne's ELO played a benefit show called Vets Aid in San Diego. I'm sure they sounded great, because mixing the band was none other than Simon Hodge, ELO Part II's former monitor man. No doubt Simon was wearing shorts, but I'll have to ask if he put Jeff's guitarist through the Hodgenizer.

LOU CLARK

From 1974 to 2021, Lou Clark arranged strings for ELO, ELO Part II and the Orchestra. Lou was the secret sauce that helped turn ELO's hits into timeless classics. I'm honored to have received the Clark treatment on my songs "Jewel And Johnny", "Over London Skies" and "Can't Wait To See You." His arrangements take my breath away with every listen. Sadly, Lou passed away February 13, 2021, after a long struggle with various ailments. There's no doubt he was a genius and one of the kindest, most gentle persons I've ever had the pleasure to know. His son, Louis Clark Jr. began performing as cellist, guitarist, and conductor with the Orchestra in April 2015, happily sharing the stage with his legendary dad for five years. Louis Jr. has now assumed Lou Sr.'s spot in the Orchestra. We miss Lou like crazy, but the Clark legacy is alive and well.

THE HILLIS IS ALIVE WITH THE SOUND OF MUSIC

Like most musicians, Orchestra bass player Glen Burtnik suffers from Gig Insecurity Syndrome, a difficult-to-treat malady which causes us to never turn down an offer to play. Besides the Orchestra, Glen performs with his proto-Beatles/original music group the Weeklings, high-bar cover band Max Weinberg's Jukebox, Beatles cover band Liverpool, and more. He's an in-demand guy. Glen's busy calendar nudged us to find a substitute bassist for the rare times Glen's commitments conflicted with the Orchestra schedule. Gordon suggested we bring in Cliff Hillis, a Pennsylvania-based power-pop multi-instrumentalist and singer. Good choice. Cliff nailed Glen's parts beautifully and, in fact, has fit in so well that we now bring him on the road as a seventh member in *addition* to Glen. Cliff gives us a fourth singer and second guitarist, making the Orchestra sound even better than the high bar we established as a six-piece.

Welcome, Cliff!

PRETTY GOOD FOR AMERICANS

Nowadays the Orchestra features Mik Kaminski on violin; Eric Troyer on keys, guitar and vocals; myself on guitar and vocals; and Gordon Townsend on drums. The four of us have been together since 2000, excepting my sabbatical. The "new guys" include Glen Burtnik (2009), Louis Clark Jr. (2015) and Cliff Hillis (2018). Our band has five Americans and two Brits. We're like an old Bentley with 71 percent AAMCO replacement parts. It's not the same car, but it still runs great.

SEASONED STARS

When I was in Rick Rock, riding my nine months of band buzz in the early '80s, we opened twice for the Romantics. Rick Rock was pretty good, but the Romantics were hitmakers on a different professional level. In 2019, I befriended Romantics guitarist Wally Palmar onboard the On the Blue Cruise. Wally generously told our shipmates that "Hux and I used to do shows together." HA! That is *not* the way it was. Wally was a star. I led the little local band that opened for him. But I love Wally's perspective.

I met Al Stewart on a rock cruise, and we had some interesting, long conversations. He remembered walking by a record shop on the Sunset Strip back in the '70s. His album *Year of the Cat* was displayed in the store window. A sign said, "500,000 record buyers can't be wrong." Al said, "Imagine how nice *that* felt." Al is a bit of a wine connoisseur. A Chardonnay he shared with me is in the running for the best thing I've tasted in my entire life. He even gave me a quote to help market my album *This Is the One*. Generous guy. His otherworldly songs "Year of the Cat," "Time Passages," and many others still sound brilliant today. Alan Parsons's production didn't hurt.

Speaking of Alan Parsons, the Orchestra played a bunch of gigs with his band, the Alan Parsons Live Project. On one particular rock cruise, his lead singer (and my friend) P.J. Olsson wasn't able to attend. Alan asked me to learn the vocal for "Don't Let It Show" from the album *I Robot*. I didn't know the song, and it took me the better part of two days to study the lyrics and familiarize myself with the melody. I sang it on two different nights in front of Alan's adoring audience. Word was that I did a good job, but I know that at least once I sang "Don't let it...*GOOOOOO!*" Oops. Maybe a cymbal crash covered up my goof.

It's gratifying when legends turn out to be fun people. Roger Daltrey struck me as a salt-of-the-earth guy when our bands both played the Moody Blues Cruise, and he delivered one of the greatest rock 'n' roll punchlines I've ever heard. One night a bunch of us were hanging out backstage. Roger had invited us into his dressing room, saying, "Come on in, boys, for Godssake I don't wanna drink alone." When we were done hanging out, Orchestra drummer Gordon Townsend stood with Roger for a picture, draping his arm around Roger's shoulders. Gordon was shocked by the 70-year-old singer's physique. Gordon exclaimed, "Jesus, Roger! You're all muscle!"

Cool as a con man, Roger said, "Well I *should be* after carrying the Who for fifty years." Boom!

GUNS & MCKAGAN

A while after we worked together at Muzak, my friend Bruce McKagan put together a benefit concert for a charitable organization in York, South Carolina. Bruce asked me to team up with his Guns N' Roses brother Duff as musical directors. The band was me on guitar and vocals, Duff on bass and vocals, Boston lead singer Tommy DeCarlo, and drummer Gary Greene from Hootie and the Blowfish. Duff and I hammered out a kick-ass set list. When Duff asked me to sing the Guns N' Roses song "Patience" how could I refuse? Fortunately, the vocal is mostly in Axl's lower range. I studied the song and noticed one funny thing about "Patience," When Axl sings "It'll work itself out *fine*," one acoustic guitarist plays an E major chord and one plays an E minor chord, a brief but noticeable train wreck. I asked Duff about it on one of our phone calls before the show. He good-naturedly said, "We were all drunk!" That would explain it, I agreed. These days, Duff is a clear-eyed unstoppable warrior, author, band leader, husband, father—the whole package. I love the guy. The benefit went down a storm, and can claim to be the first and only performance to feature a *Guns 'n' Blowfish* rhythm section. You shoulda been there.

JOB #1

I've never had a giant, everybody-knows-it, hit song. Maybe this is complete self-delusionary bullshit, but my relative obscurity has probably helped my writing. If Columbia had struck gold in 1988 with "Chance To Be Loved," I'd be forever linked to an oddly arranged song with an '80s sound, and "Chance" would still be in my live set as the number I HAVE to play. All the music I've made after "Chance" would be compared to "Chance" because it would be the one and only easy reference to my sound. No thanks.

Every album I've made since *Sunny Nights* sounds different from the last. I have a sound and a style, yes, but every new song I write is allowed to breathe on its own. That may be why I'm as invested in my music now—in my sixties—as I was in my twenties. I wake up most days with a new piece of music in my head and it excites me to no end that I am free to take it in any direction.

Would I love a hit? Sure, especially at this age and after all the music I've made. That would be a riot. But for now, I'll have to be content with four releases being named "Album of the Year," appearances on various charts, a fan base that steadily buys all my records, and singles like "Just Sayin'" from *This Is the One* that spent a year in rotation at my favorite radio station, WTMD in Towson, Maryland. For people who don't know my stuff, Paul Broucek, President of Warner Bros. Film Music, is curating a "Best of P. Hux" collection that we plan to call *Better Great Than Never*.

IMOGEN

When she was ten, my daughter Immy agreed to be a guest singer at one of my live shows. I asked her what song she'd like to do, and she said without hesitating, "'Someone Like You' by Adele." I gulped. "That's a lot of song to bite off, Boo." She was perfectly confident and stuck to her guns. I said, "Okay, fine. Let's hear your version." She nailed it and I've never doubted her since. She's writing songs on guitar now. Dad brag!

WOMAN REAPPEARS

In 2017, I had the great pleasure of sharing a bill with Damon Johnson's band, Black Star Riders, at a festival in Lahti, Finland. Prior to our show slots, we ditched the gig site and walked for miles around Lahti, catching up on everything that had happened to us since those days in Birmingham writing for Brother Cane's first album. We'd each taken a wild path through classic rock in pursuit of our dreams, me with ELO Part II and the Orchestra, and Damon with Brother Cane, Alice Cooper, Thin Lizzy, Lynyrd Skynyrd, and more. For someone I rarely see, Damon feels like a brother to me. In 2018, twenty-five years after its release, our Brother Cane song "Woman" suddenly showed up on one of my royalty statements with *fourteen million* new streams on Apple. Wow. Was I rich? I received a royalty payment of...$300. Thanks, music business. Looks like I'm still in the financial waiting room.

WHERE ARE THEY NOW?

Bev Bevan was inducted into the Rock & Roll Hall of Fame in 2017, along with Jeff Lynne and Roy Wood. He missed the ceremony due to tour dates with his friend, comedian Jasper Carrott. Bev plays with the Birmingham-based band Quill, which he joined in 2014. He married his Quill bandmate, singer Joy Brain, in 2022.

Anistatia Miller married Jared Brown, a brilliant guy almost as smart as Stashe. The pair of them lecture worldwide on the history of cocktails and have published numerous award-winning books on the subject. As Master Distiller, Jared helped create *Sipsmith Gin*, the first new gin produced in London in over 200 years. They live in the UK.

Rusty Anderson still performs and records with Paul McCartney. It's the undisputed top guitar gig in rock, and head-spinning to think that Rusty has worked with Paul for more than a quarter of the legendary Beatle's life. Couldn't have happened to a better guy.

My old manager **Michael Solomon** is managing director of Penguin Cold Caps, a company that makes hair-saving devices for cancer patients. Michael and I recently reunited in Easton, Pennsylvania, and spent five hours chatting away in the St. Luke Hospital's ER while doctors repaired my broken left hand. Do I know how to have a good time?

After the success of CC Blues King and the invention of the Hector's Greek Grilled Cheese, **Matt Barrett** married his high school crush and created greecetravel.com, a heavily-used travel website where every helpful page is written solely by Matt. He splits his time between Greece and North Carolina.

Former *Star Search* contestant **Rod** (Dash) **Abernethy** has rededicated himself to his first love, solo acoustic guitar. He releases new music, tours, and was the Overall Grand Prize Winner of the 2021 International Acoustic Music Awards.

Don Dixon lives in Ohio with his wife, singer/painter Marti Jones. He continues to write, record, perform, and produce cool music. He appears as touchy rock gossipper Alan Cox-Allen in my *Pandemic Houseguy* videos.

Mitch Easter still produces interesting artists from around the world who seek him out at his Wes Lachot-designed studio in North Carolina, The Fidelitorium.

Mark Everett releases new music and tours the world as eels. We shared a stage in 2023 (first time since the '90s) when eels played the Fillmore in Silver Spring, Maryland, about three miles from my house. I joined the band on their encore, Russ Ballard's "God Gave Rock and Roll to You." It's on YouTube.

The Blazers have performed reunion shows at the Cat's Cradle in recent years, including a third and final show in 2024. **Lee Gildersleeve** fronts the Bad Dog Blues Band, which features his son, Danlee, on scorching guitar. The fruit, the tree, falls not far, etc.

Robin Lane released a beautiful album in 2022 called *Dirt Road to Heaven*. Seek it out. Her voice always captivated me, and it sounds better than ever. **Bruce McKagan** retired from Muzak and spent years serving the underserved in his South Carolina community. He's back in Seattle and writing musicals. **David Kahne** eventually became head of A&R for Columbia. He's indie now, and still producing interesting records while leaving a trail of zen posts on social media. **Kyle Vincent**'s latest releases have found an audience in Japan and the Philippines, where he frequently tours. Young **Dan Rothchild** remains an in-demand bassist/collaborator, working with Heart, Beck, Shakira, Stevie Nicks, Carole King, and many more. With longevity and loyalty as his calling cards, **John Regna** still manages the Orchestra. **Robert Lamm** toured the U.S. in 2024 with Chicago, the band he helped form 57 years ago. **Den York** still works with the Orchestra. **Jen Condos** remains an in-demand bassist on records and on tour. She has played with *everybody*. Finally, my **mom** turned 98 in 2024. She still likes seeing The Orchestra live and enjoys hearing my new music, although after listening to my latest album she did famously say, "I'm not going to listen to this *all the time*, you know." God bless her.

ELECTRIC LIGHT ODYSSEY

COVID canceled fifteen months of the Orchestra's touring schedule. When we finally got some work on the calendar, we rehearsed at Eric's studio in New Jersey. It felt amazing to see each other—Eric, Glen, Cliff and Gordon, the stateside contingent—after being cooped up at home and stuck on Zoom calls for so long. We ran down our show, and about halfway through "Can't Get It Out Of My Head," with its breathtaking chorus, and all of us singing and playing beautifully together, I burst into tears. That moment crystallized how much I had missed being with my funny gang of band dudes, how much I'd missed hearing them play and sing, how much I loved them. After more than a year apart, we were back together to play this beautiful music we'd fought so hard to tour behind...music created by an artist I'd never met in person but whose guitar and vocal parts I knew as well as my own...an artist whose impact on me and the members of my band may never be completely known.

APPENDIX A

LEARNING THE REPERTOIRE

In preparation for my first tours with ELO Part II, I was asked to learn the songs listed here. I have included the albums from which they came.

***ELO* (Titled *No Answer* in U.S.)**
"10538 Overture"

ELO 2
"Roll Over Beethoven"

On the Third Day
"Showdown"
"Ma-Ma-Ma Belle"

Eldorado
"Can't Get It Out Of My Head "

Face the Music
"Evil Woman"
"Strange Magic"
"Fire On High"
"Nightrider"
"Poker"

A New World Record
"Livin' Thing"
"Do Ya"
"Telephone Line"
"Rockaria!"

Out of the Blue
"Turn To Stone"
"Sweet Talkin' Woman"
"Standin' In The Rain"
"Mr. Blue Sky"
"Big Wheels"
"Wild West Hero"

Discovery
"Shine A Little Love"
"Don't Bring Me Down"
"Confusion"
"Last Train To London"
"Diary Of Horace Wimp"
"Midnight Blue"

Xanadu
"All Over The World"
"I'm Alive"
"Xanadu"

Time
"Hold On Tight"
"Twilight"
"Ticket To The Moon"

Secret Messages
"Rock 'n' Roll Is King"

Balance of Power
"Calling America"
"So Serious"
"Getting To The Point"

ELO P2 *Moment of Truth*
"Whiskey Girls"
Medley Of Three Songs:
"Don't Wanna"
"Love Or Money"
"So Glad You Said Goodbye"

Acoustic Set
"Because" (Beatles, *Abbey Road*)
"Nowhere Man" (Beatles *Rubber Soul* UK LP)
"All Fall Down" (From ELO Part II *Live in Australia*)

APPENDIX B

TRAVELS WITH ELO PART II AND THE ORCHESTRA

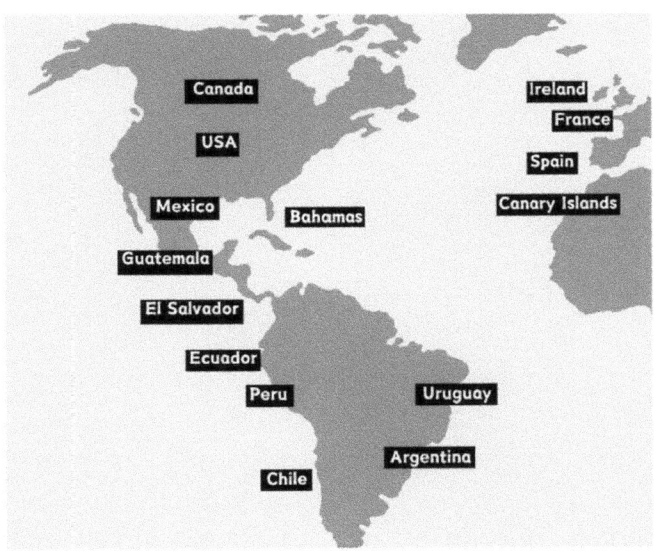

Here are the forty countries where I've performed with ELO Part II and the Orchestra.

APPENDIX C
AMAZON REVIEWS OF *NO REWIND*

David J. Spuria
★★★★★ Done As If It Was the Follow Up To "Out Of The Blue"
Reviewed in the United States on June 17, 2008

"No Rewind" is an amazing foray into the kind of music the Electric Light Orchestra was making in the late 1970's. The production captures the Beatlesque sound that Jeff Lynne successfully co-opted, combined with the orchestral elements that put an original stamp on ELO. The Orchestra may be thought of as a cover band to some, but it contains 3 original ELOers and the pop prowess of Parthenon Huxley who seems as brilliant and creative as Lynne with a certain kind of understated expertise that models the ELO pattern with a kind of authenticity that can't be duplicated by a mere cover band. "Over London Skies" is the sincerest form of flattery with it's honest to goodness replication of all the symphonic elements and pop sensibilities of anything ELO from 1976 to 1982. This is prime time ELO without any pretense. In fact, the pop elements are more consistent on "No Rewind" which means you get a more complete album and not just a couple of singles. This album is fantastic. Can you imagine how "Twist and Shout" could get better? One listen to this over covered classic, and you'll find that this is the best version since John nearly lost his voice! "Can't Wait To See You" is another perfect ELO tune with all the harmonies and lush playing and production eobed by those awesome strings. Of all the 5 star albums I've reviewed, this is the one to listen to. This album was independently produced by extremely smart men who understand the legacy behind their work. "No Rewind" furthers that legacy and even improves upon it. Find and enjoy!

Captain Packrat
★★★★★ **Classic ELO sound**

Reviewed in the United States on April 16, 2009

I'm a big fan of ELO and I've bought all of their albums. Time is one of my favorite albums, and I love the music from the movie Xanadu. In 1988, ELO drummer Bev Bevan left ELO to start his own band, which he called ELO Part II. I bought these albums as well, but was extremely disappointed. It wasn't even close to the old ELO sound. In 2000, Bevan left ELO Part II and sold his share of the ELO name to Jeff Lynne, who then sued ELO Part II over their use of the name. They eventually changed their name to the Orchestra. They have released only a single album so far, No Rewind. It was a limited release and is fairly rare. I recently came across this album being sold on Amazon. Being a packrat and one who can't stand letting a collection go uncompleted, I ordered it. And I was amazed. The album is great! It sounds almost exactly like classic ELO; the style is very reminiscent of Out of the Blue. If I didn't know any better, I'd swear it was some lost album from the 70's. This album is way better than anything ELO Part II ever did, better than Zoom, and is even better than the final few ELO albums like Balance of Power.

CDnut
★★★★★ **A nearly forgotten gem**

Reviewed in the United States on January 28, 2023

My attraction to this CD started with Parthenon Huxley. Having nearly all of his releases he brings a great pop sensibility to everything he does and this exceeds expectations. Many great reviews do it better justice, I just know what is good to these 67 year old ears. Production is crisp and clear, excellent music.

S. O'Toole
★★★★★ **Wow!**

Reviewed in the United States on October 18, 2010

As a longtime ELO fan I've collected all the sidebar projects and the albums by the assorted spinoff groups. ELO Part II was pretty good, no complaints. The Orchestra? Amazing! No, it's not Jeff Lynne but the songwriting is as tight and this, by far, outshines some of Jeff's last efforts (looking at you here "Balance of Power"). It's far more ELO than even "Zoom" (which I like quiet a bit). The band is really tight, the production is fantastic and Eric Troyer can sing circles around most vocalists out there. I miss Bev Bevan but that's simply because he's been one of my favorite drummers for decades, Gordon Townsend is great and Louis Clark's orchestration is magnificent. *No Rewind* is a remarkable achievement. An album that, at once, pays homage to its forefathers and yet takes it beyond. It's not a cheap knock-off, it's a quality package and it's shame the Orchestra never really took off. My hat's off to the whole band. Buy this CD, it won't disappoint if you're being fair to the work and not the Lynne legacy.

Willie F. Jones
★★★★★ Get it!
Reviewed in the United States on April 7, 2019
I have always been a fan on of ELO, then ELO II, and now the Orchestra. They are all a bit different, but it is all really good music. The Orchestra brought back the strings that used to dominate the early ELO stuff. Thank you, Louis Clark, who used to do the arrangements for ELO, and now, does the same for the Orchestra. Unfortunately, this is the only cd that they have released, and since, we have lost the very talented Kelly Groucutt. I have wanted to get this cd for quite some time, but the prices are ridiculous, I guess because it's a limited edition. I got my copy, however, at Parthenonhuxley.com. Mr Huxley is a very integral part of the group, and he signed my copy, and included a guitar pick. If you don't have it already, get it! It's good music!

Mark C. Meyers
★★★★★ Just Like Old Times
Reviewed in the United States on July 19, 2010
For those of you who miss new ELO recordings this should tide you over. This band of 3 ex-ELO members relives the sound of ELO with the emphasis on the string section that was missing in the 80's which was more synthesizer. Vocals are by Eric Troyer and ex ELC basist Kelly Groucutt. Any fan of 60's rock remembers the great cover by ELO with "ROLL OVER BEETHOVEN"

will love this bands version of "TWIST AND SHOUT." It starts off as a slow song and then eventually becomes the fast paced song you remember. Its been 5 years since they recorded a new CD but they still tour Europe extensively, so there's still hope. Eric's voice fits right in, like Jeff Lynne never left. This is the same band that was known as ELO Part II in the 90's but jeff wanted the ELO name for his new release so hence the name change. Kelly and Eric have solo CD's out there as well from the 80's and 90's.

Fan 1
★★★★★ That old Beatle-esque ELO-ish sound in full form
Reviewed in the United States on December 3, 2015
The Orchestra certainly recaptured the sound of the old ELO in a big way. It's a shame Jeff Lynne didn't do that with Zoom and Alone In The Universe. Even though they were good albums they didn't have that old spark of the 70's. The cellos appear only briefly in certain songs and no violins in the background from either album. The Orchestra has plenty of that in their songs which is exactly how ELO is supposed to sound hence the name Electric Light Orchestra. I only hope the Orchestra one day puts out a new album to top this classic and continue the magic.

Philip Leer
★★★★★ Couldn't agree more with these guys!
Reviewed in the United States on October 9, 2009
David's review pretty much sums it up for me: this is an incredible album filled with great songs from start to finish. While both ELO II albums had songs on each that really stood out, there were a few clunkers too; this whole album has NO fillers whatsoever (adding P.Hux was brilliant)! I really enjoyed LEO's (Bleu, Andy Sturmer, et. al.) faithful and fun homage to 70's era ELO ("Alpacas Orgling"), but this album does it even a little bit better. As much as I love the genius of Jeff Lynne, I didn't miss him at all on "No Rewind."

APPENDIX D

EVERY SHOW 1999 – 2024

Here are the 503 (and counting) shows I've played with ELO Part II and the Orchestra.

1999 (59 SHOWS)
February 25-27, 1999 Punte Del Este, Uruguay, Conrad Hotel and Casino (shows #1, 2, 3, 4, 5)
February 28, 1999 Buenos Aries, Argentina, La Movida del Verano summer TV show (6)
March 3, 1999 Antofagasta, Chile, Rock and Soccer Indoor Arena (7)
March 4, 1999 Santiago, Chile, Teatro Monumental (8)
March 14, 1999 Kiev, Ukraine, Palace of Culture (9)
March 16, 1999 Vilnius, Lithuania, Palace of Concerts and Sports (10)
March 19, 1999 Sofia, Bulgaria, National Palace of Culture (NDK Hall 1) (11)
April 7, 1999 Manchester, England, BBC National Lottery Show (12)
April 10, 1999 Toledo, OH, Stranahan Theater (13)
April 11, 1999 Columbus, OH, MEKKA (club) (14)
April 17, 1999 Bronx NY, Lehman Center Lehman College (15)
April 18, 1999 Frazer PA, Maddies Concert Club (16)
April 30, 1999 Croydon, England, Fairfield Halls (17)
May 1, 1999 Oxford, England, Apollo (18)
May 2, 1999 Liverpool, England, Philharmonic Hall (19)
May 5, 1999 Sheffield, England, Sheffield City Hall (20)
May 6, 1999 Nottingham, England, Royal Concert Hall (21)
May 7, 1999 Bristol, England, Colston Hall (22)
May 8, 1999 Bournemouth, England, BIC Windsor Hall (23)
May 10, 1999 Manchester, England, Bridgewater Hall Halle Orchestra (24)
May 11, 1999 Reading, England, The Hexagon (25)
May 13, 1999 Southport, England, Theatre (26)
May 14, 1999 Glasgow, Scotland, Royal Concert Hall (27)
May 15, 1999 Carlisle, England, The Sands Centre (28)

Electric Light Odyssey

May 16, 1999 Edinburgh, Scotland, Edinburgh Festival Hall (29)
May 19, 1999 Truro, England, Hall For Cornwall (30)
May 20, 1999 Cardiff, Wales, St. David's Hall (31)
May 21, 1999 Grimsby, England, Grimsby Auditorium (32)
May 22, 1999 Northampton, England, Royal & Derngate Theatre (33)
May 23, 1999 Leeds, England, Leeds Grand Theatre (34)
May 25, 1999 Southend-on-Sea, England, Cliffs Pavilion (35)
May 26, 1999 Portsmouth, England, Portsmouth Guildhall (36)
May 27, 1999 Eastbourne, England, Congresscentre (37)
May 28, 1999 London, England, Royal Albert Hall (38)
June 18, 1999 Arhus, Denmark, Club Train (39)
June 19, 1999 Esbjerg, Denmark, Esbjerg Rock Festival (40)
June 20, 1999 Oslo, Norway, Rockefellers Club (41)
June 25, 1999 Pittsburgh, PA, Three Rivers Rib and Music Festival (42)
June 26, 1999 Jackson, MS, The Hog Wild Cookoff outdoor show (43)
June 29, 1999 Redondo Beach, CA, Club Caprice (44)
June 30, 1999 Reno, NV, Peppermill Casino (45)
July 2, 1999 Chicago, IL, Skyline Stage at Navy Pier (46)
July 3, 1999 Traverse City, MI, Open Space Concert Series National Cherry Festival (47)
July 4, 1999 Muskegon, MI, Summer Celebration (48)
July 7, 1999 Las Vegas, NV, Fremont Street (49)
July 10, 1999 Walker, MN, Moondance Jam VIII with Cheap Trick (50)
August 6, 1999 Bonn, Germany, Museumplatz Friedrich Ebert Allee (51)
August 8, 1999 Tallinn, Estonia, Tallinn Song Festival Grand Masters of Rock (52)
September 1, 1999 San Antonio, TX, Farwest Rodeo (53)
September 3, 1999 Cumming, GA, Cadillac Ranch (54)
September 4, 1999 Kansas City, MO, Flamingo Hilton (55)
September 5, 1999 La Crosse, WI, Rockin The Ridge Festival (56)
September 6, 1999 Kenner, LA, Treasure Chest Casino (57)
November 12, 13, 1999 Atlantic City, NJ, Copa Room Sands Casino (58, 59)

2000 (43 SHOWS)

January 15, 2000 Corpus Christi, TX , Corpus Christi Symphony Orchestra Selena Auditorium (1)
January 17, 2000 Frazer, PA, Maddies Concert Club (2)

Appendix D: Every Show 1999-2024

January 21, 2000 Henderson, NV, Sunset Station Hotel Casino Two Shows 7pm 9pm (3, 4)
January 22, 2000 Clear Lake, Iowa, Historic Surf Ballroom (5)
January 24, 2000 Suttons Bay, MI, (Near Traverse City) Leelanau Sands Casino Ballroom (6)
March 9, 2000 Uncasville, CT, Mohegan Sun (7)
March 11, 2000 Hallendale, FL, Gulfstream Park Racing and Casino (8)
April 20, 2000 Toledo, OH, Stranahan Theater with orchestra (9)
April 21, 2000 Kenner, LA, Treasure Chest Casino (10)
April 22, 2000 Richardson, TX, with orchestra Greenway Corporate Office Park (11)
April 25, 2000 Biloxi, MS, Casino (12)
April 28, 2000 Robinsonville, MS, Sam's Town Hotel and Gambling Hall (13)
April 29, 2000 Marksville, LA, Mari Center Grand Casino Avoyelles (14)
May 16, 2000 Friant, CA, Table Mountain Casino (15)
May 21, 2000 Tucson, AZ, The New West (16)
May 26, 2000 Warsaw, Poland, International Film and Music Festival at Torwar Hall (17)
May 28, 2000, Jupiter, FL, Roger Dean Stadium (18)
June 1, 2000 Charleston, SC, North Charleston PAC with Charleston Symphony Orchestra (19)
June 3, 2000 St. Francisville, LA, Hemingbough Plantation (20)
July 1, 2000 Cedar Rapids, IA, Freedom Festival Kirkwood Community College (21)
July 2, 2000 St Paul, MN, Taste of Minnesota (22)
July 3, 2000 Arlington Heights, IL, Independence Day Festival (23)
July 6, 2000 Frazer, PA, Maddie's Concert Club (24)
July 8, 2000 Patchogue, NY, Theatre for the Performing Arts (25)
July 14, 2000 Irvine, CA, Orange County Fair with Jose Feliciano (26, 27)
July 15, 2000 Sacramento, CA, Radisson Hotel (28)
July 21, 2000 Madrid, Spain, Castle Courtyard (29)
July 22, 2000 Estepona, Malaga, Spain, Plaza Toros De Estepona (30)
August 24, 2000 Irvine, CA, parking lot by mall, Eric smoked me in bumper car race (31)
August 25, 2000 Springfield, OR, Springfield Filbert Festival Island Park (32)

September 2, 2000 Syracuse, NY, Cole Muffler Court New York State Fair (33, 34)
September 23, 2000 Storrs, CT, Jorgensen Auditorium University of Connecticut (35)
October 21, 2000 Lancaster, CA, Lancaster Performing Arts Center (36)
October 26, 2000 Vejle, Denmark, Vejle-Centret (37)
October 27, 2000 Copenhagen, Denmark, Vega Club (38)
October 28, 2000 Aarhus, Denmark, Musikhuset Aarhus (39)
October 31, 2000 Holstebro, Denmark, Musikteatret HolstebroHallen (40)
November 1, 2000 Aalborg, Denmark, Aalborg Kongres & Kulturcenter (41)
November 4, 2000 Hrdenberg, Netherlands, Podium Club (42)
December 7, 2000 San Salvador, El Salvador, Anfiteatro Feria Internacional (43)

2001 (15 SHOWS)

June 3, 2001 Blue Ash, OH, Blue Ash Towne Square SummerBration (1)
June 7, 2001 Frazer, PA, Maddies Concert Club (2)
June 8, 2001 Big Flats, NY, Tag's Summer Stage with America (3)
June 13, 14 2001 New York, NY, BB King Blues Club (4,5)
June 16, 2001 Falls Church, VA, State Theater (6)
June 22, 2001 Minneapolis, MN, Brewbakers Pub (7)
June 23, 2001 Eagle River, WI, Rockin' the Woods (8)
August 4, 2001 Signal Hill, CA, The Green on the Hill (9)
October 14, 2001 Manchester, England, Bridgewater Hall with Halle Orchestra (10)
October 16, 2001 Cardiff, Wales, St. David's Hall (11)
October 17, 2001 England, Fairfield Halls Royal Philharmonic Concert Orchestra (12)
October 18, 2001 Bournemouth, England, BIC Royal Philharmonic Concert Orchestra (13)
October 19, 2001 Sheffield, England, City Hall Royal Philharmonic Concert Orchestra (14)
October 20, 2001 Nottingham, England, Royal Concert Hall Royal Philharmonic Concert Orchestra (15)

Appendix D: Every Show 1999-2024

2002 (9 SHOWS)
May 10, 2002 Dublin, Ireland, Corporate gig for mobile phone company (1)
May 28, 2002 New York, NY, BB King Blues Club (2,3)
May 29, 2002 Frazer, PA, Maddies Concert Club (4)
May 31, 2002 Falls Church, VA, State Theater (5,6)
June 1, 2002 Towson, MD, Recher Theater (7)
June 2, 2002 Chester, NY, Bodles Opera House (8)
June 22, 2002 Orlando, FL, Lou Perlman's birthday party at Church Street Station (9)

2003 (7 SHOWS)
April 25, 2003 Reno, NV, Hilton Hotel with orchestra and choir World's Biggest Stage (1)
April 26, 2003 Irvine, CA, Hidden Valley Great Escape Festival (2)
July 4, 2003 Cincinnati, OH, Riverfront Park with Blue Öyster Cult (3)
August 15, 2003 Lake of the Ozarks, MO, Horny Toad Club (4)
August 16, 2003 St. Joseph, MO, Civic Center Park "Trails West! 2003" (5)
November 13, 2003 Santiago, Chile, Oz Club 18th Anniversary of Horizonte FM (6)
November 15, 2003 Santiago, Chile, Estacion Mapocho (7)

2004 (9 SHOWS)
July 3, 2004 Junction City, KS, Fort Riley, I think we followed a dog show (1)
July 4, 2004 Lake of the Ozarks, MO, Horny Toad (2)
July 23, 2004 Toledo, OH, Toledo Country Club (3)
July 30, 2004 La Coruna, Spain, Playa de Riazor with Ruben Blades for seventy-thousand concert goers (4)
August 2, 2004 San Javier, Spain, Pecata Minuta music festival in stone amphitheater (5)
August 15, 2004 Dover, DE, Classic Superstars Live at Dover Downs with CSN, Peter Frampton, Creedence Clearwater Revisited, Bo Diddley, Blood Sweat and Tears (6)
August 20, 2004 Vigo, Spain, Playa America (7)
September 25, 2004 Kansas City, MO, Rockhurst H.S. Rose Theatre (8)
November 19, 2004 Torrance, CA, Armstrong Theatre Torrance Cultural Arts Center (9)

Electric Light Odyssey

2005 (16 SHOWS)

January 15, 2005 La Serena, Chile, Florida Mall (1)
January 18, 2005 Santiago, Chile, Casa Piedra (2)
January 20, 2005 Temuco, Chile, Hotel Frontera (3)
January 22, 2005 Pucon, Chile, Gran Hotel (4)
February 4, 2005 Dubai, UAE, Philips Dubai International Jazz Festival with Mike Stern (5)
February 17, 2005 Cordoba, Argentina, PAC (6)
February 18, 2005 Buenos Aries, Argentina, Grand Rex Theater (7)
February 20, 2005 Vina Del Mar, Chile, Vina Del Mar Festival Internacional (8)
February 22, 2005 Vina Del Mar, Chile, Casino (9)
June 4, 5, 2005 Uncasville, CT, Mohegan Sun Wolf Den (10,11)
July 2, 2005 Arlington Heights, IL, Frontier Days Festival (12)
July 23, 2005 Stillwater, MN, Lumberjack Days (13)
November 19, 2005 Grenada, Spain, pop-up beerhall (14)
December 8, 2005 San Salvador, El Salvador, City Park (15)
December 9, 2005 Guatemala City, Guatemala, Grand Tikal Futura Hotel (16)

2006 (49 SHOWS)

February 17, 2006 Valencia, Spain, Sala Heineken Greenspace (1)
February 19, 2006 Castellon, Spain, Auditori i Palacio de Congresos (2)
February 21, 2006 Barcelona, Spain, Luz De Gas Night Club (3)
February 24, 2006 Madrid, Spain, Macumba Club, Plaza Estacion Chamartin (4)
April 27, 2006 St. Petersburg, Russia, Ice Hockey Arena (5)
April 28, 2006 Moscow, Russia, *Star Factory* TV show (*Russian Idol*) (6)
April 28, 2006 Moscow, Russia, Applesin Club (7)
April 29, 2006 Yekaterinburg, Russia, KKT Kosmos Club (8)
April 30, 2006 Ufa, Bashkortostan, Russia, Ogni Ufi Center (9)
May 4, 2006 Hillerod, Denmark, Frederiksborgcentret (10)
May 5, 2006 Naestved, Denmark, Gronnegades Kaserne, Kulturcenter (11)
May 6, 2006 Esbjerg, Denmark, Esbjerg '60s Festival (12)
May 12, 2006 Bradford, England, St George's Hall (13)
May 13, 2006 Ipswich, England, The Regent Theater (14)
May 14, 2006 Margate, England, Winter Gardens (15)
May 16, 2006 Reading, England, The Hexagon (16)

Appendix D: Every Show 1999-2024

May 17, 2006 Hastings, England, White Rock (17)
May 19, 2006 Liverpool, England, Philharmonic Hall (18)
May 20, 2006 Grimsby, England, Auditorium (19)
May 21, 2006 Manchester, England, Opera House (20)
May 23, 2006 London, England, Shepherds Bush Empire (21)
May 24, 2006 Bournemouth, England, Pavillion Theater (22)
May 26, 2006 Brentwood, England, Leisure Centre (23)
May 27, 2006 Oxford, England, New Theatre (24)
May 28, 2006 Torquay, England, Princess Theatre (25)
June 16, 2006 Portsmouth, England, Guildhall (26)
June 17, 2006 Basingstoke, England, The Anvil (27)
June 18, 2006 Birmingham, England, The Alexandra (28)
June 20, 2006 King's Lynn, England, Corn Exchange (29)
June 21, 2006 York, England, Grand Opera House (30)
June 23, 2006 Newcastle, England, City Hall (31)
June 24, 2006 Edinburgh, Scotland, Playhouse (32)
June 25, 2006 Leicester, England, DeMontfort Hall (33)
(Missed Truro & Cardiff shows to attend my dad's funeral)
June 30, 2006 Dartford, England, Orchard Theatre (34)
July 1, 2006 Tunbridge Wells, England, Assembly Hall Theatre (35)
September 23, 2006 Sochi, Russia, City Park (Kelly, Mik did not arrive in time for Sochi show)
September 24, 2006 Krasnodar, Russia, Prestige Hotel Rock and Roll Mansion (36)
September 25, 2006 Perm, Russia, Palace of Culture (37)
September 28, 2006 Yekaterinburg, Russia, Youth Palace (38)
September 29, 2006 Tyumen, Russia, Theater (39)
September 30, 2006 Chelyabinsk, Russia, Theater (40)
October 3, 2006 Kazan, Russia, The Pyramid (41)
October 4, 2006 Samara, Russia, Philharmonic Hall (42)
October 6, 2006 Moscow, Russia, Applesin Club (43)
October 7, 2006 Volgograd, Russia, Theater (44)
November 29, 2006 Kaunas, Lithuania, Kaunas Sport Hall (45)
November 30, 2006 Vilnius, Lithuania, Siemens Arena (46)
December 3, 4, 2006 Santa Cruz de Tenerife, Canary Islands, Auditorio de Tenerife (47, 48)
December 7, 2006 Minsk, Belarus, Palace of Culture (49)

2007 (11 SHOWS)
February 24, 2007 Antofagasta, Chile, Atacama Desert (1)
March 14, 2007 Cannes, France, Tent Gig with Rick Wakeman for UK real estate agents (2)
April 3, 2007 Zacatecas, Mexico, Plaza de Armas Festival Cultural La Jornada (3)
April 7, 2007 Coachella, CA, The Spotlight 29 Casino Showroom (4)
April 14, 2007 Tallinn, Estonia, Linnahall (5)
April 15, 2007 Riga, Latvia, Arena Riga (6)
April 21, 2007 Kaliningrad, Russia, Club gig (7)
June 30, 2007 McKinney, TX, Third Monday Trade Days (site) (8)
July 10, 2007 Colladovillalba, Ayuntamiento, SPAIN, V Festival Internacional de Jazz de Villalba (9)
August 11, 2007 Three Forks, MT, Rockin' the Rivers Festival (10)
Fall 2007 Unsure of date! Santa Fe, NM, Camel Rock Casino (11)

2008 (0 GIGS. I LEFT BAND.)

2009 (0 GIGS. I LEFT BAND.)

2010 (1 SHOW SUBBING FOR PHIL BATES.)
August 27, 2010 Bilbao, Spain, Bosca Vieja (1)

2011 (22 SHOWS. 7 SUBS FOR PHIL BATES, THEN I REJOINED BAND.)
March 28, 2011 Mexico City, Mexico, Auditorio Nacional (1)
June 18, 2011 Emmen, Netherlands, Retropop Festival (2)
July 9, 2011 Grand Falls-Windsor, Newfoundland, Salmon Festival Centennial Field (3)
August 20, 2011 Linz, Austria, Linzer Krone Fest Linz City Festival (4)
September 19, 2011 Farmingham, PA, Nemacolin Woodlands Resort (5)
October 20, 21, 2011 Orlando, FL, Disney EPCOT (6, 7)
November 6, 2011 Minsk, Belarus, Dvorec Respubliki (8)
November 11, 2011 Kaunas, Lithuania, Zalgirio Arena (9)
November 12, 2011 Klaipeda, Lithuania, Svyturio Arena (10)
November 14, 2011 Kiev, Ukraine, Palats Ukraine (11)
November 16, 2011 Poznan, Poland, Hala Arena Poznan (12)
November 17, 2011 Bydgoszcz, Poland, Hala Luczniczka (13)

November 18, 2011 Gdynia, Poland, Hala Gydnia (14)
November 20, 2011 Krakow, Poland, Auditorium Maximum (2 shows) (15, 16)
November 22, 2011 Lodz, Poland, Hala MOSiR (17)
November 23, 2011 Zabrze, Poland, DMiT (18)
November 24, 2011 Wroclaw, Poland, Hala Ludowa (19)
November 26, 2011 Warszawa, Poland, Sala Kongresowa (20)
November 30, 2011 Samara, Russia, Philharmonic Hall of Samara (21)
December 04, 2011 Yekaterinburg, Russia, Youth Palace (22)

2012 (12 SHOWS)
February 17, 2012 Coconut Creek, FL, The Pavillion (1)
February 18, 2012 Boca Raton, FL, The Royal Palm Yacht Club (2)
May 4, 5, 6, 2012 Orlando, FL, EPCOT (3,4,5)
May 12, 2012 Dusseldorf, Germany, City Hall Dusseldorf (6)
June 16, 2012 Purkersdorf, Austria, City Square (7)
July 7, 2012 Spa, Belgium, Heroes Spa Tribute Festival (8)
August 12, 2012 Littleton, CO, The Hudson Gardens (9)
August 18, 2012 Bratislava, Slovakia, Castle Devin (10)
August 25, 2012 Lewiston, Idaho, Hot August Nights Pioneer Park (11)
November 24, 2012 Feldkirchen, Austria, Stadt Saal (City Hall) (12)

2013 (31 SHOWS)
February 2, 2013 Rome, Italy, RAI TV Show *I Migliori Anni* (1)
April 19, 2013 Punta Del Este, Uruguay, Conrad Resort and Casino Ballroom (2)
April 26-28, 2013 Orlando, FL, EPCOT (3,4,5)
May 4, 2013 Bayreuth, Germany, Maisel Brauerei KG (Maisel's Weiss Beer Fest) (6)
May 15, 2013 Mexico City, MX, Auditorio Blackberry VIP en Pista (7)
May 16, 2013 Monterrey, MX, Auditorio Luis Elizondo, ITESM (8)
May 17, 2013 Guadalajara, MX, Auditorio Telmex Guadalajara (9)
May 19, 2013 McAllen, TX, McAllen Civic Center Auditorium (canceled)
June 2, 2013 Littleton, CO, The Hudson Garden and Event Center (10)
June 21, 2013 Hamar, Norway, Strandgateparken Hamar Music Festival (11)
June 28, 2013 Yorkshire Dales, England, Grassington Festival, Festival Marquee (12)

July 23, 2013 Massapequa Park, New York, John J. Burns Town Park (13)
August 3, 2013 La Junta, CO, Potter Park, Music at the Junction (14)
August 8, 2013 Hualpen, Chile, SurActiva Gran Salon (15)
August 9, 2013 Santiago, Chile, Centro Cultural Teatro la Cupula (16)
August 10, 2013 Antofagasta, Chile, Centro de Eventos Rock & Soccer Antofagasta (17)
August 11, 2013 La Serena, Chile, Plaza de Armas de La Serena (18)
August 16, 2013 Berlin, Germany, Kosmos KG (19)
August 18, 2013 Henley, England, Henley Rewind Festival (20)
August 24, 2013 Minneapolis, MN, The Epic Event Center (21)
November 1, 2013 Prague, Czech Republic, Prague Congress Centre (22)
November 3, 2013 St. Petersburg, Russia, Gorky Palace of Culture (23)
November 4, 2013 Moscow, Russia, Crocus City Hall (24)
November 5, 2013 Chelyabinsk, Russia, Palace of Culture CTZ (25)
November 7, 2013 Ufa, Bashkortostan, Russia, Ogni Ufi. Magazal Coliseo (26)
November 9, 2013 Gdynia, Poland, Sports Arena Gdynia (27)
November 10, 2013 Poznan, Poland, Poznan Congress Center Sala Siemia (Earth Hall) (28)
November 14, 2013 Lublin, Poland, Hala Globus Mori Lublin (29)
November 30, 2013, Calgary, Alberta, Canada, Southern Alberta Jubilee Auditorium, The Canadian Legacy Project (30)
December 7, 2013 Guayaquil, Ecuador, Teatro Centro de Arte de Guayaquil Fundacion Teleton Por la Vida (31)

2014 (28 SHOWS)

January 30, 2014 Clearwater, FL, Ruth Eckerd Hall (1)
February 1, 2014 Ft. Pierce, FL, Sunrise Theater (2)
February 13, 2014 Hollywood, FL, Hard Rock Live (3)
February 22, 2014 Metarie, LA, Family Gras (4)
February 28, 2014 Sheffield, England, The Plug (5)
March 1, 2014 Dundee, Scotland, Fat Slim's Live (6)
March 2, 2014 Inverness, Scotland, The Ironworks (7)
March 15, 2014 Eagle River, WI, Lake of the Torches Resort Casino (8)
March 16, 2014 St. Charles, IL, Arcada Theater (9)
March 21, 22, 23, 2014 Orlando, FL, EPCOT (10, 11, 12)
April 2-6, 2014 Miami, FL, to Cayman Island, Moody Blues Cruise II (13, 14)

Appendix D: Every Show 1999-2024

May 3, 2014 Greiz, Germany, Vogtlandhalle (15, 16)
June 14, 2014 Albuquerque, NM, Isleta Casino Showroom (17)
July 12, 2014 Los Angeles, CA, Pershing Square (18)
July 20, 2014 Rochester, NY, w/ John Fogerty and Dave Mason (19)
July 25, 2014 Park City, UT, Deer Valley Amphitheater (20)
August 2, 2014 Sydney, Nova Scotia, Canada, Concerts on the Dock (21)
August 20, 2014 Elgin, IL, Festival Park w/Deep Purple (22)
August 22, 2014 Chautauqua, NY, Chautauqua Institution (23)
August 23, 2014 Cleveland, OH, Masonic Auditorium (24)
August 24, 2014 Toronto, Canada, CNE Bandshell (25)
September 5, 2014 Atlantic City, NJ, Golden Nugget (26)
October 13, 14, 2014 Linz, Austria, Voestalpine Steel Factory (27)
December 27, 2014 Park City, UT, Silver Queen Ball 2014 Deer Valley Resort (28)

2015 (34 SHOWS)

April 3-5, 2015 Orlando, FL, EPCOT (1, 2, 3)
April 9, 2015 Ft. Pierce, FL, Sunrise Theater (4)
April 10, 2015 Clearwater, FL, Ruth Eckerd Hall (5)
April 11, 2015 Jacksonville, FL, Florida Theater (6)
April 17, 2015 St. Charles, IL, Arcada Theater (7)
April 18, 2015 Osceola, IA, Lakeside Hotel Casino (8)
May 8, 2015 Quapaw, OK, Downstream Casino (9)
May 14, 2015 Buenos Aires, Argentina, Teatro Gran Rivadavia (10)
May 15, 2015 Santiago, Chile, Teatro Caupolican (11)
May 23, 2015 Louisville, KY, Abbey Road OTR (12)
May 24, 2015 Manistee, MI, Little River Casino (13)
May 29, 2015 Lancaster, CA, Performing Arts Center (14)
July 25, 2015 Scone Palace, Scotland, Rewind Festival (15)
July 28, 29, 2015 Tel Aviv, Israel, Hanger 11 (16, 17)
July 30, 2015 Tel Aviv, Israel, Charles Bronfman Auditorium (18)
July 31, 2015 Haifa, Israel, Congress Center (19)
August 2, 2015 Seebron, Germany, Rock of Ages (20)
August 4, 2015 Tallinn, Estonia, Nordea Kontserdimaja (21)
August 5, 7, 2015 Helsinki, Finland, Kulttuuritalo (22)
August 9, 2015 Sant Feliu de Guixols, Spain, Outdoor Festival, in the rain (23)
August 17, 2015 Nashville, TN, Grand Ol' Opry (24)
September 18, 2015 Mason, OH, Year Long Bicentennial Celebration (25)

September 26, 2015 Shippensburg, PA, Luhrs Center (26)
September 27, 2015 Huntington, NY, The Paramount (27)
October 2, 2015 Danville, KY, Norton Center for the Arts (28)
October 3, 2015 Lake Charles, LA, Golden Nugget (29)
November 5, 2015 Washington, DC, Fight Night (30)
November 8, 2015 Uncasville, CT, Mohegan Sun Arena (31)
November 12, 2015 Warsaw, Poland, Arena Ursynow (32)
November 13, 2015 Krakow, Poland, ICE Krakow Congress Centre (32)
November 15, 2015 Poznan, Poland, Sala Ziemi (33)
November 21, 2015 Miami, FL, Magic City Casino (34)

2016 (26 SHOWS)

January 2, 2016 Atlantic City, NJ, Resorts Casino (1)
January 16, 2016 Quapaw, OK, Downstream Casino (2)
January 29, 2016 Las Vegas, NV, Golden Nugget Casino 52 Fridays (3)
February 14, 2016 Mizner Park, FL, Mizner Park Amphitheater (4)
February 26-March 1, 2016 Miami, FL, Moody Blues Cruise III (our second) (5, 6)
March 4-6, 2016 Orlando, FL, EPCOT (7, 8, 9)
May 13, 2016 St. Charles, IL, Arcada Theater (10)
May 14, 2016 Cincinnati, OH, Mount St. Josephs University (11)
May 21, 2016 Culiacan, Sinaloa, Mexico, Cultural Festival of University (12)
July 24, 2016 Valencia, Spain, Concert in Park (13)
July 25, 2016 Barcelona, Spain, BARTS (14)
July 26, 2016 Madrid, Spain, Concert in Park (15)
July 30, 2016 Avila, Spain, Musicos en la Naturaleza (16)
August 6, 2016 Mallorca, Spain, Yacht Harbor Port Adriano (17)
August 18, 2016 Millville, NJ, Levoy Theater (18)
August 20, 2016 Ocean Grove, NJ, Camp Meeting Association Grand Auditorium (19)
August 21, 2016 Parkersburg, WVa, City Homecoming Celebration (20)
August 27, 2016 Jacksonville, FL, Florida Theater (21)
August 28, 2016 Orlando, FL, The Plaza Live, site of tragedy (22)
October 22, 2016 Newark, OH, Midland Theatre (23)
December 3, 2016 Wilmington, DE, Grand Opera House (24)
December 10, 2016 London, England, Private Show (25)
December 29, 2016 Uncasville, CT, Mohegan Sun (26)

Appendix D: Every Show 1999-2024

2017 (26 SHOWS)
January 14, 2017 Clearwater, FL, Ruth Eckerd Hall (1)
January 28, 2017 Easton, PA, State Theater (2)
February 6, 2017 The Villages, FL, Savannah Center (3)
March 12-16, 2017 Cozumel, Mexico; Key West, FL; Ft Lauderdale, FL, Rock and Romance Cruise (4, 5)
March 23, 2017 Haifa, Israel, Congress Center (6)
March 24-25, 2017 Tel Aviv, Israel, Charles Bronfman Auditorium (7, 8)
March 26, 2017 Jerusalem, Israel, Henry Crown Hall, Jerusalem Theatre (9)
April 20-23, 2017 Orlando, FL, EPCOT (10, 11, 12, 13)
July 8, 2017 Lecben, Austria, Outdoor City Festival with Slade, Nazareth (14)
July 12, 2017 Slupski, Poland, Rock Legends Festival, Dolina Charlotty Resort, 10,000 seat Outdoor Amphitheater. Hung out with Rick Wakeman. Yes played the day after we did (15)
July 15, 2017 Lahti, Finland, outdoor town square concert with Black Star Riders (Damon Johnson), Hanoi Rocks (16)
August 6, 2017 Cheshire, England, Rewind NORTH (17)
August 19, 2017 Brookville, NY, Tilles Center, Long Island University with Orleans and Al Stewart (18)
August 25, 2017 Lancaster, PA, American Music Theater (19)
August 26, 2017 Florence, IN, Belterra Casino (20)
September 30, 2017 Morristown, NJ, Mayo Performing Arts Center (21)
November 10, 2017 St. Charles, IL, Arcada Theater (22)
November 12, 2017 Clinton, NJ, River Town Film Festival (23)
December 2, 2017 Naples, FL, Gross wedding still lots of hurricane damage (24)
December 15, 2017 Monticello, Chile, Gran Arena Chile (25)
December 16, 2017 Vina Del Mar, Chile, Valparaiso Sporting Club (26)

2018 (22 SHOWS)
January 2–7, 2018 Grand Cayman, Cozumel, Mexico, Moody Blues Cruise "Sur La Mer" with Darian Sahanaja and Zombies, Al Stewart, Alan Parsons Live Project with whom I sang "Don't Let It Show." The Orchestra closed the cruise (1, 2)
January 11, 2018 The Villages, FL, Savannah Center (3)
January 12, 2018 Jacksonville, FL, Florida Theater (4)

January 20, 2018 Queenstown, New Zealand, Winery Festival 10,000 people (5)
January 27, 2018 Taupo, New Zealand, another 10,000 people (6)
January 28, 2018 Whitianga, New Zealand, and yet another 10,000 people (7)
February 9, 2018 Easton, PA, State Theater (8)
February 10, 2018 Wilmington, DE, Opera House (9)
March 30-April 2, 2018 Orlando, FL, EPCOT (10, 11, 12, 13)
June 9, 2018 Emmen, Netherlands, Retropop Festival with Bryan Ferry and Bananarama (14)
June 28, 2018 Annapolis, MD, Rams Head on Stage (15, 16)
June 29, 2018 Atlantic City, NJ, Starlight Theater (17)
June 30, 2018 Englewood, NJ, Bergen PAC (18)
August 18, 2018 Henley-on-Thames, England, Rewind South Festival (19)
September 8, 2018 Huntington, NY, Paramount Theater (20)
September 9, 2018 Clinton, NJ, River Town Film Festival (21)
November 10, 2018 St. Charles, IL, Arcada Theater (22)

2019 (29 SHOWS)

February 4, 5, 2019 Tel Aviv, Israel, Charles Bronfman Auditorium (1, 2)
February 10 -15, 2019 Nassau Bahamas, Haiti, On the Blue Cruise, loved seeing Wishbone Ash (3, 4, 5)
February 15, 2019 Immokalee, FL, Seminole Casino Hotel (6)
March 2, 2019 Easton, PA, State Theater (7)
March 13, 2019 Lake Lucerne, Switzerland, Hotel Schweizerhof Retro Festival (8)
March 15, 2019 Lincoln, RI, Stadium Theater (9)
March 27–30, 2019 Cozumel, Mexico, Rock & Romance Cruise with Boz Scaggs, Peter Asher, War (10, 11)
April 4, 2019 Lancaster, PA, American Music Theater (12)
April 27–30, 2019 Orlando, FL, EPCOT (13, 14, 15, 16)
June 8, 2019 Southport, NC, private event for Pops (17)
June 15, 2019 Aguascaliente, Mexico, Festival Motociclista Aguascalientes (18)
June 21, 22, 2019 Bow, WA, Skagit Casino (19, 20)
July 3, 2019 Metarie, LA, Uncle Sam Jam (21)
October 3, 2019 Phoenix, AZ, Private gig at the Van Buren, Ben Hoyt subbed for Mik (22)

Appendix D: Every Show 1999-2024

October 20, 2019 Annapolis, MD, Rams Head on Stage (23, 24)
November 21, 2019 Waukegan, IL, Genesee Theatre (25)
November 23, 2019 Manitowoc, WI, Capitol Civic Center (26)
November 24, 2019 Wassau, WI, Grand Theater (27)
December 5, 2019 The Villages, FL, Savannah Center (28, 29)
December 13, 2019 Helsinki, Finland, Hall of Culture (30)

2020 (6 SHOWS. THANKS, COVID)
January 24, 2020 Stamford, CT, Palace Theater (1)
January 25, 2020 Calicoon, NY, Villa Roma Resort, with 500 NYC detectives (2)
March 6-20, 2020 Orlando, FL, EPCOT (3, 4, 5, 6)

SHOWS CANCELED OR POSTPONED BY COVID IN 2020 (16)
March 14, 2020 Jacksonville, FL, Florida Theater
March 19, 2020 Immokalee, FL, Seminole Casino
April 1–April 8, 2020 On the Blue Cruise
April 16, 2020 Uncasville, CT, Mohegan Sun
April 25, 2020 Easton, PA, State Theater
May 9, 2020 P. Hux Jackson TN, Caravan of Stars
June 9, 2020 Greensboro, GA
June 12, 2020 Atlanta, GA, with Symphony
June 26, 2020 Vienna, VA, P. Hux at Jammin Java
July 18, 2020 LA, CA, Pershing Square outdoor concert
August 15, 2020 Saskatchewan, Canada
August 22, 2020 Greven, Germany
September 12, 2020 Schenectady, NY
October 23, 2020 St. Charles, IL, Arcada Theater
October 25, 2020 Mountain Home, AR
October 29, 2020 Ladson, SC

2021 (8 SHOWS)
June 8, 2021 Lake Oconee, GA, Ritz Carlton, private gig (1)
June 11, 2021 Immokalee, FL, Seminole Casino (2, 3)
July 30, 2021 Huelva, Spain, City Cultural Festival (4)
August 26, 2021 Oostande, Belgium, "W" Festival (5)
October 28, 2021 Ladson, SC, Carolina Coastal Fair, Mom got soaked (6)

Electric Light Odyssey

November 4, 2021 Des Plaines, IL, Des Plaines Theatre, new Ron Onesti venue (7)
November 6, 2021 Schenectady, NY, Rivers Casino (8)

2022 (19 SHOWS)

March 19, 2022 Jacksonville, FL, Florida Theater with orchestra (1)
March 25-28, 2022 Orlando, FL, EPCOT (2, 3, 4, 5)
May 12, 13, 2022 Imokalee, FL, Seminole Casino (6, 7)
May 20, 2022 Morristown, NJ, PAC (8)
June 1-2, 2022 Tel Aviv, Israel, Charles Bronfman Auditorium (9, 10)
June 5, 2022 Haifa, Israel, Congress Center (11)
June 6, 2022 Jerusalem, Israel, Henry Crown Hall, Jerusalem Theatre (12)
June 19, 2022 Hollywood, FL, Hard Rock Hotel (13)
October 6, 2022 Tarrytown, NY, Tarrytown Music Hall (14)
October 7, 2022 Easton, PA, State Theater (15)
October 9, 2022 Annapolis, MD, Rams Head on Stage (16, 17)
November 12, 2022 Lafitte, LA, Jean Lafitte Seafood Festival, coldest show I ever played (18)
November 24, 2022 Biel, Switzerland, Kongresshaus (19)

2023 (18 SHOWS. I MISSED FOUR)

January 12, 2023 The Villages, FL, Savannah Center (1, 2)
January 17, 2023 San Antonio, TX, TPC San Antonio, private gig (3)
March 16–19, 2023 Rock & Romance Cruise (4, 5)
  * I missed cruise due to family situation.
March 21, 2023 Anna Maria, FL, The Center of Anna Maria Island (6)
April 22, 2023 Middletown, NY, Paramount Theater (7)
May 6, 2023 Fort Myers, FL, Brave New Pops at Barbara Mann Performing Arts Hall (8)
May 7, 2023 Punta Gorda, FL, Brave New Pops at Charlotte Performing Arts Center (9)
May 12–15, 2023 Orlando, FL, EPCOT (10, 11, 12, 13)
June 2, 2023 Santiago, Chile, Teatro Capaulican (formerly Teatro Monumental) (14)
June 3, 2023 Monticello, Chile, Gran Arena Chile (15)
June 6, 2023 Lima, Peru, Expocision Parque (16)
October 26, 2023 Easton, PA, State Theater, broke my hand, missed show (17)

October 27, 2023 Johnstown, PA, University of Pittsburgh at Johnstown Pasquerilla PAC, broken hand, missed show (18)

2024 (5 SHOWS...SO FAR)
March 22-25, 2024 Orlando, FL, EPCOT (1, 2, 3, 4)
April 19, 2024 Blue Lake, CA, Blue Lake Casino (5)

Total: 503 shows

APPENDIX E
P. HUX DISCOGRAPHY

Matt Barrett *The Ruse* (1980)
Moonlight Records vinyl EP Produced by Don Dixon
PH: Guitars, vocals

The Blazers *How to Rock* (1980)
Moonlight Records vinyl LP Produced by Don Dixon
"Top Of My World," "Country Girl," "I Can Love You," "Rock And Roll Must Be Right,""Don't Worry 'Bout It Now"
PH: Writer, guitars, vocals, more

Rick Rock "Buddha, Buddha" b/w "(I'm A Lookin' For A) Sputnik" (1982)
Big Groovy Records vinyl 45 rpm single
PH: Writer, producer, both songs plus guitars, vocals, more

Rick Rock and Various Artists *Mondo Montage* (1983)
Dolphin Records Compilation vinyl LP
"Buddha/Buddha" and "(I'm A Looking For A) Sputnik"
PH: Writer, producer, both songs plus guitars, vocals, more

Rick Rock and Various Artists *More Mondo* (1985)
Dolphin Records Compilation vinyl LP of New NC Rock
"Button (Love Is No Sentimental Journey)"
PH: Writer, producer, plus guitars, vocals, more

Parthenon Huxley *Sunny Nights* (1988)
Columbia Records LP Produced by David Kahne and P. Hux
PH: Writer all songs plus guitars, vocals, more

Parthenon Huxley "Chance To Be Loved" (1988)
Columbia Records CD Promo Single, produced by David Kahne and P. Hux
PH: Writer, producer, plus guitars, vocals

Parthenon Huxley "Double Our Numbers" (1988)
Columbia Records CD Promo Single, Produced by David Kahne and P. Hux
PH: Writer, plus guitars, vocals

Parthenon Huxley "Guest Host For The Holy Ghost" (1988)
Columbia Records 7" vinyl single Produced by David Kahne and P. Hux
PH: Writer, guitars, vocals

Parthenon Huxley and Various Artists *The Crink Chronicles* (1988)
CBS Records Promo Compilation Double Vinyl LP
PH: Writer, Producer, guitars, vocals "Double Our Numbers"

Cats in Boots *Kicked and Klawed* (1989)
EMI CD LP Release
PH: Writer "Shotgun Sally," "Evil Angel"

Stevie Salas *Colorcode* (1990)
Island Records CD LP
PH: Writer "Stand Up", "Blind", "Two Bullets And A Gun", "Over And Over Again", "Cover Me"

Stevie Salas *The Harder They Come* (1990)
Island Records CD Maxi Single
PH: Writer "Blind"

The Goosebumps (P. Hux and Sass Jordan) Various Artists *Tame Yourself* (1991)
WEA/Sire CD LP
K.D. Lang, the B-52's, the Pretenders, Fetchin Bones, Belinda Carlisle, Howard Jones and more
PH: Writer, vocals, guitars "Asleep Too Long"

P. Hux and Various Artists *For the Love of Todd* (1991)
Third Lock Records CD LP
Don Dixon, Mitch Easter, Jamie Hoover, the Woods, Bill Lloyd, and more
Producer, arranger "There Goes My Inspiration"

Appendix E: P. Hux Discography

E *A Man Called E* (1992)
Polydor Records CD LP Produced by E and Parthenon Huxley
PH: Writer, producer "Hello Cruel World," "Nowheresville" plus acoustic and electric guitars, bass guitar, percussion, finger snaps, programming

Foreigner *The Very Best and Beyond* (1992)
Atlantic Records CD LP
PH: Writer "With Heaven On Our Side"

Sass Jordan *Racine* (1992)
MCA/Impact Records CD LP
PH: Writer "You Don't Have to Remind Me"

P. Hux and Jim Jacobsen *Killer Tracks/Universal Production Music* (1992–2015)
Killer Tracks Production Music CDs and Downloads
PH: Writer, producer, arranger, guitars, more on 173 instrumental tracks with Jim Jacobsen

Stevie Salas *Bootleg Like A Mug!! Live In Japan* (1992)
Polystar Records CD LP
PH: Writer "Stand Up", "Cover Me"

E *Broken Toy Shop* (1993)
Polydor Records CD LP
Produced by E, Parthenon Huxley, Mark Goldenberg, Michael Koppelman
PH: Writer "The Only Thing I Care About", "My Old Raincoat", "Shine It All On" plus electric guitar, acoustic guitar, background vocals, bass guitar, Hammond B-3

Stevie Salas *Presents the Electric Pow Wow* (1993)
Polystar Records CD LP
PH: Writer "Wild Ride"

P. Hux, Various Artists *Yellow Pills More of the Best of American Pop* (1994)
Big Deal Records Double CD LP with Matthew Sweet, Redd Cross, 20/20, Wondermints, Kyle Vincent, the Posies, Material Issue, Shoes, more
PH: Writer, vocals, guitars "Bazooka Joe"

Stevie Salas *Back From the Living* (1994)
Polystar/Geronimo CD LP
PH: Writer "Wonderin'"

P. Hux "It'll Be Alright" (1995)
Black Olive CD Promo Single Produced by P. Hux
PH: Writer plus guitars, vocals, more

P. Hux "Every Minute" (1995)
Black Olive CD Promo Single Produced by P. Hux
PH: Writer plus guitars, vocals, more

P. Hux "Here Comes The Savior" (1995)
Black Olive CD Promo Single Produced by P. Hux
PH: Writer plus guitars, vocals, more

P. Hux *Appetizer* (1995)
Black Olive 4-song Promo CD EP Produced by P. Hux
PH: Writer all songs plus guitar, vocals, more

P. Hux *Deluxe* (1995)
Black Olive CD LP Produced by P. Hux
PH: Writer all songs plus guitars, vocals, more

P. Hux and Various Artists *A Testimonial Dinner. The Songs of XTC* (1995)
Thirsty Ear Records CD LP
The Rembrandts, Sarah McLachlan, Ruben Blades, the Verve Pipe, They Might Be Giants, Joe Jackson
PH: Arranger, guitars, vocals "Another Satellite"

P. Hux *Every Minute* (1996)
P. Hux "Deluxe" with different title and booklet art
Wagram Music France CD LP Produced by P. Hux
PH: Writer all songs plus guitars, vocals, more

Appendix E: P. Hux Discography

P. Hux and Various Artists *Come and Get It. A Tribute to Badfinger* (1996)
Copper Records CD LP
With Adrian Belew, Al Kooper, the Knack, Aimee Mann, Dwight Twilley, and more
PH: Producer/Arranger plus vocals, guitars "Perfection"

Nicklebag (Stevie Salas, Bernard Fowler) *12 Hits and a Bump* (1996)
Iguana Records CD LP
PH: Writer "Soul Search" (Mother Mix; Bonus Bump/Nicklebag Mix)

VeG *VeG* (1997)
Cactus Boy Records CD LP
Produced by P. Hux, Paul Martinez, Winston Watson, Harvey Moltz
PH: Writer all songs plus guitars, vocals, more

Kyle Vincent *Kyle Vincent* (1997)
Carport/Hollywood Records CD LP Produced by P. Hux, Kyle Vincent, Gabe Veltri
PH: Writer, producer "Arianne," "Wake Me Up (When The World's Worth Waking Up For," "One Good Reason," "It Wasn't Supposed To Happen" plus guitar, vocals, more

Stevie Salas *Le Bootleg/Live in Paris* (1997)
USG Records CD LP
PH: Writer "Stand Up"

Poptopia Vol. 3 Power Pop Classics of the '90s (1997)
Rhino Records compilation CD
PH: Writer "Every Minute" plus guitars, vocals, more

eels *Electro-Shock Blues* (1998)
Dreamworks CD Produced by E, Jim Jacobsen
PH: Writer, guitar on "Going To Your Funeral Part 1"

Jeff Foskett *Twelve and Twelve* (1998)
New Surf Limited CD
PH: Writer, vocals "Bazooka Joe"

Kyle Vincent *Sweet 16: Rare and Unreleased* (1999)
SongTree Records CD
PH: Writer, Producer "Back Off!"

Kyle Vincent *Wow and Flutter* (1999)
SongTree /Varese Sarabande Records CD LP
PH: Writer, producer, plus guitars, vocals "She Only Loves Me When She's High," "Taking Over Me," "She's Top 40"

Splendid *Have You Got a Name For It* (1999)
Mammoth/Mushroom Records CD LP
PH: Writer "Come Clean," "Come Clean (DNA Remix), "My New Tattoo"

P. Hux *Live in Your Living Room* (2000)
Nine18 Recordings CD + Download Acoustic Live Concert
PH: Writer, producer, all songs plus guitars, vocals, more

The Orchestra *No Rewind* (2001)
ART Music CD Produced by Jim Jacobsen, P. Hux, Eric Troyer
PH: Writer, plus guitars, vocals, more
"Jewel And Johnny," "Can't Wait To See You," "Over London Skies," "Before We Go"

P. Hux *Purgatory Falls* (2001)
Nine18 Recordings/Universal CD + Download Produced by P. Hux and Gordon Townsend as the Magnificent Brothers
PH: Writer all songs plus guitars, vocals, more

Pierce Turner *3 Minute World* (2001)
Punctual Records LP and CD
PH: Producer "Oh, Ireland"

Kyle Vincent and Various Artists *Zipped Up And Down Under...* (2001)
Zip Records Australia Double CD
PH: Writer, producer "Invisible Man"

Appendix E: P. Hux Discography

Persephone's Bees *Notes From the Underworld* (2002)
Columbia Records CD LP
PH: Background Vocals "Walk To The Moon," "Way To Your Heart," "Even Though I'm Fooling Around," "On The Earth?," "Paper Plane"

Rusty Anderson *Undressing Underwater* (2003)
Oxide Records CD Produced by Rusty Anderson,
Parthenon Huxley, Andrew Murdock, David Kahne
PH: Writer, producer Singer "Electric Trains"
PH: Writer, producer "Ol' Sparky"
PH: Writer "Devil's Spaceship"

Kyle Vincent *Solitary Road* (2003)
SongTree Records CD
PH: Writer "I Should Understand"

Robert Lamm *Subtlety and Passion* (2003)
CD LP Release
PH: Writer "You're My Sunshine Everyday"

P. Hux *In Your Parlour* (2004)
Nine18 Recordings CD + Download Acoustic Live Concert
PH: Writer, producer, all songs plus guitars, vocals, more

Robi Draco Rosa *Mad Love* (2004)
Columbia Records/Phantom Vox CD and LP
PH: Writer "Do You Remember"

Robert Lamm *Too Many Voices* (2004)
Blue Infinity CD
PH: Writer "Schitzoid"

P. Hux *Homemade Spaceship: The Music of ELO as Performed by P. Hux* (2005)
Lakeshore Records CD Produced by P. Hux and Michael Woodrum
PH: Arranger plus guitars, vocals, more

Helena Merikana *Helena Merikana* (1996)
Matt Barrett self-released CD EP
PH: Guitar, vocals "Old Friend," "Kafka And Camus," "Angry Man," "Wheels," "Rebuild Our Love"

P. Hux *Mile High Fan* (2006)
Nine18 Recordings/Not Lame CD LP Produced by P. Hux
PH: Writer all songs plus guitars, vocals, more

Stevie Salas *The Essential Stevie Salas Vol 1* (2006)
R and C Ltd Double CD LP
PH: Writer "Two Bullets And A Gun," "Stand Up," "Blind"

P. Hux *Kiss the Monster* (2007)
Nine18 Recordings/Beanbag1/Voiceprint CD LP Produced by P. Hux
PH: Writer all songs plus guitars, vocals, more

Stevie Salas *The Sun and the Earth* (2007)
Invisible Hands Music Double CD LP
PH: Writer "Two Bullets And A Gun," "Blind"

Kalan Porter *Wake Up Living* (2007)
Sony BMG Vinyl LP and CD
PH: Writer "Out Of My Head"

Don Dixon and The Jump Rabbits *The Nu-Look* (2008)
Dixon Archival Remnants CD LP
PH: Writer "Sputnik"

P. Hux, Various Artists *Songwriter Café* (2008)
Megatrax CD LP
PH: Writer, guitar, vocals "Beautiful"

3kStatic and P. Hux "Ma-Ma-Ma Belle" / "Showdown" (2009)
dPulse Recordings Download Produced by 3kStatic and P. Hux
PH: Arranger, plus guitars, vocals

Appendix E: P. Hux Discography

Kyle Vincent *Where You Are* (2009)
SongTree Records CD
PH: Writer, producer "Emily Standing" plus guitars, bass, vocals

3kStatic and P. Hux "Ma-Ma-Ma Belle Remix and Transmissions" (2009)
dPulse Recordings Produced by 3kStatic and P. Hux
PH: Arranger, guitar, vocals

Pierce Turner *Beyond the Blue* (2009)
Lovecat Records LP and CD
PH: Producer "Oh, Ireland"

Big Fish Audio—*A Strummer's Ball–Acoustic Rhythm Guitar* by Parthenon Huxley (2010) Loops and samples produced by Jim Jacobsen
PH: Acoustic guitar

Sony Sound Series *Parthenon Huxley's Six String Orchestra* (2011)
Loops and samples Produced by Jim Jacobsen
PH: Electric guitar

P. Hux *Tracks And Treasure Vol.1* (2011)
Nine18 Recordings CD LP Produced by P. Hux
PH: Writer all songs plus guitar, vocals, more

Kyle Vincent *The Best So Far* (2011)
SongTree CD LP
PH: Writer, guitars, vocals "Wake Me Up," "Arianne"

Sony Sound Series *P. Hux Power Trio* (2012)
Loops and samples Produced by Jim Jacobsen
P. Hux guitars, Gordon Townsend drums, Dan Rothchild bass

Parthenon Huxley *Thank You Bethesda* (2013)
Nine18 Recordings CD LP Produced by P. Hux with Mark Williams
PH: Writer all songs plus guitar, vocals, more

Edward O'Connell *Vanishing Act* (2014)
Dangerous/Oaf Ramp CD LP
PH: Background vocals "Vanishing Act"

Jonathan Rundman *Look Up* (2014)
Salt Lady Records CD LP
PH: Electric Guitar "The Science Of Rockets"

Kyle Vincent *Detour* (2015)
SongTree Records CD LP
PH: Writer "This Bed"

Arsonists Club *Static Coming Back* (2017)
Five Song Indie EP CD and Download Produced by P. Hux

P. Hux *This Is the One* (2018)
Nine18 Recordings CD + Download Produced by P. Hux with Mark Williams
PH: Writer all songs plus guitar, vocals, more

Kyle Vincent *Whatever It Takes* (2020)
SongTree Records CD LP
PH: Writer "Hard To Be Happy" plus guitars, vocals

Ed O'Connell *Feel Some Love* (2022)
Dangerous/Oaf Ramp
PH: Background Vocals "Golden Light," "M.F.C."

Sean Gaiser *Wildflower* (2023)
Self released CD LP
PH: Vocals "Help Me Out," "Simple Love"

P. Hux *As Good As Advertised* (2023)
Nine18 Recordings CD + Download Produced by P. Hux with Mark Williams
PH: Writer all songs plus guitar, vocals, more

THANK YOU

To Helle, Fiona, and Imogen for all their love and understanding of what drives a musician; Tom, Tim, and Chuck for their brotherly love and early manuscript reads; Mom and Dad for everything; Dan Levitin for his unwavering support, best-seller advice, and the confidence I could pull this off; Lauren Woolsey for her superb professional help; Sean Moran for his thoughtful feedback and encouragement; Connie Sayers for her author's eye; Robert Friedman for his early editorial input; Betsy Neill for her honest appraisal; John Mudd for his nuanced review; Paul Schneider for his expert read; Nanci Luehman, my kind, considerate, and stalwart friend of fifty-plus years, for noticing a false note; Michael Oberman for sharing his publishing experience; Pete Kennedy for the hookup with Highpoint; Highpoint publisher Michael Roney for getting it and being so enthusiastic and understanding; Carmen Tugender for our research discussions and laughs; Michael Cesarano for his eagle eye; Eric Troyer for the phone call and twenty-six years of friendship; Christine Buckley for the shock romance of the twenty-first century and her notes on my book; Mik Kaminski for all his help with the Master Gigography List; Gordon Townsend for thirty years of friendship and musical adventures; Bev Bevan for asking me to join ELO Part II; band and crew for creating stories worth writing about; John and Joyce for their endless support and incredible gigs; Nigel Osborne at Jawbone Press for his positive early take; Tyson Cornell at Rarebird Books for professional feedback and advice; Duff McKagan for sharing his publishing experience and writing me a nice blurb; my mentor Don Dixon for his blurb and large role in my memoir; dorm pal and author supreme Holly George-Warren for her review and blurb; Lee Gildersleeve for crankin' the spin; Dan Rothchild for his excellent contributions to P. Hux and book endorsement; Michael Solomon for hearing something in my demo tape; Sarah Clarehart for design and layout beyond the call of duty; Ricky, Dave and Dan for being such a ridiculously good band; and Matt Barrett for countless adventures, expert opinions, and infinite laughs. If I've left a deserving person out, it was unintentional.

INDEX

Note: Page numbers in *italics* indicate figures, and references following "n" refer notes.

#
"10538 Overture" 7, 11, 12, 64

A
Abbey Road Studio Two 82, 83, 276, 364
ABC-TV 239
Abernethy, R. (Dash) 173, 175, 377
Abrams, L. 148
Ackrill, P. 8, 12–14, 22–23, 30, 69, 278
Adams, D. 166
AKA Grafitti Man 199
Alan Parsons Live Project 364, 375
Alexander, K. 205
Alley Studios 185
"All My Loving" 79 113, 296
"All Over The World" 17, 32
"All You Need Is Love" 277
"Alright Now" 277
American Academy, Athens, Greece 343
American Idol 315
American Youth Center, Athens, Greece 326
Amsterdam 176, 178
Anchor 42
Anderson, R. 28, 196, 197, 213, 214, 233, 234, 247, 295–298, 302, 304, 377
Anderson, T. 175
Anthony, B. 194, 195, 214, 215, 230, 356
Antofagasta 41–46, 48, 300
Apple, F. 254
Applesin Club 314 316, 340
Archangel, N. 196
Arden, D. 278
Are You Experienced? 123, 183
Argentina 36, 37, 368
Arizona Daily Star 225
ASCAP 225
As Good As Advertised 311
Asher, P. 173
Athens 93, 117, 119–122, 124, 125, 127, 128, 131, 169, 176, 182, 326, 343
Atlantic City 96, 97, 269, 361
Audities 239
Axis: Bold As Love 123, 183

B
"Babe I'm Gonna Leave You" 227
"Baby Love" 114
Bad Brains 154
Ballard, G. 190
Bangles, The 191
Barrett, M. 305, 377
Bartys, A. 304
Bates, P. 16–17, 19, 34, 70, 91, 327–329, 349, 351, 364, 369
"Battleship Chains" 175
Bators, S. 152
BBC Radio 74
Beach Boys 282
Beatles 7, 21, 82, 83, 112–113, 133, 153, 154, 167, 193, 210, 211, 254, 256, 277, 295, 297, 298, 301
Beatles Songbook – Romantic Instrumentals by The Hollyridge Strings, The 79
"Beautiful Boy" 155
"Before We Go" 273, 274, 281, 282
Belarus 94, 369
Bevan, B. 8, 9, 12, 15, 16, 23, 28, 30, 31, 34, 36, 41, 45, 52, 54, 57, 59, 63, 65–71, 73–75, 79, 81, 85, 87, 89–91, 95–99, 269, 270, 274, 275, 278, 283, 284, 292, 293, 371, 377
Big Bopper 271
Big Groovy Records 161
Billboard Alternative Charts 217
Billy Joel Live in Russia 206
Birmingham 8, 15, 22, 23, 63, 69, 74, 89, 226–227, 278, 358, 359, 376
Black, G. 241
"Blackberry Way" 64, 80
"Blackbird" 302

Blackmore, R. 73
Black Olive Studios 237
Black Rock 206
Black Sabbath 8, 73, 89, 90, 124, 225, 366
Black Star Riders 376
Blazers, The 143–153, 159, 164, 189, 197, 242, 378
Blazers—How To Rock, The 147, 151
"Blind" 223
"Blinded By The Light" 137
Blood Sweat & Tears 300
Blues Period 121
Bodyguard 230
Bolois, C. 305, 306
Bonham, J. 236
Bonoff, K. 173, 185, 186, 221
Born To Run 137
Bortnick, B. 212
Bosley, M. 237
Bowie, D. 136, 203, 342
Bresky, H. 139–141, 150
Brewer & Shipley 127
Brion, J. 254
Brisebois, D. 214
"Broad Daylight" 154
Broken Toy Shop 218
Bromiley, D. 326
"Brontosaurus" 89
Bronx 63
Brother Cane 377
Broucek, P. 376
Brown, P. J. 225
Brussels 175
Buchholz, A. 91
Buckley, K. K. 303
"Buddha, Buddha" 160–162, 189, 191
Buddy Holly 271
Buffalo Records 146, 169
Buffalo Springfield 193
Bulgaria 60, 61, 63, 86
Burnett, T-Bone 310
Burr, R. 306
Burstyn, E. 218
Burtnik, G. 362, 364, 368, 373–374
"Button" 165
Byrds, The 114, 152
Byrne, D. 224

C

California 41, 94, 151, 154, 181, 182, 186, 196, 205, 213, 251, 308
"California" 237, 238

"California Dreamin'" 231
"Call Of The Wild, The" 135–136
Canadian Idol 309–311
Cannon, D. 203
"Can't Buy Me Love" 79
"Can't Get It Out Of My Head" 26, 353, 354, 372, 378
"Can't Wait To See You" 272, 282
Carlton, R. 121, 127
Carmen, E. 21, 277
Cashbox 205
Cat's Cradle, The 132, 140, 144, 146, 150, 152, 153, 155, 165, 168
CBS 120, 195, 203, 206, 218–221, 233
CCBK *see* CC Blues King (CCBK)
CC Blues King (CCBK) *102*, 126, 127, 141
Cedars-Sinai Medical Center 307
"C'est La Vie" 190
"Chance To Be Loved" 191, 195, 204–207, 376
Channel One 316
Chapel Hill Newspaper, The 147
Chapin, H. 173
Chapman, M. 156
Cheap Trick 92, 93
Cheshire, G. 151, 172, 195
Chicago 88, 91, 163, 186
Chile 41, 43, 45, 48, 52, 276, 299, 300, 342, 368
Chilton, A. 168
Chrysalis Records 171
Chubby Groove 311
Chuck Berry 11, 60, 140
Church, A. 159, 160
Clapton, E. 114, 199
Clark, L. 6, 8, 10–12, 15, 18, 19, 23, 29, 31, 34, 58, 63, 79, 81, 278, 282, 352, 373
Clark, T. 183–184
Clarke, D. 361
Clarke, G. 246
Classic Superstars Live, Dover Downs Dover, DE 300–301
Club Ahoy 176
Club Caprice 87
Club Largo 254
Club Lingerie 199, 200, 223
Cocker, J. 216
Coconut Teaszer Club 225
Cohen, J. 191, 204
Coles, B. 325–326
Coley, J. F. 241
Collins, P. 239
Colorcode 223, 225, 309

Index

Columbia Records 3, 192, 193, 195, 199, 200, 206–209, 343
"Come Clean" 4, 78
Condos, J. 182, 196, 213, 235, 307, 364, 378
"Confusion" 36, 38, 59
Connelly, M. 337
Conway, L. 167, 168, 193
Conway Studios 225
Conwell, T. 236
Cooley, A. 137
Cooper, A. 227
Copeland, M. 306
Corcoran School of Art 155
Corpus Christi Symphony Orchestra 269
Costello, E. 256
Costner, K. 187
Coue, E. 155
"Country Girl" 146
Cox, M. 81
Crashing Dream 168
Creagh, J. 171, 173
Creagh, S. 171
Creative Loafing 205
Creedence Clearwater Revisited 74, 300
Crenshaw, M. 214, 230
"Crosstown Traffic" 123
Crowe, C. 296
Cruelty Free Noodlers 234
Cyprus 129

D

Dads, The 154–155, 159
Daltrey, R. 213, 364, 375
Dan, E. 241
Dancing Hoods 212
Daniels, S. 204
Dark Side of the Moon 364
David Lee Roth Band 94
Davies, R. 114
Davis, J. E. 199
"Day In The Life, A" 254
"Day Tripper" 115
Dead Boy's 152
DeCarlo, T. 375
Deep Purple 91, 335, 341, 351-352, 399
Def Leppard 69
"Delilah" 270
DeMain, B. 311
Demon Records 175
Denmark 284, 321, 322, 325, 346
Denton, T. 325
deVillar, CJ 223, 225

Diddley, B. 300
Different Light, A. 191–192
Dillingham, M. 77, 122
Diltz, H. 247–248
"Dino's Laughing Now" 6
Dirt Road To Heaven 378
Disney 43
Disraeli Gears 123
Dixie Dregs 74, 132
Dixon, D. 141–143, 146–147, 153, 160, 165–166, 169, 175–178, 180, 206, 310, 377
Doe, J. 246
Dolphin Records 161
Donald, N. 198
Donaldson, R. 187
Don Dixon Band 177
"Don't Bring Me Down" 45, 48, 60, 80, 99, 284, 304, 347, 362
"Don't Let It Show" 375
"Don't Worry" 197, 198
Doors 123
Double Fantasy 5, 155
"Double Our Numbers" 191, 195, 204, 207, 230
Downer Channel, The 230
"Down On The Bay" 6, 154
"Do Ya" 7, 9, 10, 34, 76, 304, 372
"Dozers Away" 165
Dragon: The Bruce Lee Story 231
Dreamworks 218
Driving Rain 295
Dylan, B. 172, 208, 211, 226, 364

E

Easter, M. 142, 378
E Band *107*
Econopouly, M. 124, 133
Ed Sullivan Show, The 113
Edwards, J. 219, 220
"Eldorado Overture" 58, 80
Electric Ballroom 137
El Salvador 286, 288
EMI Studios 81, 165, 166
Enterprise Studios 203
Epic Records 289
Escher, M.C. 125
Escovedo, A. 168
Estonia 93, 94
E Street Band 137
European Southern Observatory 41
Evans, B. "Barru" 9, 20–21, 29, 30, 32, 35, 40

Evans, C. 372
Everett, M. 214, 215, 252, 378
Everybody Knows This Is Nowhere 185
"Every Minute" 237, 239
"Everything's Different Now" 351, 352
"Evil Woman" 7, 11, 12, 16, 36, 38, 87, 283, 304, 316, 325, 349, 372

F

Fab Four 277, 278
Face The Music 64
Fagan, L. 246
Falkner, J. 247
Faragher, T. 191
Fenell, M. "Fen Man" 189
Ferrari, M. 214, 230
Ferris Bueller's Day Off 240
Festival Cultural La Jornada 343
"Fifty States Of Freedom" 127
Finding Graceland 3
Finland 93, 376
Finster, H. 4
"Fire On High" 32
Flintstones Movie, The 231
Fluevog, J. 21
Fogerty, J. 74
"For Your Love" 114
Foskett, J. 5, 16, 282, 364
Fox, P. 224
Fox and Hounds, The 271
Frampton, P. 300, 325
Frampton Comes Alive 325
France 128, 239, 342, 343
Frangias, L. 128
Frasier 184
"Free Fallin'" 182
Fresh Cream 123
Friedman, R. 144–145
"Fuck Columbia" 211

G

Gabriel, P. 171
Galaxy Theater, Santa Ana, CA 305
Garden Grove Amphitheater 5
"Garden of Earthly Delights" 125
Garfunkel, A. 281
Gatton, D. 151
Geffen 5
Gene Simmons Family Jewels 365, 368
Gentrys 115
George, G. 302

Georgia 86
Germany 91, 124, 345, 358, 362
"Getting To The Point" 7, 11, 68
Giant Sand 225
Gilbert, J. 302, 306
Gilbert, K. 241
Gildersleeve, L. 139–141, 144, 146, 149, 378
Girdland, L. 304
'Girlfriend In A Coma?' 191
Glass Moon 166–167
"Gloria" 121
Go-Go 65, 225, 227–230
Goldenberg, M. 173, 174, 182, 233
"Golden Boy" 220, 221
"Golden Slumbers" 83
Gold Record 5
Goodman, D. 290–291
Goodman, J. 231
"Got To Hurry" 114
Gramm, L. 220–222
Grand Funk Railroad 193
Greece 123–125, 128, 133, 172, 174, 228
Greek Island of Ios 7
Greene, G. 375
"Green Room" 37
Greensboro Record 162
Greetings From Asbury Park 123
Gregory, D. 224
Griffith, A. 147
Gronback, S. 146, 147, 160, 161, 164–166, 171
Groucutt, K. 6, 8–12, 15, 16, 19–25, 29–31, 33–35, 38, 47, 48, 54–56, 59–64, 68, 70, 71, 75, 78–81, 85, 87–89, 91, 96, 97, 99, 270, 273–275, 278, 281–283, 287, 288, 291, 304, 312, 315, 318, 321, 325, 328, 332, 334, 338, 350, 358–360, 362, 363, 372
"Guest Host For The Holy Ghost" 196
Guns N' Roses 375

H

Hackett, B. 231
Handmade Films 200, 209, 210
"Hanky Panky" 114
Hard Day's Night, A 187
Hard Report, The 205
Harrison, G. 199, 200, 210
Harrison, S. 368
Hart, A. 258
HATNO *see* Hodgenization Across The Nation Organization (HATNO)

Index

Hay, C. 371
Head For Tall Trees 171, 172, 174, 208
Healey, J. 230
Heaney, J. 3, 72, 233, 200-203, 209-211
"Heaven Everwhere" 4
Hefner, H. 306
Heimbold, M. 237, 238
Helle 19–21, 80–83, 254–257, 349
"Hello Cruel World" 216, 217
"Hello Goodbye" 296
"Hello Susie" 284
"Help Me" 133
Hendrix, J. 123, 131, 183, 193, 247
Henley, D. 182, 213, 362, 364
"Here Comes The Savior" 237
Hey Arnold! 216
"Hey Joe" 121
"Hey Jude" 124, 295
Hillis, C. 374
"Hippy Hippy Shake" 323
Hitchcock, R. 254
Hodge, S. 39, 40, 57, 373
Hodgenization Across The Nation Organization (HATNO) 40
"Hog Wild Cookoff" 85
"Hold On Tight" 17
Holsapple, P. 172
Homemade Spaceship 303–306
"Honest Men" 91
Hooters 175
"Hot Blooded" 219, 220
"Hot Rod Lincoln" 177
Houses of the Holy 183
Howard, R. E. 140
Hughes, M. 205, 206
Hunter, L. 186–187
Huxley, A. 172
Huxley, C. 203
Huxley, H. 349

I

I Am Sam 301, 302
"I Can Love You" 144
"I Could Write A Book" 272
"I'd Really Love To See You Tonight" 241
"If Only" 272
Iggy Pop 151
"I Loved Everything" 306
"I Love You Period" 175
"I'm Looking Through You" 302
"I'm On Fire" 151
"I'm Waiting For The Man" 222

"In My Life" 277
International Fair Amphitheater 287
International Herald Tribune 7
International Pop Overthrow Festival 5
I Robot 375
I.R.S. Records 222
"I Saw Her Standing There" 277
"I Should Have Known Better" 133, 153
Island Records 165
Italy 117, 128
"It'll Be Alright" 237, 239
"I Want More" 222, 306
"I Want To Hold Your Hand" 82, 112

J

Jackson, M. 183
Jacobsen, J. 227–230, 271, 281
Jagger, M. 364
James, E. 234
James, S. 179, 180
James, T. 114
Jefferies, B. 205
Jefferson Starship 75
"Jet" 296
Jet, J. 92
Jethro Tull 132
"Jewel And Johnny" 271–272, 274, 282
Joel, B. 175, 282
John, E. 39, 72
John, N. 277
Johnson, D. 214, 226, 227, 376–377
Johnson, E. 132
Jones, K. 220
Jones, Marti 206
Jones, Mick 219–221
Joplin, J. 173
Jordan, M. 139
Jordan, S. 92
Jostyn, M. 175
JPF *see* Just Plain Folks (JPF)
Junior, L. P. 142
Just Plain Folks (JPF) 305
"Just Sayin'" 376

K

Kahne, D. 191–194, 196, 197, 199, 201, 202, 204, 207, 229, 295, 297, 298, 378
Kaminski, M. 6, 8, 10, 12, 14, 15, 19, 23, 29, 31–34, 44, 45, 47, 48, 52–56, 63, 71, 72, 75, 77, 79–81, 86, 96–98, 272, 274, 275, 278, 281, 291, 304, 312, 315, 323,

329, 332, 339, 341–343, 349, 350, 353, 361, 363, 371, 374
Keeley, D. 197–199
Keene, T. 169, 310
"Keep On Dancing" 115
Keitel, H. 3
Kinks 114, 193
Kirchen, B. 177
Kirkland, R. 143
"Kiss The Ground You Walk On" 230
Kiss The Monster 351, 352
KKT Kosmos 318
Koppelman, M. 218
Kramer, E. 183

L

LA *see* Los Angeles (LA)
Laborial, A., Jr. 296, 297
Ladd, R. 28, 169, 196, 213, 364
Lagergren, Z. 154
Lakeshore Entertainment 303, 304
LaMarca, J. 328
Lamm, R. 186, 209, 306, 378
LaMontagne, R. 182
La Movida del Verano ("The Summer Move") 37, 40
Landy, E. 185
Lane, R. 184–185, 378
Lang, J. 250
"LA's Best Kept Secrets" 225
"Last Train To London" 36, 38, 45, 343
Lawnmower and Garden Supply 241
"Lay Down Sally" 17
Leckie, J. 212
Led Zeppelin 17, 132, 133, 183, 193, 348
Led Zeppelin II 183
Lee, B. 231
Lehman Center 62
Lennon, J. 5, 7, 64–65, 82, 155, 156, 199, 203, 282
Lennon Memorial 155
"Lennon Spot" 69
Leonard, D. 203
Let It Be 277
"Let Me Fly" 272
Levy, L. 211, 214
Lies and Lullabies 233
"Life On Mars" 342
Lincoln, A. 120
Lithuania 344, 346
Little Rascals, The 215
Little River Band 75

Live In Your Living Room 302
"Live Like A King" 235
Liverpool 69
"Livin' Thing" 33, 97
Lockhart, C. 186, 187
London 77, 82, 272
Looking On 6
Lord-Alge, J. 212–214, 237
Los Angeles (LA) 3–5, 8, 18, 29, 52, 77, 86, 92, 94, 158, 167–168, 173–175, 180–187, 192, 196, 205, 207, 208, 213, 215, 219, 223, 226, 228, 233, 237, 238, 250, 271, 280, 288, 301, 305–307, 309
"Love For Nothing" 194
"Love Me Do" 83
"Loving You, Leaving Me" 65–67
"Lucy In The Sky With Diamonds" 302
Luehman, N. 128
Lynne, J. 6, 12, 34, 73–75, 91, 274–275, 290, 291, 372, 373
Lynyrd Skynyrd 144, 227

M

Maddies 62
"Ma-Ma-Ma Belle" 7, 11, 303
Mammoth Records 78, 258
Man Called E, A 216–218, 250, 302
Martin, S. 230
Martinez, L. 258
Martinez, P. 225
Masters of Rock Festival 93–95
Mateyko, J. A. 37
Matthau, W. 218, 219
Matthews Southern Comfort 167
MCA Music Publishing 3, 76, 78, 178–180, 182, 184–185, 187, 189–191, 196, 199, 211, 212, 214, 216, 219, 220, 222, 225–227, 230, 231, 234, 241, 258, 302, 306, 356
McCartney, P. 17, 91, 136, 213, 234, 278, 295–298, 301, 364
McCormack, E. 301
McCormick, K. 199, 364
McDonald, I. 312
McGhee, D. 367
McGuinn, R. 152
McKagan, B. 261, 353–355
McKagan, D. 353, 355, 375, 378
McNelis, B. 303–304
McPherson, K. 78
Medow, E. 180
Meet The Beatles 112

Mellencamp, J. 175
Melvoin, W. 199
Mercury Records 226, 241
Message From The Country 6
Messenger, D. 237
Metamorphose: M.C. Escher, 1898–1972 93
Mexico 288, 342–344
Michigan 90, 111, 151, 172, 271, 321, 328, 334, 364
Mick Jagger Centre 329
Midland Light Orchestra (M.L.O.) 74
"Mile High Fan" 212
Miller, A. 208, 377
Miller, B. B. 172, 174
Miller, G. 172
Miller, J. 64
Miller, P. 111
Miller, R. W. 111, 151, 168, 171, 236
Minneapolis 92, 93
Minnesota 90, 92, 152, 163
Minogue, K. 39
"Mirror In The Bathroom" 222
Mississippi 85, 95, 111, 274, 254
"Mister Black Sky" 311
Mitchell, J. 133
M.L.O. *see* Midland Light Orchestra (M.L.O.)
Mojo Magazine 225
Moltz, H. 225
Mondo Montage 161, 162
Monty Python's Flying Circus 122
Moody Blues 8
Moondance Jam VIII 92, 93
Moonlight Records 146, 153
Morrisette, A. 371
Morrison, J. 173
Morse, S. 73, 132
Most Of The Girls Like To Dance But Only Some Of The Boys Like To 175, 176
Mother's Right: The Elizabeth Morgan Story, A 233
Moulding, C. 224
Move 6–9, 30, 64, 65, 71, 73, 74, 80, 88, 89, 92, 93, 98, 125, 154, 167, 257, 283–284
"Mr. Blue Sky" 18, 97, 359, 372
Mrs. Lambert Remembers Love 218, 219, 233
"Mr. Stoneface" 212
"Mr. Tambourine Man" 114
Mrvos, J. 193, 204
Mull, M. 184
Murphy, E. 301

Musi-Call 164
"My Baby's M-M-Makin' Me Dance" 141, 143, 153
"My Old Raincoat" 218
"My Sweet Nothing" 257

N

Naked Gun II 215
National Academy of Songwriters, The 185
National Lottery Show 40
National Symphony Orchestra of Ukraine 58
NC *see* North Carolina (NC)
Neill, B. 128
Neilson, R. 93
Nevada 41
Nevil, R. 190
"New Age" 212, 214
New Guy, The 43
New Jersey 19, 82, 112, 115, 117, 124
New Line Cinema 301, 302
New Orleans 96
Newsweek 137
New York 158, 163, 173, 174, 178, 192, 207
New Zealand 159, 371
Nicks, S. 182, 364
"Night I Left Her, The" 118
Non-Stop Pop Roadshow 239
"No Reply" 153
"No Rewind" 272, 274, 281, 282, 288, 325, 344, 385–388
Noroeste Pop Rock Festival, Playa de Riazor, La Coruña Spain 299
North Carolina (NC) 98, 151, 154, 158, 161, 163, 164, 175, 186, 307
Norway 176
Nottingham 69, 292
No Warning 222
No Way Out 187
"Nowheresville" 216
Nu-Look, The 153
"Nuptials, The" 277

O

O'Brien, C. 270
Ocean Way Studios 241
O'Connell, H. 72, 255–257, 289, 307
O'Connell, J. 255, 281
O'Connell, T. 300
"Offer You The World" 251
Ogni Ufi Center, Ufa 320
"Oh, Pretty Woman" 113, 114, 146

Olivo, N. 237
Olsson, P. J. 364, 375
Omega School of Recorded Arts, The, Rockville 352
"One More Day In The Life" 235, 236
"Only Thing I Care About, The" 218
"On The Run" 284
Operation Kiss 366–368
Orbison, R. 113
Orchard Theatre 329
Orchestra, The 275–278, 299, 307–308, 316–318, 327, 337, 338, 368–374, 376, 378
Orson, S. 214, 230
"Out Of My Head" 310
Out of the Blue 4–6
"Over London Skies" 68–72, 80, 88, 90, 91, 282
"Over Midland Skies" 67–68

P

"Pages Of Love" 166
Palace Theater 186
Palmar, W. 374
Parker, G. 176
Parker, R. 237
Parsons, A. 364, 374, 375
"Parthenon Huxley" 28, 171–172, 200, 206–208, 238, 240
"Patience" 375
Paul, L. 111, 226
"Pavanne" 64
"Pay To Cum" 154
Penis mugs, 43-46
Penn, S. 301
Pennsylvania 62
Petersson, T. 92
Peter the Great 314
Petty, T. 182
Phenicie, D. 357
Philbin, R. 37
Phillips, W. 230
Phillips Jazz Festival Dubai, UAE 299–300
P. Hux 5, 21, 76, 96, *107, 108,* 235–236, 238, 241, 247–248, 254, 302, 309, 407–416
P. Hux "Deluxe" 238, 239, 253, 271, 302
P. Hux II 248, 250
Pickett, W. 178
Pierone, N. 87, 248, 276, 304
Pink Floyd 206, 207, 335, 364
Pioneer Records 239

Pittsburgh 85
"Play" 220, 228
"Plexiglass" 127–128, 133
Poland 280, 344, 345–347, 369
Polish Telecommunications Music and Film Festival 280
Pompidou Center 10
Poptopia: Power Pop Hits of the '90s 239
Porter, K. 309–311
Portsmouth 75
Powwow Highway 200, 203, 209–211
"Praying Mantis" 175, 176
Pressure Boys 169
Pretzel Logic 237
Prog Band 154
Prolepsis 132
"Psychic Waitress" 167
Pucon Gran Hotel, Pucon, Chile 300
Pulp 69
Pulp Fiction 229
Punta Del Este 28, 31, 39, 42, 45, 368
Purgatory Falls 22, 77, 252, 257–258, 271, 302, 306
"Purple Haze" 123
Pusha Ozerna 53, 54
Puterbaugh, P. 162

Q

Quidd, J. 154

R

Rage Against The Machine 225
Rain Parade 168
Ralbovsky, S. 172
Raspberries 193
Ray, B. 296
Raye, J. 73
"R.E.D." 212
Redding, O. 141, 169
"Red Eyeliner" 258
Reed, L. 141
Reflection Studios 310
Regna, J. 99, 269, 274, 279, 289, 301, 378
Resorts Superstar Theatre, Atlantic City 361
"Restless" 142, 143, 153
Rhino Records 239
Rhodes, E. 180
Rialto Theater 206
Rich Bitch 8
"Rich Man's War" 199
Rick Rock 162–164, 169, 172, 191, 374

Riedel, J. 205
Rigby, E. 179
Rigby, W. 141
Robert, D. 146
Robertson, R. 211
"Rock And Roll All Nite" 365
"Rock 'n' Roll Is King" 363
Rock 'n' Roll Mom 203
"Rock And Roll Must Be Right" 145
Rock 'n' Roll To The Rescue 246
"Rockaria!" 7, 11, 33
"Rock Drummer To Be Reckoned With" 284
"Rockin' Little Angel" 146
Rockin' The Rivers 349
Rogers, P. 136
Rolling Stone 91, 114, 162, 205, 236, 306
"Roll Over Beethoven" 60
Romero, A. 236, 239–240
Ronson, M. 353
Ronstadt, L. 173, 183, 185, 186
"Rosalita" 137
Roth, D. L. (DLR) 93–95
Rothchild, D. 250, 302, 361, 364, 378
Rothchild, P. 173–174
"Roundabout" 133, 343
"Round And Round" 185
Roxy Music 171
Royal Albert Hall, London 21, 63, 75–79, 81, 85, 87, 325, 355
Royal Philharmonic Orchestra (RPO) 77, 79, 80, 282
RPO *see* Royal Philharmonic Orchestra (RPO)
"Rubble" 257
Rundgren, T. 216
"Running Out" 211, 218
Ruse, The 153
Russia 93, 206, 313–315, 319, 321, 322, 331–350

S

Sadler, M. 121, 123
Salas, S. 28, 214, 222, 225, 226, 309–311, 364
Salmon Festival, Grand Falls 364
Samara 339–340
San Antonio 95, 96
Sand, C. 122
Sandbox 237
"Sandy" 137

San Francisco 158, 163, 204, 205, 213, 219, 225, 248
Santiago 45–49, 51, 57, 300
"Satisfaction" 114, 122
"Savatage" 215
"Saving The Planets" 195, 201
"Say Goodbye" 272
Scandanavia 81
Schallert, W. 219
Schock, G. 227, 230, 231
Schultz, T. 169
Scotland 326, 371
"Seth Material, The" 195
"Set Me Free" 114
Sex, Lies & Videotape 210
"Sexy Senior Citizen" 256
Shazam 6
Sheffield 69
Shelby, C. 159, 160
"She's Not There" 114
"Shine A Little Love" 359
"Shine It All On" 218
Ship Handling Research and Training Centre 348
Shipp, J. 288, 337
"Shoebox" 197, 202
Shoemaker, R. 76, 78, 178–181, 189, 191, 204, 205, 214, 230
Shondells 114
"Showdown" 72–74, 80, 372
Sigersson, D. 216
Simmons, G. 365
Simon, C. 175
"Simple Things" 235
Simpson, O. J. 215
"Six Miles From The Cage" 121
"Six Pack" 153
Smith, E. 254
Smyth, P. 362
Smythe & Co. Studios 282
Soderbergh, S. 210
Solberg, C. 217
Solihull 8, 12, 23, 69
Solomon, M. 173, 178–180, 185, 187, 191, 192, 194, 195, 205, 206, 213, 224, 377
"Something In My Heart Stopped" 166–168, 197
"Son of Beatles" 7
South America 40, 51, 63, 86
Souther Hillman Furay Band 280
Spain 29, 124, 312, 343, 362, 363
Spectator Magazine 150–151, 155, 158, 161, 164, 168, 172, 173, 195, 250, 357

Spheeris and Voudouris 343
Springsteen, B. 17, 137, 138, 208
"Sputnik" 161, 162, 189
"Stairway To Heaven" 227
Stamey, C. 141, 142
Stanley, P. 365
Star Factory 315, 316, 318
Starr, R. 236
Starship 75
Stashe 157–158, 161, 163, 164, 171, 172, 174, 181, 208
Stawarz, J. 209
Steely Dan 237
"Steer Clear" 254
Stein, B. 240
Stewart, A. 364
Stewart, R. 214, 222–223, 226, 364
Stills, S. 300
Stoeger, R. 372
Straight Outta Krasnodar 345
Stranahan Theater, Toledo 62
"Strawberry Fields" 82
Subtlety and Passion 209
Suckerpunch Studio 310, 360
Sullivan, E. 113
Sundance Film Festival 210
Sunny Nights 196, 197, 199, 203–207, 209, 211–213, 219, 222, 223, 229, 237, 238, 295, 376
"Sunshine Of Your Love" 123
Supremes 114
Sussman, M. 154
Swap, E. 246
Swartzwelder, S. 154, 223
"Sweet Talkin' Woman" 14, 17, 89, 90, 99, 303, 304
Swinging Blue Jeans ("Hippy Hippy Shake") 323
"Symphonic Beatles" 79
Szabo, G. 35, 39–40, 48, 55, 57, 75, 271

T

Talking Book 123
Tallinn 93–95
Tandy, R. 372
Tate, S. 144
Taylor, C. 179
"Telephone Line" 304, 316
"Tenderness" 222
Texas 85, 94, 95, 134
TGS Studio 142, 146, 160, 161, 164, 168, 171

Thank You Bethesda 360–361
That '70s Show 93
Thin Lizzy 227
This Is The One 374, 376
Three Dog Night 301
Throb 183, 184
"Ticket To The Moon" 60, 315, 316
Til Tuesday 351
Time 137, 315, 364
Tobias, J. 258
Tony Fucking Iommi 89
Too Many Voices 209
"Top Of My World" 148
Town Hall 132, 144, 146
Townsend, G. 76, 235–236, 302, 304, 374, 375
"Train Leaves Here This Morning" 127
Tripps, J. 21
Troubles, The 273
Troyer, E. 5–10, 12, 15–19, 21, 23–25, 29–36, 38, 48, 52, 54, 57, 61, 64, 65, 69, 71, 78–80, 87, 90–93, 95–96, 99, 258, 271–275, 278–279, 282, 287, 291, 296, 297, 300, 312, 315–319, 322, 325–326, 331, 332, 342–343, 349–350, 352, 358, 361, 363, 365–369, 374, 378
Trudell, J. 199, 200
Tuesday Night Music Club 241
Tune Up In-Store 239
Turkey 128, 129
Turner, P. 4
Turn of a Friendly Card, The 364
"Turn To Stone" 97
Twain, M. 182
TWA Records 239
"Twilight" 59
Twilley, D. 4, 151
"Twist And Shout" 274
"Two Bullets And A Gun" 223

U

Ukraine 51–55, 58, 59, 61, 86, 313
Ume Digital 306
United States (U.S.) 15, 63, 290
Uruguay 13–16, 15, 25, 28, 29, 36, 40

V

Vagnini, S. 239
Valens, R. 271
Vassilopoulos, A. 158

VeG 77, 225–226
Vega, C. 202
Vega Club 286
Vela, R. 291
Velvet Underground 222
Very Best and Beyond, The 221
"Victoria" 154
Vina Del Mar Festival, Vina Del Mar, Chile 299, 351
Vincent, K. 241, 308, 378
Virgin (V2) Records 302

W

Wagner, R. 231
Wainwright, R. 254, 310
"Wait" 154
Waits, T. 173, 187
Wakeling, D. 214, 222, 306
Wakeman, R. 342, 344
"Wake Me Up (When The World's Worth Waking Up For)" 241, 242
Wake Up Living 310
Wales 72, 270
Walsh, B. 193
Waran, S. 187, 201, 202
Ware, C. 214
Warner Brothers 143, 210
Warner Brothers Television 307
Warner Chappell Publishing 78, 258
Warner Curb Records 143
Watson, W. 28, 223, 354
Webb, A. *103*, 148
Weiland, S. 353
"What It Was, Was Football" 147
Whitney, B. A. 305
"Who Is Bruce Springsteen and Why Are We Saying All These Wonderful Things About Him?" 123
Wilde, M. 323
"Wild West Hero" 64
Willett, T. 111n2
Williams, M. 310, 360
Wilmington Opera House, Delaware 19, 21, 22
Wilson, B. 185, 364
Wiltern Theater 185
Wisconsin Conservatory of Music 228
Wise, R. 357
"With Heaven On Our Side" 221
"Woman" 65, 227, 377
Wonder, S. 123, 183
Wood, R. 64, 74, 75, 92, 141
Woodrum, M. 304, 305
Woodstock 125
World Entertainment Associates 278
Worthy, J. 194
WQDR 147, 148
Wyngate Elementary School 309

X

X 158
"Xanadu" 16, 277, 359
XTC 212, 224

Y

Year of the Cat 364, 374
York, D. 16, 23, 34, 57, 58, 61, 68, 80, 284–286, 378
Young, N. 185, 193
Young Rumblers 236

Z

Zander, R. 93
Zombies 114
Zoom 289–291

www.ingramcontent.com/pod-product-compliance
Ingram Content Group UK Ltd.
Pitfield, Milton Keynes, MK11 3LW, UK
UKHW022132231224
452783UK00011B/522